Doctor's Diary

Doctor's Diary

Dr James Le Fanu

ROBINSON
London

Robinson Publishing Ltd
7 Kensington Church Court
London W8 4SP

This collected edition first published in the UK by Robinson
Publishing Ltd 1996

Collected writings from *The Times* and *Sunday Telegraph*,
1990–96

A copy of the British Library Cataloguing in Publication data
is available from the British Library

ISBN 1-85487-728-3

Printed and bound in the EC

10 9 8 7 6 5 4 3 2 1

Contents

Contents

Acknowledgements

My greatest debt is to the readers of my columns in *The Times* and *Sunday Telegraph*, who have expressed their appreciation – which is always flattering – but more importantly whose comments, suggestions and experiences have inspired so much of what I have written.

I am grateful too to the many colleagues, past and present, on these newspapers, whose editorial skills and encouragement have been invaluable: Trevor Grove, Graham Patterson, Philippa Ingram, Stuart Reid, Virginia Hampton, John Morgan, Marsha Dunstan, Lisa Friedmann, Rebecca Nicolson, Robert Matthews, Victoria McDonald, Lucy Percival and Calli Emiris.

Thanks too to the amazing secretarial skills of Vanessa Adams, and to all at Robinson Publishing for making this anthology possible.

J. L. F.

For my readers

Introduction

Anthologies, like old silent movies, can appear jerky and disjointed so I have arranged the contents into four parts which may be read in different ways.

The first section – In Sickness and in Health – offers a perspective on the difficulties encountered in interpreting symptoms, making diagnoses and deciding on treatment. This part can be read 'straight through' as a sort of self-help guide to the perils and pitfalls of dealing with doctors and illness. How, for example, does one distinguish serious symptoms from the trivial? What to do if the doctor cannot find out what is amiss? When and why might new and more costly drugs be better treatment than cheaper ones? When might 'heroic' surgery be justified? What are the merits and drawbacks of private or and of 'alternative' medicine? Should there be an age limit on 'high technology' treatment?

Section 2 – A Portfolio of Diseases – describes the history, causation and treatment of common diseases with a few esoteric ones thrown in. Leaving aside those with a morbid preoccupation with all manner of illnesses, I imagine most readers will only be interested in those diseases by which they themselves are afflicted, or some friend or relative.

Section 3 – The Hazards of Everyday Life? – is intended for all those who over the years have felt anxiety or guilt induced by the constant stream of medical scare stories and advice which seek to implicate each and every aspect of our lives – the air we breathe, the food we eat, what we drink and many others in some dreadful disease. This section is an antidote to such anxiety-mongering about health and I hope everyone will feel a good deal better having read it.

Section 4 – Diversions – is for late-night reading as here will be found the more curious aspects of our lives: whether it is natural to believe in ghosts, why criminals are so fond of tattoos, do-it-yourself brain surgery, links between sex and sneezing and much else besides.

Part 1

In Sickness and in Health

1

Sorting Things Out

There is a virtually limitless number of ways of falling ill, and the most demanding of medical tasks is to make sense of the tide of symptoms that sweep through the surgery every day. This is not an easy task. In 'Is it Serious?', I suggest some criteria by which people can decide whether their ailments merit medical attention. 'Telling Your Story' and 'The Truth Is In the Details' emphasise the importance of giving as full an account as possible of what is wrong. The moral of 'Age – A Cause of Confusion' and 'Surprising Symptoms' is that not all illnesses fit in to neat boxes. 'A Second Opinion' may sometimes be necessary in difficult cases.

Is it Serious?

People's perception of the significance of their medical symptoms varies enormously. A man in his mid-seventies staggered breathlessly into the surgery, apologised profusely for wasting my time, but said he now found it difficult to climb the stairs to his flat because as he put it: 'I'm a bit puffed.' The cause of the problem was obvious from a cursory examination: he had a fast pulse, swollen ankles and fluid in the lungs, which all added up to a diagnosis of gross heart failure. My next patient was a woman in her forties, who had been afflicted with a headache for a few days and wanted to know if she could have a brain scan to make sure she did not have a brain tumour. This discrepancy between individuals in their threshold for seeking medical advice is largely attributable to personality. Some people are stoics, others hypochondriacs.

Nonetheless, for the majority somewhere in the middle, the question remains: how can you tell whether your symptoms are due to some trivial minor illness, the 'aches and discomforts of passing years', or herald something more sinister that would benefit from medical attention? There is no difficulty in making this distinction when struck down by some medical or surgical catastrophe – a heart attack, stroke or perforated bowel. The body, through its network of pain fibres, has no hesitation in making it clear that the sooner you get to hospital the better.

But how can you be sure that a headache is *not* caused by a brain tumour or that an attack of constipation may *not* be due to cancer of the colon? Are those aches and pains just 'old age', or a condition like polymyalgia, which is readily curable with steroids? Then there are those subtle changes in physical ability – like breathlessness, tiredness or loss of energy – which can be too readily dismissed as 'I'm feeling a bit run down', when there might be a remediable underlying cause – anaemia, an underactive thyroid or even depression.

The point about all these symptoms is that most of the time they are transient manifestations of some self-limiting illness, but they may also be the sign of something more sinister and if they are shrugged off, the subsequent delay in seeking help can be serious. This is well illustrated by cancer of the colon where, on average, six months elapse between the first symptoms – usually a change in bowel habit, whether constipation or diarrhoea – and the diagnosis being confirmed by a barium enema or colonoscopy. This may, in some cases, make all the difference between a tumour that is operable and one that is not.

Every day, millions of people with a multitude of different symptoms seek medical advice, and probably the most intellectually challenging task confronting doctors is to make exactly this distinction between the trivial and the potentially serious which may require further investigation or hospital referral. They do this essentially by applying three cardinal criteria of 'novelty', 'persistence' and 'deterioration' which act as a red-alert system, so if one or more are fulfilled, danger bells should start ringing.

Is the symptom new? If a middle-aged man wakes with a pain in the chest, which he has had on and off over the years, the likelihood is that it is not desperately important. If this is the first time he has pain, there is a greater probability that it is significant.

Has the symptom persisted? Most illnesses get better of their own accord, often before a proper diagnosis is made, and it is usually reasonable to let things run for a week or so before deciding to take action.

Is the symptom getting worse? This applies to those that markedly deteriorate over a day or two or a longer period, like a fortnight, and strongly suggest it is necessary to find out what is really going on.

It would be very unwise to advise people whose symptoms fail to fulfil these criteria not to seek medical help. They are not foolproof and require medical skill to be properly interpreted. However, those whose symptoms do fulfil these criteria will be well advised to obtain a medical opinion urgently. The stoical 70-year-old who complained of being a 'bit puffed' would have been helped a lot earlier if he had done so. His fast pulse turned out to be due to atrial fibrillation, a rapid uncontrolled coordination of the heart muscle which had forced fluid into the air sacs of the lungs, making them waterlogged. Three days of digoxin and a water pill and he was running up the stairs again.

As for the woman with a headache, this could of course have been due to a brain tumour, but headaches are the commonest pain for which medical advice is sought and it is completely unreasonable to expect that they should all be investigated with a brain scan just in case there may be a brain tumour present. If, however, she had rarely suffered from headaches before, or this one had lasted for ten days, or it was noticeably getting worse, or any combination of these criteria, not only would she have been right to seek medical advice, but it would have merited prompt investigation.

Telling Your Story

A woman wrote to tell me how for two and a half years she suffered from early morning headaches made worse by movement, and subtle personality changes. Several doctors she saw during this time all fobbed her off by saying she was suffering from, variously, tension headaches, migraine, depression and, that old standby, stress. It was only when she finally secured a referral to a consultant neurologist that a brain scan was arranged which – lo and behold – revealed the true cause of her complaint. She had a benign brain tumour, otherwise known as a meningioma. So, she asked, why do doctors jump to conclusions? Why indeed?

I have come across many similar cases. A young journalist returned from the Far East with bloody diarrhoea which was attributed to some bug he had picked up on his travels. Two months later he was no better, so half-heartedly his general practitioner sent him for a barium enema, which showed a typical picture of an infiltrating cancer of the colon. There was a man in his thirties who noticed he was getting short of breath climbing stairs. He did at least get a see a specialist, who told him he had asthma. Two days later he had a massive coronary, from which he never recovered.

It requires little imagination to summon up the nightmare of these cases. Initially the patient may be grateful for reassurances that it is nothing serious. Then doubt sets in, the symptoms fail to improve, so what then? Go for another consultation, only to get the same verdict? There is a natural reluctance to make a fuss, so time passes and anxiety deepens, until belatedly the true diagnosis is finally arrived it.

So, why do doctors jump to conclusions and get it wrong? They are guided by the laws of probability, the most certain of which is that common things occur commonly. A GP who sees on average two patients a week with headaches, will, in thirty-five years of practice probably diagnose a brain tumour only twice. The likelihood that either a traveller returning with diarrhoea is harbouring a cancer of the colon or that a young man is about to have a heart attack is small. So the doctor opts for the common diagnosis, justifying his decision not to investigate further on the grounds that to do so often causes great inconvenience and is a waste of resources.

As it usually takes around three months to get to see a consultant neurologist, a GP will be doing a disservice to his patients if he clogs up the system by referring all his headache patients on the off-chance that they might have a brain tumour. This is the conventional explanation why for some there is a delay between initial consultation and diagnosis. Most readers will no doubt say: 'Fair enough, but I do not want that sort of thing to happen to me.'

To minimise this possibility, it is only necessary to appreciate that symptoms are highly specific. It is a common belief that no proper diagnosis can be made without the help of some fancy piece of high-tech hardware. This may sometimes be necessary, but in over 90 per cent of cases the suspicion that something is seriously amiss can be deduced from the patient's account of his symptoms. The distinction, for example, between the many types of headache can be made solely by differentiating its site, type, periodicity, and exacerbating or mitigating factors. Simply saying: 'I've a bit of a headache' is useless, as the busy doctor working on the basis of probabilities will just check your blood pressure and issue a prescription for painkillers. By contrast: 'I don't usually get headaches, but for the past month I wake every morning with a real crasher which usually gets better during the day but is made worse by stooping or coughing,' will, unless the GP is a complete idiot, ring sufficient bells for him to take it seriously. An examination and prompt referral to a neurologist should follow.

So be self-confident, reflect on the precise nature of your symptoms – and tell the lot. The importance of this is illustrated by the story of a woman blind since birth, who had developed a bat-like sixth sense for objects close to her. She would mentally tick off the lamp-posts as she walked to work so she knew when to turn into her office. One day she realised she could no longer 'see' the lamp-posts and feeling this a little sinister, persuaded her doctor to arrange a brain scan. She too had an early meningioma. So, if you have a stable personality and are generally healthy, the development of any symptom, no matter how unusual, is unlikely to be a figment of your imagination.

The Doctor Must Listen

At one time I saw quite a lot of a man in his mid-forties who strenuously maintained he became so breathless travelling around on bus and Tube that old ladies would regularly stand up to offer him their seats. The trouble was that neither I nor several other doctors could find anything wrong with him. He certainly did not appear breathless, his chest X-ray and tests of lung function could not have been more normal. From this we could only deduce that either he was having us on, or his symptoms were psychological. He took this in good part because he was as puzzled as us by the disparity between the severity of the symptoms and his apparent A1 physical fitness.

Before he was packed off to the psychiatrist, his case was presented at a Grand Round of all the local heart and lung specialists, who agreed with the diagnosis of psychogenic breathlessness – until a bright young medical student enquired about a very faint line in the region of the heart on the chest X-ray. We all crowded round his X-ray and realised that the faint line was his mitral valve connecting the chambers of the heart, which had been narrowed by a thin layer of calcium. This usually produces a quite characteristic rumble as blood whooshes through the tight aperture, but we had all missed the diagnosis because our patient's valve was so narrow that only a trickle of blood was passing through it. No wonder he was short of breath! When I saw him a couple of months later, after a valve replacement, he commented ruefully that the offers of seats on public transport had dried up.

In the hierarchy of medical sins, misdiagnosing a genuine complaint as 'being all in the mind' comes near the top of the list. In retrospect such mistakes are usually quite obvious – the problem being that the doctor has failed to pay attention to precisely what he was being told. Thus my patient's complaint was of being breathless on exertion but he had always been examined after he had been sitting quietly in the outpatients' department. If he had been encouraged to climb a flight of stairs, there would have been no doubt about the reality of his symptoms, and further tests – such as an ultrasound examination of the heart – would have revealed the diagnosis much earlier.

Margaret Turner-Warwick, former professor of respiratory medicine at London's Brompton Hospital, discovered an important variance of asthma by following the golden rule of listening to what the patient has to say. Several of her patients complained that they woke early in the morning extremely short of breath, but when they were seen during day-time surgery hours examination and tests were completely normal. Professor Turner-Warwick thought it would be interesting to given them a small hand-held peak-flow meter and instruct them to blow into it at regular intervals. The pictures that emerged resembled a roller-coaster – most of the recordings were excellent but there was a massive precipitous decline in lung function in the early hours of the morning. This pattern was abolished by taking a drug last thing at night which kept the airways open. Her patients, needless to say, were very grateful to learn that their symptoms were not just imaginary and to be able to enjoy an undisturbed full night's sleep. This type of brittle asthma is now well recognised, and it is difficult to overstate its clinical significance because (again, obvious in retrospect), it certainly explains some of the tragic and previously unexplained instances in which apparently healthy young people died suddenly in the middle of the night.

A final example concerns a young woman with severe aching pain in her upper thigh whose investigations also turned out to be normal. This time, however, she was believed, and although her orthopaedic surgeon admitted to being a bit foxed, he advised an exploratory operation on her lower back to see if something might be pressing on a nerve. Just before going down to the operating theatre, she was visited by the senior registrar, of whom she enquired, in the nicest possible way, why it was that her spine, hips and knees had all been X-rayed, but not the part of her thigh from which the pain arose. This was duly done and, sure enough, there was a large, but fortunately benign, bone tumour. Such cautionary tales have a simple moral: if you are really convinced your symptoms are genuine, they almost certainly are.

The Truth is in the Details

A doctor's diagnostic skills are sometimes compared to those of a good detective, seeking 'the truth' by picking up on clues, little details, that might easily be overlooked. An ageing East End GP, to whom I was apprenticed in my early days as a medical student, maintained that the truth always lay in the details, a point well illustrated by the greatest diagnostic triumph of his working life. One of his friends had progressively severe headaches with early-morning vomiting. This was before the days of brain scans and, as examination revealed signs of a mass in the brain, he was told he had a tumour about which 'nothing could be done'. My GP mentor visited him and in the course of their conversation the friend described a trip he had taken to a favourite pub in Southend just before developing his fatal illness. It had been a very nice day; he had eaten oysters, gone for a swim, etc, marred only, he remembered, by bumping his head on a low beam in the pub. My GP picked up the phone, rang St Bartholomew's Hospital and told the neurosurgical registrar that his friend with an 'incurable' brain tumour almost certainly had a blood clot pressing on the outside of the brain following a mild head injury. And so it turned out; the clot was removed and a full recovery followed.

Nowadays, no doubt, the friend would have had a brain scan early on and the truth would have emerged that way. But despite modern diagnostic aids, the details can still be crucial as a reader's story shows. His mother's mental state started to deteriorate until, after a few months, she was admitted to hospital where a doctor told him she was suffering from dementia due to a series of 'mini strokes' that had caused 'loose connections' in her brain. He advised it would be best if she were placed in a nursing home and that he should 'get on with the rest of his life'. He refused and took her home, where she 'improved with the stimulus' though 'uttering the most incredible nonsense at times'. Three months later she fell and broke her arm, requiring another period in hospital. By this time, the reader writes

'I was very depressed with things. All the doctors I consulted tried to reconcile me to coming to terms with the problems of my mother's old age.'

In the end he decided to get a second opinion privately. Dementia is a dead-end diagnosis but very occasionally there is a treatable underlying cause, which the private specialist picked up on almost immediately. How? The clue lay in two details. One year before her mental deterioration the mother's walking had become 'uncertain' and her handwriting less fluent. She had also become incontinent of urine, which was attributed by her GP to cystitis and treated with antibiotics.

Clearly this is not the clinical picture one would expect with 'mini strokes'. Abnormalities of gait and incontinence followed by mental deterioration are typical of only one condition, known as normal pressure hydrocephalus, where the fluid circulating through the ventricles of the brain markedly increases, putting pressure on the brain from the inside. The insertion of a shunt draws off the fluid, allowing the tissue to recover. The specialist's diagnosis was confirmed by the brain scan and there has been a good response to treatment.

The Rewards of Persistence

'Magic,' the genial oldie replied to my query about the efficacy of the pills I had prescribed for him the previous week. He had dropped into the surgery with a flu-like illness and, by way of conversation, added that he knew that decrepitude was imminent, as his arms were now so weak he could no longer comb what little hair was left on his head. It was not necessary to examine the affected limbs to know this was a classic case of *polymyalgia rheumatica*. I could do nothing about his flu, but I told him that in 24 hours the strength in his arms would be wonderously restored if he took a healthy dose of steroids every morning – and so it turned out. There is so much to be impressed with in modern medicine, but nothing beats performing 'miracles' like this, where the cure is unexpected, instantaneous and complete.

Patients with *myasthenia gravis* – a deficit of a chemical transmitter in the nerve endings – find the simplest of tasks, such as eating, speaking, turning over in bed, increasingly difficult. It used to be incurable until the drug neostigmine was discovered. A woman with myasthenia for ten years described the day in February 1935, when, aged twenty-eight, she was first given it: 'Until that time there was no treatment, but many things to try – gold, thyroid extract, ephedrine – all disappointing. Then came the day I shall always remember. I was lying on the sofa after tea and my fiancé came in late, saying he had yet another possible remedy. I submitted to the injection with complete indifference, and within a few minutes began to feel very strange . . . When I lifted my arms they shot into the air. Every movement I attempted was grotesquely magnified until I learnt to make less effort. It was wonderful, and we danced twice around the room. This was my first meeting with Neostigmine, and we have never been separated.'

The drama of the 'miraculous' cure is heightened further when the patient's illness has previously been diagnosed as hysterical or incurable. A couple of years ago, Patricia Mills, a doctor in Tunbridge Wells, described in the *British Medical Journal* how her mother's progressive weakness and difficulty in swallowing had been diagnosed by a neurologist as myotonic dystrophy – an inheritable form of muscle weakness. The prospect that she and her children might succumb to it led to a nervous breakdown and admission to psychiatric hospital. After this, Dr Mills read the classic monograph on the disease, and began to question the diagnosis. She expressed her doubts to the neurologist: 'He wrote back saying he was sure; but to oblige would arrange a muscle biopsy, though he did not think this absolutely necessary.' The specimen showed a florid inflammation of the muscle known as polymyositis and her mother was promptly started on steroids. 'She had thought she would not survive another winter. She has survived ten more. My sister and I each have two fine children. How different it would have been if I had not questioned the original diagnosis,' Dr Mills observes.

It is fanciful to suppose that many patients diagnosed as having some incurable illness may in fact be afflicted with some curable condition – but it does happen. A woman in her early fifties complained of an unusual symptom – a constant faecal odour, for which there was no physical cause. Reading back through her notes, I discovered that she had seen a hospital specialist ten years earlier for the same complaint, which he had concluded was psychological. As my patient had just buried her husband, I presumed that depression had exacerbated her condition and suggested hypnosis might be helpful. Two months later she developed weakness down one side of the face, and a brain scan revealed a large tumour pressing on the olfactory nerve – almost certainly the cause of her original complaint. It was by now too late to do anything about it, but she would have been cured had the correct diagnosis been made a decade earlier. Such cases underline the need to challenge every diagnosis, no matter how eminent its source.

Age – A Cause of Diagnostic Confusion

When responding to a request for a home visit by a woman with severe colicky pains in the upper abdomen, I found that she had an exquisitely tender spot just under the right rib cage. Both the nature of her pain and examination were strongly suggestive of a stone in the gall bladder. But she was only twenty-one, and people of that age do not get gallstones, which characteristically occur in those who are 'fat, fertile and over forty'.

Ruminating on my diagnostic uncertainty, my mind went back to a clinical meeting at Whipp's Cross Hospital when the consultant paediatrician had presented a case of a young boy with the very rare condition of Kawasaki's disease – an inflammation of the arteries, which impedes the blood flow, resulting for this unfortunate child in gangrene of the foot which required amputation. The paediatrician said sadly that he would have made the diagnosis earlier, and perhaps amputation would not have been necessary, if he had only listened more closely to what the boy had been telling him. After walking a short distance he would develop a severe pain in his calves which disappeared when he rested and recurred when he moved off again. In a 65-year-old man this could only mean one thing: narrowing of the arteries to the leg with atheroma which deprives the calf muscle of oxygen. But exactly the same symptoms in a five-year-old seemed inexplicable, so the paediatrician had ignored them until the boy's foot turned gangrenous.

This case from almost two decades ago seemed to have a clear lesson for me. Even if it is unheard of for a 21-year-old woman to have gallstones, if that is what her signs and symptoms point to, then that is what she must have.

There is a more generalised and important message that arises from this story, concerning the way that the probability of different diseases changes with age. The common illnesses of childhood like measles and chickenpox are rarely seen in adult life – and when they do occur they are usually unaccountably ferocious. Similarly, illnesses that may develop in the middle years, such as multiple sclerosis or diabetes, are different again from the chronic degenerative diseases of ageing – cataracts, arthritis, prostate problems and so on. So, when confronted by a patient with say, chest pain, which has many causes, a doctor, on the basis of probabilities, will instantly discard several possibilities on the criterion of age alone. Put simply, this means that chest pain in a young man is most likely to be due to a collapsed lung; in someone in their fifties, angina; and in the over-seventies angina again, or arthritis of the spine.

This ranking of diagnostic probabilities by age group is obviously very useful, focusing the doctor's attention on what is the most appropriate investigation to reach a definite verdict, and preventing him from being sidetracked. The problem, as can be imagined, is when people have diseases inappropriate to their age group. This is a particular hazard for those in their thirties or forties with potentially serious illnesses such as heart trouble or cancer. Their chest pain is misinterpreted as being due to indigestion, or their breathlessness may be attributed to asthma. Then suddenly, out of the blue, they have a heart attack, at which point the true significance of their symptoms becomes clear. Similarly, a change of bowel habit for two or three weeks' duration, which in an older age group is readily recognisable as a potentially sinister harbinger of a bowel tumour, does not produce similar alarm signals in a younger man. The necessary investigation to confirm it – a barium enema – is not requested and so the diagnosis is delayed.

In the older age group, the reverse of this situation may occur where a 'chronic degenerative' disease is mistaken for one that is eminently treatable. Thus, a smoker in his sixties who is short of breath, with a cough and a wheezy chest, will be told he is suffering from emphysema and that there is little to be done for his damaged lungs. But he may have late-onset asthma. The distinction is made by prescribing a short course of steroids at high dosage or a longer course at a low dose, which will both markedly improve the breathlessness and make his airways more sensitive to drugs such as Salbutamol, which, by dilating the bronchi, will allow oxygen to pass more readily in and out of the lungs.

Alternatively, those afflicted with pain and stiffness in the joints may too readily be dismissed as suffering from 'arthritis' and treated with painkillers and anti-inflammatory pills, while their symptoms are actually due to late-onset rheumatoid arthritis which responds, often dramatically, to gold injections. So, next time you are told you are either 'too young' or 'too old' to suffer from some illness or other, be sure to ask your doctor – in the politest possible way – how he can be so certain. Most of the time he will be absolutely right, but exceptionally he may not be – and that can make a lot of difference.

Second Opinion

Compared with our elitist National Health Service, those of western Europe and the United States are positively plebeian. Over there, any doctor can erect his plaque as a specialist after hanging around a teaching hospital for a few years and passing an exam or two. In Britain, the accolade comes only after stiff competition and rigorous evaluation by one's peers. Only the best make it to the top. A British specialist knows his trade and the standard is such that, whether in Bolton District Hospital or London's finest, patients will almost invariably get a good opinion. Almost invariably, but not always. The limitation of our elite system is that with fewer, albeit better trained, specialists, their workload is heavier and opportunities thoroughly to evaluate each case are thus restricted. This does not matter and indeed may be a bonus when the problem is straightforward, as it protects patients from being over-investigated. But when it is more abstruse then mistakes can be made. This situation and what can be done about it can be considered under three headings – Time, Interest and Expertise.

Lack of time to sit down and think through a difficult case can result in a faulty diagnosis. This can happen even to doctors themselves. Dr Stanley Freedman, a consultant physician in Enfield, described in the *British Medical Journal* last year how he was wrongly told he had motor neurone disease. It all started with a difficulty in walking due to weakness in his right foot, which a neurologist put down to a 'back problem'. His condition deteriorated, he fell off his bike a few times and was admitted to hospital, some tests were done and the gloomy verdict delivered. Dr Freedman, however, knew enough about motor neurone disease to realise that, first, he did not have at least one classical sign, 'fasciculation' – a rippling of the muscles – and that his rate of physical deterioration was too fast to be compatible with the diagnosis. A thorough rethink of his case then followed and the possibility raised that the results of his tests – on which the diagnosis rested – might be in error. He was given a small dose of the drug used in the treatment of another neurological disorder, *myasthenia gravis*, and 'the effect was magical. The following day I could walk comfortably, albeit at a slow pace but with few stops.' In a couple of months he was back at work.

It is easy to see that if, right at the beginning, the neurologist had the time to reflect on how the clinical symptoms and signs were incompatible with the lab results, this whole sorry saga would have been avoided. There is really only one way for people to avoid this happening and that is to buy a specialist's time and go privately for a second opinion. Then with a leisurely hour to take a thorough history and perform a systematic examination, the possibility of misdiagnosis will be minimised. It does not really matter who the specialist is, but it is always good to have a name and here *The Good Doctor Guide* by Martin Page is very useful. It contains names and addresses of over 500 specialists.

This takes me to the second heading. It is always striking what a difference it makes when the doctor has a specific interest in a condition, especially if it is chronic and not readily amenable to treatment. Many doctors find this type of problem – migraine, pre-menstrual syndromes, itchy bottoms, and so on – rather boring and they will give standard advice, but not much more. But a gynaecologist enthusiastic about PMS will not only have a greater placebo effect, but, having read the literature, will know details of management which will have passed his colleagues by. Here too, *The Good Doctor Guide* is useful, though its references to 'special interests' are not as comprehensive as they could be. The alternative way of discovering an enthusiast for your ailment is to visit the library and look up your condition in the index of the *BMJ* or *The Lancet*. This should guide you to articles whose authors can usually be assumed to be better informed than most. The next stop is the *Medical Directory*, also usually available in libraries. Look up his or her name, check the age (doctors in their forties tend to be the best enthusiasts), and suggest politely to your GP that you might benefit from a consultation and ask for a referral.

Lastly, we come to 'expertise'. This, of course, is related to 'passion'. The surgeon fascinated by hips and who spends all his time putting in hip replacements will get slightly better results than the one who only does a couple a month. This is fairly obvious, though one needs to be rich enough or covered by private medical insurance to take advantage of this fact. There is another related issue here which is particularly relevant for those with a potentially serious, but treatable, illness. It is a curious fact that hospitals or units that concentrate on one type of disease have a better cure rate than others, even though patients are given exactly the same treatment. Young men with cancer of the testes at the Western Infirmary of Glasgow, which deals with half the cases in Scotland, have an 87 per cent five-year survival rate, while for those at other hospitals the figure is 73 per cent. Nothing better illustrates what a tragedy it will be for British medicine if specialist hospitals are forced to close.

Surprising Symptoms at the Surgery

There is no difficulty switching to autopilot during a busy morning surgery. The sort of problems are usually so routine that scarcely a flicker of intellectual activity is necessary in deciding what is wrong and how it should be put right. And then every so often someone comes to the door with a story so curious that my initial suspicion is that I am being taken for a ride, were it not for the indefinable authenticity of the matter-of-fact way in which it is recounted. Scepticism in these circumstances invariably makes a doctor appear very foolish, as I discovered when I encountered the clicking-ear syndrome. 'My daughter says her ears are clicking,' the bemused mother told me. 'Oh yes,' I said, inspecting them with my auroscope, 'they seem fine to me.' 'But if you listen closely, you can hear it!' she replied. And so, for the only time in my life, I found myself placing my stethoscope over a patient's ear – and there, sure enough, was a quite deafening 'click' about every five seconds. Subsequent enquiry revealed that this rare but luckily self-limiting condition is caused by the rhythmic oscillations of the minute bones of the middle ear.

Then, a young man told me his wrist 'creaks so badly it must need oiling'. He wiggled it up and down quite cheerfully and I was about to comment 'Seems fine to me', when he said 'Go on, doc, feel it'; and sure enough, placing my hand on his wrist elicited a sensation just like a rusty hinge. This turned out to be another rare syndrome – crepitating tenosynovitis. There seems no limit to which a doctor's credulity can be challenged. How, for example, could anyone take seriously a complaint of itchiness at the tip of the nose after sex? And indeed just such a patient recently described in a medical journal was fobbed off with 'reassurance and tranquillisers'. He returned to say that his nasal itchiness now came on after carrying the shopping. Only then did the penny drop. This was a most unusual form of angina, and, sure enough, X-rays of the arteries to the heart showed them to be seriously narrowed. After a coronary bypass his nasal itchiness disappeared. Similarly, it took a young man almost five years before anyone took any notice of his unusual complaint – that after walking 50 yards he always developed an erection which would subside only after he sat down. He eventually developed other symptoms, including weakness in the legs, which took him to a neurologist who diagnosed narrowing of the lower part of the spinal canal. An operation restored strength to his limbs and abolished his ambulatory erections.

Very occasionally, bizarre symptoms, though obviously genuine, remain utterly inexplicable. A Canadian doctor, Stephen Sullivan, wrote to *The Lancet* asking for help in diagnosing (and treating) a 28-year-old woman who, a couple of times a week, had 'attacks' lasting a few hours. He described these as follows: 'They start with a sensation of intense warmth followed by a generalised itchiness. Within an hour nausea develops followed by vomiting so copious she has to carry a plastic pail with her. Both she and her friends then notice an unusual body odour like 'smelly feet' which she attempts to eradicate by taking frequent cool baths, after which she notices there is an oily film on the water.' Dr Sullivan's request for help went unanswered. Presumably the unfortunate patient can find some consolation in the fact that, though her symptoms are very unusual, most debilitating and apparently untreatable, they are at least unique.

2

Putting Things Right

The first piece in this section reflects on the wisdom of Hipprocrates' aphorism – 'To do nothing is also a good remedy'. In the past, age has been considered justification enough for 'doing nothing'. 'Never Too Old' explains why this is no longer acceptable. Private medicine is a luxury that regrettably few people can afford (unless, like lunch at Claridge's, someone else is paying). 'The Price of Private Care' explains why. 'Get Up and Get Better' draws attention to the dangers of taking to one's bed when ill.

The Virtues of Doing Nothing . . .

The most appropriate medical treatment is, very often, to do nothing. The best prescription is the friendly reassurance that whatever ails you is passing, that it is unnecessary to swallow pills to make it better, and that a slug of stoicism and quiet rest at home are all that is needed. Hippocrates was the first to articulate this important insight: 'To do nothing is also a good remedy.' Over the centuries this has been reformulated in many different ways: good surgeons, it is said, know how to operate; better surgeons know when to operate; and the best surgeons know when *not* to operate. Some doctors are very keen on doing nothing. They pride themselves on being therapeutic minimalists, dismissive of the claims for wonder drugs (rather they 'wonder' what their side effects might be): they put their trust in the body's ability to heal itself.

For virtually every ill, no matter how insignificant, there is a pill, and the harm of potent remedies is certainly greater than that caused by under-treatment. This applies to everyday minor problems like a sore throat or upset stomach, but can be extended almost indefinitely. Sleeping badly? You don't need sleeping pills. A touch of gastritis? A couple of glasses of milk four times a day are preferable to drugs that reduce acid in the stomach. Strained your ankle? A few aspirin are as likely to work as a powerful anti-inflammatory drug. But, personally, I think this therapeutic conservatism can be overplayed. Virtuous as it may seem for a doctor to decide on principle not to prescribe certain types of drugs – such as hypnotics, tranquillisers, or potent pain-killers – they are short-changing those of their patients who suffer from insomnia, anxiety, or whose arthritic pain is poorly controlled by simple remedies. There is also a suspicion in these cost-conscious times that perhaps therapeutic conservatism towards newer, more expensive types of drugs is actually a ploy to help doctors cut down on their drug budgets.

It is not possible to give specific advice on this issue other than to alert readers as to why the treatment they receive may be so different from and so much less – or indeed more – effective than that of acquaintances with a similar complaint. It is important to emphasise, however, that in this modern age the criterion against which a doctor's treatment should be judged is whether it minimises or eradicates the symptoms that need alleviating. To be sure, there are times when this is not possible, but before that point is reached one should try to make certain that the best drugs have been given at the highest tolerable dosage. The implications are clear. It may well be a good thing to have a therapeutically conservative-minded doctor, but if his remedies do not work there is little point in personally making a virtue out of stoically tolerating one's ailments. He or she should be gently badgered – in the nicest possible way, of course – to prescribe something 'a bit stronger'.

Never Too Old

Back in 1974 an editorial in the *British Medical Journal* described open-heart surgery in those over 60 as 'not feasible'. Twenty years on a report from America describes an 87-year-old women who not only had three obstructed coronary arteries bypassed but also, for good measure, had her narrowed aortic valves replaced at the same time. Commenting on the operation in an article significantly entitled 'You are never too old', Dr John Wong, of Tufts University School of Medicine in Boston, criticises those doctors who would have left this 'poor old lady' to die peacefully, on the ground that patients of this age who survive the operation would be likely to live four years longer than if they were merely given symptomatic medical treatment. Geriatric cardiac surgery, contrary to past medical opinion, has not only proved highly feasible but also increasingly popular for the simple reason that potential candidates for the operation are to be found in greatest numbers among the old and very old. This has been made possible by the greater skill of the surgeons themselves – which has come with experience – and the increasingly sophisticated technology that helps to keep the old and frail alive during and after major surgery.

But not everything that is technically feasible is desirable both in a strictly medical sense and in overall terms of the nation's health. 'Every choice requires a sacrifice,' says Kierkegaard and if we choose to perform expensive open heart surgery on oldies in their eighties, then something else has to be given up to pay for it. Recognising this, the cash-limited NHS has systematically discriminated against the old. In Britain even if this particular 'little old lady' had been ten or even fifteen years younger, she would have been very lucky to have been offered an operation. But it seems as if oldies are increasingly irritated by this policy. According to Dr John Grimley Evans, professor of geriatric medicine at Oxford University: 'Although it can be difficult to prove, many consultants practise an implicit form of age discrimination.' What is the evidence for this and how pervasive is it? Discrimination operates at two levels. The first is easier to show – the official or unofficial refusal of certain investigations or treatments on the ground of age alone. The second, probably more important, is rationing on the basis of expectation – it is not expected that, for example, those over 70 warrant certain types of medical intervention and so they are not offered them.

The national screening programmes for breast and cervical cancer provide a clear example of official 'age discrimination', neither being routinely available to women after the age of 65. This cannot be justified on medical grounds as the incidence of both these cancers rises incrementally with each passing decade. Similarly, a survey of coronary care units in Britain discovered that just under half set an upper age limit of 70 for giving the clot-busting drug Streptokinase to patients following a heart attack. This policy could be defended on the grounds that there is a modest increased risk of stroke following the use of this drug in the older age groups. However, in the words of Keith Fox, professor of cardiology in Edinburgh, 'this level of risk is far from that required to negate the overall benefits of the drug on mortality and morbidity in older patients.'

Then, comparisons with other Western countries show there is a definite – if unofficial – practice of age discrimination with high-technology treatments like kidney dialysis. In Germany, France and Italy about a quarter of new patients accepted on to dialysis programmes are over the age of 65, whereas the figure in Britain is around 8 per cent. It is a similar story with bypass surgery which cannot be justified on the basis of the results obtained in the older age group. Indeed, those lucky enough to be offered open heart surgery do remarkably well: a recent review of 117 such operations in those over 65 at Papworth Hospital was associated with a post-operative mortality rate of zero. Age discrimination is equally evident in the provision of services for the chronic degenerative diseases of ageing, particularly arthritis. The longest waiting lists are for just those procedures – such as cataract surgery and hip replacements – which almost uniquely are a cause of disability to oldies. 'The older age group tend to be given palliative and symptomatic care rather than a proper diagnosis and intervention,' observes Professor Grimley Evans. What more is there to be said?

The Price of Private Care

A visit to Harley Street (or its equivalent elsewhere) is, without doubt, one of life's little luxuries. Instead of the local NHS surgery with its narrow lino-covered staircase, there is a capacious Georgian entrance hall and a comforting carpet underfoot; instead of a surly receptionist defying you to make an appointment ('Sorry, nothing until next week'), a long-legged beauty in a nurse's uniform tells you the doctor will be available 'in just a moment'. Instead of a waiting-room crowded with despondent faces, the Harley Street reception room is almost empty, there are pleasing pictures and the *Financial Times* and *Country Life* on the table. And instead of a three-minute hurried consultation with your GP, the besuited paragon of the private doctor leaps up from behind his desk, his outstretched hand carrying with it the promise of a least half an hour of his undivided attention. It is pretty bogus really, if pleasantly so. However, except for the well-off or those whose insurance premiums are paid for by their employers, the cost of private medicine is seen by many as prohibitive. Like lunch at Claridge's, it is an extravagance that, regretfully, one has to do without.

Now it appears that an important reason why those on middling or fixed incomes must deny themselves the convenience of private medicine is that the British doctors are too greedy and charge too much. How else can one explain that a hysterectomy will cost £160 in Ontario, £400 in Sydney, £600 in New York, will set you back £830 in London; or that much-sought-after operation, the hip replacement, which costs more than £1,000 in Britain can be had for a mere £300 in Canada. Resentment at the considerable sums charged by doctors is a recurring theme in Western literature (well evoked by Hilaire Belloc's famous lines, 'They answered as they took their fees/There is no cure for this disease'). The bad feeling will be fuelled by rumours that some senior consultants can make £4,000 a day, or the average national wage in one five-day week. The whiff of scandal associated with these inflated fees has attracted the attention of the Monopolies Commission, which seems to think that British doctors have been keeping them artificially high. Were the Commission to break this price-fixing cartel by opening up private practice to 'competition' – magic word – it would become more readily affordable to the benefit of the public generally but also to the insurance companies, who would be able to lower their premiums and thus attract more customers.

But it will be some time yet before the ordinary customer can take the trip to Harley Street for a cut-price hysterectomy or hip replacement. First, the relatively high fees charged by British specialists are a covert subsidy for the NHS. The average consultant earns around £50,000; private fees, on average, might double this. If their private earnings were to fall, the NHS would have to increase this basic salary which would prove very costly (and politically unacceptable) to the Treasury. The high price of private medicine in Britain is also driven by 'quality'. Doctors in Europe and America need only complete four years' training in their chosen speciality to style themselves as 'specialists' and wait for the customers to roll in. But, in Britain, specialists must first come out on top of the highly competitive battle to get an NHS consultant post. British specialists are, thus, relatively few in number but very good, an elite that has maintained Britain – and London in particular – as the medical capital of the world. The prospect of ready access to private medicine through lower fees does seem to require a major revolution in the whole structure of British Medicine.

Get Up and Get Better

Almost fifty years ago the distinguished physician, the late Richard Asher, wrote a paper with a deceptively simple title. 'The Dangers of Going to Bed', which was to transform medical practice. At the time compulsory bed rest was prescribed for all manner of illnesses: for acute infections such as polio and diphtheria, for tuberculosis and rheumatic fever, following heart attacks and major surgical operations, for peptic ulcers, and much else besides. The premise was simple. In the absence of more potent remedies, the best advice a doctor could give was that the patient should rest in bed, thus harbouring his energy and promoting the natural healing powers of the body.

Taking his theme from Hymn No 23 in Ancient and Modern – 'Teach me to live that I may dread/the grave little as the bed' – Dr Asher set out to show that the consequences of lying in bed could too easily lead to an early grave. First there was thrombosis – 'the most disabling and lethal catastrophe that bed rest can bring to a patient'. Then there was muscle wasting and contractions of the joints. The bones lose calcium at a tremendous rate during bed rest, leading to osteoporosis, so that when the patient does finally rise dizzily from his sick bed, he falls over, fractures a hip, and then has to be put back to bed again.

The other hazards of bed rest include kidney stones, constipation, loss of co-ordination when walking, and depression. 'Look at a patient lying long in bed, what a pathetic picture he makes,' Dr Asher exclaimed. 'The blood clotting in his veins, the calcium draining from his bones, the faeces stacking up in his colon, the flesh rotting on his buttocks and the spirit evaporating from his soul!' Dr Asher's warning had a dramatic effect. The compulsory six-week bed rest for victims of heart attacks fell to a fortnight, then a week until, as is now the common practice, they are up and about in a few days. Following surgery the swing has been even more marked, with almost a quarter of patients not only getting up but going home on the same day as their operation.

Science has amply confirmed what Dr Asher deduced from clinical observations. Autopsy studies show that the risk of thrombosis followed by a lethal pulmonary embolism is directly related to the duration of time spent in bed prior to death. Experimental studies have confirmed that bed rest slows the contractility of the gut, leading to constipation, while a group of volunteers confined to a setting simulating a hospital room, with 'little social interaction and meaningful visual or auditory input', reported sensory distortions and depression.

There remain, however, a couple of conditions where bed rest may still be appropriate. The first and commonest is for acute back pain with sciatica, where the usual advice is complete rest for a week or more. This is undoubtedly the best policy for the minority where the pain is caused by a prolapsed disc pressing on the spinal nerve, but for most the problem is inflammation of the muscles and ligaments up and down the spine. Clearly bed rest, by reducing biomechanical stress, should permit such injuries to heal, but for how long?

Dr Richard Deyo of the University of Texas compared the outcome in patients advised to rest for either a week or just two days. He found, rather to his surprise, the former group recovered more slowly, perhaps because they mistakenly believed the injunction to rest for a prolonged period meant their back pain was serious and disabling.

The second situation where bed rest continues to be prescribed is for the late complications of pregnancy, and particularly for women thought to be likely to go into labour too early, resulting in the delivery of a premature infant. In such circumstances some obstetricians have continued to recommend admission to hospital from around the 32nd week, to avoid precipitating labour. The validity of this advice has also been examined in a clinical trial where 'at risk' women were either admitted to hospital or allowed to continue as normal. A study of mothers pregnant with twins published in the *British Journal of Obstetrics and Gynaecology* found that 'no beneficial effects of bed rest could be identified in prolonging the pregnancy or improving foetal outcome.'

In retrospect the advocacy of the virtues of bed rest was based on a fundamental misunderstanding of the close links between physical activity and physiological function. Man is a mobile animal and most of the body systems are strengthened and fine-tuned by movement. There is no alternative other than to rest during acute and serious illnesses, but once the crisis is passed recovery is accelerated by getting moving as soon as possible. Dr Asher subsequently reworked Hymn No 23: '*Teach us to live that we may dread/ unnecessary time in bed. Get people up that we may save/ our patients from an early grave.*'

3

A Pill For Every Ill

Most people are reluctant pill-takers so if they 'really must' it is only sensible that they should have to take as few as possible with a minimum of side effects. Here newer drugs are consistently better, but inevitably more costly. The first three pieces in this section – Easy to Swallow' and 'New Drugs for Old – 1 and 2' shows how to encourage the family doctor to prescribe the most appropriate remedies. 'Over the Counter' looks at the increasing number of drugs that can now be obtained without prescription. In 'Steroids' I present a balanced view of the virtues and vices of the most potent of all modern medicines.

Easy to Swallow

The British have serious reservations about taking pills. Even for those with a grave illness, like rheumatoid arthritis, a recent survey from the Royal London Hospital found that 'more than four out of five spontaneously expressed their dislike at having to take drugs at all'. As one woman put it: 'If there was something else I could do instead, I would.' The same survey reveals that fewer than half took their medication 'as per instructions'. Most compromised by taking their drugs at a lower dose or less frequently; some just did not bother to take them at all. In medical-speak, this is 'a problem of non-compliance', with the obvious implication that it is due to a combination of fecklessness, obstinacy and ignorance. The two commonest excuses for non-compliance revealed by the survey were 'convenience' – it is difficult to remember to take the pill three or four times a day – and 'side effects'. If one examines these excuses, it appears that much of the 'problem' of non-compliance lies not with the patient but with the doctor, for failing to prescribe intelligently.

The treatment of raised blood pressure is notorious for non-compliance. First, hypertension itself rarely causes any symptoms, so the motivation for taking the pills is essentially theoretical – that it will reduce the risk of a stroke, which may or may not occur at some time in the future. Then, once started, treatment must be continued indefinitely, which encourages the thought that if these damned pills have to be taken for fifteen years, it does not matter if the occasional dose is missed. Finally, it is often necessary to take more than one drug to control the blood pressure effectively.

There is no doubt that the cheapest way of treating hypertension is with the generic form of, for example, a beta-blocker like propranolol, which stays in the bloodstream for only about eight hours, so it has to be taken three times a day. Then, if this does not do the trick, it is necessary to add a diuretic or water pill or other medication which again have to be taken once or twice a day. Thus the patient with hypertension is expected to take four or five doses of medication at separate intervals during the day. The inconvenience factor is very high, as is the likelihood of non-compliance. It would be much more sensible and the likelihood of compliance would be much higher if a doctor were to prescribe a drug, Inderex, that combines the three doses of propranolol and a diuretic in one long-acting preparation, which only has to be taken once, after breakfast.

It is equally possible to circumvent many of the side effects, associated with drugs. A minority of those taking beta-blockers, for example, complain of a certain lassitude, which may just mean that the skip is taken out of their step, but which can be quite debilitating. This effect should be entirely avoidable, as there are four completely different drugs that also reduce the blood pressure and it should be possible to find one that is effective without making life a misery. Similarly, the anti-inflammatory drugs like ibuprofen and indomethacin, which are very good at relieving the pain and stiffness of arthritis, cannot be tolerated by a significant minority because they irritate the lining of the stomach, causing nausea and indigestion. There are several ways round this. They can be taken as suppositories, or in slow-release form where the active ingredient is only released once it has passed through the stomach. They can be combined with the acid-lowering drug cimetidine, or with another compound, misoprostol, both of which counteract the irritant effects in the stomach. So, by one means or another, almost all patients with arthritis should be able to take anti-inflammatory drugs and so benefit from their indubitable pain-relieving properties.

The moral seems obvious. If an illness or symptom is sufficient to warrant medication, then it should be prescribed in a form that is most convenient and has fewest side effects. The failure to do so is really the doctor's. In these cost-conscious times, it is considered almost a point of honour to prescribe the cheapest generic form of a drug rather than a more acceptable – though more expensive – equivalent. And some doctors, I suspect, lack the imagination to appreciate the degree to which side effects explain the public's reluctance to take their drugs. The cost of 'non-compliance' – that is, of drugs being prescribed but not used – has been calculated at around £300 million a year. Lurking in the bathroom cabinet of virtually every home in the country are little brown bottles half filled with pills that will never be taken. Some, perhaps, should never have been prescribed in the first place. But it is also true that such wastage could be minimised if doctors were to prescribe more intelligently.

New Drugs for Old – 1

Throughout the Fifties and Sixties, every year, miraculous 'wonder' drugs were discovered for previously untreatable illnesses. This was the high point of medical discovery and innovation – an epoch of human achievement unprecedented in the history of science. For complex reasons and despite research budgets running to billions of pounds, that epoch is now well and truly over. New drugs are still being produced, but the majority are alternatives to those that are already available. The pharmaceutical industry encourages doctors to prescribe these new drugs on the grounds that they are 'better', which indeed they might be. The trouble is they are often more expensive. In these cost-conscious times and with constraints on the family doctor's drug budget, this inevitably means that patients are being given the older, cheaper drugs rather than the new, costlier ones.

This is a matter of great importance and one about which people should be more aware. Consider, for example, the latest outbreak of flu-like illnesses, coughs and colds. Some of these may have been caused by the bug *Mycoplasma pneumonia*, which needs treatment with an antibiotic, notably erythromycin. This drug, like the majority of the antibiotics currently in use, was discovered in the early 1950s. It is astonishingly effective against a whole range of organisms and the cost of a standard week's course of treatment is just under £1:

amazing. It has, however, a short duration of action so must be taken four times a day. It also has the unfortunate side effect of stimulating the gut, so patients, besides having the symptoms of flu, may also suffer from abdominal discomfort, nausea, vomiting and diarrhoea. Recently a drug company launched a variant to erythromycin called Zithromax. This need only be taken as one single dose on three consecutive days – which is more convenient and easier to remember – and is also reported to have fewer side effects. But a course costs £13.43. Given the chance, any flu-ridden patient would naturally plump for this new, improved variety, but likely as not he will be prescribed erythromycin. Unless, that is, he reads this and, knowing the score, exerts gentle pressure on his GP to write Zithromax on the prescription pad.

This is a relatively trivial example, and to appreciate what is really at stake it is necessary to examine drugs used to treat depression, where the question of cost is even more important because treatment needs to be for at least six months and often indefinitely. The most commonly prescribed drug is amitryptyline, which was also discovered in the 1950s and works very well at a mere 20p for a day's treatment. It is undoubtedly very effective, but its side effects include a dry mouth, constipation, lethargy and dizziness. These symptoms are undoubtedly a problem as they discourage patients from taking their medication, especially in the first three weeks, before the benefits, in terms of improved mood, become apparent. By contrast, the new anti-depressants such as Prozac, which are taken as a single dose once a day, are much better tolerated, but cost almost six times as much, at £1.13 for a day's treatment. Once again, given the choice of prescribing a course of treatment for six months that could cost either £180 of £18, the prudent GP will be strongly tempted to save £162 by prescribing amitryptyline. Is he right to do so?

Professor Ian Hindmarch of Surrey University argues that patients on amitryptyline are prone to accidents (the effect of one pill on a patient's reaction times is similar to that of being over the legal limit for drinking and driving), are more likely to die from overdosage, less likely to be able to work satisfactorily and less likely to 'comply' with treatment (that is, take their pills regularly) and so reap the benefit. When all these 'hidden' costs are added up, the total for a course of treatment is the same or even greater than for Prozac. This analysis, it must be said, is disputed and others maintain that there is 'only questionable benefit' from the more expensive Prozac. So, as with the example of Zithromax, it is essential for patients to be well informed and by insisting on discussing 'the options' make it quite clear they are aware of the trade-off between costs and side effects. The GP will start to feel guilty about not providing the best possible treatment and will write a prescription for the more expensive Prozac.

The best source of information about drugs is the *British National Formulary*, which is available through many booksellers (ISBN 0-859369-258-0). It has a bias in favour of the older, cheaper, more established drugs, but also gives a fair analysis of the merits of newer ones. The expert authors also give their opinion on the best treatment for any condition, so for those who might have a mind to, this is an excellent opportunity to check your doctor's treatment against that of the pundits.

New Drugs for Old – 2

The standard treatment for migraine is quite straightforward and usually involves taking an anti-nausea drug, Maxolon, along with a strong pain-killer. Many sufferers may also gain relief from the drug ergotamine. Then they retire to some quiet haven and sleep off the attack. Now along comes a new, magic treatment, sumatriptan, whose efficacy, according to *The Lancet*, goes 'far beyond that of placebo or other acute treatments, symptom relief from "severe or moderate" headache to "mild or no" headache is achieved in less than an hour in 75 per cent of attacks'. Such a glowing commendation from so dispassionate a source leaves little doubt that many patients suffering migraine headaches should receive the new drug. There is a catch, however. Sumatriptan costs £20 a shot, which is 40 times more than ergotamine and 200 times more than Maxolon and painkillers. If everyone with migraine and its variants were to receive it, the total cost to the NHS would be £1.35 billion a year or one-thirtieth of the total NHS budget.

In the old days, when doctors didn't know how much drugs cost and were not responsible for their bills, this would not have been a problem. Now, however, fundholding GPs are given a defined budget to provide health care for their patients. A new drug like sumatriptan poses an unanticipated and unacceptable charge against that budget – a strong disincentive to prescribing it. Thus the responsibility for rationing expensive treatments has been shifted from the Treasury, where it is something of a political embarrassment, to the GP. The sumatriptan case demonstrates an increasingly common ethical dilemma facing doctors. Is it justifiable to prescribe a relatively ineffective drug for an unpleasant medical condition when one knows full well that another much better, albeit more expensive, treatment would be more appropriate?

There is a further equally important issue at stake. Drug research is a very uncertain and capital-intensive business. It probably cost Glaxo £100 million and ten years of hard slog to bring sumatriptan to the market. By definition, a new drug is likely to be considerably dearer than standard remedies, many of which are no longer protected by patent and thus can be produced very cheaply.

Once doctors feel they are unable to prescribe new and better drugs for reasons of cost, the pharmaceutical industry will have no alternative but to discontinue its programme of research-based innovation. At that point, we who have benefited from the products of this remarkable industry over the past forty years can kiss goodbye to any prospect of cures or better treatments that are waiting to be discovered. So the Government's commitment to fundholding GPs will certainly control drug costs but may well have the effect of killing off the goose that has laid so many golden eggs.

The French government has taken a more sophisticated approach with the view that Glaxo's price tag for sumatriptan is unreasonably high and refuse to give the drug a product licence unless the company reduces the cost. This seems to be a reasonable negotiating position, and if it succeeds it means that many more French citizens than British are likely to benefit from the drug. Meanwhile, those afflicted with migraine or its variants should not hesitate to ask their family doctor for the best possible treatment for their headache. If this does not result in a prescription for sumatriptan they might like to ask why.

Over the Counter

Afflicted by sinusitis while travelling through France, I dropped into a chemist's in search of the Gallic equivalent of Night Nurse – only to have Madame la Pharmacienne offer me a course of antibiotics which I know to be among the most expensive available. A brief negotiation followed and she finally let me have a much cheaper but equally effective brand, which worked wonders. The 'over-the-counter' availability in France of drugs which can be had here only on prescription probably explains why the French spend four times – four times! – as much on pharmaceuticals as we do.

This cannot be a good thing, but it certainly has the advantage of convenience – obviating the need for medical consultation for many minor ailments. In Britain over the past few years, some drugs have changed category from 'prescription only' to general release, including steroid creams for eczema, antihistamines, and most popular of all, the pain-killer Nurofen. Subsequently the Medicines Control Agency has radically extended this to include a further 50 drugs for illnesses which, taken together, occupy a fair slice of the GP's time, herpes, impetigo, conjunctivitis, piles, asthma, mouth ulcers, irritable bowel, peptic ulcers, nausea, vertigo and arthritis.

Buying these drugs directly from the chemist – many of them are almost household names, including acyclovir, Intal and Zantac – will cost as much as if they were obtained on prescription, but for those not keen on hanging around in doctors' dismal surgeries, this might well be a price worth paying. It will, of course, require patients to take a stab at diagnosing their own symptoms, but their guess is often as good as the doctor's. Anyway, self-diagnosis takes place much of time already – most patients know if they are suffering from piles or acne, or, if puzzled by a rash, seek the opinion of a family member or a helpful neighbour.

High-minded 'leaders of the profession' have warned of the possible dangers of people treating themselves with, for example, the anti-ulcer drug Zantac, when in fact their indigestion is caused by something altogether more sinister, but their main fear seems to be that these proposals threaten the doctors' monopoly of medical matters. Most doctors will be pleased to be liberated from the grind of diagnosing and treating routine problems, which, in turn will give them time to counsel the lonely and unhappy – or to read the *Investors Chronicle* to find the best use for their large salaries. The main justification for these proposals is undoubtedly financial. The NHS drug bill now runs at more than £3 billion a year. Both the Treasury and GPs – who are now responsible for their own drugs budgets – will be grateful if the public start paying for drugs out of their own pockets.

Steroids

My views on steroids have been sought by a reader from Bolton. 'We hear so many dreadful stories about their side effects,' he writes, 'yet several of my friends have been told they absolutely must take them. Your comment on this matter would be most welcome.' I will try to oblige. When first introduced in 1948, steroids proved to be so powerful in treating previously untreatable diseases as genuinely to warrant the description 'miracle cure'. The first patient was a woman in her mid-twenties with painful swellings of her joints due to rheumatoid arthritis of such severity she had been confined to bed for the previous 18 months. Dr Oswald Savage, emeritus physician at the Middlesex Hospital, was working at America's Mayo Clinic in Baltimore when the crippled woman was given her first large dose of cortisone. 'It was a revelation to see her walking again within two days of starting treatment,' he recalls. Her swollen joints became painfree virtually overnight.

When Dr Savage returned to the clinic the following year, however, he found the chief physician 'depressed by the increasingly numerous reports of side effects . . . My generation will never forget the severe complications they produced – the moon face, the perforated and bleeding ulcers, the bruising and crushed vertebrae. It was clear these drugs were so powerful it was imperative to learn to use them safely.' In the succeeding decades, steroids have been found to be similarly effective in an enormous number of different illness, yet their fearsome reputation from the early days lives on. To understand why, it is necessary to grasp what they do. Common to all diseases is a process known as 'inflammation' which is a precursor to healing. 'Inflammatory cells' migrate to the site of the noxious stimulus which might be an infection like tonsillitis, or the trauma of a broken bone, or heart muscles suddenly deprived of oxygen following a heart attack. The inflammatory cells secrete potent enzymes that dissolve the injured tissue. The enzymes may, for a short time, appear to worsen the effect of the original stimulus, but they are essential to get rid of the damaged tissue to allow it to be replaced with the new and healthy. Sooner or later everything settles down and health is restored.

Now there are many illnesses, whose cause is usually not known where the inflammation spirals out of control and actually becomes destructive. This is the case with rheumatoid arthritis, in which the body's defence mechanisms – the inflammatory cells – turn on the healthy tissues of the joints and ligaments. The potent enzymes whose function it is to remove injured tissue attack the normal, and so nature's mechanism of healing becomes itself a noxious stimulus.

Inflammation is thus analogous to a fire which, when confined to the grate, performs the useful function of giving off heat but, if it escapes, threatens to burn the house down.

Steroids dampen down the process of inflammation. They will not cure the illness itself, but they can control the symptoms of pain or loss of function in the hope that the illness will eventually lessen in severity. The Catch-22 of steroid treatment is that it achieves its effect by interfering with the healing mechanisms of the body so that, inevitably, the side effects include increasing susceptibility to infection which can at times be so devastating that even trivial illnesses, such as chickenpox, may turn lethal.

Steroids have many other useful physiological functions – controlling the level of glucose in the blood, the balance of salts and the absorption of calcium – all of which are disturbed by giving steroids over and above natural requirements, resulting in diabetes, raised blood pressure, thinning of the bone and much else besides. Thus, the public perception of steroids as powerful and potentially unpleasant drugs is correct. Too often, however, they are also thought to be unnecessary when they are, in fact, irreplaceable. Every year they save the lives of thousands suffering asthma attacks and acute allergic reactions. They stop people going blind, relieve paralysis, are essential for organ transplants and for curing cancers like leukaemia and lymphoma. As for the dreadful side effects to which Dr Savage referred, it is clear that these were due to the very high doses used in the early days – up to ten times higher than those commonly prescribed today. Nowadays, indeed, the optimum dosage of steroids is the irreducible minimum needed to control symptoms. A standard textbook puts it: 'The initial dose should be small and gradually increased until the symptoms have been reduced to tolerable levels. Complete relief is not sought. At frequent intervals, the dose should be gradually reduced until the recurrence of symptoms signals that the acceptable dose has been found.'

4

The Surgeon's Knife

Modern surgery is a marvel, but as 'Heroic Surgery' points out, its practitioners can at times be a bit over-enthusiastic. 'Suitable Day Case' looks at the increasing popularity of convalescing at home rather than in hospital. Sometimes it is not at all clear what the best thing is to do as illustrated by 'A Surgical Conundrum'. The next two pieces 'Heart Operations for Oldies' and 'Am I Too Old For a Transplant' point out there is now virtually no age limit for the most complex of operations. The last two pieces 'Modern Miracles' and 'The Gift of Life Can Be a Burden' examine the difficult problems of transplants in children.

'Heroic' Surgery

The sheer chutzpah of surgeons can be breathtaking. Mr Katsuhiko Ynaga, of Kyushu University's Department of Surgery in Japan, had a problem. His 49-year-old male patient had a tumour of the colon successfully removed but was subsequently found to have a solitary metastasis in the liver. Normally it would be possible to remove this, in which case the prognosis would be excellent. But it was buried deep inside, and surgical intervention was potentially disastrous because of the danger of uncontrollable haemorrhage. So what did Mr Ynaga do? He temporarily tied off the liver's blood supply and its other connections and took out the whole organ just as if he were removing an engine from a car. He could then carefully cut out the metastasis without any danger of bleeding, after which he replaced the organ and connected up the arteries and veins again. A year later his patient was doing fine. Mr Ynaga's operation was courageous but really it was just an exercise in lateral thinking, the skills necessary to remove and replace livers having been refined over the years in transplant programmes. All Mr Ynaga had to do was use the same techniques to give the patient back his own liver minus its cancerous growth. So obvious in retrospect – but so elegant.

A similar exercise in lateral thinking led to the first successful lung transplant ten years ago. I was working in a department of respiratory medicine, at that time, with several patients suffering from terminal chronic lung disease whose only hope would have been a transplant. But several attempts had ended in disaster – the lung just seemed too delicate and its connections to the heart too complex. Bruce Reitz, a surgeon at Stanford University, found the solution. Rather than attempting to transplant a single lung, he did something much more ambitious but technically much simpler: He transplanted both lungs and heart all together. This innovative operation, which is now fairly routine, had an added bonus. As the recipient had both his working heart and his damaged lungs removed to make room for the transplant, his heart was now available to be transplanted into some other patient who might need it.

Surgeons must have a certain personality to attempt this type of heroic surgery – enormous self-confidence, assertiveness and singlemindedness – but this can have its drawbacks. A report from the Royal College of Surgeons – *The National Confidential Enquiry into Perioperative Deaths* – drew attention to the regrettable surgical habit of performing 'heroic' operations on patients 'whose death is inevitable and imminent'. In one instance a 68-year-old man with inoperable cancer of the brain was recommended for surgery and then required a second operation the same day to release the build-up of pressure within the skull. He died soon afterwards. Another example of a 'hopeless' operation was a 74-year-old woman with a head injury who ended up on the operating table even though she appeared lifeless at the time. She later died from bronchial pneumonia. A 34-year-old woman dying from kidney failure due to cancer of the cervix was subjected to a hysterectomy and multiple bowel resection by a gynaecology registrar. There are many others. Why did they do it? Professor John Blandy, chairman of the committee which produced the report, commented that sometimes operations were done on the very sick to reassure relatives that 'no stone was being left unturned'. This may be true but there is another deeper reason. Surgeons like doing things. In particular they like operating, and the more technically difficult the operation, the greater the challenge and the greater the buzz they get from it. This blurs their clinical judgement.

The problem is less for those whose prognosis is gloomy – such as the cases cited in the report – than for patients who have to live with the consequences of the operation for some time. 'I was fine until they started mucking about with me' is not an uncommon observation by, for example, patients with a tumour of the lung found to be inoperable at the operation. With modern X-ray techniques it should be possible to determine whether a lung tumour is amenable to operation, and the failure to ascertain this means that the patient ends up both with the symptoms of the tumour and the sometimes severe and debilitating pain of having had his chest opened to no good purpose. It is difficult to give specific advice about this further than to suggest that if a major 'exploratory' operation is proposed, or the surgeon seems equivocal about the likelihood of success, then a second opinion should be sought.

A Suitable Day Case for Treatment

The working life of an anaesthetist has been described as 99 per cent boredom and 1 per cent panic. The patient is trundled into the operating theatre, a slug of barbiturates in the veins sends him to sleep, another drug relaxes the muscles, a tube is popped down the throat and connected up to the gas and air, and the operation can begin. Besides keeping an eye on a few knobs on the anaesthetic machine and monitoring the blood pressure, the anaesthetist has little else to do other than engage the surgeon in polite banter. Unless, that is, the patient turns blue or the heart stops beating, when all hell breaks loose. There is, of course, more to the life of an anaesthetist than this, but it contains an element of truth – general anaesthesia for most routine operations is not difficult. Suddenly, however, everything has changed. The shift towards day-case surgery combined with technical advances has transformed anaesthetic practice, with undoubted benefit to all.

Virtually everybody seems to be in favour of day-case surgery. It cuts costs by half, frees hospital beds for others (thus reducing waiting lists), and boosts the productivity of surgeons. Patients can convalesce in the comforting environment of their own bedroom, and it allows them greater freedom to choose when to have their operation. The trend seems unstoppable. Although it currently accounts for only 15 per cent of operations, the Royal College of Surgeons has recommended that this should rapidly increase to as much as 50 per cent. The trend has been accelerated by dramatic changes in surgical technique. Large incisions allowing direct visualisation and manipulation of structures are on the way out. They are being replaced by inserting slender endoscopes through punctures in the skin to remove gall bladders from the abdomen and repair torn meniscuses in knee joints. Fine catheters can now dilate blocked arteries to the heart, achieving the same results as major surgery. None of this would be possible without a fundamental rethink of the practice of anaesthesia. The goal is 'street-fitness': the patient must have recovered sufficiently to be able to walk out of the hospital the same evening, and the side effects of an operation – pain, nausea, headache, and general debility – must be minimised. King's College Hospital in south London has been a pioneer of day-case surgery, and consultant anaesthetist Dr Anthony Fisher has summarised their experience in some detail.

The process starts with a visit to the day-surgery centre to check on fitness for the operation, and to perform some simple screening tests. Any potentially difficult problems are assessed by a consultant, and a date is fixed.

When the big day comes the patient returns to the unit, where he is provided with an armchair to relax in and a trolley which will also serve as bed and operating table. The standard sedative 'pre-med' is no longer routinely given, but a very short-acting anti-anxiety drug, midazolam, neutralises the stressful period of waiting. The essential question is whether the operation should be done with the patient awake under some form of anaesthesia, or asleep. Both methods have their advantages, but at King's a general anaesthetic is still the preferred option, though with important modifications. Anaesthetic sleep is now induced with propofol, which allows for a much more rapid recovery, and is maintained with a laryngeal mask rather than a tube down the trachea, thus eliminating the post-operative sore throat. During the operation adequate pain relief without excessive sedation is usually provided by the short-acting opiod drug, fentanyl. At the close of the operation local anaesthetic is infiltrated into the wound (or, in the case of orthopaedic surgery, injected into the joint) to provide immediate post-operative pain relief. This is supplemented by the non-steroidal anti-inflammatory group of drugs, such as ibuprofen (Nurofen), rather than the conventional morphine or pethidine, with their side effects of dizziness, vomiting and constipation. Most patients take only a few minutes to wake up. They are then transferred for a short period to a fully equipped recovery area. Once they can show the nursing staff that they can walk without difficulty and tolerate fluids without vomiting, they are sent on their way in the company of a responsible adult.

The main limitation of general anaesthesia remains, however – a sense of tiredness and debility which may persist for two to three weeks. Increasingly patients are requesting alternatives, of which there are several. Virtually every operation below the waist can be performed by injecting a local anaesthetic into the spinal cord. This is thus a good option for prostate problems, stripping varicose veins, and operating on the genital organs and the rectum. An even more restricted type of anaesthetic is possible for operations on the arms and legs, which can be rendered numb by injecting local anaesthetic into the plexus of nerves or, with a cuff around the limb, into a vein. However, these techniques require considerable skill and can be very time-consuming, so for the foreseeable future they are unlikely to replace general anaesthesia. The only fly in the ointment of this success story is that nobody really knows how well patients do in fact cope after their operation. When Adrian England, reader in anaesthetics at the Chelsea and Westminster Hospital, followed up 50 women after day-case laparoscopy by phoning them regularly, he found that a week later almost a quarter still had 'moderate or severe pain', while a significant minority also complained of nausea, headache and similar minor symptoms. Another survey, by surgeons at Oxford's Radcliffe Infirmary, of 18 patients following day-case hernia repair, found that eight 'experienced more pain than expected', and ten said they would have preferred to have stayed in hospital after the operation. Clearly there is still room for improvement in the anaesthetising of day-case patients.

A Surgical Conundrum

Here is an intriguing medical conundrum. For almost a year a 60-year-old barman experienced a crushing pain in the chest whenever he walked upstairs and more recently whilst walking to the corner shop for his morning paper. His doctor arranged for him to have an electrocardiogram, which showed that he had already had one heart attack and, from his symptoms, there was a strong possibility that he was about to have another one. It was arranged that he should have a coronary angiogram – an X-ray of the arteries to the heart – with a view to performing a bypass operation. But on the day before this was to take place, our barman woke to find that both his right arm and leg were weak and that it was difficult to find the correct words when talking. This was discovered to be due to a narrowing of the carotid arteries in the neck, which carry blood to the brain. So, in addition to an impending, potentially fatal heart attack, he was also about to suffer a full-blown stroke that could leave him paralysed.

Clearly our barman now needed two operations: a bypass to restore the bloodflow to the heart and 'decoking' of his carotid arteries (opening them up and scraping out the sludge within) to restore the bloodflow to his brain. Although theoretically these operations would prevent him having a heart attack and stroke, in practice the blood supply to both heart and brain was so precarious that they could have the opposite effect and precipitate either or both misfortunes. So what were the doctors to do? There is no 'right answer', as it is not possible to predict what may happen. But when a group of doctors were presented with this case, they gave a wide range of opinions. Most suggested that nothing be done other than to thin the blood with anticoagulant drugs and for everyone to keep their fingers crossed. Dr Graham Jackson, cardiologist at Guy's Hospital, argued that decoking of the carotid artery should take priority, while Philip Hornick of the Hammersmith Hospital in London believed that both the decoking and the bypass should be done simultaneously in one combined operation. There are several reason why judicious medical opinion should vary so widely. While some doctors are by instinct and experience conservative, others favour action, which in extreme circumstances is usually justified as 'there is nothing to be lost'. The doctor's experience is a powerful influence as the highly skilled surgeon may be able to perform an operation that would not be possible or would carry an unacceptably high risk of complication were it to be undertaken by anyone else.

In the end, the decision on our barman was to take further X-rays of both the carotid arteries to the brain (the one on the right side was completely closed, while the one on the left was 95 per cent narrowed), and the heart, which showed that all three blood vessels were severely restricted. With so little blood getting through, it was imperative, no matter the risk, for something to be done and the following day the patient had a successful decoking operation, his signs of paralysis retreated and he was left with only 'mild impairment of fine finger movements of the right hand'. He is now awaiting his bypass operation. So the interventionists were vindicated – although it required nerves of steel and immense skill even to begin to contemplate such a procedure where the carotid arteries were narrowed to the extent they were in this case. This is not something to be attempted by a surgeon working at a district general hospital doing ten such operations a year. Rather, anyone in such a situation should insist on being transferred to a unit that specialises in vascular surgery. This almost inevitably will increase the chances that the operation will be done, but more important, that it will also be successful.

Heart Ops for Oldies

There are many reasons why someone in their seventies should be short of breath. They could have bronchitis or pneumonia or anaemia or heart failure. Whatever it is, there is little difficulty in finding out what is amiss, and the appropriate treatment falls well within the competence of the ordinary family doctor. Sometimes, however, the matter proves more complex, and then it is natural to seek a specialist opinion. But this is not without its problems. A couple of years ago, I visited a man who lived on the second floor of a block of flats. The lifts worked only intermittently and he had been unable to get out for a while because, as he said, 'I get puffed just walking across the room.' We had not met before for the simple reason that, being eighty, he was one of a generation that did not like to bother the doctor. He was quite heavily tattooed, a sure sign that at some time he had been in the armed forces – and, indeed, he had spent the war chasing Rommel back and forwards across North Africa. His wife had died, his children had moved away and he gave the impression that he thought his own life was drawing to a close.

He had the classic signs of heart failure, which improved with a water tablet that drained the fluid off his lungs, so that his symptoms were quite a lot better on my next visit. As I examined him for the second time, the underlying causes of his problem became apparent. The valve through which blood flows from the heart into the major artery was narrowed, a condition known as aortic stenosis. It was not possible to say how narrowed – for that he would have to undergo specialist investigations to identify exactly the diameter of his aortic valve, but there would be no point in having such tests, unless he was prepared, despite his age, to undergo open-heart surgery to have the valve replaced. So we talked about the various possibilities for a while, during which he asked the fairly obvious questions, to which

I did not have the answers: how long might he live if he did not have the operation and, were he to have it, what was the chance of getting off the operating table alive?

Coincidentally, the following week, one of the medical journals described a very similar case in a woman of eighty-seven, and reviewed the results of replacing the aortic valve in octogenarians. From this, I gathered that my patient's prognosis was about 18 months, but were he to have surgery, his life expectancy would be little different from that of anyone else in his age group – that is, about another five years. The risks of open-heart surgery are considerable at this age, and there is an 'immediate' mortality rate of about 20 per cent. The 87-year-old woman had done very well and, after a month's stay in hospital – her operation was complicated by kidney failure and depression – she was described as 'back doing the housework!' and 'having resumed an active social schedule'. Inspired by this, I rang the cardiac surgeon at the local hospital and asked whether he took kindly to the idea of performing open-heart surgery on my patient now beginning his ninth decade. He did not dismiss the idea, but pointed out that the length of his current waiting-list oscillated somewhere between six and nine months. Were GPs like myself to make a habit of referring patients in their eighties, this waiting time would rapidly escalate to a year or more, he said. The inevitable consequence would be that some of those waiting – still in their fifties and sixties – would die before the date of their planned operation.

There was much to discuss on my third visit and, rather to my surprise, I found that I was the more enthusiastic. His reluctance, I suggested, was because he had already reconciled himself to the inevitable, and not 'having an active social schedule', he was not quite sure what he would do with the extra three or fours years a successful operation would allow him. He countered with the 'fair innings' argument. Having already made it to eighty, he thought it wrong that the few extra years he might gain could be at the cost of denying an extra decade or more to someone quite a lot younger. As time passed he actually became quite a lot better, capable of making it (lifts permitting) to the corner shop and back again for his daily paper. When I next raised the subject of his seeing a cardiologist, he agreed. Whether he did so to please me or because being out and about had changed his mind, I do not know.

He made it past the first hurdle, the investigations which confirmed severe aortic stenosis – but never made it to the operating table. A few weeks before his operation was due, he awoke very short of breath in the middle of the night, summoned an ambulance but, sadly, was dead by the time he reached hospital. Had I been a bit pushier earlier on, he would probably still be around. In retrospect, it seems a mistake in such circumstances to raise the question of whether serving the best interests of an individual might be at the expense of others – for example, by lengthening waiting-lists for some procedures. Since the health service reforms, so much money is frittered away that it seems important to focus attention on what medicine can achieve. Aortic valve replacement is technically feasible at virtually any age. If, as with my patient, there are no other serious medical problems, the benefits both in prolongation of life and its quality are substantial.

Am I Too Old for a Transplant?

Modern medical advances pose tricky problems of etiquette. If, for example, you are knocking seventy with a dicky heart or failing kidneys, do you politely ask whether you might be put up for a new organ, or wait to be offered the option in the form of a referral to the local transplant surgeon? Clearly, it is bad manners to appear to be too pushy and there are always those younger than you to consider, whose call on spare hearts or kidneys might be thought greater. On the other hand, those who don't ask, don't get.

When I worked in a kidney transplant unit 15 years ago the accepted, if never articulated, demarcation line was that all those over the age of 50 were 'too old'. Since then, the survival rates have markedly improved, thanks mainly to better immunosuppressive drugs – so, theoretically, there is no reason today why anything other than extreme decrepitude should be a barrier. It is a tricky subject, though. There was a major political row in Canada when a senior government minister in his mid-seventies – the lucky recipient of a heart transplant – was accused of having used his privileged position to get preferential treatment.

This whole matter has been clarified in an article in *The Lancet* by Mr Raymond Tesi of Ohio State University on 'renal transplantation in older people'. Mr Tesi has reviewed the results of 1,200 transplants analysed according to the age of the recipient and found, unexpectedly but very significantly, that whereas one in three kidneys were rejected in those under the age of 60, the figure for those older than this was one in ten. That is, the older one becomes, the greater the success rate – presumably because, with time, the immune system becomes more tolerant. Not surprisingly, however, overall survival was down 20 per cent in the older recipients because they were more likely to die from other causes, such as a stroke or heart attack. Still, 70 per cent of the 60-plus age group were fit and well five years after their operation. Mr Tesi concludes: 'It is not justified to prevent access to renal transplantation based on age.'

This seems fair enough, but with transplants for kidneys in short supply, it seems a bit wasteful to offer one to someone, only for that person to drop dead from a heart attack even though the kidney is still working. Mr R. W. S. Chang of St Helier Hospital in Carshalton has suggested that this possibility can be minimised if potential recipients are first medically assessed. Those found to have heart disease should first have a heart bypass before their transplant. 'Since introducing this policy,' he writes, 'we have not had a single unexpected death in our kidney transplant patients.'

Alternatively, a heart surgeon from the University Hospital in Zurich, Miralem Pasic, has proposed that where a patient dies with a functioning transplant, it should simply be re-used. One such patient was a 47-year-old man who had a massive stroke five days after his transplant. Accordingly, Mr Pasic whipped out the kidney and re-tranplanted it into a 58-year-old who, a year later, 'is fully active and without symptoms'. This situation, he admits, is unusual, but it shows just how routine this type of surgery has become if surgeons are now transplanting what are essentially third-hand organs.

As for the question of etiquette over whether to ask to be considered for a transplant, Professor J. S. Cameron of Guy's has set a useful precedent in giving a new kidney to a 78-year-old. Anyone in and around this age group should take note . . .

Modern Miracles

In July 1993 the world's longest living heart transplant patient, Arthur F. Gay, an American postal worker, died of cancer of the oesophagus at the age of 56. Back in 1973 Mr Gay had become seriously ill with terminal heart failure from a diseased valve, for which he was offered a heart transplant. In those days only a small fraction of patients survived the operation; the techniques were crude and the problems of organ rejection still not fully overcome. But Mr Gay took his chances and bought an extra twenty years of life with someone else's heart beating in his chest, before his premature demise from a completely unrelated condition. Nowadays it is all much less of a gamble: 70 per cent of patients survive at least five years and most of these return to full time employment. And, as a recent upbeat report from the University of Utah describes, young women now think nothing of following up their transplants by having a baby – despite the increased strain on the heart and the need to take a cocktail of immunosuppressant drugs. James Scott, an obstetrician, describes no less than 25 women who, following heart transplants, have had 27 babies – including two sets of twins – with no foetal or neo-natal misfortunes and no congenital abnormalities.

There is a double significance in Mr Gay's death: first it symbolises how, in a very short period of time, what in any other era would have been considered a miracle has become straightforward and almost routine. But, secondly, such 'miracles' have become so commonplace that they scarcely merit comment. Indeed, Mr Gay's obituary featured as a single paragraph tucked away on the inside pages of the *Journal of the American Medical Association*. Future medical historians will surely appreciate that this phenomenon, in which the miraculous within a few years becomes commonplace, as an extraordinary human achievement.

And it is happening all around us. Consider, for example, children with biliary atresia, born without a bile duct to drain bile from the liver into the gut. Bile salts build up and corrode the liver leading to cirrhosis, liver failure, coma and death by the age of 18 months. Well, that was the case up until 1989, when Dr Deirdre Kelly, a consultant in the Liver Unit at the Children's Hospital in Birmingham, decided to try to cure these babies with a liver transplant. This was helped by certain technical developments which meant that the transplanted liver could now, like buying a suit, be cut to the right size, so it was no longer necessary to rely solely on suitable donors from the same age group.

In the three years up to December 1992, 27 babies under the age of one year received a liver transplant at the Children's Hospital. They were terribly ill, 20 having reached the stage of hepatic encephalopathy, or inflammation of the brain, due to the accumulation of liver toxins in the blood. Post-operatively, they had the usual problems of infection and rejection, and indeed three had to have a second transplant after the first had failed. At the end of all this, one would expect their chances to be at best 50:50 – but it is not. The survival rate of these tiny babies following this massive and complicated operation was 88 per cent. So a child born with biliary atresia in 1987 – only six years ago – would certainly have died, but now, with almost equal certainty, he is likely to live. Here we have another medical miracle right under our noses. Such things are not easily achieved, and Dr Kelly specifically acknowledges at the end of her report in the *British Medical Journal* the enormous work and dedication of all 'whose skill has brought these children back to health'.

The Gift of Life Can Be a Burden

Doctors are reluctant to criticise each other openly. The dignity and authority of the profession are best maintained by presenting at least a façade of unanimity and common purpose. Every so often that façade cracks, and what can be glimpsed behind is most revealing. Two papers in the *Archives of Disease in Childhood* on heart-lung transplants in children illustrate this point. The results are remarkably similar, but the interpretation of their significance is diametrically at odds. Dr Peter Helms, from Great Ormond Street Hospital, finds the results 'encouraging', while Professor John Warner, of the National Heart and Lung Institute, talks of a 'nightmare ending in disaster'. What is going on?

Heart-lung transplants have been increasingly thought of as the definitive treatment for cystic fibrosis. Cystic fibrosis is one of the commonest hereditary diseases and causes an abnormality of secretions, especially in the lungs. The airways become plugged with mucus behind which small segments of lung collapse and become infected. The outcome used to be very poor, but the combination of powerful antibiotics, steroids and physiotherapy means that many sufferers now live well into their thirties. None the less, for the most severely affected, the recurrent infections take their toll, destroying the delicate structure of the lung air sacs, so sufferers become progressively short of breath and die from respiratory failure in their early teens. This gloomy prognosis could be transformed if it were possible to give these children a new pair of lungs. Nobody suggested it would be easy. Lungs are fragile organs and the operation itself is very difficult as their connections to the heart are so complex. As we have seen, this latter problem at least was resolved by deciding to transplant lungs and heart together, which is both simpler and has the added advantage that the recipient's own healthy heart can then be given to someone else. In the two years up to March 1990 the transplant team at Great Ormond Street had assessed 45 children, 19 of whom were considered unsuitable for a variety of reasons. At the time of writing the result of the remaining 26 were: 10 had died waiting for a transplant and 11 had been transplanted, of whom 6 survive, and 5 are still on the waiting list. Predictably, those who received a transplant have been plagued by episodes of rejection and serious lung infections, requiring repeated readmissions to hospital. Looked at optimistically, the transplant programme has benefited 6 out of 45 children with an improved quality of life for an indefinite period. Dr Helms goes further, to argue that it actually benefits all children with serious cystic fibrosis by 'letting in some hope when only inevitable deterioration and death seemed possible'.

Professor Warner's results are very similar: out of 26 children originally referred, 6 have had viable transplants and their lives have been 'miraculously transformed'. The question he poses is whether this is sufficient to justify 'the anguish and suffering that has been borne by the children and their families'. This transplant programme, he maintains, can never benefit more than a very small minority of children with cystic fibrosis, while for the rest it is little more than a cruel hoax. What, for example, are the feelings of those who are assessed for a transplant only to be told they are unsuitable? Or of those parents whose children die on the waiting list? What is the emotional cost of the hospitalisation periods necessary for the initial assessment, the subsequent transplant (for the lucky few) and its aftermath? How can one grasp the feelings of children on the waiting list? 'A more exquisite form of torture could not be devised,' he says, 'than to give a child a bleep that will sound once a week as a check, and will go off once at any time in the future to indicate that suitable organs may have been found.' And what of those children whose apparently successful transplants fail? Professor Warner describes one girl who before her transplant 'had been totally resigned to her fate and able to face death in a remarkably mature way.' For twelve months after her operation she was remarkably well until things started to go wrong. 'In her last six months, she became a frightened, desperate girl; she was assailed with morbid guilt about the donor of her heart and lungs.'

Superficially, Professor Warner's dispute with the doctors at Great Ormond Street centres on how the transplant programme has distorted the priorities and care that all children with cystic fibrosis should receive. But the substance of his charge is deeper than this – they are guilty of self-deception. Professor Warner's paper is called 'Heart-lung transplantation: all the facts', with the implication that up until now those involved have not provided them. So convinced of the importance of what they have achieved, they have hidden the true costs of this high-risk high-tech medicine. Behind the bare statistics of success and failure the agonising reality has been hidden away.

5

Prevention – Better than Cure?

It would be nice if 'prevention' was, as is frequently claimed, 'better and cheaper' than 'cure' but regrettably this is rarely the case, as is made clear in the third part of this anthology, 'The Hazards of Life?' This section examines an important aspect of prevention – 'screening' – the search for hidden problems in the hope of catching them early. The scope of screening is outlined in 'Checking out the Check-ups' which is followed by two pieces on preventing strokes. Probably the most successful, but paradoxically least practised form of screening is the detection of an aortic aneurysm before it bursts, which is discussed in 'A Screening Test that Works'.

Screening is particularly appropriate for those in whom a serious disease runs in the family and the following three pieces discuss the merits of screening for cancer of the colon, stomach, and cervix respectively. Screening for lung cancer is discussed on p. 257 and prostate cancer on p. 230. Finally the most contentious, expensive and least effective form of screening is discussed in 'The Cholesterol Controversy'.

Checking out the Check-ups

The New Year would not be the same without the opportunity for self-improving resolutions. But, as virtually everyone nowadays seems to have given up smoking, drinks only moderately and takes a spot of exercise, there is precious little to be resolved about. So what about splashing out on a really thorough private health check-up? The rationale is plausible enough. Three main illnesses, stroke, heart disease and cancer, account for nearly two-thirds of all deaths, so it seems sensible to invest the relatively modest sum of around £200 to enable doctors, with their sophisticated tests, to catch them early enough to be treatable or even cured. Theoretically, of course, a health check could turn up any number of illnesses, the pulse might betray an abnormality of heart rhythm, a pale complexion might suggest anaemia, or a yellow one jaundice. But in reality all these conditions would produce symptoms sufficient to take you to the doctor and so would not need a health check to find them.

Rather, the purpose of health check-ups, or screening, is to find 'hidden' illnesses but this in turn depends on how thorough the search is. Whereas a chest X-ray is easy to do and can be used as a routine screening test to find an early lung tumour, a barium enema is more difficult and so is of no value in screening for early bowel tumours. With this caveat, what can a private check-up reveal? It starts with a head-to-toe examination – looking in the eyes, listening to the chest, testing the reflexes and so on, which is reassuring in its thoroughness and can pick up two potentially serious conditions. The first is raised blood pressure, which if treated will prevent a stroke. The second (almost exclusively in men) is an aneurysm, or ballooning of the main aorta, suggested by a pulsating mass in the abdomen. The chance of this rupturing after it has reached a certain size – with maybe lethal consequences – is quite high.

To discover more 'hidden' diseases it is necessary to do some tests on the urine (the presence of sugar indicates diabetes) and the blood. Blood tests are now fully automated and generate a mass of data about the functioning of the kidneys, liver and thyroid gland and results look impressive on the final report. Again, however, it is most unlikely one might be suffering from, say, kidney disease without knowing about it and the only blood test that is a true screening test is for a raised blood cholesterol which may be a risk factor for heart disease. Then, the lungs will be further investigated with a chest X-ray which might conceivably catch a tumour of the lung early enough for it to be operated on. After this the heart is investigated with an electrocardiogram or ECG. The problem here is that this can be entirely normal even in the presence of heart disease and it may be necessary to do an 'exercise ECG', while the patient walks on the treadmill. This can bring out evidence of narrowing of the coronary arteries which otherwise would not be apparent. Finally, for women, a cervical smear may pick up an early cancer, and a mammogram an early breast tumour. Two further screening tests can also detect cancer early, but cost extra as they are not part of the 'standard' health check-up. An ultrasound of the pelvis may reveal a cancer of the ovary and testing the stool for blood may point to an early tumour of the bowel.

A week of so after the check-up you will receive an impressive-looking letter containing the findings from your physical examination along with a sheaf of your test results. But the number of 'hidden' diseases that might have been discovered is limited. Further, as discerning readers will realise, they could save their money as virtually all the useful tests are available anyhow on the National Health Service. The practice nurse at your local surgery will happily check your urine and measure your blood pressure every two years. Your GP will be equally happy to arrange a cholesterol test if there is a history of heart disease in the family and can be persuaded to arrange regular chest X-rays for smokers who are worried about getting lung cancer. National screening programmes provide regular cervical smears and mammograms for women up to the age of 65. For those who wish to carry on after this, most GPs will be happy to arrange it.

All the other screening tests not done on the NHS – the exercise ECG, the ovarian ultrasound and testing the stools for blood – have to be paid for anyhow as extras in addition to routine private health checks. The sensible thing then is just to dispense with the routine private health check-up while taking full advantage of what is available on the NHS.

Preventing Strokes – 1

At the time, the resignation of Russian Prime Minister Pavlov because of 'raised blood pressure' one day after the abortive Soviet coup was highly significant. Such an obvious diplomatic illness was a clear indication that the counter-revolutionary leadership was in serious disarray. Pavlov's blood pressure may indeed have been raised by his part in the coup, but it was an unconvincing reason for making his excuses and stepping down. It is becoming apparent that due to the stressful circumstances under which many millions in the West have been told they have raised blood pressure (hypertension), the validity of this diagnosis may be as unsound as that of Mr Pavlov's.

The main problem is that most people find it stressful visiting their doctor's surgery. By the time the doctor gets round to taking their blood pressure, the reading may be misleadingly high. Then, being labelled as suffering from hypertension, with its clear risk of a stroke in the future, can also be stressful, so that a return visit to the surgery may also produce inappropriately high readings.

The potency of 'doctor-induced hypertension' was revealed clearly by one of my patients whose raised blood pressure I had been trying – unsuccessfully – to treat for over a year, with a wide array of different drugs. He turned up at the surgery one day to tell me he had bought his own blood-pressure machine, and presented me with the results of four weeks of twice-daily measurements, all entirely normal. Since then, I have told as many patients as can afford it to buy one of these machines as the only sure protection against having to take unnecessary amounts of drugs.

Doctors should adhere to certain strict criteria if patients are not to be told wrongly that they have 'hypertension'. Before the diagnosis is made, the patient's blood pressure reading has to be consistently elevated when taken – at rest – on at least three separate occasions, preferably at monthly intervals. But perhaps even this is insufficient. One of the most surprising findings (to doctors) of a large Australian trial of the treatments of patients with mild hypertension was that the blood pressure of more than half of the placebo group (those not given drug treatment), reverted to normal over a period of two years. The fact that many with mild hypertension probably have normal blood pressures explains why the benefits of treatment appear so modest. The largest study undertaken by the British Medical Research Council found that 850 people had to be treated for one year to prevent one stroke.

If, over the years, doctors have been too enthusiastic about diagnosing hypertension, the obvious question is whether those now taking drug treatment could stop without any untoward consequences. Dr Malcolm Aylett and Dr Stuart Ketchlin, from Northumberland, have tried just this with nine patients and found that two years later, eight still had normal blood pressure. The implications of this are phenomenal. As the doctors point out, two million adults in Britain are currently being treated for hypertension, at a total cost of £104 million. Stopping treatment in even a small number of cases would save enormous sums, while the patients themselves would be relieved of the burden of a diagnosis that many find very worrying.

Preventing Strokes – 2

A reader writes that, following her husband's severe stroke, she has been reading medical books and now realises there were warning signs whose significance they had failed to appreciate. Had they done so, the stroke might have been prevented. I would, she suggests, be doing a great service if I passed on this vital information.

There are two main reasons why strokes occur. In the first, a blood vessel in the brain bursts, causing haemorrhage into the surrounding tissue. This occurs most commonly in those with raised blood pressure or hypertension, and is preventable by taking drugs. The second is due to a blood clot, or embolus, in the small arteries of the brain, impeding the flow of blood so that the tissue beyond it dies. These may be preceded by one or more mini, or transient, strokes.

Preventing strokes caused by raised blood pressure seems quite straightforward. You should go to the doctor every two or three years, have your blood pressure checked and, if it is raised on three separate occasions, take pills to lower it. It is not quite so simple as that. What, after all, is 'raised' blood pressure? For the young and middle-aged the consensus is that it is anything over the arbitrary measurement of 140/90 millimetres of mercury. But as one ages, the blood pressure naturally rises, so for older people it is much more difficult to decide what is 'high'.

Nonetheless it seems sensible to err on the side of caution and take the pills: with two important provisos. The pills that lower blood pressure generally need to be taken indefinitely, but for a significant number of patients the underlying hypertension seems to get better. The only way of telling is by stopping the pills and seeing if the pressure stays down. In a recent Swedish study of 333 patients between 70 and 84, 20 per cent of those who stopped treatment still had a 'normal' blood pressure five years later. Then, as I have already explained, there is the problem of 'doctor-induced hypertension' – when people see their doctors, they tend to be anxious, and this pushes up the blood pressure. This is particularly important as it might suggest the medication is not working, or that it needs to be taken at a higher dose, or that stronger pills have to be substituted. It is obviously undesirable to take more or stronger pills than necessary, and the only way round this is to buy your own blood-pressure machine, or electronic sphygomanometer, and measure it yourself in the comfort of your own home.

The second preventable kind of stroke, from an embolus, is often preceded by a 'shot across the bows' in which the signs of a stroke – paralysis, loss of sensation, vertigo and double vision or blindness in one eye – last for 24 hours or less. These are known as Transient Ischaemic Attacks (TIAs), where the embolus has temporarily interrupted the blood flow to part of the brain before dispersing. The danger is that a further embolus may be too large to disperse; and indeed, following a TIA, there is a one-in-ten chance of developing a major stroke within a year. Clearly TIAs have to be carefully evaluated to find the source of the embolus. If it comes from the heart, further ones can be prevented by taking blood-thinning drugs such as aspirin or Warfarin. The other major source of embolus may be a small fleck of atheroma breaking away from the inner wall of the arteries to the brain – the carotid arteries. If X-rays show these arteries to be narrowed by more than 70 per cent, an operation to scrape away the atheroma may be recommended. Both the operation and the drugs carry some risk of causing a stroke, but this is obviously considerably less than if the TIA goes untreated. Despite all this hassle, avoiding a stroke is so intrinsically desirable that every one should make the effort to have their blood pressure checked regularly and their TIAs treated promptly.

A Screening Test that Works

Farmer Alfred Edwards will always be grateful for an attack of bellyache three years ago which forced him to take to his bed. Lying on his back, stroking his stomach to ease the pain, he felt a pulsation just under the ribcage he had never noticed before. 'It felt like a balloon pumping away in tune with my heartbeat,' he recalls. For six months Mr Edwards dithered before going to the doctor, but then things moved very quickly. An ultrasound test at hospital confirmed that the major artery that runs the length of the abdomen just in front of the spine – the abdominal aorta – had ballooned outwards under pressure from the blood surging through it to form an aneurysm. 'By all accounts, it was a whopper,' says Mr Edwards. He describes the surgical resection of his aneurysm and its replacement with a Teflon graft as 'not pleasant, but infinitely preferable to the alternative'.

The 'alternative' would have been that at some time in the next year or two, his aneurysm would have burst, spurting blood into his abdominal cavity. Most patients die rapidly, but even if Mr Edwards had been lucky enough to get to hospital his chances of surviving the operation would still have been only 50–50. It is easy to imagine why emergency repair of a ruptured aneurysm should so frequently be unsuccessful. First, the patient is in shock with several litres of blood swirling around his guts, making it difficult to see what is going on. The surgeon has to clamp off the aorta, cut out the aneurysm and spend an hour or more meticulously sewing the graft in place. Then those lucky enough to get off the table alive run the risk of developing a heart attack or acute kidney failure from prolonged low blood pressure. In the words of Peter Harris, a surgeon at the Royal Liverpool University Hospital: 'Despite extravagant consumption of scarce health service resources, the impact of emergency surgical treatment is slight. This is either because massive haemorrhage from the rupture is immediately fatal, or there is damage to vital organs from which there is little chance of recovery despite diligent intensive after-care.' He does not believe the situation is likely to improve. But, if the aneurysm is diagnosed before such a catastrophe – as in Mr Edward's case – the chance of successful repair is much higher. Indeed, there is a memorable simplicity about the statistics: 95 per cent of those with a leaking aortic aneurysm die, whereas 95 per cent of those whose aneurysm is repaired before it leaks will survive.

Mr Edwards's experience would suggest that it might be sensible were all men (the condition is much rarer in women) to check for a pulsating balloon-shaped mass in the abdomen. The number of aneurysms detected in this way is surprisingly high. In a study of just under 500 men between the ages of 65 and 74, Jack Collin, vascular surgeon at the John Radcliffe Infirmary in Oxford, found twenty-two had a suspicious pulsation in eight of whom an ultrasound test confirmed the presence of an aneurysm. Mr Collin calculates that if these findings were to be extended to the whole country, 22,000 men would be found to have a life-threatening aneurysm while a national screening programme in which all men at the age of 65 had just one ultrasound test would prevent '6,000 unnecessary deaths from ruptured aortic aneurysm'. The main impediment to such a screening programme is the cost, which is estimated as being about £11 million for England and Wales. This might seem expensive but when calculated as the cost of every life saved, it turns out to be a hundred times cheaper than screening for breast cancer.

For the moment there seems little hope that the Health Department will agree to a national screening programme, so what else can be done besides periodic self-examination? When men in their sixties go to the surgery for their annual blood pressure check they should ask the GP to perform an examination of the abdomen and if he detects a pulsating mass this should be followed by an ultrasound test to exclude (or, rarely, confirm) the presence of an aneurysm. This approach is particularly commended for those whose close relatives may have had or died from a ruptured aneurysm since the condition runs strongly in families. Though not approaching the ideal of a nationwide screening programme, the involvement of family doctors in detecting aortic aneurysms, either on their own initiative or at the instigation of their patients, would still reap substantial rewards.

Screening for Cancer – 1

The Papal abdomen is heavily scarred. First there was the assassin's bullet that entered one side and exited the other. Then there was the operation to remove a benign 'grapefruit-size' tumour from his colon. We know what happened to the bullet, It was retrieved from the arm of a nearby pilgrim and has now found a home under the crown of the statue of the Virgin Mary at Fatima, and become an object of veneration for the faithful. The passing pilgrim – from the southern United States – has also become something of a celebrity as the experience of being wounded by a bullet which has just traversed the Papal gut seems to have given her considerable prestige among fellow Catholics back home. The ultimate destination of the Papal tumour remains uncertain. In earlier times, no doubt, it would have been mounted in a glass case, to be worshipped as a holy relic. Now it is more likely to end-up bathed in formaldehyde in a plastic box as a prime exhibit in a pathology museum at the Vatican hospital.

The Pope was lucky to have survived the assassin's bullet. Now he had been lucky again. At his age, it was much more likely that the tumour would have been malignant than benign, in which case the prognosis would have been very different. The fact that it had already reached the size of a grapefruit before causing symptoms serves to emphasise just how difficult it can be to detect tumours of the colon early enough for them to be curable. In theory, this is possible. Both benign and malignant tumours leak small amounts of blood which can be detected by a Haemoccult test – where a specimen of the stool is placed on a specially treated piece of paper which changes colour if blood cells are present. Those testing positive undergo a colonoscopy, in which a flexible tube is passed around the colon until the source of the bleeding is identified. Nearly half of the colon cancers detected by the Haemoccult test are diagnosed at the earliest stage when they can be cured by surgical removal. Were this type of testing to become widespread, there would be a substantial fall in the toll of 75,000 deaths a year from colon cancer. And there is no doubt it works. A pilot project in Birmingham, co-ordinated by Dr Richard Hobbs with the help of five local practices, detected six early colon cancers in almost 2,000 patients.

Despite this, early detection of cancer by these means is not readily practicable for two reasons. The public, for aesthetic reasons, seems reluctant to take part, with only a quarter of the target population in the Birmingham study agreeing to do the test. Moreover, even if social attitudes were to change and more people wanted the test, there would not be nearly enough doctors skilled in colonoscopy to perform the necessary investigations in those whose tests turn out to be positive. Nothing illustrates better the enormous gulf between the potential of modern techniques to detect cancer early enough for it to be cured, and the reality of how difficult it is to achieve.

The prospect of early detection of cancer at the top end of the gastro-intestinal tract – the stomach – is more encouraging. Only one in twenty of those diagnosed with stomach cancer live longer than five years. The main reason is delay in making the diagnosis, because common symptoms of the cancer, such as loss of appetite or indigestion, are often interpreted by patients and their GPs as due to dyspepsia and treated with antacids. Time passes, the symptoms do not improve, so a special X-ray or endoscopy is finally performed which reveals, too late, the dread disease. The Japanese, who have a very high rate of stomach cancer, have a policy of rigorously investigating anybody with dyspepsia and by early detection have pushed the cure rate up to 50 per cent. Taking a leaf out of the Japanese book, a British surgeon, Mr J.W.L. Fielding, has set up a service where GPs can refer any patients over the age of 40 with the first symptoms of dyspepsia for an immediate endoscopy. The number of cancers detected in the earliest stage soared, and the proportion suitable for curative surgery rose from 20 to 65 per cent.

Those wishing to maximise their chance of surviving these types of cancer therefore need to do two things. They need to enquire from their doctors how to get hold of Haemoccult test strips and test their stools every two years: if the test is positive they will have to encourage their GP to arrange a colonoscopy to reveal the source of the bleeding. And anyone who develops dyspeptic symptoms for the first time over the age of 40 should ask their GP for an early referral for an endoscopy.

Screening for Cancer – 2

After I had made an inspired diagnosis of athlete's foot in a young man with itchy rash between his toes, he solemnly informed me that his father had the same condition, and so he presumed it must 'run in the family'. Many common maladies – headaches, menstrual disorders, varicose veins, and so on – appear to 'run in families', for which there are two possible explanations. First, these illnesses are, by definition, common, so it might just be coincidence that both parent and child are affected. Alternatively, genetic inheritance may in some subtle way be involved, not in causing the condition but in increasing susceptibility to it. Perhaps those with a family history of athlete's foot may have some subtle inherited defect of the skin between their toes, making it less resistant to fungal infections.

Needless to say, it is not easy to distinguish between 'coincidence' and 'inheritance', and in practical terms it makes no difference which it is. None the less, when some condition does affect more than one family member, many people seem to prefer to believe it is a family trait, because at the very least this offers some sort of explanation. For migraine-sufferers, the fact that an aunt or grandparent 'suffered terribly from headaches' can be quite consoling, as it makes sense of why they are so afflicted.

It is a different matter when a close relative has a serious illness, such as cancer or heart disease, because here the popular belief that illnesses run in families can be a potent cause of unwarranted fears. At one time I saw a lot of a woman in her mid-thirties, with vague and changing symptoms of abdominal discomfort and nausea. I could find nothing wrong, and the specialist to whom I referred her could find nothing wrong, while intensive investigations all turned out to be normal. Dissatisfied with this verdict, she asked for a second opinion. She was convinced she had cancer, she told me, and the failure of both myself and the specialist to find it was only because we had been insufficiently diligent. Indeed, her uncle had died from a tumour in the colon, she said, only because his doctors had not discovered it until 'too late'. Over the years I have seen several patients with similar 'cancer phobia', invariably induced by this belief that cancer runs in families, and so that if a relative is struck down, it is only a matter of time before they themselves succumb. It is difficult to be completely reassuring in these circumstances, since some cancers, a minority of around 5 per cent, are indeed caused by a genetic defect, and thus occur more frequently in some families than others.

Breast cancer is the best-known example, where the risk markedly increases with the number and closeness of relatives with the disease, and the age it becomes apparent in them. The discovery of two breast-cancer genes now allows the prediction of this risk to be made even more accurately, and those with the defective gene have an 87 per cent chance of getting the disease in their lifetime. It is thus possible to distinguish between families with a 'moderate' risk and a 'high' risk of breast cancer, and plan appropriate screening tests at regular intervals in the hope of catching it early enough for it to be curable. A similar approach can be taken with ovarian cancer, and since it now appears that the genetic defect may be the same as that of breast cancer, women from affected families should be screened for both diseases.

So whenever cancer does appear to 'run in the family', and particularly if it occurs at a young age, further steps need to be taken. A report into 34 first-degree male relatives from families in which 2 brothers had developed prostate cancer turned up 'previously unsuspected' and clinically relevant cancer in 8 of them. This might sound quite straightforward, but it is fraught with uncertainty, both in establishing a definitive genetic link, and in deciding how to act on that information. Further, the opportunities to generate unwarranted anxiety are considerable, because inevitably some people will find themselves living in the shadow of a potentially serious illness that they will never get. Advice can be obtained from several family cancer clinics that have been set up around the country, or from a consultant clinical geneticist.

Screening for Cancer – 3

A cheery newspaper headline announces *Smear tests save 2,000 lives a year*, summarising a report from the national cervical cancer screening programme. The exact words of the programme's Secretary, Dr Muir Gray, were slightly less emphatic: 'I believe we are saving between 1,000 and 2,000 lives a year,' he is quoted as saying. This, in turn, was an optimistic gloss of the precise figures for England and Wales for the four years from 1988 to 1992 which show that deaths from cervical cancer are falling at the rate of 300 a year. This is certainly an over-estimate of the benefits of screening as the incidence of cervical cancer has been falling at a similar rate since the war. A more accurate headline might have been *Smear tests may save one hundred lives per year*. Put another way, despite 40 million smears taken over 25 years, screening has, at best, reduced mortality by about 10 per cent. Professor E.G. Knox of Manchester University has called this an 'unprecedented failure' and James McCormick, professor of community medicine at Trinity College, Dublin, describes it as 'an expensive contribution to ill-health because the harm screening causes exceeds any possible benefits by a substantial margin'. Throw in the occasional scandal, when the reliability of the smear or its interpretation have been questioned, and the reports of women being found to have cancer after a 'normal' smear, and Dr Muir Gray's optimism appears rather misplaced.

Even if cancer screening is not as effective as might be hoped, there is naturally a feeling that it must be a good thing. It might be, but any benefits must be balanced against the costs as screening and, particularly the treatment of 'pre-cancerous' changes in the cervix in the hope of preventing them from progressing, can be traumatic and unpleasant. First there is the initial reaction to the news that the cervical smear is abnormal. As Nicky Britten, a lecturer in medical sociology, expressed it in the *British Medical Journal*: 'Surprisingly, despite my belief that early detection was a good thing, I reacted badly. For several days I could think of nothing but death. I saw myself dying in the near future and was only consoled with the thought that it might be better to die young surrounded by loved ones than old and alone.' This is followed – usually after a long and anxious wait – by colposcopy, the direct visualisation of the cervix to allow biopsies to be taken, which, in Miss Britten's case, was complicated by severe haemorrhage requiring two hospital admissions. Laser treatment is not pain-free, and, as cervical cancer has been linked to sexual activity, most women find that at some time or other they are interrogated about previous episodes of venereal disease and the number of sexual partners. As one women put it: 'I had to pause to make sure I gave the right answer, and a look I have never been able to interpret passed between doctor and nurse which made me feel very small indeed.'

More than 10,000 women go through this experience every year, far greater than the mortality figures for cervical cancer before screening was introduced, and many – perhaps 95 per cent – are being treated unnecessarily, as even without laser treatment, the abnormalities in the cervix would not have progressed to cancer. If nothing else, cervical screening must be generating misery and psycho-sexual problems on a substantial scale. Now this might be acceptable if screening was having, as claimed, a major impact on the disease, but clearly this is not the case.

There are probably two reasons for this. First, the smear is not a very good test because it identifies 'abnormalities' which may or may not be significant; and as it is not possible to tell, all must be treated. Further, it is assumed that mild pre-cancerous changes become more aggressive, so early treatment nips the cancer in the bud. This may be the case in some instances, but clearly cancer can also arise very rapidly in the interval between one cervical smear and the next. Secondly, all women must have a regular smear if screening is to work. This is relatively easy to organise in countries or districts with well-defined, well-educated, stable populations, but Britain is a different matter. The logistics of trying to reach the deprived in the inner cities who are most at risk from the disease are daunting. When Dr Rosemary Beardow of London's St Mary's Hospital tracked the fate of just under 700 letters sent to women asking them to attend for a smear, she found that in over half the address was incorrect and in a further fifth, the request was inappropriate. Only 90 women ended up having their cervical smear.

Theoretically cervical cancer could be prevented in Britain, but at impossible financial cost and then only by exposing ever more women to the miseries of unnecessary treatment. I wish there was some way out of this impasse, but there is not. It may eventually be possible to devise a test which would reliably identify those at special risk, thus making prevention on a large scale a realistic possibility, but that time has not yet come.

The Cholesterol Controversy

Mr C. G. from Middlesex is a man of habit. For five decades he started the day by treating himself to a proper breakfast – eggs and bacon, thickly buttered toast, marmalade and fresh coffee. Then he had his cholesterol measured: it was 7.6, and life has never been the same since. The morning egg is boiled and the smell of sizzling bacon is just a memory: indeed he has cut out virtually all animal fats, and soya margarine now covers his toast. The result? He has lost 7 pounds, his cholesterol is down to 6 and 'I've lost my former sense of wellbeing'. Mr C. G. had read that low cholesterol levels are associated with depression and wondered whether this might be the explanation.

For more than a decade the medical profession has persuaded itself that the cholesterol question was all sorted out. Cholesterol whooshes around the circulation, furring up the arteries, and as a result far too many people keel over from coronaries before their time. A rigorous low-fat diet can certainly lower cholesterol, and if it were widely adopted the nation's arteries would remain squeaky clean. For those with very high cholesterol, this is insufficient and they have to take cholesterol-lowering drugs. The implication of all this is that cholesterol consciousness will prevent thousands of premature deaths, make a lot of money for the drug companies, and everyone will live happily ever after.

But is it true? The experience of a couple of octogenarians is very useful in illuminating the general controversies over the value or otherwise of reducing fat in the diet in order to reduce one's level of cholesterol in the blood. The first is an 88-year-old man living in a retirement home in America who for 15 years or more has been eating twenty to thirty eggs a day. According to the nurse attached to the home he takes delivery of two dozen eggs a day which he always eats soft boiled. He keeps a careful record, egg by egg, of his intake, which must be compulsive. Dr Fred Kern of the University of Colorado School of Medicine has taken an interest in his case because, despite a cholesterol intake 40 times greater than that recommended for a 'healthy diet', his blood cholesterol level is normal and he has no clinical evidence of atherosclerosis. How does he do it? Dr Kern uncovered three main mechanisms. First, his gut has adapted by absorbing only a fraction of the cholesterol content of the eggs and excreting 80 per cent. Second, his liver metabolism has reduced the amount of cholesterol it synthesises. Third, the volume of bile – which contains cholesterol – travelling down the bile ducts is much greater than normal. This octogenarian's highly efficient methods of disposing of the excess cholesterol from his two-dozen-eggs-a-day habit means that the actual amount of cholesterol circulating in his blood is no different from that of someone on a low-fat and low-cholesterol diet. This in turn reflects a vital nutritional truth which is too often ignored: attempts to influence physiological variables, such as cholesterol level or blood pressure, by changing one's diet are extremely difficult as there are so many adaptive homeostatic mechanisms conspiring to maintain them in a steady state. Indeed it must be so, for man could not survive for long if minor environmental changes like what and how much he eats every day readily perturbed the *milieu intérieur*.

The second case is that of an 86-year-old woman whose unusual Christmas present from her family was a visit to a private hospital for a 'cardiovascular risk assessment'. This included measuring her cholesterol, which turned out to be 7.3. She was accordingly advised to reduce the amount of fat in her diet – which usually means cutting out eggs and bacon for breakfast, only eating low-fat cheeses and drinking skimmed milk. Her GP, Dr John Justice, commented in the *British Medical Journal* recently: 'This would not have lengthened her life, but would certainly have made it more miserable. She was greatly relieved to be told to eat what she liked.' There are two interesting aspects of this story. Blood cholesterol levels rise with age, so though 7.3 might be on the high side for people in their forties, it is optimal for those over the age of 70, anything lower being associated with an increased risk of strokes and cancer. Clearly the medical advice given to this woman was not only ludicrous but potentially harmful. Further, if she had followed the advice given, her life, as Dr Justice observes, would have been made more miserable.

No doubt it must be a bit depressing to be bullied into sacrificing the much loved pleasures of bacon and eggs for breakfast, but that is not all. Many of those forced into a low-fat diet and take cholesterol-lowering drugs report, like Mr C. G. of Middlesex, a loss of their usual sense of wellbeing. The reason may lie in an observation by Dr Hyman Engelberg of the Californian Arteriosclerosis Research Foundation in *The Lancet* that altering the blood cholesterol might have an effect on neurotransmitters in the brain, particularly in altering the physical shape of the receptors for serotonin, which influences the mental state. In fact there is quite a lot of evidence, none of it reassuring, linking cholesterol and personality. It has been noticed that anti-social criminals – youths with 'aggressive conduct disorders' and murderers who are 'habitually violent when intoxicated by alcohol' – all have lower than average cholesterol levels. The simple answer to Mr C. G.'s query, then, is it is not possible to say for certain whether lowering cholesterol causes depression. But the evidence is highly suggestive. Further, as his boiled eggs and soya margarine are unlikely to be doing him much good I urge him to revert to his proper breakfast without delay.

6

The Alternatives

Helping Hands for Healing

A general practitioner in St Albans is offering to heal her patients by the laying on of hands. Dr Jean Robertson, who has been in practice for twenty-six years, had had little time for alternative therapies until a healer turned up at her daughter's funeral. 'She touched us all, including our district nurse, who had a chronic whiplash injury, and her friend who had an arthritic hip. They both recovered immediately.' Now Dr Robertson runs a special clinic with the help of three regular healers. Her patients are enthusiastically reporting various improvements in arthritic joints, palpitations and headaches. This laying on of hands presupposes that some sort of energy is being passed on from the healer, but this is not very different from the way patients feel better when touched by the doctor. So, a doctor taking a patient's pulse may ostensibly want to know how fast the heart is beating, but in reality is touching the wrist to convey a feeling of reassurance. Nurses have been observed to touch their patients, usually on the wrist, shoulder or forehead, twice as frequently as anyone else. This is especially noticeable in intensive care units, where patients, surrounded by wires and gadgets or on ventilating machines, are likely to suffer sensory deprivation.

It would be interesting to know whether this type of physical contact – often without overt therapeutic intent – might itself help recovery. Touch has been shown to have quite remarkable effects in rats. Those that are regularly handled and caressed from an early age put on weight more rapidly and grow faster. They recover more quickly from stress and operations and live longer. For obvious reasons it has not been possible to demonstrate similar effects in humans, except for one intriguing study by Dolores Krieger, a professor of nursing at New York University. Seriously ill patients are often anaemic with low levels of haemoglobin in the blood which improve as they get better. Ms Krieger encouraged one group of nurses to stroke and caress their patients while a second group were told to limit physical contact to normal nursing procedures. The haemoglobin levels in the caressed patients rose significantly faster.

The therapeutic value of touching must derive from the pleasure it gives. An American psychiatrist, Dr Marc Hollender of Vanderbilt University School of Medicine in Nashville, Tennessee, has found that the desire to be touched has many of the attributes of a physical craving as one woman put it. 'I get the sensation across my upper chest. It's not like an emotional longing for some person who is not there, it's more of a physical feeling.' This 'wish to be held', he suggests, may even lead to a life of sexual promiscuity, leading a woman to seduce strangers just to satisfy this need. Of twenty women who had three or more illegitimate children by different fathers, eight confessed that sexual intimacy was the price they were prepared to pay for this physical contact. They said 'cuddling' was more pleasurable than sexual intercourse which was merely 'something to be tolerated'.

Feels Good, but Does It Do You Good?

Much the most popular alternative medical therapy favoured by my middle-class patients at the moment is reflexology – the 5,000-year-old Chinese art of foot massage. The body is divided into ten longitudinal zones, which apparently correspond to specific anatomical points on the foot. To stimulate the pituitary glands, the fleshy pad of the big toe is massaged; the length of the spine corresponds to the arch of the foot, and so on. The effect of an hour's worth of reflexology is reputedly immensely invigorating and after a while almost addictive, with some people maintaining they cannot get through the month without the fix of a reflexology session. There is a strong 'feel good' component in all this, but reflexologists' claims to be able to influence distant organs and parts of the body must be deemed more contentious and here a scientific paper in the journal *Obstetrics and Gynaecology* is particularly interesting. Dr Terry Oleson has studied the effects of reflexology in women with severe symptoms of pre-menstrual tension but whereas in one group the area of the foot was massaged that corresponded to the 'relevant' organs for PMT – such as the ovary and the pituitary – in another group the area massaged corresponded to the ear, nose and shoulder region. Virtually any treatment works for a fair proportion of women with PMT, and, indeed, in both groups there was a strong placebo element, with many women going to sleep during the session and feeling much more relaxed after it. But the improvement in symptoms was much more marked in those who had been massaged in the appropriate part of the foot and persisted for two months or more.

Many of those who practise alternative medicine are antipathetic to this type of experimental testing, maintaining that every treatment has to be individualised, as no two patients are ever the same. But the tale of two alternative treatments for eczema shows how vital it is if properly evaluated. Back in 1982 Dr Steven Wright, dermatologist at Bristol Royal Infirmary, reported in *The Lancet* that evening primrose oil 'modestly' improved atopic eczema in children and adults. Now eczema is a distressing condition, being itchy, painful and unaesthetic and treatment, even with strong steroid creams, is not very successful, particularly in severe cases. Consequently doctors tend to jump on any new treatment like evening primrose oil in the hope that it might help a bit. There is also considerable pressure from patients to prescribe the remedy, mainly because of the belief that as it is a 'natural' product, it must be better than steroid ointments. Over the years evening primrose oil must have been prescribed hundreds of thousands of times at a cost of £25 for a month's treatment. There have been rumblings for some time that evening primrose oil does not really work, and that the positive results of the trial were misleading, because the two groups in the eczema study were not strictly comparable. Anyhow, in June 1993, Dr John Berth-Jones, dermatologist at Leicester Royal Infirmary, published a paper, again in *The Lancet*, which reports absolutely and unequivocally that evening primrose oil is useless in the treatment of eczema.

By contrast, the effectiveness of a treatment offered by a Chinese practitioner in London, consisting of a traditional Chinese herbal tea, has amazed dermatologists. Most of the ingredients of the tea are described in the ancient Chinese herbal manuscript, *The Inner Classic of the Yellow Emperor*, compiled by unknown authors between 300 and 100 BC. John Harper, professor of dermatology at Great Ormond Street, first became interested when children under his care started turning up at his clinic in a much improved condition, thanks to the tea. 'We have seen many children with moderate-to-severe eczema, in all of whom the response is undoubtedly impressive, with a noticeable improvement in the skin and a reduction in itchiness within seven days,' he wrote in *The Lancet* in 1990. These initial anecdotal impressions were confirmed in a formal study two years later. 'Substantial clinical benefit in patients unresponsive to conventional treatment' was the verdict. This is a seriously significant development, and many parents are now taking their children to Chinese medical clinics for the tea. But Professor Harper warns that these children should still remain under strict medical supervision as, like any medicine that works, the tea does have side effects, and there are several reported cases of damage to the liver. So, contrary to the prejudices of most doctors, alternative therapies clearly can work, often dramatically so, but they must be properly evaluated if costly mistakes are to be avoided.

Pot and Meditation

What with Transcendental Meditation (TM) on the television – courtesy of the colourful Natural Law Party – and the Association of Police Officers proposing that possession of 'small amounts' of cannabis be decriminalised, life is full of echoes of the glory days of the Sixties. TM certainly had a powerful effect on my contemporaries, transforming boring scientists and left-wing activists alike into hairy, soft-spoken mystics. The technique is, by all accounts, easy to learn and does not require any intellectual concentration – it is a 'silent state of awareness, devoid of any specific thought content'. Not quite my scene, as we used to say in those days.

TM, however, is certainly not all bogus, as it is associated with quite profound physiological changes. The pattern of the brainwaves, as monitored by an EEG, change in a way that would be expected when falling into a state of 'restful alertness', and this, in turn, almost certainly explains the fall in heart rate, decline in blood pressure and dilation of the airways, the last two of which are particularly useful for those with hypertension and asthma respectively. The overall benefits of regular TM are so staggering as to be almost unbelievable. Psychologist David Orme-Johnson examined the health statistics of 2,000 participants in the TM programme of the Maharishi Mahesh Yogi and found that, over a five-year period, they had half the number of in-patient admissions to hospital than would have been expected. In particular, they had 55 per cent fewer admissions for benign and malignant tumours, 87 per cent fewer admissions for heart disease and a third fewer admissions for infectious disease and mental disorders. Even allowing for the probability that, as a self-selected group, these meditators were likely to be healthier than average, these findings are remarkable.

As for that other great symbol of the Sixties, cannabis, the momentum for its decriminalisation has been helped by the growing evidence of its therapeutic properties. Indeed, the President of the Royal College of Anaesthetists, Professor Alastair Spence, has argued that legalising the supply of cannabis is essential for 'controlled and comprehensive studies of its potential medical benefits'. Cancer specialists in the United States, according to a survey three years ago, regularly recommend that their patients should smoke cannabis illegally to mitigate the side effects, particularly nausea and vomiting, of chemotherapy. Cannabis is also available under special licence to glaucoma patients, because it reduces the pressure within the eyeball, and has been recommended in the treatment of asthma as it opens up the bronchi. Because its active component binds to specific receptors in the brain, cannabis has also been tried for a variety of neurological conditions, including Huntingdon's Disease and Parkinson's. The most dramatic of the many anecdotal reports of its usefulness concerned a 40-year-old man confined to a wheelchair with severe multiple sclerosis, causing spastic paralysis of all four limbs, bladder problems and impotence. According to the *Journal of Neurology*: 'After smoking a cannabis cigarette, he noticed an instantaneous improvement lasting several days. Since then, he has regularly taken cannabis each week, which allows him to climb stairs, walk on even ground and to have erections. He now has a quite satisfactory sex life.' These improvements were confirmed by objective physiological tests and the report concludes: 'Cannabis has powerful beneficial effects that urgently warrant further evaluation.'

Part 2

A Portfolio of Diseases

1

Bugs

Coughs and Colds

The usual seasonal round of colds and respiratory complaints has been aggravated by the appearance of an apparently new and very aggressive 'mystery' virus. My first patient was an otherwise healthy man in his forties whose only symptom was a cough – but what a cough! Dry, painful and persistent, it racked his chest for minutes at a time. The slightest stimulus – a whiff of cigarette smoke or a small change in temperature – would precipitate another attack. I tried everything to help him – two different kinds of antibiotics, the most powerful of cough suppressants in heroic amounts, anti-asthma treatment on the slim chance this might reverse the spasm in his airways, and finally large doses of steroids. All were entirely ineffective and he carried on hacking away for a further three weeks before getting better with tantalising slowness. The following week, two more patients turned up in the surgery with exactly the same symptoms, and then the floodgates opened. Over the next fortnight I now had at least a couple of dozen. All have been very decent about my therapeutic impotence and stoically accepted my reassurance that they will get better eventually. In the circumstances patients seem particularly grateful to be told 'there is a lot of it about', for, if many people have the same symptoms, it can be presumed that whatever ails them cannot be too serious.

It seems logical to suppose that my first patient passed the virus on to others but he had not, in fact, had any contact with the later victims. Indeed, watching the way this illness has passed through the community reminds me just how poorly we understand this type of infectious illness.

To start with, it is not easy to determine which virus is responsible, but it is obviously new because the symptoms it causes are so distinctly unusual. So the first question is: 'Where has it come from?' Then, the curious thing about these viral epidemics is that they start almost simultaneously in many different parts of the country or, indeed, in different countries – a flu epidemic in London will synchronise with one in Prague. In a notorious flu pandemic that followed the First World War, killing 30 million people, the first cases were reported at the same time from cities as far part as Boston and Bombay.

Next, even those whose solitary lives mean they have little chance of 'catching' a virus from others are affected by these epidemics. Shepherds in the mountains of Sardinia developed their symptoms at the same time as those living in cities many miles away, while sailors who have spent weeks at sea can suddenly be struck down by the same virus. Finally, it has actually been very difficult to demonstrate the spread of something presumably as infectious as the common cold from one person to another. When, in a specially designed experiment by the Common Cold Research Unit, twelve volunteers marooned on a Scottish island for three months were visited by five people from the mainland with streaming colds, not one of them developed a sniffle. Indeed, it is a common observation that rarely more than one in ten of those living in close communities like public schools or prisons will be affected in any single outbreak.

So, although viruses can spread by nasal droplets or physical contact, this is only a small part of the story. It is equally necessary to explain why viral epidemics arise when they do, affecting many different people at the same time who have never been in contact with one another. Two radically different theories have been proposed. It could be possible that many people harbour the common flu and cold viruses throughout the year without knowing about it. Something happens – a change of temperature or the amount of solar radiation – and these latent viruses become activated to cause symptoms. This would certainly explain the marked seasonality of these illnesses and a tendency for epidemics to start simultaneously in many different places.

Alternatively, and more speculatively, the distinguished astrophysicist Sir Fred Hoyle has proposed that viral particles from passing comets are deposited in the upper stratosphere and dispersed around the globe. This would explain the periodicity of viral epidemics, the fact that it is not necessary to be in contact with other humans to catch these illnesses, and the source of apparently new viruses. The existence of these theories only underlines the inadequacy of scientific knowledge about something as apparently simple as the transmission of viral illnesses.

The Flu

Sweating and shivering in bed pole-axed by a virulent attack of flu, I have spent a lot of time reflecting on what the best treatment should be. My first priority was to control the two worst symptoms: a crashing frontal headache and profuse sweating. For this I chose Coproxamol, which combines potent analgesia with the antipyretic (temperature-lowering) effect of paracetamol. I was surprised to find this drug was not as effective as I had imagined: it gave relief from my vice-like headache for only two hours at a time – and as the dose is limited to two tablets four times a day, this left a further four hours of pain. Accordingly, I also took ibuprofen – an anti-inflammatory drug – which seemed to have a moderate additive effect.

I was equally surprised to discover that when my temperature came down I felt worse, with shaking chills and pains in the back. There are some who will argue that it is wrong to try to lower the temperature, because such a consistent response to infection must have some useful biological function. The seventeenth-century physician Thomas Sydenham called fever 'a mighty engine which Nature brings into the world for the conquest of her enemies'. Like so many doctors before him, he was struck by how his patients would recover only when their illness had passed through the crisis phase of sweating and delirium. Indeed at the turn of the century, the deliberate induction of a temperature – known as fever therapy – was a standard treatment for syphilis and gonorrhoea. The patient would be placed in a hot bath or wrapped in heated blankets until his temperature reached 41 degrees centigrade. An Austrian physician, Julius Wagner-Jauregg, won the Nobel Prize for medicine in the Twenties by taking this idea a step further – deliberately injecting malaria parasites into the veins of patients with chronic infections. Temperature-lowering drugs such as aspirin and paracetamol are taken by millions with no obvious harmful affect. In the long watches of the night, however, I did wonder whether the Coproxamol might be protracting my flu for an extra day or two. I also suspect it exacerbated my profound apathy and anorexia; even though it was essential to replenish my energy stores, I could only average one boiled egg a day.

The current belief that there is no specific treatment for flu is actually wrong – there is, in fact, a very effective remedy – the anti-viral drug amantadine. Taken as one capsule twice a day, it reduces the duration of the illness by half and, taken prophylactically, it prevents the infection in almost 100 per cent of cases. This is a very well kept secret for obvious reasons – were everyone with flu to ask for this wonder drug, the nation's drug bill would rise by at least a percentage point or two. In retrospect, I should have put myself on it straight away but did not, partly out of apathy and partly because it took a couple of days to realise just how debilitated I was going to be. The first signs of fever and headache in my nearest and dearest, however, and I will be signing the prescription immediately. And why did I not have the flu jab? Doctors spend a lot of time having germs breathed all over them, but rarely catch the infection – perhaps because their immune system is so well stimulated. They therefore tend to believe they are resistant to the common viral bacteria infections, and so do not bother with flu jabs. My experience has shown that this is, regrettably if predictably, untrue. Next year, I will be first in the queue with my sleeve rolled up.

All in all, it has been a salutary experience. I have learned that the drug doctors commonly prescribed for flu – Coproxamol – is not very effective in controlling the headache and needs to be supplemented with some other medication. I suspect, too, that it may prolong the duration of flu and, by causing apathy and anorexia, hinder recovery. But above all, I now realise that flu must be among the most serious acute infectious illnesses that we doctors come across, and there is a good case for treating many more people with the most effective remedy – amantadine.

Fungal Afflictions

Few medical problems are more routine than a young woman with an attack of vaginal thrush, perhaps following a course of antibiotics. The diagnosis is self-evident – an itchy white discharge – and the treatment – one dose of the anti-fungal pill Diflucan – could not be more straightforward. Scarcely intellectually challenging; yet the great pleasure of practising medicine is that virtually every ailment, no matter how trivial, opens a window on to the sublime mysteries of the natural world.

The yeast that causes thrush, *Candida*, is only one of 80 species of micro-organisms – fungi, bacteria and protozoa – to be found in their hundreds of millions in or on the healthy human body. As in any other habitat, each species struggles to maintain its foothold against adversaries. The presence of so many micro-organisms in such close symbiotic relationship to man protects and maintains human health in myriad subtle ways. So resident bacteria in the throat, such as *Strep. viridans*, secrete an antibiotic-like compound, bacteriocin, which prevents infection by other, more toxic pathogens which cause pneumonia and abscesses; *Lactobacilli* in the vagina secrete hydrogen peroxide, which is toxic to *Candida* species and so keeps thrush at bay and protects against gonorrhoea and other sexually transmitted infections; normal flora in the gut generate short-chain fatty acids which are toxic to organisms that cause dysentery, such as cholera and salmonella.

Yet the role of these organisms is not entirely benign, and nowhere is this better seen than with human fungal infections responsible for such diverse, if minor, ailments as ringworm, athlete's foot, dhobie itch (ringworm of the groin) and dandruff. Fungi are an evolutionary anomaly. Their chief function is as recyclers of the detritus of the organic world, and they can flourish in the most hostile of environments. They have been recovered from acids, inorganic solutions, distilled water bottles, and even pathology museum specimens. There are more than 100,000 types, eleven of which have adapted to living on humans, feeding off the tough fibrous protein, keratin, which is present in hair and skin cells. The keratin itself is encased in a strong membrane but, true to their destiny as recyclers, the fungi do not find this an impediment. Their narrow, thread-like protuberances or hyphae literally push their way in and secrete a group of digestive enzymes which make the keratin edible.

The fungi are ubiquitous. Everybody harbours one or two strains on their skins, which usually cause no symptoms. But if the integrity of the skin is breached and they get a hold, particularly in some warm, moist area or inaccessible site, they are astonishingly resilient and difficult to eradicate. *Tinea corporis* or ringworm is the simplest form found on humans, from the Arctic to the equator to the Antarctic. The term 'ringworm' reflects the manner in which it spreads from the site of infection outwards in a centrifugal fashion to form characteristic red, scaly and itchy rings. Another form, *Tinea versicolor*, is more generalised. This fungus interferes with manufacture of skin pigment, leading to dark patches in Caucasians and pale ones in dark-skinned people. Ninety-two per cent of the population harbour the organism responsible, *Malassezia furfur*, either on the scalp or chest. As with many other fungal infections, the reason why it should cause symptoms in some but not others is not at all clear.

This is the case with athlete's foot. The toe webs would seem to provide the ideal environment for fungal proliferation, but attempts experimentally to induce the condition by regularly immersing the feet of volunteers in water laden with fungi have failed to produce a single case. This suggests that athlete's foot is not a contagious disease spread from one person to another, but rather that the fungus is almost universal, and symptoms develop only in those with a genetic predisposition, or in the very favourable circumstances found in heavy footwear, which generates the right degree of sweaty humidity.

Nor indeed are fungi solely responsible for the smelly discomfort of athlete's foot. Rather, athlete's foot has been described as an 'ecological wonderland' of competing organisms. First come the fungi which alone can break through the tough cell wall to get at the keratin. Other resident bacteria in the vicinity are killed off by naturally secreted antibiotics, such as penicillin. The bacteria, however, hit back, first by becoming resistant to the fungi's antibiotics, and then by overwhelming them with force of numbers. One bacterium in particular also inhibits fungal growth and, by synthesising a variety of foul-smelling gases with evocative names like putrescine, gives rise to the unpleasant, cheese-like odour found in those badly affected. Thus, interestingly, in some of the worst cases of athlete's foot, fungi can be detected in less than a quarter of cases. Treatments must be directed first at killing off the bacteria, and only then against the fungi. Pliny recommended 'sow's gall and bull's urine' as the best antifungal remedy. More mundane domestic cures include antiseptics, and iodine salts, but for really difficult cases modern drug therapy is always necessary.

The subtle and often mutually beneficial relationships of man and his natural flora falls apart when the immune system is compromised by infection with the HIV virus. Indeed, much of the distress of Aids patients, particularly in the later stages of their illness, is due to these otherwise innocuous micro-organisms. In the words of Philip Mackowiak of the University of Texas: 'The natural microbial flora cannot be viewed in absolute terms according to their capacity to benefit or menace the hosts. Given the appropriate circumstances, each species can either help or harm.'

Psittacosis and Other Pet Perils

There is a long list of diseases we can catch from animals, usually through intermediaries such as fleas and other insects. There are only a handful – rabies, anthrax, brucellosis and psittacosis – where an illness in an animal is directly transmissible to man. These diseases are thus exceptions to the general rule that infections found in one species rarely occur in another. Whatever the reason for this – and it is usually attributed to variations in the immune system between species – it is certainly a good thing, as otherwise the range of human illnesses would be much increased.

Human psittacosis, a lung infection contracted from birds – usually parrots – was imported into Europe at the turn of the century, as a consequence of the trade in exotic birds from South America. As always with a 'new' disease, it proved markedly virulent and in the first recorded outbreak in Paris in 1892 more than half of the patients died. Psittacosis is certainly highly infectious, in one case being caught by a man who had spent ten minutes buying dogmeat in a pet shop which also housed two blue-winged parakeets who died the day after his visit. The symptoms in an infected bird can be highly variable. Sometimes it may only seem to be out of condition, but owners should be particularly suspicious if their pet develops a croaky voice and has shivering attacks and diarrhoea. The bacteria that cause psittacosis – chlamydia – are excreted in urine and faeces, and the infected dust from the litter is then inhaled, causing the infection in man. This usually takes the form of a very bad dose of flu, with a high temperature, restlessness, insomnia and sometimes delirium. More seriously, it may attack the lungs causing pneumonia, when the chest X-ray will have a 'snowstorm' appearance.

Of the four other infections direct transmissible between animals and man, anthrax and rabies are gratifyingly very rare, while brucellosis (from cattle) and Weil's disease (from cattle again, or through contact with the infected urine of rats) are essentially occupational hazards for farmers and their families.

A most unusual outbreak of Weil's in four prisoners sharing a cell in a jail in Barcelona has been reported in *The Lancet*. The prisoners were trying to escape by building a tunnel, but after a few days became ill one after the other with a feverish illness and muscular aches and pains. They were duly admitted to the prison hospital, developed jaundice, leading to the appropriate tests, which found they were all infected by leptospirosis, the organism responsible for Weil's. The authorities initially thought the prisoners' water supply must somehow have become contaminated, but no further cases were identified and it began to seem rather suspicious that all the four patients shared the same cell. This was duly inspected and the tunnel discovered, which led directly to a sewer full of stagnant water.

Given the intimacy of the relationship many people have with their pets, it is remarkable how infrequently animals are a source of human infection. The public perception of the threat of infection from pets is dominated by fear of the two toxos – toxoplasmosis from cats and toxocariasis from dogs. Toxoplasmosis is much more frequent, with almost 8,000 cases over a ten-year period in England and Wales. In adults, it results in a trivial infection, usually a mild temperature with a transient swelling of a few lymph nodes. But in pregnant women, the organism can cross the placenta to cause terrible damage to the foetus, particularly its brain, which not infrequently leads to neonatal death. Toxocara is much rarer: there are only ten cases a year, and in children it is usually acquired by the accidental ingestion of soil contaminated with larvae, which migrate through the liver to the eye where they can damage the retina. Both toxos are preventable by elementary hygienic precautions – pregnant women should not handle cats or empty the litter trays, and pets should be vigorously excluded from children's play areas.

Travellers' Woes

Having spent good money to get away from it all to some exotic location, there is nothing more disheartening than waking on the fourth or fifth day with violent tummy pains, heralding an attack of the runs. For the next few days a disproportionate amount of time is spent staring at the bathroom floor, feeling faint and nauseous, and wondering whether it might be preferable just to die. Sixty million people every year travel from the West to the developing world, and between a third and a half will be struck down by travellers' diarrhoea. Travel doctors maintain it is preventable if only people took the elementary hygienic precautions of sterilising drinking water and eating only well-cooked food, summarised in the slogan 'boil it, cook it, peel it or forget it'. But such admonitions are rarely realistic, or effective.

Raj Bhopal, professor of public health at Newcastle University, became interested in travellers' diarrhoea on a visit to India. He asked all the foreign travellers he came across to fill in a health questionnaire. When he got back and analysed his results he was amazed to find that those who took rigorous water precautions 'at all times' reported the same frequency of diarrhoeal illness as those who took 'none at all'. His misgivings over standard medical advice were reinforced by a British professional couple in their mid-twenties who had spent fifteen months on a round-the-world trip, which he described in the journal *Travel Medicine International*. 'Meticulous by nature, they sought advice from their general practitioner, the local hospital physician, a centre for infectious and tropical diseases, and from a variety of books and journals,' he writes. They boiled or chlorinated all drinking water, including that for brushing their teeth. They avoided milk, cheese, yoghurt, uncooked vegetables and peeled all fruits. They ate only in 'hygienic tourist restaurants' where they dried their own dishes with their own dishcloths.

Despite all this, the woman had nine separate attacks of diarrhoea, lost so much weight she stopped menstruating and 'suffered many minor health problems'. Her husband had severe, apparently life-threatening bacillary dysentery *Giardiasis*, and two further episodes of diarrhoea. As Michael Farthing, professor of gastroenterology at St Bartholomew's Hospital has commented in the *British Medical Journal*: 'Sadly, the standard advice for preventing travellers' diarrhoea almost always fails.' The main reason seems to be that several of the pathogens are remarkably resilient, and able to survive extremes of temperature.

Yet most cases of travellers' diarrhoea are preventable, and readily curable, as they are caused by bacteria which are sensitive to antibiotics. At a meeting of the British Society of Gastroenterology, Professor Farthing described the results of a study of Marine commandos in Belize given either a single dose of the antibiotic ciprofloxacin, or a placebo, as soon as they developed diarrhoea. Those given the antibiotic passed half as many stools, and the average length of their illness was reduced from three days to less than 24 hours. Travellers' diarrhoea will, given time, usually cure itself, but why should people allow their holidays to be ruined waiting for it to do so? The travelling public should, he suggests, take the initiative and ask their GP for a course of ciprofloxacin before they leave – which they should be prepared to pay for.

Hygiene Rules, OK

Much of what now passes for medical research involves identifying previously unknown hazards to health in our everyday lives. Nothing escapes scrutiny. Indeed, a curiously named American scientist, Dr Bruyninckx, reported in the most prestigious of all science journals, *Nature*, that the oxygen we breathe can cause cancer – at least, oxygen had tested positive in the standard tests investigating the cancer potential of chemicals. Clearly, if oxygen is dangerous (and many chemicals have been banned on the grounds of similar findings), then we will all have to stop breathing.

There is one area, however, where despite intensive investigation, scientists have been unable to identify a threat to human health; it is apparently very difficult, if not impossible, to catch infectious diseases from inanimate objects. Letters and parcels were obvious candidates for spreading such infections, especially smallpox and scarlet fever. Throughout western Europe and particularly the United States, elaborate attempts were made to disinfect the mail by baking it in an oven with formalin or chlorine gas, by dipping letters in vinegar, or by punching them with holes to let in disinfecting fumes. The practice was not popular with the recipients of correspondence tampered with in this way – a General F. E. Spinner, formerly Treasurer of the United States Government, replied to a friend: 'Your very kind letter came from the pure air of the Green Mountains, but the criminal fools at the fumigating station seized it, punched it full of holes so it is almost illegible and then pumped an unbearable stink into it.' In spite of anecdotal reports that the first case of an infectious epidemic was contracted from a letter sent by a victim of the disease, the idea that viable viruses or bacteria might be transmitted by these means was eventually discredited and the practice fell into disrepute.

More recently, the lavatory seat has been suspected as a potential source of sexually transmitted diseases. An American venerealogist, Dr James Gilbaugh, took swabs from hundreds of public lavatory seats in hotels, department stores and hospitals but was unable to culture sexually transmitted organisms from any of them. Indeed, there is only one case ever reported – and that was over 50 years ago – where such a mode of transmission has been documented. After several weeks confined to a hospital bed with both legs in plaster, a sailor developed the symptoms of acute gonorrhoea. His circumstances precluded the possibility of his having acquired the infection by the usual means, and further investigation revealed the source to be a recently arrived patient in the next bed with whom he had shared a bedpan.

Now, Dr Sara Brook of Georgetown University has shown that library books are also free of hazard. The only bugs she was able to grow from a large random sample of children's library books was the harmless *Staphylococcus epidermidis*. 'Library books are safe,' she concludes.

If physical contact with inanimate objects is not a source of contagion, contact with human hands certainly is, as they provide a ready source of nutritional factors which enable bacteria to flourish. In everyday life, this is probably of no importance but in hospitals, with their nasty bugs and susceptible patients, it is a different matter. Hence the significance of an editorial in *The Lancet*: 'Hand-washing – the Semmelweis lesson forgotten.'

Ignac Semmelweis was the Viennese doctor who discovered the cause of childbirth fever. In the Vienna General Hospital in the 1840s, there existed, side by side, two obstetric departments, exactly the same in every way, each delivering approximately 3,500 babies a year. The only difference was that in one department all the deliveries were by obstetricians and students, and 800 mothers died each year from childbirth fever; while in the second, the deliveries were conducted by midwives and there were only sixty deaths a year. The reason, Semmelweis speculated, was that the doctors conducted several autopsies a day, from which they must be transferring on their hands 'some cadaver particles' to women while assisting them in labour. (These 'particles' we now know to be the *streptococcus* bacterium.) He instituted a simple measure of washing hands with chlorine and within a year the mortality rate fell to that in the wards run by the midwives.

In *The Lancet* editorial, Dr William Jarvis of the National Center for Infectious Diseases in Atlanta, Georgia, argues that this vital element of prophylactic hygiene is ignored in modern hospitals. Despite repeated campaigns to encourage the practice, doctors and nurses 'seldom wash their hands before patient contacts'. 'Excuses include being too busy, skin irritation, or not thinking about it,' Dr Jarvis says. 'Some believe they have washed their hands even when observations indicate they have not.' He proposes a radical solution. On admission to hospital, patients should be informed of the importance of hand-washing in reducing infection rates. 'How many doctors and nurses would ignore a patient's request that they first wash their hands?' he asks.

Florence Nightingale's Mysterious Illness

The drawback of spending time in exotic places is the possibility of contracting some exotic disease, requiring a panoply of tests on one's return to determine which malevolent organism might be responsible. A family doctor from the north-west of England spent a month working in Saudi Arabia: 'It was great – five-star luxury, trips to the desert, and the skin-diving in the Red Sea was divine,' he reports in the doctors' journal *Medical Monitor*. A fortnight after his return, however, he felt unwell with a high temperature, and ended up in hospital. 'During the night I developed rigors. The chills came first, then I was cold, very cold, and I covered myself with blankets. The shakes followed. The morning found me caked in sweat.'

His consultant ordered a 'complete battery of tests', and everyone sat back to await the results. 'A week passed and the rigors continued, but no diagnosis was made. The consultant went off on holiday, and I was left to the mercy of his registrar, who wanted to do a liver biopsy.' The patient dissuaded him from doing this, suggesting instead that the registrar might contact the hospital in Saudi Arabia to find out if anyone else had gone down with a mysterious ailment. 'I was in my second week of hospitalisation and had lost 22lbs in weight when the diagnosis finally arrived. Brucellosis was prevalent in Jeddah and I had attended the delivery of a febrile Bedouin woman. The midwife, the nurse and myself had all caught brucellosis from her. A quick course of tetracycline cured the rigors, but it was six months before I regained my weight and previous state of health.'

One wonders how many of those intrepid founders of the Empire must have returned to a life of chronic ill-health, whose cause was never identified and for which there was no treatment. This reflection is prompted by the news that the Nightingale School of Nursing at St Thomas' Hospital had finally closed its doors. The tradition of nurse training established by Florence Nightingale has been one of Britain's most substantial contributions to Western civilisation, bringing to the care of the sick the inestimable virtues of discipline, attentiveness, compassion and cleanliness. And yet the reputation of this extraordinary woman has always been tarnished with the charge of hypocrisy. While her public life was devoted to humanitarian ends, in private she was regarded as cold, tyrannical and a malingerer. Following her return from the Crimea, Florence Nightingale took to her bed for 20 years. 'Her indeterminate illness did not give her doctors much to work on,' observed the historian F.B. Smith. 'It remains indisputable that whenever Miss Nightingale announced herself to be ill, she was busy.'

But in a masterly piece of medical detective work, the former principal scientist at the Wellcome Foundation, David Young, has shown this cruel verdict to be quite unfounded. Soon after arriving in the Crimea, Florence Nightingale was struck down by 'as bad an attack of fever as I have ever seen', wrote the chief medical officer, Dr Anderson. Her recovery was slow, and three months later she was described as being 'white-faced, extremely weak and looking much older than her age'. Her 'Crimean Fever' is now known to have been none other than the very same brucellosis that affected the doctor in Saudi Arabia. It is caused by the bacterium *Brucella melitensis*, which gains entry to the body through the tissues of the mouth and pharynx, and spreads through the bloodstream, causing rigors and debility.

Following the acute illness, *Brucella* can remain in the body, causing recurring symptoms over many years. Reviewing the description of Florence Nightingale's symptoms in the years after she returned to England, Dr Young has found them to be 'entirely consistent' with this chronic form of brucellosis, punctuated by acute relapses every few years. The weakness and pain that forced her to take to her bed was almost certainly because the nerves of her lower spine were affected. This has been described as 'one of the most incapacitating and painful maladies that can affect man', and which, in Miss Nightingale's case, could only be relieved by injections of opium. Nor was that the total of her misfortunes, because chronic brucellosis may also cause sleeplessness, depression, palpitations and nervous tremors, precisely the sort of symptoms that have been cited as evidence that her illness was neurotic.

'After the age of 60, Miss Nightingale's depression – the last symptom of her brucellosis – lifted,' writes Dr Young. 'Gone was the cold, obsessed tyrant who rejected as inadequate the devoted services of her closest allies. As her character blossomed into benevolence, this thin, emaciated woman became a dignified, stout old lady with a good-humoured face.' In the absence of antibiotics, her physicians could do nothing to relieve her suffering other than recommend rest. She followed this advice for 20 years, and nothing in her life generated more censure.

Thank God for Bugs

What is the role of microbes – bacteria, viruses and fungi – in the Grand Order of Things? The common perception is that they are essentially malevolent 'germs', whose purpose seems to be to make life a misery for humans and, indeed, all living things. Despite being the most primitive of all organisms, they sometimes seem to be remarkably intelligent in pursuing this aim, spreading around mysteriously and changing their antigenic spots periodically to elude the immunological mechanisms we have developed to combat them. Some are benign, indeed, positively beneficial – the role of yeasts in brewing alcohol springs to mind – but in any balance sheet, the harm they do much outstrips the good.

Britain's eminent science writer Bernard Dixon, in his book *Power Unseen: How Microbes Rule the World*, suggests a very different role for 'germs'. Quite simply, life on this planet would be impossible without them. They are essential for all our food requirements, from both plants and animals. For plants to grow they must have nitrogen, which they cannot get from its most abundant source – the air. Rather, the nitrogen must first be 'fixed' into soluble salts that can then be absorbed in water. The 'fixers' are bacteria: cyanobacteria on the paddy fields of Asia; rhizobium in the vegetable patches of England; azospirillum in the grasslands of South America.

Cows, sheep and goats could not survive on their herbaceous diet, were it not for their ruminant stomachs in which the principal constituent of grass, leaves and other green plants – indigestible cellulose – is fermented by bacteroides and ruminococcus into cuds before passing to the stomach proper to be absorbed with the help of digestive enzymes. Yeasts like saccharomyces convert sugar to alcohol and carbon dioxide, giving us bread, wine and beer; add the bacterium leuconostoc to pasteurised milk, and you get cottage cheese. The fungus *Penicillium roqueforti* gives us Roquefort and is the main ingredient of Stilton and Gorgonzola. So a meal of steak, chips and salad, washed down with claret, followed by a selection of cheeses, is utterly 'germ-dependent'. As, indeed, is the digestion of it, which should generate astonishing litres of methane and hydrogen gases per day whose elimination would require humans to be eructating and passing wind almost continuously. Thanks to the tens of millions of bacteria in our colons, most of these gases are converted into non-volatile substances so the average amount of daily flatus is a mere one litre.

In the cycle of life, growth is balanced by decay, but growth could not happen if the decay of organic life were not recycled, and here Dr Dixon tells us that bacteria 'make a massive contribution to global cleansing, attacking the waste that arrives in an unceasing stream at sewage disposal plants, rendering it safe and innocuous ... microbes accept this cocktail of filth and turn it into water sufficiently pure to be discharged into the cleanest of rivers'. Thus man, in all his glory, is utterly dependent on these, the most primitive single-cell organisms on the face of the earth. The elegance of it all is awe inspiring. Dr Dixon provides many other instances of how germs preserve food, eliminate pests, protect the ozone layer and prevent global warming. Set against this beneficence, the harm caused by the malevolent disease-causing germs is trivial indeed.

In the past, the infectious diseases, in all their diversity, might well have been seen as part of the Grand Order of Things – a salutary warning sent in dramatic fashion by the Almighty to remind mankind of its morality. But I prefer a less apocalyptic, more biological explanation. For 'germs' to carry out their myriad different functions, they have to be enormously adaptable to different environments. Some grow and multiply in distilled water, others in formaldehyde used to preserve anatomical specimens; they can be found in the heart of a bubbling volcano or buried deep in a glacier. And so it is that, when they come across human hosts, some, such as the malarial parasites, will make their home in the red blood cells; others, such as herpes, have a predilection for nervous tissue; while streptococci favour the soft tissue just beneath the skin. Thus the harm they cause is an almost inevitable corollary of their ability to do good. Germs have been around for some 3,500 million years, and will continue to colonise the planet for aeons of time after we have gone. Microbes rule the world!

2

Ears, Eyes, Noses and Throats

The Mystery of the Senses – Smell

In a famous court case the defence sought to rule the evidence of the main prosecution witness – Ben, a nine-year-old German shepherd dog attached to the Thames Valley Police – as unacceptable, because he could not be cross-examined and might have been acting mischievously. Following a raid on a British Legion club, Ben had picked up the scent, which led him 200 yards down an alley to a leather shoulder-strap, later matched to the telltale strapless bag found at the home of the burglars. The presiding judge, Lord Taylor, after hours of complex legal consideration, ruled Ben's evidence to be admissible in a 17-page judgement.

In general, I would have thought that well-trained police dogs, with their phenomenal ability to discriminate between odours, are more reliable witnesses than most humans. It has been shown, for example, that they can identify steel tubes touched by a human hand for fewer than five seconds, or lightly fingerprinted glass slides that have been kept in the open for a fortnight. Further research into odour perception has revealed that homing pigeons navigate by smell, relying on the odours specific to their locality for homeward orientation. Humans can discriminate between up to 10,000 different odours, but with much less specificity and accuracy, because we have methods other than following our noses when it comes to foraging for food, picking our mates and finding our way around.

It was therefore with some incredulity that I read a paper by Dr Claus Wedekind of Berne in the prestigious journal *Proceedings of the Royal Society* in which he asserts the contrary. Dr Wedekind asked forty-four male students to wear the same T-shirt on two consecutive nights, and to minimise the chances of it being tainted by aromas other than their own body odour, they were also requested not to use perfumed deodorants, to avoid spicy food and alcohol, and 'to sleep alone'. The T-shirts were then placed in separate sealed boxes with a hole cut out of the top, and forty-nine female students were invited to sniff and rate the odours on the grounds of intensity, pleasurableness and sexiness. Dr Wedekind claims, astonishingly, that the most highly favoured T-shirts belonged to men with a different set of immunity genes from the sniffer. Theoretically, then, were a woman to act on this instinctive attraction by jumping into bed with a male with the sexiest-smelling T-shirt, any resulting offspring would be better able to resist infection.

Frankly, I don't believe it. Why, if odour is so important in selecting a mate, are women so keen to put potential suitors off the scent by wearing perfumes derived from the pungent odours of a small deer in Tibet – musk – or the follicles of a beaver – castor. Odours are not a sexual cue in humans, except in the most general sense, where different types of diet influence smell and so encourage mating within one's social and racial group. Indeed, it has always been a matter of curiosity to Europeans and Americans that the Chinese claim Westerners have a distinctly unpleasant smell of sour milk. Ellis Douek, formerly a consultant at Guy's Hospital, and a great smell expert, tells the story of a group of Chinese women returning home after a year in the United States. As soon as they boarded the ship, they insisted on eating only Chinese food, explaining that it would take several days before they lost their 'Western' smell, as they had learnt, to their cost, on a previous visit home.

Human odours have a useful biological function only in infancy – to compensate for the lack of development of the other senses. They help babies find their source of food, while encouraging mothers to love their babies. Dr Heili Varendi, from Tartu University Children's Hospital in Estonia has reported an ingenious experiment in *The Lancet*. Immediately after delivery, thirty mothers were asked to wash one breast thoroughly with an odourless liquid soap, while leaving the other untouched. Their new-born babies were then placed face down between the breasts. Virtually all rooted to the unwashed side. 'Naturally occurring maternal odours from the breast may have a role in guiding the infant to the nipple, and thereby contribute to early sucking and attachment,' Dr Varendi concludes. Just as maternal smells help an infant find the nipple, so the infant's smell binds the mother to the baby. This, at least, is believed to be the explanation for the quite characteristic smell exuded by babies in the first six months – often described as being like 'crumpets or vanilla' – which encourages mothers to kiss them so often and enthusiastically.

Besides this, the role of human odours in our social and sexual lives is really very disappointing, certainly when compared with other mammals. Male rhesus monkeys temporarily deprived of their sense of smell by having plugs of cotton wool stuffed up their nostrils show no interest in potential female partners, but start copulating immediately the cotton wool is removed. Female sexual smells do not serve the same function in humans. Another mystery then, for the evolutionists to explain. Why should we have lost such a valuable cue for the propagation of the species?

The Mystery of the Senses – Taste

Jancis Robinson, oenophile extraordinaire, has been tilting at some of the shibboleths of wine-buffery. There is, she says, no point in opening the red an hour before the guests arrive to let it breathe: 'It makes no difference to the taste as so little of the surface area of the wine is exposed to air.' Corks, too, are a gratuitous piece of wine mythology – 'superfluous stoppers' – and a screw top will do just as well. No doubt Miss Robinson knows what she is talking about, being one of the privileged few with a sophisticated palate that allows her to appreciate the subtleties of aroma and taste. Although it is not known how she and her fellow masters of wine can discriminate between so many distinct taste experiences, recent research has identified some people as 'super-tasters' with twice as many taste-buds as anyone else.

But taste is not perceived primarily through the taste-buds in the mouth but rather through the sense of smell in the nose. The complex relationship between these two organs of 'taste' has been reviewed by a leading authority on the subject, Dr Linda Bartoshuk of Yale University. Imagine, for example, that you are enjoying a plate of steak and chips and a glass of claret. The oak and vanilla odour molecules from the claret percolate up through the nose where they come across millions of minute hairs on the surface of the olfactory nerve. These hairs are studded with receptors into which the odour molecules fit like a lock and key, thus initiating nerve impulses to the taste centres in the brain. Simultaneously, the odour molecules released by chewing on the steak and chips pass up through the back of the mouth into the nose, where they come across their appropriate receptors, so the impression of the taste of steak is also mediated by the same route. This major contribution of the sense of smell to taste becomes obvious during a heavy cold, which causes both a loss of smell and an inability to taste food and drink.

By comparison the contribution of the taste-buds in the mouth to 'taste' is very limited with only four main types – salty, sour, sweet and bitter – evenly distributed around the tongue and palate. Indeed, their primary purpose has little to do with the appreciation of food, but rather seems to serve more basic physiological functions. Thus the 'salt' taste-buds are highly sensitive to the amount of salt in the body and induce a craving for the mineral if the blood becomes salt depleted. The role of the 'sweet' and 'bitter' taste-buds explains why parents are so often driven to distraction by their children's aversion to healthy green vegetables and their inordinate yearning for anything sugary. Children, it seems, are born with an innate antipathy to anything that tastes bitter. This is certainly a good thing, as most toxic compounds tend to be bitter, and so, if inadvertently stuffed into the mouth, they will be promptly spat out. But most green vegetables also tend to stimulate the bitter taste-buds, so these, too, tend to be rejected for the same reason. To compensate for the lack of calories from bitter-tasting foods, young children are also highly responsive to anything that tastes sweet, hence their enormous appetite for all sorts of confectionery.

Although the taste-buds themselves contribute little to the appreciation of food and drink, none the less the sensation of taste does indeed appear to emanate from within the mouth. This apparent paradox has been clarified by an ingenious experiment described by Dr Bartoshuk. A young man was first asked to chew on some tasteless, odourless gum. Next, a tube was placed between his teeth leading to a reservoir of chocolaty syrup. As the odours of this entered through the back of his nose, he reported that his gum had suddenly started to taste of chocolate. From this, Dr Bartoshuk infers that the physical sensation of objects within the mouth must somehow redirect the odours perceived by the nose so taste seems to be coming from within the mouth itself.

We are, of course, unaware of how we actually taste food and drink until something goes wrong. Not surprisingly virtually all those seeking medical advice for loss or alteration in their sense of taste turn out to have some problem in the nose: either the nerve has been damaged by a virus, or there is some other local problem, such as nasal polyps or sinusitis. When the sense of smell is intact, then abnormalities of taste are rare and usually take the form of a persistent metallic or 'repugnantly sweet' sensation at the back of the tongue. Drugs taken for conditions such as arthritis or hypertension are usually responsible. The abnormal taste should disappear, albeit slowly, if they are discontinued. Temporary relief can sometimes be obtained with local anaesthetic mouth sprays or lozenges. Zinc supplements have also been advocated in the treatment of taste abnormalities, but the benefits claimed for them have not been confirmed.

Don't Shut Your Eyes to Glaucoma

The fluid in the eyeball that keeps it round and bouncy just like air in a football is secreted by tissue behind the iris and drains out of the eye through minuscule channels at the side. If this drainage is blocked, the amount of fluid and the pressure within the eyeball rises – a condition known as glaucoma. This in turns damages the optic nerve carrying visual messages to the brain. Patients with glaucoma lose their peripheral vision: a normally sighted person standing in the middle of a road can see both oncoming traffic and pedestrians on the pavement on either side; those with glaucoma cannot see the pedestrians. Failure to reduce the pressure within the eyeball further compresses the optic nerve and the visual field becomes steadily narrower.

The progressive loss of vision is slow and insidious – hence the need for regular eye checks to detect it early. The diagnosis is readily made by a machine that measures the pressure within the eyeball, and the condition is readily treatable with drops which reduce the amount of aqueous fluid produced within the eye. By necessity this is an over-simplified account and some cases of glaucoma seem to progress relentlessly, irrespective of how well it is treated. Blindness from glaucoma is thus not necessarily preventable, but for most it is. Those close to retirement age would thus be well advised, if they can afford it, to have a regular eye check every two or three years.

Alternatively, there is always the possibility of testing oneself for glaucoma by standing in the middle of the road and noting whether one can see pedestrians on the pavement on either side. If not, then a visit to your GP complaining of loss of peripheral vision should lead to a prompt referral to the local eye hospital. This method of do-it-yourself eye-testing is, for obvious reasons, not without its hazards and those attempting it should be careful not to be knocked down by passing traffic.

Cataracts – Dazzling Impressions

'Take off that bandage, nurse, and let's find out what he can see,' boomed the voice of the senior surgeon at Moorfields Eye Hospital, London. 'I can remember that moment to this day,' recalled the patient, Dr A. E. Clark-Kennedy, a distinguished physician from the nearby London Hospital who, a few days earlier, had had a cataract removed from his left eye. 'The first thing that struck me was the face and particularly the colours of the pretty girl who took the bandage off. The second was the almost dazzling whiteness of the registrar's white coat. Third, it was the brilliant blue of the surgeon's suit – and I always thought he dressed so discreetly. And then I realised the appalling vulgarity of my multi-coloured striped pyjamas.'

Dr Clark-Kennedy's initial reaction was very typical. The most striking impact of the operation is of being overwhelmed by the sense of colour. But not just any colour. Cataracts have a yellow discoloration which both makes the world seem dirty and cuts off light at the blue end of the spectrum – and over the years the retina tries to adapt by increasing its sensitivity to blues and greens. So when the cataract is removed, the world appears clean and blue. 'On the drive home, the countryside had gained a brilliance I did not know it possessed,' Dr Clark-Kennedy wrote. 'I had no idea the sky was so blue or the grass so green. All the roads now looked blue. Smoke looked a lovely blue, as did distant clouds.'

This blurring of visual acuity and alteration in the perception of colour is dramatically illustrated in the paintings of the great French impressionist Claude Monet (1840–1926). The same subject – the Japanese bridge in his garden at Giverny – painted first at the age of 60 is full of detail and subtle shades, but ten years later the colours are confused, and the shape of the bridge itself is scarcely discernible. Writing in 1918, Monet observed: 'I no longer perceive colours with the same intensity. Reds appear muddy to me, pinks insipid. What I paint is darker and darker, and when I compare it to my former works, I am seized by a frantic rage and slash at my canvases with a penknife.' He was reduced to reading the labels on his tubes of paint to distinguish the colours and maintained a regular order of colours on his palette to avoid mistakes. A French critic at the time commented: 'Monet's coloured symphony becomes increasingly monochromatic.'

Monet's visual problems reached a climax in 1920 when he was persuaded by the French Prime Minister, Georges Clemenceau, to paint a series of the waterlily pond at Giverny as a gift to the nation. He soon realised that he could not successfully complete the project. 'I was no longer capable of making something of beauty,' he wrote. Clemenceau urged him to seek the help of a Paris ophthalmologist, Charles Coutela, who advised an operation. By modern standards, cataract surgery was very primitive. The eye was anaesthetised with cocaine, the knife went in at the margin of the iris and the lens with its cataract was scooped out. In skilled hands, the technique took five seconds. To ensure adequate healing of the wound, the patient then lay immobilised for ten days with bandages over the eyes. Monet's stepson later described this post-surgical ordeal: 'Lying flat in bed, without even a pillow, sandbags were placed on either side of the head to ensure it did not move. A guardian watched over him at night to converse with him, so he did not succumb to psychosis from lack of contact with the outside world.'

With his visual acuity restored, Monet was now afflicted with a problem of colour perception. 'I now see blue,' he wrote. 'I no longer see red or yellow. This annoys me terribly, because I know these colours exist, I know that on my palette there is some red, some yellow and a certain violet. It's filthy, it's dispiriting, I see nothing but blue.' And indeed in the period immediately following his operation Monet's paintings are very blue. One, of his house at Giverny, contrasts very sharply with almost the same picture painted a year previously which is full of reds and yellows. To restore an appropriate sense of colour, Monet was advised to wear glasses with a yellow/green tint that would partially simulate the colour interference of his yellow cataracts, but would at least mitigate the 'filthy blueness' which now overwhelmed his perception of the world. This seemed to work: a year before his death, he was able to write to Dr Coutela: 'I'm very happy to inform you that finally I have recovered my true vision. In brief, I'm seeing everything again and working with ardour.'

Almost 30 years after Monet's operation, the modern era of cataract surgery was inaugurated by Harold Ridley, an ophthalmic surgeon at St Thomas'. During the Second World War he had observed that penetrating glass injuries to the eye sustained by fighter pilots elicited virtually no inflammatory reaction. Why not, he speculated, remove the dirty yellow lens and replace it with a plastic implant, thus obviating the need to wear spectacles or contact lenses. Cataract extraction with an intraocular implant is now much the commonest of all eye operations – over a million are performed every year in America alone. It takes longer – fifty minutes rather than five seconds – but thanks to micro-surgical stitches the patient can usually return home the same day. Bandaging the eye is no longer necessary. Still, for those with a heightened artistic sensitivity to colour, it is advisable to have a pair of tinted yellow glasses to tone down the overwhelming blueness of their new-found world.

The Laser Cure for Short Sight

As we have just seen, fifty years ago, Harold Ridley, ophthalmic surgeon at St Thomas' Hospital, made an astute observation that ushered in modern eye surgery. While treating fighter pilots who sustained penetrating glass injuries to the eye, he was struck by how little inflammatory reaction these foreign bodies seemed to evoke. Glass, more than any other substance, is remarkably non-allergenic and the immune system makes little effort to reject it. Meditating on this phenomenon, Mr Ridley realised that it should be possible to cure poor sight due to cataracts by replacing the cloudy lens with one made of glass or plastic.

His colleagues were horrified, arguing that it was courting disaster to place such objects in an organ as delicate as the eye. Initially their misgivings were justified, for, as with any pioneering surgical technique, things did go wrong – the artificial lens became displaced, the aqueous humour that keeps the eyeball round and bouncy leaked out, and some patients ended up worse off than before the operation. But now, half a century later, cataract extraction with an intraocular lens implant has become much the commonest of all eye operations with more than 100,000 performed every year in Britain.

Now we have another pioneering operation which in the years to come will probably prove even more popular than cataract extraction. This, too, has originated from St Thomas', where Professor John Mitchell has been curing short- and long-sightedness by vaporising a layer of cells from the front of the cornea with a laser – a technique known as a photorefractive keratectomy or PRK for short. PRK is not quite so daring as placing an implant within the eye, but the stakes are higher as it requires submitting patients to an irreversible procedure whose success cannot be guaranteed for a visual defect that is readily correctable with glasses or contact lenses.

After preliminary trials in blind volunteers, for whom it did not matter whether the laser caused some unanticipated damage to the eye, the first operations on a group of short-sighted patients were performed in 1989. By 1991 four private clinics were offering the treatment; now there are fifty, and by the end of the decade there will be 200. The spiralling popularity of PRK is something of a self-fulfilling prophesy, as the more people who have it the greater the public confidence in the procedure. This is reinforced by the justified belief that, in these litigious times, eye surgeons would not be performing PRK if they did not think it was safe, and patients are sufficiently pleased with the result not to demand their money back.

The principle could not be simpler. The curved cornea at the front of the eye, along with the lens, focuses images on the retina. For the short-sighted, the image falls short, so flattening out the cornea by removing a thin layer of cells from the centre will bend the light rays outwards, causing the image to fall further back. For those with long sight, the reverse applies. The image falls 'behind' the retina, and so making the cornea slightly more concave, by removing cells from around the sides of the eyeball, will bring the image further forward. Sophisticated technology calculates precisely where the laser should be directed to achieve maximum benefit and defines its precise range so that it only skims the top layer of cells to a depth of 0.05 millimetres.

Success depends on the pre-existing visual defect, and some apparently are disappointed that the improvement is not so great as they had hoped. There may be initial problems with haze and glare when looking at a bright light, but this resolves within six months. There have been a few reports of increased sensitivity and eye irritation, especially on exposure to smoke or dust. PRK seems a sensible and straightforward operation – especially for those who, for any reason, cannot wear glasses or are intolerant of contact lenses. At £1,500 per eye, the operation is undoubtedly expensive, but this is little different from what one would pay for a decade's worth of contact lenses.

The Bells of Hell – Tinnitus

'My ears whistle and buzz continuously day and night. I can say I am leading a wretched life,' poor old Beethoven complained about his tinnitus. Had it been available at the time, a Walkman mini-stereo might have helped, for, as Aristotle observed: 'Buzzing in the ears ceases when a greater sound drives out the less.' Aristotle's observation is also the explanation for the apparently miraculous cure for tinnitus sufferers who made the pilgrimage to the Breton town of Stival. There the handbell of the Celtic saint St Meriadec was (and, on request, still is) rung loudly in the suppliant's ears and then placed over his head. When the bell was removed they noticed the buzzing had stopped.

Tinnitus is the amplification of the noise that can be induced by placing both hands over the ears. Many people experience it – especially those like Beethoven who have some form of hearing impairment – but few complain of it. For some, however, it comes to dominate their lives. Why? It is easy to understand how tinnitus might be more of a nuisance for the gloomy than for the optimistic and indeed over a half of those seeking medical help are suffering from depression. But here we are caught in a classic chicken-and-egg conundrum. For some, tinnitus can take the form of a high-pitched whistling, or loud 'machinery' noises. Such patients seek a medical opinion, expecting there to be a reason and a solution, only to be told the cause is not precisely known and that there is no reliable remedy. This response can easily be interpreted as indifference on the part of the doctor, and the resulting frustration then causes depression. Next thing, patients are being offered anti-depressants and psychotherapy, with the obvious implication that it is their fault for not coping. This only makes them more miserable.

From this it can be fairly surmised that tinnitus is difficult to treat. A positive attitude from the doctor is very helpful – not just 'You'll have to learn to live with it', but a proper examination, an explanation and reassurance that it should get better. The use of tinnitus maskers or a Walkman to drown out the noise is useful for some, and the anti-epileptic drug Clonazepam in low dosage has its advocates. For the anxious, the much maligned Valium is the drug of choice, and for the depressed, Nortriptylene. Professor R. Hinchcliffe of London University recommends a form of psychological treatment called cognitive therapy, while those much afflicted by tinnitus in bed at night can drive it out of their consciousness by simply repeating in mantra-like fashion the same words over and over again. A number of tinnitus sufferers find yoga a relief, taking a leaf out of the book of Eastern mystics to exploit the naturally occurring tinnitus induced by placing the hands over the ears. 'The ears are closed by the fingers and attention is focused on the sounds that are heard. With practice the mind is able to hold on to progressively finer and subtler sounds until eventually liberation is reached.'

There is no doubt that the numbers complaining of tinnitus have risen markedly in recent years, which suggests that the threshold at which people are prepared to tolerate it must have fallen. This might be because of the considerable adverse publicity tinnitus has received and the frequently repeated rumour that it can so sap morale as to lead to suicide. Health education programmes focusing on the dangers of noise at work may have contributed, especially as those seeking compensation for occupation-related hearing loss receive much larger sums if they are also suffering from tinnitus. According to the British National Study of Hearing, 8 per cent of the population have tinnitus that is bad enough to cause 'moderate or severe annoyance'. It is, however, virtually unknown in India. Is this, Professor Hinchcliffe asks, 'because they have a lot of things to worry about, or because they have not been subject to the maleficent effects of the mass media?'

Curable Deafness – Earwax

In an epigram that would no doubt have appealed to his son Oscar, the eminent Dublin ear surgeon Sir William Wilde once observed: 'There are only two types of deafness. One is caused by wax and is curable. The other is not due to wax and is not curable.' One hundred years on, his verdict almost still holds. Those of my older patients complaining of increased deafness who have a discrete plug of wax in each earhole can have their hearing miraculously restored by dislodging it with a fine jet of warm water. But if examination shows the auditory canal to be clear, then the diagnosis is almost certainly presbyacusis or 'the deafness of old age' for which the only answer is a hearing aid or an ear trumpet (which are still available, apparently, on the NHS).

Doctors who spend a lot of time looking down earholes comment on the remarkable variation in the quantity and consistency of wax that is produced, although they rarely bother to ask what it is doing there in the first place. This interesting question has been resolved by a Mr R. J. Canter, senior registrar in the Ear, Nose and Throat Department of Bristol Royal Infirmary. As he points out: 'The external ear provides a warm, dark, moist environment which favours the growth of fungi and bacteria, yet infections are relatively uncommon.' The explanation, he suggests, 'must be due to the protective effect of human cerumen' (or earwax). He had confirmed this elegantly by showing that dollops of earwax placed on culture plates teeming with bacterium like *Staph. aureus* and the fungus *Candida albicans* effectively inhibit their growth. So those who feel the urge to twiddle a cotton-tipped Q-tip into their ear to get rid of their wax should be warned that they risk causing an ear infection.

Tonsils and Grommets

It is not unusual to suffer partial deafness after a bad cold – for which the Eustachian tube is to blame. This must qualify as one of the least prepossessing structures of the body. A mere inch in length and a few millimetres in diameter, its function is to drain small amounts of fluid from the middle ear (the bit beyond the eardrum) into the back of the nose. The trouble, as can be imagined, is that being so short and narrow, the Eustachian tube tends to get blocked by the inflamed tissues of the nose associated with a cold, the fluid in the middle ear can no longer drain away and accumulates leading to deafness. In adults this usually resolves within about four weeks. As the swelling of the nasal tissue subsides, the Eustachian tube re-opens, the fluid drains freely and normal hearing is restored.

In children it is a different matter. Here the tube is, in relative terms, even shorter and narrower, making it even more vulnerable to blockages by the recurrent colds to which they are so prone. The fluid stuck in the middle ear becomes viscous, causing the condition of Serous Otitis Media, or glue ear, which in turn leads to a more permanent hearing impairment and recurrent acute ear infections. The partial deafness associated with glue ear may cause learning difficulties due to inattentiveness in the classroom because the child cannot hear what the teacher is saying – or, alternatively, the child's failure to meet their parents' expectations of scholastic achievement may be blamed on glue ear. Either way, considerable pressure is exerted on general practitioners to 'do something about it', which means the referral to an ENT surgeon who makes a hole in the eardrum and inserts grommets to allow the viscous fluid to escape.

ENT surgeons' enthusiasm for this operation has increased in leaps and bounds over the past ten years, with a doubling in the number of operations performed. Certainly the resulting improvement in hearing and the reduced frequency of ear infections can dramatically improve the quality of children's lives, and indeed that of their parents. It has been alleged that perhaps half of the 90,000 operations performed a year are unnecessary, that most children improve without any need for surgical intervention, and that when measured objectively the evidence of serious hearing impairment is minimal. Grommet insertion for glue ear appears to have become a fashionable operation in the same way that removing tonsils used to be.

Indeed, the rise in the popularity of grommet insertion may even be related to the decline in popularity of tonsillectomy as ENT surgeons have sought alternative outlets for their surgical skills. This might sound implausible, but it should be recalled that less than 5 per cent of children now have their tonsils removed compared with 95 per cent in the 1950s and 1960s. In a fascinating study of surgical decision-making from that time, 1,000 children were examined by a group of ENT surgeons who decided that 611 needed a tonsillectomy. The remaining 349 were re-examined and a further 174 of these were then judged to need the operation. That left 215 with apparently normal tonsils, but when they were examined again, ninety-nine were recommended for the operation. The remaining 116 were examined for a fourth time and – surprise, surprise – fifty-one were said to need their tonsils out. A contemporary ENT surgeon candidly admits that 'many of the reasons for tonsillectomy in the past were plainly ridiculous and it is embarrassing to read about them now in the medical literature'.

To curtail the current epidemic of glue ear operations it has been recommended there should be a 'cooling off period' in which children with glue ear are initially observed for a year or more and the degree of hearing loss is objectively measured by appropriate tests. A compulsory waiting list will be introduced which will mean that those who improve spontaneously are more likely to avoid unnecessary intervention while those in greatest need should not encounter delays in getting surgical treatment. Doctors at the Royal Throat, Nose and Ear Hospital in London have found that in eight out of ten children, the reason for the blockage of the

Eustachian tube and the accumulation of fluid in the middle ear is an allergic inflammation of the nasal passages, or nasal rhinitis. If this is treated energetically with a steroid nasal spray then only one per cent finally end up requiring grommets.

Snoring Solutions

The nearest most men or women get to murder is when they are woken yet again by stentorian snoring from the adjoining pillow. Lying there alone in the darkness, a beguiling fantasy passes through the mind, of replacing their noisy partner with some altogether more considerate lover. It is, however, no longer necessary to find a hired assassin, as Ear, Nose and Throat surgeons are increasingly willing to perform the snoring curative operation known as an Uvulopalatopharyngoplasty, or UPPP.

The grunting sounds of snoring are caused by obstruction of the air being inspired into the lungs by the soft tissues at the back of the throat which have collapsed in on themselves. Thus for much of the night the heavy snorer is being deprived of oxygen. In its extreme form this causes a condition known as Obstructive Sleep Apnoea (or OSA), where between inspiratory efforts breathing stops altogether. A person with OSA is, as it were, suffering from self-strangulation. The oxygen concentration in the blood sinks steadily until the respiratory centre in the brain initiates a further heavy intake of breath. Those with OSA are not only heavy snorers, but also getting insufficient restful sleep. They wake with a headache and are hyper-somnolent during the day, falling asleep at the slightest opportunity – at work, in church, while driving a car and sometimes in the middle of a meal.

Snoring is, of course, very common – affecting about one-third of all adult males, although they do not suffer from OSA. But research from the Osler Chest Unit at Oxford's Churchill Hospital suggests that heavy snoring, even without a disturbed sleeping pattern, may be a cause of daytime sleepiness and is an independent risk factor for heart attack. It would be inappropriate and utterly unrealistic to suggest that every snorer required surgery. It is initially more sensible to try various self-help measures.

Heavy drinking and over-weight are important contributory snoring factors and these can be corrected in the obvious ways. For other people the simplest 'cure' is to tape the offender's mouth at night, thus forcing the snorer to breathe through his or her nose. If there is a degree of nasal obstruction, this can be relieved by nightly use of Xylometazoline, a decongestant spray. If this is ineffective, a nasal dilator, made of springed plastic, inserted into the nose, will keep it open. Where the obstruction is due to an allergy, such as hayfever, sufferers should use such anti-inflammatory agents as Rynacrom and Beconase. Snoring is most common and loudest when the sleeper is lying on his back, which can be discouraged by sewing a marble or tennis ball into the back of a pyjama jacket or T-shirt. When the snorer rolls over the resulting discomfort between the shoulder blades forces him back on to his side, usually without waking him up. Alternatively, the disturbed sleeper can always plug the ears at night.

If these simple methods are unsuccessful – which regrettably they often are – there is no alternative but to seek the help of a surgeon. His examination may reveal some relatively straightforward and correctable anatomical defect, like a deviated nasal septum or (unusual in adults) enlarged tonsils. But he will usually recommend further investigations in a specialised sleep laboratory before considering an operation. At the sleep laboratory the snorer is linked up for a night to a polysomnograph, which records brainwave activity and the heart beat. A special device attached to the skin detects how much oxygen is getting into the blood. During the night a trained observer records the sleeping pattern and objectively assesses the severity or otherwise of the snoring.

Snorers suffering from OSA will often find their symptoms of daytime sleepiness dramatically relieved by wearing an oxygen mask at night, where the pressure of the incoming air forces, or 'splints', the airways open. The Uvulopalatopharyngoplasty is best reserved for those whose main problem is socially destructive snoring, unrelieved by the simpler measures already considered. The operation is a sort of glorified tonsillectomy, where the tissues on the side of the pharynx, the uvula and part of the soft palate are removed. It has a cure rate of around 95 per cent. The complications are few. Some find that with the soft palate removed, fluids regurgitate up the nose, which makes playing the trumpet or other wind instrument more difficult, as the expelled air escapes through the nose.

Curing Sinusitis

It is surprising how few people resort to inhalational treatment for the commonest of all ailments – the common cold. Ten minutes with a towel over the head, breathing in the steam from a flat pan of boiling water spiced with menthol, works like a miracle for unblocking the nasal passages. At the same time it prevents the most grievous complication of the cold – sinusitis. The sinuses are large air-filled holes in the skull on either side of the nose, whose prime function is to humidify and warm air on its way down to the lungs, while filtering out bacteria, viruses and other particulate matter. By protecting the lungs from damage, however, the sinuses themselves are vulnerable to infection. Repeated attacks damage their linings, resulting in chronic sinusitis – a constant source of misery for those afflicted.

The sinuses become filled with a sort of infected glue that drips down the back of the nose, causing sufferers to wake in the morning with a vile taste in the mouth. They feel, and indeed are, 'bunged up'. The head feels heavy, headaches are common, and there is a curious deadening of mental function that makes it difficult to concentrate. To compound their misfortune patients often lose their sense of smell, and with it the ability to enjoy food. But probably the worst problem for those with chronic sinusitis is that in the past it has been so difficult for both family doctors and specialists to treat successfully. Such pessimism is no longer warranted. Ear, nose and throat (ENT) surgeons now realise that the condition is not intractable and past failures may have been due to a poor understanding of the working of the sinus. This has now been corrected and as a result 'the treatment of chronic sinusitis has been revolutionised in the last decade', says Robert Slack, ENT specialist at the Royal United Hospital, Bath. 'Eighty-five per cent of patients can now expect to have a good or very good outcome.'

In order to appreciate the significance of this development, it is necessary to clarify the function of the sinuses. Air enters through an opening, or ostium, at the back of the nose and then circulates to the four main groups of sinuses. Bacteria and other particles are trapped in a fine layer of mucus on the inner surface of the sinuses and then expelled back out through the nose by the action of millions of minute hairs, or, cilia, beating rhythmically about 700 times a minute. Damage to this 'mucociliary transport', as it is known, lies at the heart of chronic sinusitis. If, for any reason, the opening into the sinuses is narrowed, this reduces the amount of air flowing through them, depriving the mucus lining of oxygen. This renders the mucus secretions more acidic, which in turn impairs the action of the cilia. A vicious circle then sets in where the sinuses become more vulnerable to infection and the mucociliary transport is further impaired so the infective organisms cannot be removed. 'As the disease progresses the mucus lining becomes increasingly damaged, with a decrease in the rhythmic movement of the cilia to less than 300 beats per minute,' says Kathryn Evans, consultant ENT surgeon at the Gloucester Royal Hospital.

For almost a century ENT surgeons sought to treat this problem with the Caldwell-Luc operation, named after its pioneers. This involves making a hole in the lower part of the sinuses and allowing them to drain downwards. The limitation of this approach has become clear as a result of two important technical advances which in turn have led to the revolution in treatment. The first is the CT scanner, which has given surgeons a much better understanding of the anatomy of the sinuses and particularly the crucial part played by any narrowing or obstruction of the ostium in treating the vicious cycle of chronic sinusitis.

Second is the nasal endoscope, a thin metal tube which allows a thorough inspection of the internal structures of the nose. David Kennedy, an ENT surgeon in Baltimore, summarises the new approach to treatment: 'The conventional opinion has always been that the lining of the sinuses becomes irreversibly diseased and needs to be completely removed. But now we have come to realise that chronic sinusitis is primarily a disease of obstruction of the ostium.' The priority now is to relieve that obstruction, which is also performed through the endoscope – an operation known as Functional Endoscopic Sinus Surgery, or FESS. The ostium is directly seen and is widened by cutting away the tissue surrounding it. This enormously improves the ventilation of the sinuses and the damaged lining should then heal spontaneously. 'After surgery it may take many months for the mucosal changes [damage to the lining of the sinuses] to reverse,' said Dr Evans, 'so supplementary treatments with regular inhalations, antibiotics and steroids will be necessary during this time.'

3

Skin

Childhood Eczema – Do Diets Work?

There are few things more gratifying in a busy clinic than a child with a rash. Neither a thorough examination nor protracted investigations are necessary to establish the cause; a quick glance will usually suffice to determine whether it is chicken-pox or eczema, a fungal infection or scabies. Treatment is straightforward and rapidly effective. So, in just a few minutes, mother's worries have been allayed, the rash given a name, a prescription signed and mother and child depart happily.

I anticipated just such a satisfactory consultation when a young mother brought her five-year-old son with an itchy rash around his elbows. From his notes, it was obvious that he had suffered from eczema in the past and this was his problem again. I said something along the lines of: 'It looks as if the eczema is back again.' 'No it isn't,' said the child's mother. 'It can't possibly be.' When I asked why not, she told me that her son's eczema had been cured by the homeopathic medicines she was giving him, and therefore his rash had to be something else. This was clearly a tricky one, as any suggestion on my part that perhaps the homeopathic medicine was not quite so effective as she believed would have gone down very badly indeed. A compromise was clearly needed. Recent evidence suggests that eczema may be associated with a low-grade infection of the affected skin, so I suggested that the elbow rash was a skin infection, exacerbated by an underlying predisposition to eczema. This allowed me to prescribe a cream combining a mild steroid to make the eczema better and an antibiotic, which was probably useless. A bit unethical, perhaps, but there seemed no other way of resolving the problem.

Regrettably, in some children, eczema can be so severe as to be refractory to even the best of modern medicines, and then the allure of alternative remedies is perhaps more understandable. Every avenue is worth exploring to see if 'it might help'. Some children's eczema certainly does improve when dairy foods are excluded from their diet, but in those who are severely affected a more drastic option is often proposed – the 'few-foods' diet, which excludes all foods except six: lamb, potatoes, rice, pears, broccoli and tap water. This is so unappetising that forcing children to eat it is tantamount to child abuse – unless, of course, it works. But does it?

This type of dietary treatment of eczema has been advocated by 'alternative nutritionists' and, indeed, some paediatricians for 15 years or more, but no one – up till now – has formally tested it by comparing its efficacy with a 'control' group of children eating normally. This has now been done by Tim David, professor of paediatrics at the University of Manchester, and the results published in *Archives of Disease in Children*. The 'few-foods' diet is predictably very unpalatable; over half of the sixty children taking part in the study were withdrawn as they were unable to comply. Those who stuck it out were assessed after six weeks by an independent observer, who recorded a fall in the average amount of daytime itchiness and night-time sleep disturbance. Taken together, their eczema was less extensive. This would seem to make the diet worthwhile, were it not that exactly the same improvement was noted in the control children eating normally. From this, it would seem that the act of participating in a study of eczema treatment is enough to produce an improvement, but the specifics of the diet involved are irrelevant. 'The study failed to show benefit from a "few-foods" diet,' concludes Professor David.

This would seem to be fair comment, but buried deep in his report is one observation that makes me wonder whether this method of scientific analysis, where the changes in the severity of the eczema in all the children are aggregated together and presented as 'an average', might actually be concealing something important. A detailed examination of Professor David's paper reveals that the eczema improved in fifteen out of the twenty-four children who remained on the diet. Indeed, Professor David remarks elsewhere on 'the occasional dramatic response to diet'. Readers will no doubt find this all very puzzling. Certainly, it seems ridiculous to believe so passionately in the curative power of homeopathic remedies as to refuse to recognise that they are ineffective in controlling your child's eczema. But it is no more ridiculous than scientifically testing the benefit of a few-foods diet in a way that fails to bring out the crucial fact that in some children it does actually make them better.

What to conclude? If your child has any chronic condition like eczema or asthma that is readily treatable with modern drugs, there seems no point in giving them 'alternative' remedies. If, however, it is severe, then other avenues are worth exploring. But, bear in mind that whatever one does, the condition might improve anyway, and only if it improves dramatically should the therapy be continued.

Embarrassed by Rosacea

There is a riveting regular feature in one of the medical journals called 'My Worst Moment' where doctors write in to tell of the most toe-curling, embarrassing incidents of their careers. A recent contributor urged his colleagues to make absolutely sure a patient was indeed dead before passing on the sad news to the nearest and dearest. Summoned at 2 a.m. to attend an elderly man struggling for breath with heart failure, the doctor gave him a slug of morphine, at which point 'the patient promptly stopped breathing and collapsed back on the bed'. In view of his age, he decided not to attempt resuscitation and the next ten minutes were spent consoling the wife in the room next door. The doctor then returned to the bedroom to collect his bag, 'when, to my utter amazement, I found the poor man was making attempts to breathe. The wife reappeared in the doorway, and all I could think of to say was "actually he's not quite dead after all".' By the time the ambulance and 'perplexed' relatives arrived, the recently deceased was sitting up and talking. The doctor concludes: 'It seems comical now, but at the time I would gladly have sold my soul to be anywhere other than in that room.'

It would have been very odd if he had not been so embarrassed. Here, perhaps, lies a clue to the apparently purposeless phenomenon of blushing, which only serves to compound the discomfiture of embarrassment. The person who fails to blush when he should gives the impression of being indifferent to the fact he has broken important social rules of behaviour by being inept, immoral or rude. As the distinguished sociologist E. Goffman elegantly puts it, someone who shows their discomfiture 'demonstrates that, while he cannot present a coherent self on this occasion, he is at least disturbed by the fact and may prove worthy at another time.' Confirmation of this explanation is provided by an experiment involving people watching a videotape of a shopper in a large store who inadvertently topples a tier of toilet-paper rolls and then either appears embarrassed and stops to rebuild it, or is unaffected and just walks away. Those watching the videotape rated the 'embarrassed shopper' much more favourably. In the dreadful terminology of psychology-speak, 'blushing serves to repair people's public image after a self-presentational predicament'.

In other circumstances – being publicly praised or stared at, or having others sing *Happy Birthday* – the common feature is that the blusher is the centre of attention. Blushing is therefore very rare in children under the age of five, who have no inhibitions about attention-seeking behaviour, and it becomes rarer with the passing of years when the opinions of others seem less important. Some unfortunate people, usually women, are 'chronic blushers', in whom the slightest stimulus can 'crimson the face' and often the front of the chest as well. In its extreme form, this can lead to Erythrophobia – a painful fear of blushing – for which the only escape is to become a social recluse. There is not much that can be done to help chronic blushing, but the social anxiety associated with fear of blushing is itself an exacerbating factor. The paradoxical treatment for those with Erythrophobia is thus to encourage them to try to blush as often as possible, so they become desensitised and the number of serious blushing episodes rapidly diminishes.

Chronic blushing is important for another reason: it is associated with the skin condition Rosacea – a permanent, disfiguring reddening of the face. This starts with episodes of flushing and, as the blood vessels under the skin dilate, fluid leaks out into the surrounding tissue, which becomes boggy and liable to acne-like infections. Over time, the face becomes permanently reddened, dotted with rose-red papules and little pustules, and the nose acquires the characteristic bulbous appearance made famous by W. C. Fields. The cause is not known, although any other reason for facial flushing – alcohol, the menopause, temperature extremes and 'chronic blushing' may exacerbate it. Chronic blushers therefore need to take preventative steps, by being cautious about flush-inducing foods (such as hot curries), avoiding exposure to extremes of cold, heat and sunlight, and having regular facial massage to disperse the accumulation of fluid under the skin.

Though established Rosacea is often thought to be rather intractable, the world's leading authority on the condition, Dr Jonathan Wilkins, asserts in the journal *Archives of Dermatology* that, with a combination of antibiotics, lasers and a little plastic surgery, 'it is a treatable disorder'. Antibiotics taken by mouth control the infection, and if they do not work singly, then combinations must be used. Once the Rosacea is under control, it is prevented from recurring by the daily application of an antibiotic lotion. As the reddening of the skin subsides, the cheeks can be seen to be covered with tiny blood vessels which have become permanently dilated. These are known as Telangiectasia and can be eradicated with laser therapy. As for the disfiguring bulbous nose, it can be pared away with a technique known as electrodesiccation.

The Itch

It is a great joy of practising medicine that the humblest of symptoms can be a source of endless fascination. Consider itching or, as we call it, pruritus. Besides itchy feet, itchy genitals and the common itchy skin conditions such as eczema, scabies and ringworm, I've seen patients who itched after drinking a glass of red wine, going for a run, having a hot bath, getting into bed with their husband, and wearing elasticated knickers. This is only, as it were, to scratch the surface of the diversity of itching conditions. Skin specialists will see, in addition, a host of other rare skin complaints and obscure causes of itching that most doctors would only ever read about in textbooks.

And yet, despite the ubiquity of itching, its mechanism and purpose is utterly mysterious. It has some relationship to pain whose nerve fibres it shares, but whereas pain is usually useful in forcing withdrawal from a painful stimulus, the instinctive response to an itch is to scratch – but to what end? Then there is the curious way that scratching or rubbing an itchy area not only brings relief but pleasure, so there is an urge to carry on, even though it is absolutely certain that once the relief has worn off, the itching will return with a vengeance.

These paradoxes may intrigue the inquisitive medical mind, but for patients the only really interesting thing about an itch is what is causing it and, more importantly, how to get rid of it. The doctor should be able to identify the skin complaint responsible, treatment of which should eradicate the itch. There are, however, situations where a straightforward solution is not possible. This can cause a lot of misery, so it is useful to take a closer look. There may be no obvious cause for the itching, no skin rash, no history of taking drugs that may cause itching as a side effect, and no jaundice or kidney failure. There may, however, be a hidden cause which can be overlooked. Thus, both an over- and an under-active thyroid can cause itchiness, as can anaemia, due to insufficient iron, and diabetes, all of which can be diagnosed by appropriate blood tests. Very occasionally, itching may be the first symptom of Hodgkin's disease, preceding its clinical appearance by a year or more.

Once all these conditions have been considered and excluded, we are left with 'idiopathic' pruritus, or itchiness of unknown cause. This is especially common in the older age group, and the only treatment is symptomatic, directed at minimising any potential irritation of the skin. Baths should be limited to once a week. A steroid cream, Synalar, is helpful, along with regular medication of antihistamine drugs. The acquisition of a suntan seems to be of real benefit, whether on some foreign beach or in a tanning parlour on a local high street. The two most intractable sites of itching are the anus and the vulva, known respectively as *pruritus ani* and *pruritus vulvae*, which can be so severe and profound as utterly to dominate the patient's life. A specialist opinion is essential, as the strong reassurance that only an expert can give is very helpful in counteracting the psychological problems that often result. It is essential to minimise irritation in the affected area, so, after washing, hairdryers are preferable to towels, and loose-fitting cotton underwear is helpful, as is a mild steroid ointment. There are two other specific points. Coffee seems to be an important exacerbating cause of *pruritus ani* and should be avoided. Less convincingly, beer, chocolate, and tomato ketchup have been implicated in a similar way. As for those with unrelenting *pruritus vulvae*, they should enquire about more drastic treatment. Alcohol injections or laser therapy (under anaesthetic) kill off the local nerve fibres. The vulva will be anaesthetised but blissfully itch-free.

4

Hormonal Disharmony

The Dissimulating Thyroid

Syphilis used to be known as the Great Dissimulator. After the primary sore or chancre in the genital region has healed, the disease's relentless progress, over 20 years or more, through its secondary and tertiary stages, involved every organ in the body, and produced a protean variety of symptoms. So, whether a patient's complaint was a fever or a rash, swelling of the lymph nodes, laryngitis or inflammation of the eye, anaemia, or hepatitis, heart failure or any of a bewildering variety of neurological syndromes, a wise physician would always start his investigations by ordering the Wassermann test for syphilis, and only if this turned out to negative would other possible causes be considered.

Nowadays, syphilis is so rare, and penicillin so effective a remedy, that these late manifestations are hardly seen, and the title of the Great Dissimulator has passed to diseases of the thyroid gland. These, too, can result in many different symptoms, although less florid than in syphilis. The deception rather is that they can be so subtle, so difficult to distinguish from the normal state, that they are easily overlooked. To emphasise the point, Dr Mary Church, a family doctor from Blantyre, has described two cases in the *British Medical Journal* – one, a female colleague with an over-active thyroid (thyrotoxicosis), and herself with an underactive thyroid (myxoedema).

The hormone thyroxine, secreted in minute quantities by the thyroid gland, primes the metabolic rate of the cells. Too much, and the body (and the psyche) goes into overdrive; too little, and it becomes sluggish and unresponsive. Describing her friend's illness, Dr Church writes: 'Recent conversations I had with her were all one-sided. I could never get a word in edgeways. Her best ideas came to her at four o'clock in the morning, and she would leap out of bed and bash the keys of her word processor until it was time for

111

work.' From this it would appear that her friend was just a bit manic, although there were other tell-tale symptoms, such as a voracious appetite. The penny only dropped belatedly, when her eyes seemed to start bulging out of their sockets, and eventually a diagnosis of thyrotoxicosis was made by an opthalmologist. Dr Church comments 'I was appalled by my bloomer [for having missed the diagnosis], and embarked on a course of soul-searching: was I in the right profession? How many other cases had I missed?'

Two years later the two colleagues went to a medical conference, and this time it was the friend who commented that Dr Church seemed inordinately tired and sensitive to the cold, and suggested that she have her thyroid function tested, which showed she had myxoedema. 'The symptoms had been there for many months for all to see,' Dr Church writes. 'I woke up tired, I dragged my body to work, always wrapped up, I fell asleep before the children while reading their bedtime story. The skin on my hands looked more like it belonged to my 90-year old granny.'

The danger for doctors – and for their patients – is that the early symptoms of both under- and over-active thyroid are virtually undistinguishable from the waves of trivial complaints that wash through the surgery every day: fatigue, anxiety, palpitations, diarrhoea, weakness, shortness of breath (thyrotoxicosis); lethargy, depression, aches and pains, heavy period, constipation (myxoedema). Explaining the frequent delay in the diagnosis of myxoedema, the late Dr Richard Asher points out: 'The symptoms tend to be dismissed as minor inconveniences rather than as major complaints. The mental slowness of the illness itself smothers self-criticism, and so changes may pass unnoticed by the patient. Not one of the symptoms – whether tiredness, aches and pains or poor memory – is a constant feature of the illness, and all occur in patients without myxoedema.'

The message is clear: if you feel you are manic, or gratuitously depressed, or if you are suffering from virtually any symptom your doctor has failed to diagnose, suggest gently you should have your thyroid function tested. Who knows, in a couple of weeks you could be a changed person!

Diabetes and the New Insulins

In 1921, a 13-year-old boy, Frederick Thomson, was admitted to Ward H of Toronto General Hospital, terminally ill with diabetes.

One of his doctors later commented: 'He was a pathetic, emaciated figure, lying quietly in his bed, too weak to show any interest in the activities of a large busy ward. All of us knew he was doomed.' But he was not. Two young scientists who had just extracted purified insulin from a dog's pancreas were looking for a young patient to act as their first human guinea-pig. Frederick Thomson was an obvious candidate for the daily injection. 'These results were certain. The condition of this dying boy was dramatically changed – he literally came back to life.' It was as a 'sturdy young man' that he was eventually discharged two months later.

Over the past 70 years, millions of diabetics have been able to live near-normal lives thanks to insulin. For years the pig and the cow have been the mainstay of diabetics' lives, their pancreases ground up and purified to produce, respectively, porcine and bovine insulin. A decade ago, the drug manufacturers realised that the new technology of genetic engineering enabled them to make human insulin. The American drug giant Eli Lilly extracted it from the bacterium *E. coli*, into which they had inserted the human insulin gene. More elegantly, a small Danish company, Novo, manipulated the pig insulin molecule, removing one of its amino acids and substituting the human equivalent. The close chemical similarity between pig and human insulin meant that any putative benefits to diabetics were likely to be trivial. Human insulin, however, could be presented as 'more natural' or 'purer' and so it was likely to take the lion's share of the insulin market. To encourage this process, both companies cut back drastically on their animal-based insulin.

Commercially this strategy has been very successful; 80 per cent of British diabetics now use the human insulin. Medically, it is a different story. Just over half of the respondents to a questionnaire from the British Diabetics Association reported they felt 'worse' for the change. Typical comments were: 'I feel off colour for a week or two at a time' and 'Now I rarely feel like a well diabetic.'

Human insulin is claimed to increase the number of hypoglycaemic attacks in diabetics, where the blood sugar falls to low. It is said to alter the severity and nature of these episodes – from sweating and palpitations, which can be rapidly relieved by a cup of sweetened tea or a biscuit, to more disturbing symptoms such as headaches, difficulties in concentration and disturbances of speech and vision. Some say they seem to lose these warning signs altogether and collapse into coma – with potentially lethal consequences – before they can take the necessary precautions. Those who revert to using animal-based insulins find the control of their diabetes rapidly improves.

Most diabetics become very skilled at balancing their insulin injections and food intake to allow them to lead a normal life. Many are quite rightly resentful that their careful routines have been disrupted by the introduction of human insulin for what appears to have been a marginal benefit. But perhaps the real moral of the story is how neatly it illustrates the illusory nature of what often passes an 'important advance' in modern medicine. It is remarkable that drug companies should have invested hundreds of millions of pounds to develop a new type of insulin only slightly different from – and for a substantial minority a lot worse than – that which plucked Frederick Thomson from the jaws of death 70 years ago.

Brittle Diabetes

While working as a medical registrar in a hospital in the East End of London, I became fairly skilled at treating diabetic coma, thanks to the misfortune of one girl in her late teens who must have been admitted a dozen times or more over a period of 18 months. Her problem was 'brittle' diabetes. No matter how frequently her regime of insulin injections was modified to achieve normal levels of glucose in the blood, her diabetes would veer out of control, leading rapidly to dehydration and coma. The unpredictable life-threatening pattern of diabetes in this young woman was naturally a source of enormous concern for all those who came into contact with her. In pursuit of some underlying cause that might explain the brittleness everything was considered: chronic infection, hormonal problems, resistance to insulin were all suspected and in turn excluded. The obvious explanation eluded us.

Writing about the problem of brittle diabetes in *The Lancet*, Dr Judith Steele of Victoria Hospital, Fife says: 'In clinical practice, it is clear that almost all these patients are manipulating both their diabetes and the people around them. The lengths to which they can go are extraordinary. They omit their insulin or use too much, inject it into the mattress, dilute it with water, hide it in concealed bags or up the vagina. They seek and gain attention.' Dr Steele's comments are based on a survey of 26 brittle diabetics followed up over a decade. Five have died and, of the remainder, nine were all known to omit their insulin injections deliberately, or admitted doing it. Further evidence for the fictitious nature of the disorder is that, with time, their diabetes stabilised, usually in association with some 'positive life event' like marriage or pregnancy. In retrospect, it is surprising that it has taken so long for the hidden cause of brittle diabetes to be revealed. 'Even now, many doctors are unwilling to confront the problem,' writes Dr Steele. 'There is a natural reluctance to believe that patients would deliberately cheat, and an understandable worry about making false accusations.' Now that the secret is out, the number of cases can, predictably, be expected to fall – to everyone's benefit.

This saga illustrates the dangers of ignoring the many psychological problems associated with chronic illness. Robert Tattersall, diabetic specialist at the University of Nottingham, has listed some of them. The parents (particularly mothers) of diabetic children may be either over-anxious or rejecting, or an intricate mixture of the two. The father is often excluded, to the detriment of the marriage. Siblings resent the attention paid, and seek vengeance in the usual fashion. The child may use the illness as a shield against growing up, never being well enough to take part in normal activities, or may rebel, 'which invariably involves striking out at the cause of their frustration, the diabetes'. During the teenage years, 'many at some time or another falsify their urine test, go on eating binges, quarrel with parents and doctors and show varied combinations of hostility, rebelliousness and provocative attitudes'.

In general, the emotional burden of having insulin-dependent diabetes is almost unimaginable, with its regime of daily injections, tightly controlled diets and rigid meal times. The responsibility of success or failure in achieving adequate control of blood glucose levels rests with the patient, and cannot readily be displaced onto the shoulders of medical advisers. Lastly, there is always the apprehension that the blood glucose may fall too low, resulting in wild mood-swings, and aggressive behaviour, which may be readily interpreted by bystanders as incipient (or actual) madness. Taken together, it is surprising that the severe psychological maladaptation, as represented by brittle diabetes, is not much more common. It certainly says something about the resilience and force of personality of those with the illness that so many manage to lead 'normal' lives.

Classy Gout

At one never-to-be-forgotten period of my life, there was on my list a middle-aged man of quite pathological unpleasantness – a bully, manipulator and braggart all rolled into one jowly, sweaty frame. A doctor before me had stupidly started him on some pills for 'angina', and nothing I or anyone else could say would persuade him he was not afflicted by heart disease. When the cardiologist's tests failed to show narrowing of the arteries to the heart, he consulted a medical textbook in the local library and convinced himself that he had a variant of angina caused by spasm rather than narrowing of the arteries – and clung to this self-diagnosis like a drowning man to a log. He certainly believed it was good enough reason not to work, and I learned from his wife that, whenever he was crossed at home, he would get his own way by having a dramatic attack of chest pain. Aware of my scepticism, he was defensively jocular and would address me as 'the quack', as in 'you quacks always think you know best' and 'what quack remedies are you peddling today.' To preserve my sanity, I realised I had no alternative other than to throw him off my list, but before I had an opportunity to do so, his personality changed quite dramatically. He hobbled into surgery one morning complaining of a pain in his big toe and, as it was red, swollen and exquisitely tender, I had no hesitation in telling him he had gout. As with so many sufferers, he had gone to bed the previous evening feeling fine and woken in the middle of the night with a pain usually depicted as a small red-skinned devil tearing at the flesh with teeth and talons. The acute attack ranges through the full spectrum of the sensations of pain – tearing, gnawing, burning, stretching and tightening. I managed to resist the temptation to torture him by manipulating his toe up and down, but seized the chance to get my own back with a ten-minute lecture on his slob-like ways. I told him these were to blame for the gout, and that if he wanted to avoid another episode he would have to lose weight, stop drinking, take regular exercise and so on. I then gave him a prescription for the most powerful of the anti-inflammatory drugs – indomethacin – and sent him on his way.

From then on he was a reformed character, a change I could only attribute to the same sort of conditioning reflex that Pavlov demonstrated in his dogs: the association in his mind of an acutely painful stimulus – his swollen big toe – with my admonitions, reinforced by the relief from the pills I prescribed, had had an extraordinary salutary effect. He lost weight, cut down on his drinking and, presumably because he had experienced what pain could really be like, his fictional angina faded away. In view of this gratifying outcome, I never got round to telling him the truth: that gout is only tenuously linked to self-indulgence, and that I was being less than honest in blaming his misfortune on his slobbish habits.

Certainly, the purines present in meat and alcohol are metabolised to uric acid which, in high concentrations, precipitate out as crystals in the joint of the big toe. None the less, the reason most people get gout has less to do with the amount of meat they eat or alcohol they drink than with an inherited tendency by which they fail to excrete adequate amounts of uric acid in the urine. The link between gout and high social class, which made the affliction very respectable in the eighteenth and nineteenth centuries, is usually attributed to the belief that those who suffered did so because they were rich enough to eat and drink to excess. It seems, however, that gout was more likely to be an inherited predisposition, due to a trait common in upper-class families, as the distinguished medical historian Professor Roy Porter has observed: 'Gout did not idly choose the eminent, it was hereditary, running in good families.' He quotes Sydney Smith: 'Gout loves ancestors and genealogy; it needs five or six generations of gentlemen or noblemen to give it full vigour.' Gout's reputation as an upper-class malady was reinforced by the belief that diseases were mutually exclusive and jealous of each other. So no matter how grievous an attack might be, at least it protected against something worse. 'Gout prevents other illnesses and prolongs life,' observed Horace Walpole. 'If I could cure the gout, should I not have a fever, a palsy or an apoplexy?'

The decisive shift in medical thinking about the disease came with the accidental discovery in 1963 of the drug allopurinol, which blocks the synthesis of uric acid, and which is much more effective in preventing further attacks than attempting to encourage people to lead a more sober and ascetic life. The concept of gout as primarily a biochemical disorder has never really penetrated the public consciousness, most people still believe the malady is a just desert for past indulgences. Still, I doubt very much if my pathologically unpleasant patient would have been so wondrously reformed if, rather than exploiting that belief, I had sympathised with him for having a biochemical disorder.

5

Neurological Nuggets

Restless Legs

Restless Legs Syndrome is an obscure affliction in which an unpleasant creeping sensation is felt deep within the bone and muscle. 'It feels as if my whole leg is full of small worms,' is how one sufferer described it, and another 'as if ants were running up and down my bones'. Movement of the legs provides the only solace, and sufferers find it impossible to keep still. Thomas Willis, the great English neurologist, provided the first, and most colourful description in 1695. 'For some when being a Bed and betake themselves to sleep, presently so great a restlessness and tossings ensue, they are no more able to sleep than if they were in a place of greatest torture.' This torture is psychological as well as physical. The creeping may persist for hours at a time, keeping the tormented victim up till four or five in the morning, and this forced insomnia unsettles the mind, inducing hallucinations and depression. Come morning, the discomfort usually disappears, but will recur if the sufferer is forced to stay immobile, as on a visit to the theatre or on a car journey. Some find it impossible to sit still at all; they are unable to get even a moment's peace relaxing in an armchair. Rather their discomfort forces them to walk up and down constantly 'like a lost soul', as one woman put it, or, in the words of another, 'like a caged bear'. Torture indeed.

Neurological examination of sufferers reveals no abnormalities; nor do other investigatory tests. No pathological abnormalities of muscle or nerves have been identified. The cause is unknown, though it is presumed there must be some area deep in the brain from where the crawling sensation originates. The syndrome may, however, be a feature of other, unrelated conditions. Pregnant women – almost one in ten of them – may find the last third of their pregnancy made a misery through the syndrome, though the sensation disappears immediately the baby is born. A quarter of those with anaemia due to iron deficiency may be victims. It may also be a symptom of kidney failure, which can be resolved with dialysis or a transplant.

For those for whom there is no obvious cause, treatment must be empirical. Heat is sometimes helpful – a hot bath or a hot-water bottle and bed socks. Blessed relief may come with a viral illness such as influenza, which pushes the temperature up a few degrees for several days. Others prefer the cold, pouring icy water over the legs and, whenever the opportunity arises, walking barefoot in the snow. Thomas Willis favoured opium, but in general, strong sedatives are of little use as they cannot overcome the abnormal sensation. Those taking large doses still find themselves staggering around the bedroom in the middle of the night. Drugs developed for the treatment of epilepsy and Parkinson's are useful in most cases. Two years ago Dr Peter Bateman, an Australian anaesthetist, reported that he was completely cured through taking 250 to 500 milligrams of magnesium supplements before retiring. 'I suffer from the condition myself,' he writes, 'but nowadays only if I forget to take my tablets.'

No one could confuse restless legs with that other disorder that prevents a good night's sleep – recurrent and painful nocturnal cramps – which can wake those affected several times a night. Cramp sufferers are advised to keep their legs flexed in bed by, for example, placing a pillow under the knee or against the foot. This prevents the leg muscle from relaxing completely and producing a spasm. Treatment with quinine usually, and quite dramatically, reduces the frequency of these cramps, though there have been doubts recently as to whether it is as effective as claimed. The problem may be that the standard dose – one tablet at night – is too low and should be doubled. This may, however, produce quinine toxicity with tinnitus, hearing loss, dizziness and visual disturbance.

Tales of Epilepsy

One of the more unusual of medical reports concerns the case of the lying Eurocrat. A 51-year-old Frenchman based in Brussels was involved in 'adversarial negotiations' with his counterparts from other EC member nations, which required him to be economical with the truth. Unfortunately, every time he had to tell a lie, which was apparently several times a day, he came out in a hot flush, had auditory hallucinations and even, on occasion, fell off his seat and had a convulsion. As in the tale of the wooden puppet Pinocchio, whose nose grew longer every time he told a lie, this particular Eurocrat's dishonesty was perfectly transparent to his fellow negotiators. When he eventually sought medical advice, he was diagnosed as suffering from epilepsy. Late-onset epilepsy is often a sinister sign of some serious pathology in the brain, and sure enough the scan revealed a benign tumour or meningioma pressing on the temporal lobe. This was operated on, and the Eurocrat started taking anti-epilepsy drugs. Since then he has had no further trouble. He is now back at the negotiating table, presumably lying away with impunity.

Epileptic fits are usually precipitated by flashing lights, hunger or tiredness, but emotions – including, as in this case, guilty feelings brought on by telling lies – may also be involved. The commonest of 'reflex epilepsies', as they are known, are probably orgasmic fits brought on by the intense feelings aroused by sexual passion, though they may also occur under the stress of having to take difficult decisions – or even as a result of reading a particularly gripping or moving novel. Sentimental feelings associated with a particular piece of music may also be responsible – one clergyman only had his attacks when playing *Now Thank We All Our God* on the church organ. In another well-documented case, a 62-year-old civil servant had his fits at exactly the same time every day while listening to the radio. Both he and his doctors were mystified as to the cause of the fits, until it was pointed out that they coincided with the playing of a peal of the Bow Bells commonly used as an interval signal by the BBC.

Clearly, if the precipitant cause of an epileptic seizure can be identified, then avoiding this, combined with taking anti-epileptic drugs, is usually sufficient to prevent attacks occurring. None the less, for most epileptics, their seizures usually come out of the blue and this lack of predictability is obviously a source of considerable anxiety. Enter, man's best friend. Mr Andrew Edney, president of the World Small Animal Veterinary Association, has been systematically collecting reports from epilepsy sufferers whose dogs anticipate their owner's fits. In a typical case, Sandy – an 11-year-old mongrel, whose owner, a Mr Dennis Appleby, developed epilepsy after a stroke – barks and nuzzles him for several minutes before a fit occurs and then finds Mrs Appleby and barks until she comes to look after her husband. According to Mr Edney, 'the dog may look anxious or restless and start behaving strangely. Some try to herd their owners to safety and encourage them to lie down'. Rarely, apparently, do they get it wrong. One owner pretended to have a fit just to see what happened and was 'politely ignored' by his dog.

Mr Edney speculates that dogs may have the ability to detect the very early electrical disturbances in the brain that precede an epileptic fit. Alternatively, he says, 'it may not be necessary to search for complex explanations. Most dogs have up to 24 hours a day to observe the behaviour of their owners, and it is easy to forget that they can detect tiny changes which would not be noticed by most humans.' In the United States, 'epilepsy' dogs are being trained to give clear signals to their owners of an imminent seizure. And, interestingly, as a result, the owners often have fewer fits. This is probably because, as one of the dog trainers points out, 'the well-being of the patient and their peace of mind is enhanced by the dog's companionship'.

Parkinson's Holidays

Dwight C. McGoon was at the peak of his career as a heart surgeon at the world-famous Mayo Clinic in the United States when he developed Parkinson's disease. Initially, he had noticed only that he seemed to be slowing down, so an operation which should have taken three hours stretched to four. Then one day, while delicately separating tissues with the blunt edge of his scissors, he sensed a slight tremor in his right hand. From that moment, he realised his working days were over, and although still in his early fifties, resigned his post. Mr McGoon's misfortune, however, is our gain – for he has written a remarkable book about his illness which will be a boon to many thousands of his fellow sufferers.

Parkinson's disease might seem quite straightforward. The nerves in the control centre, or gearbox, of the brain gradually die off, leading to the three cardinal symptoms of tremor, rigidity – where the muscles feel stiff and inelastic – and bradykinesia – a slowness in initiating and carrying out movements, interspersed with episodes where the patient is caught in a state of frozen animation. The treatment is with the drug levodopa, which corrects the deficit in the amount of the neurotransmitter dopamine. Within half an hour the body is suffused with a feeling of warmth and the inelastic muscles loosen up, and while these beneficial effects last the patient feels cured.

But after a while the miracle of levodopa turns out to be a mirage. First, the duration of responsiveness dwindles from around six hours to less than half an hour, and as the drug wears off, the patient who, one moment may be completely mobile, finds himself frozen as if in a block of ice. Secondly, while the drug is working with maximum effectiveness, the benefit it confers it vitiated by its main side effect, a painful, uncontrollable twisting of the limbs. The patient's disease thus becomes highly unstable; a small increase in the dose brings its toxic effects to an unbearable pitch, a small decrease results in severe immobility. In this cat-and-mouse game, the treatment becomes worse than the disease. In these circumstances, there is no alternative other than to stop the treatment altogether for a fortnight or more in the hope that when levodopa is reintroduced the brain's responsiveness is improved. This is known as a 'drug holiday', although for the untreated, immobilised patients it is anything but a holiday.

To simplify matters, I have not described the value of other, less effective drugs, but it should be clear that juggling around with a dose of levodopa and other medications in pursuit of the best relief of symptoms is a very complicated matter indeed. It is certainly well beyond the competence of the average general practitioner to give good advice, while a twice-yearly visit to a consultant neurologist – which is the best most patients can hope for on the NHS, is clearly insufficient. Patients with Parkinson's are very much on their own. The achievement of Mr McGoon's book and what distinguishes it is that it gives readers the self-confidence to pursue the only possible alternative course: to become their own physician and treat themselves.

As an example, he describes his own solution to the problem of the diminishing effectiveness of levodopa, which I suspect will markedly improve the lives of many sufferers. He incorporates the concept of the 'drug holiday' into his daily treatment schedule, taking his levodopa for only four or five hours in the afternoon, during which time his muscles 'miraculously regain their useful vitality, I can walk freely again and a smile comes easily'. By evening, the stiffness and rigidity returns and worsens throughout the night. In the morning his mobility is quite seriously impaired. The advantage of this regime is twofold. It should prolong, probably almost indefinitely, the brain's sensitivity to the drug. Secondly, it allows him to plan his day, sure of at least four hours of near-normality.

And what of the rest of the time? Here, Mr McGoon provides

another major insight. The disability of Parkinson's is not a loss of muscular power but the loss of integration of many different movements previously performed instinctively. Might it be possible, he wondered, to re-educate his brain to perform such tasks? In the afternoon, while enjoying the benefits of levodopa, he found he could tie his shoelaces without hesitation, but in the morning and evening he had to ask his wife for help. Accordingly, he examined in detail while under the influence of levodopa the intricacies of shoelace-tying, how the fingers hold the strings and manipulate them. Once the effectiveness of the drug had worn off, he then practised his new-found knowledge. Gradually, with the same trial-and-error process as a child, he has re-learnt how it can be done. Applying similar principles to walking, he has improved his ability to move about during his drug-free period. This inspiring volume gives more useful advice than could be gleaned from a cohort of physicians.

(*The Parkinson's Handbook*, by Dwight C McGoon MD is published by W. W. Norton & Co Ltd.)

Guillain-Barré Syndrome

It may not be a lot of fun lying on your back in hospital unable to move a muscle below the neck, but as 40-year-old Laurence Knott reflected soon after his admission to the Royal Free Hospital in London, things could be a lot worse. Certainly he found it a nuisance that he was unable to feed himself, and humiliating to require nursing assistance for basic physical needs, but at least his diagnosis, Guillain-Barré Syndrome, is one of the few catastrophic neurological illnesses that tend, eventually, to get better of their own accord. His phlegmatic reasoning was no doubt helped by the fact that he is a family doctor in Enfield, north London. The first sign something might be wrong came when visiting a patient after morning surgery. 'By the time I got to her room, I was more breathless than she was,' he recalls. 'We made a sorry picture, she wheezing on one side of the bed, me gasping on the other.' As soon as he got home he made straight for his medical textbooks. 'There seemed to be just one condition that fitted all my symptoms of tingling in my hands and feet, breathlessness and difficulty in walking.' Dr Knott rang the local hospital and told the physician on duty that he had developed Guillain-Barré Syndrome (GBS).

Gullain and Barré were two French physicians who in 1916 together described this syndrome of progressive ascending paralysis for the first time. The underlying problem is acute inflammation of the motor and sensory nerves, which can be induced by a variety of causes including viral and bacterial illnesses. The commonest of these is campylobacter infection, which can be contracted by eating undercooked chicken or by drinking milk from bottles that magpies or jackdaws have pecked at. The paralysis starts in the hands and feet and then moves up slowly towards the neck. The main life-threatening complication is asphyxiation from paralysis of the respiratory muscles of the rib cage. About a quarter of patients need mechanical ventilation, sometimes for a month or longer, until the power to breathe unaided returns. Most cases recover spontaneously over a period of two to three months but recovery may be speeded by a process called plasma exchange where the blood plasma is removed from the body and filtered to remove the antibodies that are attacking the nerves. Alternatively human immunoglobulin given directly into the vein may be equally effective.

In Dr Knott's case it was decided to proceed with plasma exchange, but the first attempt almost killed him: 'As the needle plunged into my chest, I suddenly felt as if everything was getting further away,' he remembers. 'Someone said "his blood pressure has gone down to zero". Someone else shouted "call the resuscitation team".'

Dr Knott survived and after a short stay in the intensive care unit he returned to the general ward. But after his brush with death, his phlegmatic optimism had evaporated. 'For the short period I thought I was going to die, I consoled myself with the thought that I'd had my life, and that it had not been too bad,' he says. 'But when the crisis was over, I was overwhelmed by despair at the prospect of my continued dependency. I was assailed with morbid thoughts that perhaps I would be one of the unlucky few that did not recover, that perhaps I would be spending the rest of my life in a wheelchair. If I had the strength or opportunity I would willingly have thrown myself under a bus.'

After six weeks, right on cue, came the first signs of recovery. 'It happened in the physiotherapy department when in response to the command "move your legs", I looked down and amazingly saw the first flicker of movement in my feet.' Dr Knott was transferred back to his local hospital, Chase Farm in Enfield. 'I graduated from the wheelchair to walking with sticks and to this day I will never

forget when I was able to get around on my own two feet again.'
Dr Knott's prolonged convalescence at Chase Farm had another
quite unexpected bonus in restoring his sense of medical vocation.
He had a steady stream of visitors, patients from his practice who
went out of their way to drop in to see him before going on to their
outpatient appointments elsewhere in the hospital. 'I realised then I
was not just a technician sitting behind a desk signing prescriptions.
I felt appreciated, almost loved. It was very moving.'

Terrifying Tremor

In a classic study of war neurosis published in 1941, Dr John
Sutherland, lecturer in psychology at Edinburgh University, found
the commonest physical symptom to be 'tremor and jumpiness',
especially in reaction to sudden noises. Fear of death was the
major precipitant, especially in those whose fathers had died in
the First World War. Fear and tremor are virtually synonymous:
'Work out your own salvation with fear and trembling,' wrote
St Paul in his Epistle to the Philippians, and we shake with fear,
and 'tremble like a leaf' after a shock. This fear-induced tremor is
caused by the chemical adrenalin, which exaggerates and amplifies
the normal physiological tremor readily demonstrable by the fine
oscillations of a sheet of paper placed on the back of the hands
when the arms are outstretched. This fear-induced, exaggerated,
physiological tremor is of particular concern to musicians prone
to stage fright, as it can so readily compromise their performance.
Nearly a third of professional musicians regularly take a beta-blocker
which, by antagonising the effect of adrenalin, reduces the tremor
and other symptoms of anxiety. Dr Ian James of the Royal Free
Hospital, London has found the drug's benefits to be especially
marked in string players, because of the adverse effect that tremor
has on bowing.

There are, however, several other types of tremor which are
unrelated to fear or anxiety, but of particular interest to neurologists,
because the sufferers are frequently labelled neurotic and denied
adequate treatment. These tremors are not present at rest, which
distinguishes them from those associated with common neurological
disorders such as Parkinson's disease, but rather become apparent
during the maintenance of a fixed position. In the commonest –
benign essential tremor – the hands start to shake uncontrollably
whenever they assume a fixed or stable position, such as holding a

cup or fork, during writing, or in other types of fine manipulation such as doing up buttons. Benign essential tremor runs in families, can come on at any age, and gradually deteriorates over time. Predictably it can have a disastrous impact on social life, discouraging sufferers from visiting restaurants or pubs, while speaking in public or even a handshake is an ordeal. A schoolteacher in her late thirties observed that on being introduced her hands shook so forcefully that men would be under the misapprehension that they were exerting a strong emotional effect upon her.

Quite remarkably this tremor is abolished completely, albeit temporarily, by alcohol. This is clearly very useful for those worried that they might be embarrassed by their tremor during a social event, but carries the risk of ending in chronic alcoholism. As one neurologist observed rather censoriously: 'The fact that a dose of spirits will temporarily check the tremor appears only too often to serve as an excuse for habits of intemperance.' Alcohol is, however, of little use for those whose tremor threatens their livelihood, either because it interferes with the manual skills of, for example, tool makers or lorry drivers or simply because it damages their prospects of promotion. The mainstay of current medical treatment was discovered quite fortuitously by a female patient of Dr Gerald Winkler, a physician at Harvard Medical School. Back in 1974, soon after his patient started taking the newly discovered drug propranolol for an abnormality of heart rhythm, she realised that her severe essential tremor had disappeared, allowing her to sign her name for the first time in five years. Dr Winkler promptly tried the drug on a further 24 patients with essential tremor and found it to be very useful in three-quarters. Propranolol reduces the intensity of the tremor sufficiently to allow patients to eat and drink in public without undue embarrassment and to continue in their jobs.

The second type of tremor poses problems for people when standing still. They have no trouble when sitting or walking, but when they have to maintain a fixed position, such as standing at a supermarket checkout or waiting for a bus, their legs start shaking, they become increasingly unsteady and have to take a step in order to regain their balance. This condition is known as primary orthostatic tremor and, according to Dr Thomas Britton, senior registrar at the National Hospital for Nervous Diseases in London, 'many patients are initially labelled as suffering from a psychiatric illness'. He describes the case of a 25-year-old woman whose symptoms had started four years earlier, and for whom 'unsteadiness began a few seconds after having to stand still. If forced to stand for long periods, the shaking would become so pronounced as to make her fall.'

Regrettably neither alcohol nor propranolol are of any use, though some of the drugs used for treating epilepsy have occasionally been successful. 'Most patients are just pleased to know the diagnosis,' says Dr Britton, 'particularly if a psychiatric cause has been suspected.' He advises patients to buy a shooting stick with a rubber end so that, whether doing the cooking or standing in a bus queue, they can sit in comfort without fear of toppling over. Tremors have always fascinated neurologists, and even if their cause is often uncertain and their origins disputed, accurate diagnosis and appropriate treatment can transform the lives of victims.

Mistaking Myasthenia

Doctors can get it spectacularly wrong in two quite distinct ways. They may insist there is nothing wrong when in fact there is. Or the patient is gravely told he has an incurable disease for which there is no treatment when in fact it is eminently treatable. Those suffering from the muscle disease myasthenia seem particularly prone to both types of error.

Myasthenia gravis is a disorder of the junction between nerve and muscle. The message for muscular movement passes as an electric current down the nerve, causing a small package of the chemical acetylcholine to be discharged from the nerve ending. This then crosses the junction to the muscle, locks onto a receptor and, as a result, the muscle contracts. For reasons as yet unknown, the body can produce antibodies to the receptor, so the message cannot get through. This results in weakness or, more precisely, fatiguability of different muscle groups. So, patients wake up feeling spry and energetic but as the day progresses they begin to tire. They start seeing double or find it difficult to carry on a prolonged conversation as their speech becomes slurred. Meals become something of an ordeal, with sufferers spilling their food as they find problems in constantly moving the fork from plate to mouth. They also develop pain around the shoulder girdle from the strain of trying to keep their head upright. By the early afternoon they often feel exhausted and retire to bed, after which they feel their batteries have been recharged, albeit temporarily.

127

The description of this pattern of symptoms is characteristic and there should be little difficulty in reaching the right diagnosis. Like any illness, however, myasthenics have a spectrum of symptoms and it is at the two extremes of the very mild and the severe that patients may be told that they are either neurotic or have a rapidly progressive fatal muscle disease. The experience of Marianne Mcphie, falls very much into the first category. Indeed, it took nearly 20 years before she finally discovered what was wrong. Mrs Mcphie's main problem was tiredness. She married in her early twenties and had two children in quick succession but found that, unlike her friends and to her own surprise, it was very difficult to cope. By the end of the day she was simply exhausted. 'Myasthenia is a very irritating illness because it does not allow excess in any form and behaves like a reprimanding nanny if you overdo it,' she says. 'The trouble is, life does not come in measured doses, so Christmas holidays, late nights, excitement or emotion could leave me exhausted, and frustrated and guilty as a result.'

Mrs Mcphie and her long-suffering husband always believed there was something physically amiss and badgered her doctors to find out what it was. Several GPs she consulted over the years were, she says, 'an uncurious lot. They took one look at me and concluded I must be an unhappy female.' She was referred to one neurologist who 'took half an hour to decide I was the healthiest specimen of womankind he'd ever seen'. A second neurologist did at least consider the possibility of myasthenia, but told her she did not have it. Eventually a friend of the family came to tea and noticed her squinting across the room and advised she consult John Richmond, professor of neurology at Sheffield University. 'I'll never forget the afternoon he came flapping down the corridor in his white coat and said "I've found what is wrong, you have myasthenia",' she recalls. 'I leapt out of bed and did a little dance of joy much to the astonishment of his entourage – but it was the most wonderful feeling to be believed at last and to know I was not going mad after all.'

Dr Stanley Freedman, 58-year-old consultant physician in chest diseases at Chase Farm in north London, had exactly the opposite experience. He found difficulty riding his bike to work one morning, saw a neurologist that afternoon, had a special test of his muscle function and was told he had motor neurone disease. 'It was like receiving a death sentence. I felt an unbelievable sense of shock. My heart rate must have fallen to ten beats a minute.' The gloomy diagnosis was confirmed by a second neurologist a few days later. 'I gave all my suits to Oxfam, resigned from all the committees I was on and settled down to expect the worst.' Dr Freedman's symptoms deteriorated rapidly, which should not happen with motor neurone disease, and a friend at Charing Cross Hospital poured scorn on the diagnosis. He suggested that Dr Freedman see the world's leading expert on myasthenia, Professor John Newsom-Davis at Oxford's Radcliffe Infirmary. 'The correct diagnosis was swiftly made and, with treatment, I gradually regained my strength.'

The vital clue to myasthenia in both instances lay in the nature of the main symptom of weakness. Mr Mcphie's tiredness was different from that which is so often a feature of a neurotic illness because it became gradually worse throughout the day. Further, there was always a dissonance between her great desire to be active and her physical inability to do things. Dr Freedman's weakness also fluctuated throughout the day. The essential mistake of the two neurologists he initially consulted was in placing too much faith on a misleading test. As so often happens, the correct answer lies in a fastidious attention to the details of the patient's story. Dr Freedman was treated with steroids and is now back at work. 'Following my experience, I now treat my patients differently and understand much better why they sometimes complain that doctors do not listen to what they are saying.'

Gloomy Alzheimer's

Alzheimer's is a gloomy subject, albeit an important one and two issues in particular merit comment. The first concerns the value or otherwise of the drug Tacrine, and the second, the NHS's responsibility of caring for those with this illness. Tacrine increases the concentration of the neurotransmitter acetylcholine in the brain, thus theoretically compensating for the loss of nerve cells by boosting the action of those that remain. Over the past eight years, many studies have evaluated its efficacy, some making unbelievable claims that it is a miracle drug, allowing patients to return to work or take up golf again, while others have found it completely useless. Little wonder there is some confusion about its merits. The best quality studies done in this country show that if the drug is given in sufficiently high doses for long enough, then almost half of the patients will show 'significant' improvement. It must be said, however, that not all Alzheimer specialists are impressed by its efficacy. Tacrine is not available on the NHS because it has not yet been granted a product licence. There is a suspicion that this is being blocked on grounds of cost as, at £80 for a month's treatment, it could easily add £10 million to the nation's drug bill. Tacrine is, however, licensed in the United States and France, and some patients in Britain are obtaining the drug from these countries. In theory Tacrine can be obtained in this country by private prescription from a specialist.

With or without Tacrine, all people with Alzheimer's need considerable care and attention, which used to be provided free by the NHS. Now, by a sleight of hand, the Government has decided that it should be paid for out of the patient's funds, or those of their relatives. So those who have been prudent throughout their working lives can easily find their savings and the capital invested in their homes whittled away in a couple of years. Consider, for example, Mrs Dorothy Hay, who for the past five years has cared for her husband, in his early seventies. He does not recognise her, is aggressive, incontinent and difficult to lift. He falls, breaks his leg, and goes into hospital. She decides she can no longer cope, but finds that her health authority has divested itself of virtually all its long-term nursing-care beds and she finds the only option is a private residential home. This must be paid for by their joint savings, specially put aside in case she was left on her own, along with Mr Hay's occupational pension. Her only means of support in the future will be the state pension. To cap it all, she finds out that a similarly placed couple in the neighbouring health district are having all their needs provided for by the NHS.

What should Mrs Hay do? To answer this question it is necessary to fill in some background. In 1994 the Health Ombudsman ruled that Leeds Health Authority had a 'duty to care' for a man with profound brain damage following a stroke, who had been discharged from hospital to a nursing home at a cost to the family of £6,000 per year. After this case, the Government sought to clarify its responsibilities, and in August 1995 the NHS executive issued new guidelines. These acknowledged that for those 'with complex and multiple health-care needs', the NHS has a responsibility 'for funding their care'. But, crucially, the guidelines go on to say that 'the significant majority who require continuing nursing care are likely to have their needs met through social services'. That is, they will be placed in private nursing homes and, following a means test, the cost of their care must come from their own assets. Now, does

Mr Hay have 'complex and multiple health-care needs', entitling him to free NHS care, or does he require only 'continuing nursing care', which must be paid from his assets?

This is a fudge, as any decision will be entirely arbitrary. According to Mervyn Kohler of Help the Aged, cynical health authorities will use these guidelines to save money by closing their long-term NHS beds for the elderly on the basis that, at this time of life, they need only 'continuing nursing care'. It might have been more honest to establish the principle that everyone is entitled, for example, to six months' free NHS care, after which the NHS could charge a fixed fee based on a percentage of that charged in the private sector.

For the moment, however, these are my suggestions. First, the middle class could follow the example of the rich and hand their assets over to their children, though there are restrictions on this. The state, whether the NHS or social services, will then have to foot the bill for any long-term care, if it is needed. Alternatively, they could try to exploit the ambiguity in the wording of the guidelines and, with their doctor's affidavit that their relative has 'complex and multiple health-care needs', insist on the statutory right to free NHS care. This will involve mobilising the support of the Community Health Council, the local MP, the Health Ombudsman or, indeed, threatening the health authority with legal sanctions. Good luck!

Vertiginous Vertigo

I was summoned recently to the bedside of a woman in her early thirties who had woken that morning and lifted her head from the pillow only to be overwhelmed by a sensation that the room was spinning around and around. As she collapsed back on the bed, sweat pouring off her brow, she realised she needed to throw up, but the bathroom seemed a million miles away. Very slowly she rolled onto her side, slipped out of bed and crawled on her hands and knees towards the lavatory bowl. After a protracted bout of vomiting, she crawled back, phoned the surgery and managed to slip back into bed where she lay absolutely still.

It sounds serious – and, indeed, my patient was convinced she was dying, the only question being whether it was from a stroke, haemorrhage, brain tumour or heart attack. There are few enough circumstances where a doctor can be genuinely reassuring that the most catastrophic symptom is actually benign, but this is one of them. My patient had an acute inflammation, probably caused by a virus, in the part of the inner ear that controls balance – the vestibule. A few days in bed, some pills to stop her feeling sick, and all would be well. An episode like this is a reminder once again of how utterly dependent we are on the most sophisticated of physiological mechanisms about which, when we are healthy, we have absolutely no knowledge. How do we resist the force of gravity and stay upright? Why, when we move the head from side to side, do we not feel dizzy? How do ballroom dancers twirl round and round without staggering about?

The balance mechanism in the ear is only part of the story. Here, three semi-circular canals, set at right angles, are filled with lymph. As the head tilts to left and right, or forwards and backwards, the fluid swishes around, brushing against minute hairs, instigating nervous impulses to the brain. This information has to be co-ordinated with the position of the eyes, so that as the head swings one way, the eyes move in the opposite and the world appears stationary. Then, from the soles of the feet upwards to the spine and the neck, there are millions of sense organs monitoring the position of the body. Microsecond by microsecond, these three sources of information about our position are co-ordinated in the mid-brain. With such a necessarily complex process, it would be surprising if subtle deterioration in one or other of these symptoms with the passage of years did not result in dizziness – and thereby hangs an interesting tale.

Dizziness is, indeed, a very common symptom in the older age group but, unlike my patient's acute symptoms, the abnormality can be so subtle that it is difficult to define its source, even with specialist investigation. Treatment is not very satisfactory, because there are no drugs that can correct subtle abnormalities in the processing of sensory information. Lastly, dizziness can also be a neurotic symptom. It is common, for example, in those with agoraphobia who, as soon as they put their head out of the door, start feeling panicky, nauseous and vertiginous. The matter is complicated by the fact that dizziness itself can cause anxiety, so that simple movements such as bending down or turning sideways have to be performed carefully. In addition, the world outside is suddenly full of hazards. This is particularly true when vertigo is caused by contradictory visual messages leading to a feeling of disorientation. Thus, when he or she is standing on an escalator, the messages from the legs are that they are stationary but from the eyes that the body is moving. The result is a bad attack of dizziness, and after a few experiences such as this, the patient soon becomes fearful of going out, which may readily be misinterpreted as agoraphobia.

When doctors find it difficult to locate the source of dizziness, are unable to treat it and cannot readily distinguish it from neurosis, it is not surprising that most patients get a rough deal. At best, they may be told they will have to live with their condition, but too frequently they are labelled as neurotic. Help is at hand. Lucy Yardley, a psychologist at University College London, has written a book, *Vertigo and Dizziness*, which analyses with clarity the ramifications of this very difficult problem. Further, and this was certainly news to me, she points out that there is, after all, a method of treatment originally proposed 50 years ago for soldiers with profound dizziness following injuries to the vestibular apparatus in the ear. The treatment relies on the remarkable ability of the brain to compensate for misleading information derived from the sense organs. Ballroom dancers can twirl around and gymnasts do their exercises without feeling dizzy because the balance centre in the brain adapts to the greatly increased stress placed upon it. Similarly, the patient with vertigo can teach the brain to make up for imperfections in the balance receptors by deliberately and repeatedly performing the movements that induce the sensation of dizziness. In 80 per cent of patients, this results in an improvement in symptoms, and in a third they are eliminated completely.

(*Vertigo and Dizziness*, by Lucy Yardley (Routledge £11.99).)

Fickle Finger of Faints

People faint for all manner of reasons – hunger, excessive heat after standing immobile too long on the parade ground, the sight of blood or some other stomach-churning spectacle, exhaustion, shock or dehydration. In a minute or two before it happens, and in quick succession, the victim feels nauseous, claustrophobic, dizzy, sweaty, spots dance in front of the eyes, then everything goes black. In popular terminology this is a blackout, and no cause for alarm. Recovery is spontaneous and immediate and little further needs to be done other than to offer reassurance, a blanket and a glass of water.

If, however, an ambulance is summoned and the now recovered fainter is transported to hospital, matters become more complex. For as Dr M. C. Petch, cardiologist at the famous Papworth Hospital, put it in the *British Medical Journal*: 'While any ordinary person can recognise a common faint, regrettably doctors seem to find the diagnosis difficult.' The trouble is that they know too much. There is actually quite a long list of potential causes of blackouts for the concerned physician to consider. This includes narrowed heart valves, disturbances of heart rhythm, epilepsy, and anything that can reduce a continued flow of blood to the brain. Investigating these possibilities requires an extensive series of tests, all of which almost invariably turn out to be normal. The medical verdict is that the blackout was 'just a faint' – or, in scientific jargon, 'a vasovagal attack' – and that nothing more needs to be done.

For Dr Petch, common sense rather than arcane medical investigations is the best guide to action. The distinction between a common faint and other more serious causes, he argues, is made by paying attention to the circumstantial evidence. Common faints are precipitated by one or other of the physical or emotional factors already considered. These act via the nervous system to dilate the blood vessels throughout the body. As a result blood pressure falls, oxygenated blood can no longer make it from the heart up to the brain, and the result is a blackout. As the victim collapses to the ground his brain is now at the same level as his heart, and so blood once again reaches the brain and recovery is immediate. This whole cycle, from premonitory symptoms to full recovery, usually takes two or three minutes. By contrast, most of the more serious causes of blackouts are something to do with the heart. They come out of the blue without any precipitating cause, are instantaneous, and recovery is slower.

Investigating this type of blackout, known as 'cardiac syncope', with a continuous recording of the heart rhythm may reveal episodes where it suddenly speeds up or slows down, and for which the best treatment is a pacemaker. Alternatively it may be due to a narrowed heart valve or disease of heart muscle known as cardiomyopathy, which requires treatment with drugs or an operation. The crucial distinction between the common faint and these more serious types of cardiac syncope is the absence of an obvious precipitating factor, and it is these patients who require more thorough investigations.

That, at least, was the fairly clear-cut situation until doctors Adam Fitzpatrick and Richard Sutton of London's Royal Brompton Hospital focused their attention on a group of patients who seemed to fall somewhere in between. Their blackouts were preceded by premonitory feelings, like those who were about to have a common faint, but they were recurrent and occurred in the absence of a precipitating cause. They thus resembled cardiacsyncope, though there was nothing wrong with the heart. Those with this type of faint invariably recovered rapidly, but they were prone to minor lacerations and bruising, or serious complications such as fractured bones in road traffic accidents.

Drs Fitzpatrick and Sutton found these fainting episodes could be replicated by tilting the patients backwards on a table at an angle of 40° for about an hour. This suggests an impairment of the mechanisms which maintain steady blood pressure, and has been called malignant (i.e. serious) vasovagal (faint) syndrome. This problem is difficult to treat, but in a recent issue of the *British Heart Journal*, Drs Fitzpatrick and Sutton report a study of 37 patients treated with a pacemaker in whom the total number of faints per year fell from 137 to 11. This 'massive reduction', they argue, is 'powerful evidence' for the value of identifying and treating this particular group of patients. Fainting therefore covers the entire spectrum, from the trivial to the potentially life-threatening. The crucial clues lie, as always, not in complex tests but in listening to the patient's description of what has happened.

Making Sense out of a Stroke

From time to time doctors – like cosmologists or physicists – are brought face to face with the central awe-inspiring mysteries of life. Take, for example, the case of a 65-year-old woman from New York with an impeccable Bronx accent who was admitted to hospital after a small stroke. Much to her relatives' surprise, her intonation of speech seemed to have changed entirely and her accent was now pure Irish brogue. Her mother, it transpired, had been a first-generation Irish immigrant, and it was from her that she had acquired an accent as a child, losing it when she had started going to school, only for it to emerge again clearly 60 years later. As she recovered, so her Irish accent faded. Simplistically, one might think that, as a person's accent changes over time, it would displace earlier ones, but here we find the whole manner of speech is preserved, unsullied, deep in the brain.

This is, however, only the beginning of a voyage into the complexity of language. It is well known that, following a stroke, a person may lose the ability to talk in an acquired language but remain entirely fluent in a mother tongue – which may not have been spoken for many years. And then there is singing which – again simplistically – one might imagine is simply a matter of putting words to a tune: but no. It is possible to lose the power of speech after a stroke but still be able to communicate effectively by singing. In a classic case in 1836, a French patient who could say only the single word 'tan' was quite capable of singing the Marseillaise.

The commonest speech defect following a stroke is when a patient knows what he wants to say but is unable to translate it into meaningfully constructive sounds. At one extreme there may be just an inability to name certain objects like a chair or a watch, or to use small words like 'the', 'if' and 'is'. At the other, the loss of speech may be virtually complete except for one or two words – usually profanities – though, if asked, the patient can repeat perfectly, with normal articulation, spoken sentences. In a different type of speech defect, speaking remains fluent with normal rhythm and cadences, but its content is abnormal, words are jumbled together, used unnecessarily or reduced to a level of meaningless jargon. This type of problem occurs with damage to that part of the brain where spoken language is recognised, so patients can still talk but cannot understand what others say to them – or, indeed, what they are saying themselves. And here we come to the subtlest level of all. Language is not just about words but it is also the main avenue for the expression of feelings and emotions. Astonishingly there are patients who cannot understand what is being said to them, but know when they are being lied to. As Oliver Sacks puts it: 'Though the words might convey nothing, spoken language is suffused with "tones" which transcend the verbal – and it is precisely this expressiveness, so deep, so various and so subtle, that can be perfectly preserved.'

We know there are two separate parts of the brain concerned with speech – Broca's area, involved in articulation; and Wernicke's area, involved in comprehension of the spoken word – but we might as well say we know nothing. The many different types of speech defect that can follow a stroke cannot be explained mechanistically in terms of the coding and connections of neurones. Rather we are dealing with a network, a system like a spider's web, in which a perturbation at any point changes the tension of every strand right back to its anchorage in the blackberry bush. The gap in our knowledge is not merely unbridged but unbridgeable – and our ignorance will remain ineluctable. By the same token, man's ability to communicate through language must cast doubt on the validity of Darwin's theory of evolution, a point made forcefully by his contemporaries but which has subsequently been overlooked. For Darwin there was no problem: the faculty of articulate speech, he wrote, offers no insuperable objection to the belief that man has evolved from some lower form. Not so, said the philologist Professor Max Muller, who wrote: 'Language is something more palpable than a fold of the brain or angle of the skull. It admits of no cavilling; no process of natural selection will ever distil significant words out of the notes of birds or the cries of beasts.'

6

Heartaches

Fibrillating Hearts

Medical prognostications can be as imprecise as any form of crystal-ball-gazing, but this story about one Frederick Loftus Townshend – as recounted by Dr I.G. Anderson from Harare, in the *Central Africa Journal of Medicine* – takes a lot of beating. Freddie, as he was known to everyone, was just 17 when the First World War broke out. Being patriotic and not flat-footed, he promptly volunteered for military service. It took some time for the medical authorities to get around to giving him a routine physical examination and, when they did, he was found to be afflicted by a rapid and uncontrolled contraction of the heart muscle, known as atrial fibrillation. 'The thrifty military authorities promptly discharged him from active service before being put to the expense of burying him,' writes Dr Anderson, 'and he was advised to go to some warm climate and take it easy for whatever short space of time was left to him.'

Freddie emigrated to Rhodesia, where he became a prosperous farmer and founded the Commonwealth Sports Club in the capital. As he grew older, he was frequently to be seen with his gang of 'bandits', prisoners from Salisbury's main prison, tidying up the gardens of the General Hospital. He never married, nor was he ever able to take out life insurance on account of his heart, which none the less kept him in good health and vigorous until his death at the age of 87. Dr Anderson estimates that Freddie had lived for at least 65 years with his supposedly lethal heart condition – 'a classic example of the fallaciousness of prognosis in heart disease,' he comments.

Now we know better, and the discovery of atrial fibrillation in a young, healthy person is viewed as a benign condition and, as in Freddie's case, quite compatible with a normal life. By contrast, the onset of atrial fibrillation in later years is not only very common but also debilitating. There are, as most people know, two chambers on either side of the heart, the atrium and the muscular ventricle. The atrium contracts first, expelling its blood into the ventricle, and the same electrical stimulus a fraction of a second later causes the muscles of the ventricle to contract, which pushes the blood out into the circulation. In atrial fibrillation, the walls of the atrium resemble a wriggling pack of worms and the disordered electrical signals transmitted to the ventricle have the effect of making it contract fast and irregularly.

This has two main consequences. It reduces the amount of blood travelling to the brain and the muscle, and the patient is overwhelmed by a sense of lassitude. It also puts a strain on the heart, causing an accumulation of fluid in the lungs, otherwise known as heart failure. Easily exhausted and seriously short of breath, someone with rapid atrial fibrillation feels, and often thinks, he is at death's door. There are few things as pleasing in the practice of medicine as to be able to say quite genuinely that within a couple of days he will be 'back to his old self again'. The mainstay of treatment is digoxin, one of the oldest remedies around, originally derived from the leaf of the foxglove – *Digitalis purpurea*. This slows down the pulse and increases the contractility of the heart muscle, energy bounces back and the breathlessness vanishes as the fluid of the lungs is dispersed.

Until a few years ago this would have been considered quite adequate treatment, but the onward march of medical progress is relentless and there have been two further substantial recent developments. The ideal solution for atrial fibrillation would be not just to slow the heart rate, but to convert it back to a normal rhythm. This can be reliably achieved by an electric shock to the heart as used for resuscitation following a cardiac arrest. Then the problem is how to prevent the fibrillation returning. There is now a long list of effective drugs that can achieve this, such as amiodarone and propafenone, but their side effects can be quite hair-raising, so they should probably only be prescribed, at least initially, by a specialist.

The second, very important development has been the realisation that patients with atrial fibrillation are particularly prone to strokes. As blood gets trapped in the fibrillating atrium, it forms clots which then pass into the ventricle and shoot up to the brain where they get stuck in a small artery with predictably disastrous consequences. Blood-thinning drugs, such as the rat poison Warfarin and aspirin, substantially reduce the risk of this, but again this is not without its own dangers. Indeed, they can cause precisely what they are intended to prevent – a stroke – by inducing a haemorrhage in the brain. The balance of benefit versus risk is a very difficult one and, again, expert advice is necessary. Nowadays, given the right treatment, there is no reason why virtually everyone with atrial fibrillation should not, like Freddie Townshend, live out their natural life-span. There is no doubt that those hoping to fulfil this worthwhile ambition must seek expert advice on the most judicious combination of drugs.

To Bypass, or Not to Bypass

While skiing down a mountain in Oregon, an American heart surgeon in his mid-fifties experienced a twinge of chest pain which he promptly diagnosed as angina. He carried on to the bottom of the slope, packed up his skis, checked out of his hotel, took a train back to his home town and that evening was on the table of the cardiac laboratory of his own hospital having the arteries of his heart X-rayed. The X-rays showed, not surprisingly for a man of his age, a moderate degree of narrowing, but it was enough for him to persuade a colleague that he needed bypass surgery – which was duly performed the next day.

Justifying this drastic self-treatment to a conference of heart specialists several months later, the surgeon commented that there was not a narrowed coronary in the country that would not be better off being bypassed. With this logic, virtually anyone over the age of 55 will be a candidate for bypass surgery, and America is not far off that goal. From 15 operations a year in 1968, to 150,000 in 1980, to more than 400,000 currently, approximately 4 million American citizens now carry the hallmark of the operation: a long scar over the sternum on the front of the chest.

This is not the British way. Here, patients are only deemed worthy of a bypass if the anginal chest pain is so severe as to interfere with daily life, despite treatment with nitrates (which dilate the arteries) and beta-blockers (which reduce the heart's demand for oxygen). Nobody denies that bypass surgery is an excellent operation, relieving symptoms in 90 per cent of cases, but it is a sensible rule that simple treatments should be tried first. The more cautious British approach is more a matter of making a virtue out of necessity, as there are not the resources in the NHS to perform the operation on the same scale as America. But it has the

140

bonus of protecting people from the discomforts of major surgery – in this case a painful chest and aching legs (from which the veins for the bypass graft are removed), a small risk of stroke, or death, and a slight danger of permanent subtle neurological damage, loss of memory, concentration and mild personality changes.

Over the past decade arguments over the merits of the American and British approach have raged, with ground gradually being ceded towards the benefits of bypass surgery sooner rather than later. The reason can be found in an article in *The Lancet*: 'Effects of coronary artery bypass graft on survival.' This confirms what many suspected: that bypass patients survive longer. The difference is not great: after ten years, 974 out of 1,324 surgery patients are still alive, compared with 921 out of 1,325 just given medical treatment – but it is more marked in those with the more severe heart disease. Nonetheless, it does support the contention of the skiing American heart surgeon that, in general, narrowed arteries to the heart are better off being bypassed.

The practical implications are daunting if Britain is to increase the scale of bypass surgery to take account of this survival advantage. It may not, however, be necessary, because technology has moved on and there is now an alternative: dilating narrowed arteries with a balloon, known as coronary angioplasty. Back in 1979, a Swiss cardiologist, Andreas Gruntzig, reported in the *New England Journal of Medicine* that a balloon-tipped catheter inserted into the femoral artery in the groin, manoeuvred up towards the heart, and then dilated with air, would flatten the obstructing atheroma in coronary arteries 'like a footprint in the snow', allowing blood to flow freely again to the heart muscle. The advantage of this technique is that it generally requires only a day in hospital – the complications and prolonged convalescence of bypass surgery are obvious – and the popularity of angioplasty has increased in leaps and bounds.

It has not, however, replaced bypass surgery because the results are not so good. In about a third of patients the arteries have narrowed again within six months, and the symptoms of angina have returned. Further, the relative simplicity of the technique does not prevent there being serious complications – including rupture of the artery, which would require surgery, and heart attacks – in about one in 20 patients. Finally, angioplasty could never replace bypass surgery unless it were made to work in the more serious cases in which the survival advantage from active intervention was most marked.

It has not happened yet, but an assortment of technological gizmos could be the answer. These have been reviewed in the *British Medical Journal* by Dr Laura Corr of Guy's Hospital. First the problem of 'restenosis' – where the artery narrows again soon after having been dilated by the balloon – has been overcome by leaving behind a delicate stainless-steel mesh stent that embeds itself into the artery wall, so keeping it permanently open. The initial risk of a clot forming within the stent is minimised with the help of several anti-clotting drugs. Stents have reduced the rate of restenosis by about half. The problem of arteries being too tight, or too extensively narrowed, to be amenable to dilation by the balloon can now be surmounted by the use of cylindrical cutters rotating 750 times a minute and shaving the atheroma from within the artery. Alternatively, the Rotablater, an olive-shaped burr studded with micro crystal diamonds rotating 200,000 times a minute turns the atheroma into particles so small that they can pass into capillaries to be consumed by scavenging white cells.

This wizardry is expensive, being individually handmade and non-reusable, so angioplasty is currently no cheaper than bypass surgery. But it is more patient-friendly and as its result is the same – the restoration of normal blood flow to the muscles of the heart – it can be predicted that these techniques will both relieve angina and prolong life. The future direction of the treatment of heart disease is now clearly signposted.

Clotted Lungs

The number of girls under the age of sixteen seeking contraceptive advice at family planning clinics leapt by 37 per cent in 1994. No doubt the news gladdened the heart of the then Secretary of State for Health, the saintly Mrs Virginia Bottomley, as being a 'sign of progress' in reducing the rate of teenage pregnancies – one of the 'health targets' advocated by her department. Regrettably, life is rarely that simple. No matter how apparently rational and desirable the goal of stopping young girls becoming pregnant, state promotion of under-age sex is likely to have perverse consequences. At an inquest into the death of a fit and healthy 16-year-old schoolgirl, Nancy Berry, it was revealed she had died from a pulmonary embolus, a blood clot in the lung, within a month of having started on the Pill. There has been a rash of such cases, prompting the south London coroner Sir Montague Levine to write to the drug manufacturers and the Department of Health urging that more prominent warnings be placed on the packets – not that I imagine it will do much good.

In young girls such as Nancy Berry, blood clots of any sort are staggeringly rare, so any that do occur are almost certainly attributable to the Pill – but why so soon after starting it? Professor J. L. Beaumont of the Inserm Research Centre in Creteil, France, believes he knows the answer. He has identified an antibody against the synthetic oestrogen component of the Pill in eighteen teenagers who developed thrombosis within a month of first starting on it. This antibody, he maintains, damages the wall of the veins in some way, reducing the free flow of blood and thus increasing the likelihood of a blood clot.

While the Pill remains a rare cause of thrombosis, the question of how to prevent the majority of cases – estimated to cause 19,000 deaths a year – has exercised the minds of doctors for the past two decades. There is no simple solution but there have been significant advances in two areas. The first is treating those at high risk of thrombosis – such as patients about to undergo a surgical procedure – with the blood-thinning drug heparin. The combination of lying flat on one's back on the operating table for several hours and the trauma of surgery, which increases the clotability of the blood, produces thrombosis in the leg veins in a significant proportion of patients following operation. These may then break off, travel to the lung and cause a fatal pulmonary embolus in one in 100 patients. This danger can be minimised when the blood-thinning drug heparin is injected under the skin before, and for seven days after, an operation – or alternatively, by taking aspirin in low doses.

The second approach has been to improve the accuracy with which a pulmonary embolus is diagnosed, as once treated it prevents a further potentially fatal episode. The efficacy of treating a pulmonary embolus with heparin was demonstrated convincingly in what, in retrospect, appears to have been an ethically rather dubious trial conducted by doctors in Bristol; none of fifty-four patients treated with heparin had a further fatal embolus, compared with five out of a group of nineteen patients who acted as controls. One cannot get a more clear-cut result than that, but it seems a bit tough on those who drew the short straw and were not given the heparin.

Before instituting this life-saving treatment, it is necessary to diagnose a pulmonary embolus in the first place. This can be straightforward when the patient obliges by having the symptoms that point to the diagnosis – a sore, swollen leg and pain in the chest, combined with characteristic changes on the X-ray. But the leg may not be swollen or the chest pain may be misinterpreted as pneumonia or a heart attack. When in doubt there is no alternative other than to proceed to more complex investigations including, if necessary, injecting dye directly into the veins entering the lungs to look for evidence of a clot. It is well worth the trouble, however, for – as the Bristol trial so eloquently confirmed – it is quite literally a matter of life or death.

Walking through Angina

Exertion increases the need for oxygenated blood. But if the arteries to either the heart or the leg are narrowed, this increased demand cannot be met and the result may be a pain of such intensity there is no alternative other than to desist. In the heart this is experienced as the crushing pain of angina pectoris, and in the legs a cramping pain in the calves known as intermittent claudication. After a short period the pain subsides and exercise can be resumed until it recurs again. Those with either angina or claudication, therefore, have to learn to pace themselves and live within the limits of their disability.

But, paradoxically, those who defy these limits and exercise regularly through their pain are often rewarded with a marked improvement in their symptoms. The first clinical account of angina by the English physician William Heberden, published in 1772, described a man who 'set himself the task of sawing wood for half an hour every day and was nearly cured'. This improvement in angina has been attributed to two important physiological adaptations of the heart to regular exercise – a slowing of the heart rate and a fall in blood pressure which together reduce the heart muscles' need for oxygen. Hence the threshold of the amount of exercise that can be done rises before the onset of pain.

Regrettably this prescription of 'exercise' for those with angina is not without its hazards. Heavy exertion (the equivalent of shovelling snow, slow jogging or, indeed, sawing wood) increases the risk of a heart attack even among the fit, and by as much as one hundredfold among the unfit, according to two separate studies published in the *New England Journal of Medicine*.

The specific risk in those with angina has not been established but it must be substantial as post-mortem examinations of those who collapse and die during a marathon invariably show narrowing of the arteries to the heart. The unfortunate angina patient is, therefore, transfixed by the cruel dilemma that regular exercise may either cure or kill. The most that can be said is that it may contribute to a fitter life but not necessarily a longer one.

The same dilemma does not arise, at least to the same extent, in those whose mobility is restricted by the vice-like calf pain of claudication. This too, often improves dramatically with regular exercise. Thirty years ago, Andre Larssen, a Danish physiologist, instructed a group of seven patients to spend one hour every day walking for as long as their claudication pain would allow, to rest until it disappeared and then to walk again as energetically as possible. After six months, their average walking distance had increased by 300 per cent and the time elapsed before the claudication pain came on had increased threefold. Meanwhile the symptoms in a control group had actually deteriorated, albeit slightly.

The most plausible explanation would be that Dr Larssen's exercise regime opened up some of the smaller arteries to the leg, but to his surprise he found blood flow to the muscle had remained unchanged and was no different from that in the control group. In the subsequent thirty years several reasons have been put forward for this apparently paradoxical finding, which has focused attention on what happens to the blood once it gets into the muscle. In essence the arteries divide into ever narrower capillaries until ultimately they are only the diameter of a single red blood cell which then gives up its supply of oxygen to diffuse across the capillary wall into the muscle. It is at this level of microcirculation that regular exercise has its beneficial effects by increasing the network of capillaries, improving the efficiency with which the oxygen is delivered to the muscle. In addition, exercise seems to fluidify the blood, reducing its sludginess, so it travels with greater ease and rapidity through the capillaries.

The two other medical treatments for claudication also work at this level of microcirculation. Smoking is the single most important exacerbating factor because the constituents of cigarette smoke increase the stickiness of the blood and its tendency to clot. Those who quit are rewarded by an almost immediate improvement in the amount of exercise they can take; and, more importantly still, they reduce the chances that their symptoms will deteriorate to the point that the viability of the limb is threatened, which can lead to gangrene and the need for amputation. In general, drug treatment has not proved very successful.

The management of patients with claudication can thus essentially be encapsulated in the five-word axiom 'Stop smoking and keep walking!' This advice will provide measurable improvement in 90 per cent of sufferers. Only if it fails will the more drastic option of surgery become necessary where the narrowed section of the artery is bypassed with a graft.

Post-cardiac coition

It is true after all. Just as the Victorian doctors claimed, sexual excess – what Hippocrates called 'immoderate venery' – really does cause blindness. Dr Thomas Friberg of the University of Pittsburgh has reported six cases of 'sudden visual loss associated with sexual activity'. Thus, 'a 39-year-old man describes sudden blurring of vision in his left eye while he was gazing out of the window'. After more detailed questioning, he related that a dark spot had appeared centrally in his field of vision while his partner was performing 'a variant of heterosexual intercourse on him'. Clinical examination showed evidence of haemorrhage from a burst blood vessel in the retina at the back of the eye. The precipitating cause in this and the other five cases, Dr Friberg believes, was the marked increase in blood pressure that accompanies sexual activity. 'The risks of blindness with sexual stimulation would be minimised by refraining from undue physical exertion,' he writes, adding: 'Age must play a role, as five of the patients were over 40.' Luckily, the haemorrhages cleared spontaneously and most recovered normal vision within a few weeks.

Another equally dramatic and worrying complication of 'immoderate venery' has been highlighted by a personal account of a young doctor. While in bed with his partner, he writes: 'All had gone uneventfully, until at the point of orgasm I suddenly experienced a pain in the back of my skull akin to being struck on the back of the head with a sledgehammer. My poor girlfriend looked on in horror as with a cry of pain I sat up and then promptly fell to the floor.' Such headaches are typical of a subarachnoid haemorrhage, where a surge of blood pressure bursts an aneurysm in a blood vessel at the base of the brain. It was much more likely, however, that the good doctor's headache was a variant of migraine – 'benign coital headache'. Although the headache may feel anything but benign, recovery is rapid and there is no damage to the brain. It is also, as Dr J. W. Lance, neurologist at the University of South Wales, points out, highly capricious. 'The headache might develop on several occasions in succession, and not trouble the patient for several months, or even years, even though there has been no alteration in sexual technique.'

Such curiosities aside, the substantive and difficult to resolve question is whether the significant haemodynamic changes that accompany intercourse – the rise in blood pressure and heart rate – present a significant threat to those who already have had, or might be at risk of, a heart attack or stroke. The usual answer is that if a person can manage two flights of stairs, there is nothing to worry about. A more precise evaluation of the risk can be gained from the results of exercise-testing in patients who have, or are suspected to have, heart disease. According to Dr Barry Franklin, a cardiac rehabilitation expert from Michigan: 'With maximal exercise-testing in which people are achieving their peak capacity for 10 to 15 minutes, the risk is one death in 10,000 tests. As sexual activity for most represents only a third of their physical capacity for a short period of time, people have little to fear.' He concludes 'If someone can walk a mile in 17 minutes comfortably and without adverse signs or symptoms, he or she can safely engage in sex . . .'

Even those who do get symptoms of either angina or palpitations during intercourse should not be discouraged. Dr Graham Jackson, cardiologist at Guy's Hospital, advises that such patients should only avoid sex after a meal or a hot bath, as this puts an extra strain on the heart. The symptoms of angina can be prevented by taking a glyceryl trinitrate (GTN) tablet under the tongue, which dilates the arteries to the heart, and fortuitously also increases the firmness of an erection. Palpitations can be controlled with beta-blocker drugs. He reports a study of 35 patients with angina, 29 of whom had intercourse at least once a week, 19 of these developing angina on most occasions. With this combination of drugs, they were able to have intercourse without angina, and four of the six who had abstained resumed sexual activity. 'Sexual activity is safe for patients with heart disease, who enjoy intercourse with their spouses at home,' he said. The same may not, however, be true for middle-aged men 'engaging in extra-marital relationships'.

The Preventative Vitamin

One of the more amusing things about medicine is the circulatory nature of fashion in treatment. In an interesting article in the science journal *Nature* from 1956 called 'The effect of vitamin E in coronary heart disease', two cardiologists, doctors Vogelsang and Shute, described the effects of administering large doses to patients with congestive heart failure and angina. The result, they said, was an increase in the amount of exercise that could be taken and 'a diminishing or abolition of anginal pain'. From this arose the idea that if healthy people took vitamin E supplements it would protect them against heart disease. Since then there has been a bewildering variety of other preventative measures. In the 1950s the rat poison Warfarin was advocated (because it stops the blood clotting); in the 1960s oestrogen (because heart disease is rarer in women) and the hormone thyroxine (because those with under-active thyroids have high cholesterol levels). Then there was a vogue for drinking glassfuls of polyunsaturated fats, which was replaced by enthusiasm for 'low-fat diets' – cutting down on meat and dairy products. In the past decade we have been advised that fish, garlic and even porridge might be useful. Finally, 37 years after the article in *Nature*, the *New England Journal of Medicine* reports that 'high doses of vitamin E halve the risk of heart disease'.

Now, just because the fashion in treatment comes full circle does not mean that it is correct, especially in the case of vitamin E, whose precise role in the body is so mysterious. In *Nutrition Today* Dr A. Tappel writes, 'The more research that is done on the vitamin, the more intriguing it appears. There is a nagging suspicion it must be important, but we are just not smart enough to see why.'

The problem in defining its role is that unlike scurvy, rickets or beriberi, which are caused by a deficiency of vitamins C, D and B6 respectively, there is no comparable deficiency syndrome for vitamin E. This is because it is so widely distributed in foods that whatever one eats provides sufficient quantities of it. This mystery surrounding vitamin E has encouraged doctors to prescribe it for many different conditions – to premature infants, for cancer, to counter the effects of ageing and environmental pollution, and for rare muscle and skin disorders, though extravagant claims of benefit have never been properly confirmed. Indeed, the ubiquity of vitamin E and the absence of a specific deficiency syndrome strongly suggest there is nothing to be gained from taking it.

But now Dr Eric Rimm and his colleagues from the Harvard School of Public Health have found, in a study of 40,000 men and 80,000 women that taking 400 or more International Units of vitamin E per day are much less likely to keel over from a heart attack. Their results, it must be said, are infinitely more impressive than any other preventive measure such as cutting down on fat in the diet.

Vitamin E apparently goes around mopping up the dangerous-sounding 'free radicals' – molecules with an odd number of electrons. I cannot say I really understand the significance of this, but it seems that these 'free radicals' interact with fat in the cell wall and cause a lot of damage. So perhaps vitamin E protects the smooth lining of the arteries from being damaged and narrowed by atheroma, thus preventing heart attacks. It sounds plausible. It certainly seems that those at 'high risk', with a history of heart disease in the family, should take a dose of vitamin E every day.

A word of caution, though. When vitamin E supplements were first widely advocated, a doctor from California, Harold Cohen, and his partner both decided to take it themselves, as well as handing out to all their patients. After a week Dr Cohen 'began to feel an amazing weakness and fatigue as if I were suffering from a severe bout of influenza. The symptoms stopped after withdrawal of vitamin E; I resumed the vitamin and the symptoms promptly returned.' His partner had a similar experience, as did 'virtually all the patients and colleagues I started on the therapy'. Dr Cohen found that dosage levels were critical and that at 400 IU per day the vitamin caused 'only minimal fatigue'. Those who do not like popping vitamin pills should know that the main dietary sources of vitamin E are vegetable oils – but there is obviously a limit to the amount that can be swallowed daily.

7

Gut Aches

Dealing with Gallstones

A reader has asked for my view on gallstones and what to do about them – a much more interesting subject than one might imagine. Mrs P, a Dorset woman, reports that she is 'fit and active at 72'. Her gallstones are not causing her much nuisance 'apart from gently burping' – in particular she has no pain, sickness or other symptoms. She has so far declined to have the stones removed, although has agreed to see her surgeon for a further appointment. Meanwhile, she is taking homeopathic tablets of *Berberis vulgaris* in the hope of dispersing them. The simple answer to Mrs P's query is that she should sit tight and politely decline any offer from her surgeon to remove them. Ninety per cent of those like Mrs P whose stones are causing no, or minimal symptoms, stay that way – and so there is nothing to be gained by taking them out. It will be better to wait and see whether she joins the remaining 10 per cent in whom stones cause serious pain or discomfort before even thinking about surgery.

This seems so obvious that it is mystifying why her surgeon should already have proposed an operation. One possibility is that she is seeing him privately, so his advice may have been influenced by the prospect of financial gain. Certainly American surgeons remove three times as many gall-bladders per head of population as do British surgeons, and the only way they could achieve such a figure is by operating on those without symptoms. This can happen in one of two ways. The patient may have complained of some vague abdominal problem and gallstones were found to be present even though they were not the cause. Alternatively, they may have been discovered incidentally during investigation for some other medical problem. Either way the surgeon advises the gallstones would be 'better off in the bucket', the patient is exposed to the unnecessary risk of an anaesthetic and the surgeon pockets his fee.

If we imagine, for the sake of argument, Mrs P becomes one of the unlucky 10 per cent whose gallstones do start to cause problems, what should she do? The commonest symptom of gallstones is pain under the ribs on the right side caused by a stone lodged in the duct that connects the gall-bladder to the biliary tree down which bile flows from the liver into the duodenum. This pain may, but does not invariably, start after a meal and last for several hours. Once gallstones start to cause pain it is likely to get worse and the risk of complications, such as gall-bladder infection, increases. The time has come to act.

There are several options. The first is to try to dissolve the stones with drugs. Only a minority are suitable for such treatment, which works in less than 50 per cent of cases, and in half of these the gallstones will recur. I find it hard to believe that Mrs P's homeopathic remedy would do any better than this, so dissolving gallstones is essentially a non-starter. The alternative is surgery, of which there are two types. With the standard operation, an incision is made under the right ribs, the gall-bladder is identified under the liver and removed. This requires at least five days in hospital to allow the wound to heal. This procedure is now rapidly being replaced by what is known as 'minimally invasive surgery', where five fine metal tubes are inserted through holes in the abdominal wall through which the gall-bladder is dissected and removed. The patient is then usually fit enough to leave hospital the next day. There is no doubt about which is the 'better' operation, although as everyone should now know, this type of surgery requires considerable skill and should be carried out only by the properly experienced.

One might imagine there will be some adverse consequence of being deprived of one's gall-bladder, but this is not the case. Some patients will however experience heartburn, dyspepsia and diarrhoea, which usually settles with time, but might not – yet another reason for not removing the gall-bladder without good reason. Finally, gallstones look very attractive arranged on the mantelpiece or in a bowl, where they will gain the attention of friends, providing an excuse for those who wish to discuss their operation with others.

Curing Constipation

On a visit to the splendidly named St Mark's Hospital for Diseases of the Colon and Rectum I looked further up someone's bottom than I ever have before – three feet in fact, all the way up one side of the colon and down the other. Though the colon's owner was in her seventies and a bit wrinkly, her innards looked in peak condition, pink, healthy and amazingly clean. St Mark's is a typically British medical institution: small, intimate, staffed by a handful of great enthusiasts who apply their considerable intelligence to problems that most of us do not like to think about. Over the past ten years the doctors at St Mark's have, among many other things, been investigating constipation. This might seem a rather mundane topic, but it is very common (450,000 people visit their doctor every year solely because of it), causes a lot of distress and turns out to be rather interesting.

Watching the tip of the colonoscope weaving its way around the lady's colon, it was striking to observe how the walls were in almost constant movement. These contractions are of two sorts: rhythmic movements which mix the contents of the colon, bringing them into contact with the wall so that water and salts can be reabsorbed back into the body; and powerful coordinated waves that impel the colon contents forward. In most cases of constipation, these latter contractions are attenuated, for which there are two possible solutions. The first is to take laxatives, such as senna, which stimulate the nerves in the colon wall. This type of laxative has fallen out of favour with doctors since it was shown that, taken in large quantities over many years, it ended up destroying the nerves themselves. This is a typical example of medical over-reaction, and in my experience senna used sensibly is much to be preferred over the current fashionable treatment of constipation – fibre.

Increasing the fibre content of the diet certainly speeds up the bowel by increasing the bulk of the stool and 'exercising' the colon. But the dietary changes necessary to achieve this are substantial – an effective 'dose' requires eating two Weetabix and four large, thick slices of wholemeal bread – and many find this, not surprisingly, fairly unpalatable. Purified fibre supplements, such as Fybogel, may be more acceptable but often lead to the distressing side effect of flatulence, abdominal distension and colicky pains. Further, fibre is useless in those with severe, persistent constipation – usually young women – and experimental investigations by the doctors at St Mark's over several years have discovered why. These women not only have sluggish colons, but also problems with the muscles in the pelvis which do not relax when the urge comes to defecate, so the stool is not passed.

This condition has proved intractable to any sort of medical therapy and the surgeons at St Mark's have spent much time evaluating whether operative intervention might be useful. Various operations have been tried, but they have proved to be valueless. The more drastic procedure of simply removing a large segment of colon does seem to improve the chronic abdominal pain that is so often a feature, but can have the undesirable side effect of severe and persistent diarrhoea. Although this might seem disappointing, it is just as important to discover whether an experimental treatment is a failure as it is to find out whether it works.

There is, however, some hope for these patients in the technique of bio-feedback training, in which they are taught to exert conscious control over the muscles of defecation. Here a balloon is introduced into the rectum and connected up to an oscilloscope so the contraction and relaxation of the muscle can be observed on the screen. So we should all be very grateful to institutions such at St Mark's for clarifying our understanding of such an important, if neglected, part of the body.

Dyspepsia

Standing in a queue at my local pharmacist, I overheard a grey-haired customer ask the pharmacist for, and be refused, the 'anti-ulcer' drug Tagamet (which can now be purchased without prescription), on the grounds that he was too old, as it could only be sold to those under the age of 45. A packet of Rennie tablets was suggested as an alternative, which was duly purchased. When I finally got the pharmacist's attention, I asked about the etiquette of refusing to sell a drug on the grounds of age. How could he be sure that someone *was* over 45, and might customers be offended at being thought older than they really were? Apparently not. The sensible rationale for this ageist discrimination is that from about the mid-forties, there is an increasing likelihood that the dyspeptic symptoms for which people usually take Tagamet are more likely to be due to some potentially serious cause, such as an ulcer, and so it is better that they first consult their doctor.

Dyspepsia encompasses the symptoms of stomach pains, heartburn, nausea, bloating, belching and easy satiety. It is very common, affecting approximately 30 per cent of people at one time or another, and accounts for more than half of the patients referred to gut specialists. In some, the dyspepsia is found to be due to an ulcer or gallstones, or a hiatus hernia, or, very rarely, a gastric tumour, and appropriate treatment is usually effective. For the vast majority, however, investigations fail to reveal any obvious cause, and these patients are said to have 'functional dyspepsia', which can, in turn, be sub-divided into three main further categories, dependent on the characteristics of the symptoms.

In the first two of these sub-types, the symptoms simulate those of acid reflux and a stomach ulcer respectively. With *reflux-like* dyspepsia, patients have the sort of problems that would be expected from the reflux of acid up from their stomach into the lower oesophagus – heartburn and regurgitation. However, on inspection, the lining of the lower part of the oesophagus is not obviously inflamed. Similarly, those with *ulcer-like* dyspepsia, tend to be woken at night by a severe pain in the upper abdomen, which is relieved by milk or antacids, symptoms characteristics of a stomach ulcer, but there is no ulcer to be seen. The cause of both *reflux-like* and *ulcer-like* dyspepsia is presumed to be excessive acid from the stomach, and improves with drugs like Tagamet, which block acid secretion.

The third type of 'functional dyspepsia' is related to an abnormality of gut motility, the forward propulsion of the stomach contents downwards into the intestine. Here, the main symptoms are a sensation of bloating and distension, nausea is common and may be accompanied by retching. This is known inelegantly as 'dysmotility dyspepsia'. After a meal, food usually stays in the stomach for around 60 minutes, where it is broken down into its digestible constituents. Then, the pylorus, a sphincter connecting the stomach to the duodenum and beyond – relaxes, and rhythmical co-ordinated contractions of the muscles in the stomach wall impel its contents onwards. This process can be profoundly disturbed in those with dysmotility dyspepsia, and the muscles of the stomach wall alternate between contracting feebly and in high frequency spasms, leading, not surprisingly, to the symptoms of pain, nausea and bloatedness.

The source of dysmotility lies in a disruption of nervous control of the muscles in the stomach wall. This may be psychological – there is a close, if complex relationship between the psyche and the gut – and dysmotility seems to be commoner in those with an anxious or depressive personality.

Alternatively, the defect may be at the level where the nerves connect to the muscles in the gut wall, and, indeed, operations in which the nerves are cut are frequently followed by dysmotility symptoms. The pain, nausea and bloatedness of dysmotility are frequently misinterpreted as being caused by one or other of the acid-related functional dyspeptic syndromes; but, predictably, treatment with Tagamet or similar drugs, whether prescribed by the doctor or bought over the counter from a chemist, provides little relief.

The solution lies rather in improving gut motility, and the most important first step is to establish that this is the problem. A sensible explanation of what is happening is itself highly therapeutic, especially for those who, up until then, have been told there is nothing wrong with them. Where appropriate, treatment of the underlying depressive or anxiety states may be useful, but virtually everyone – 80 per cent or more – benefits from drugs that increase the strength of muscular contractions, and improve the speed of emptying the stomach contents. There are several to choose from, including Maxolon (metoclopramide) and Motilium (domperidone).

The Ulcer Breakthrough

Medical science truly understands the cause of less than one per cent of the hundreds of ailments to be found in a standard medical textbook. This does not stop doctors being fairly successful at treating many of them, but makes medicine an empirical science – short on theory if quite good in practice. So complete is this black hole of ignorance that one wonders whether medical researchers might be overlooking something fairly obvious. There must be a reason why one person is struck down by rheumatoid arthritis, another by multiple sclerosis and a third by diabetes. The point is important, because unless we know the cause we can rarely offer a cure. Diabetes can be treated with insulin, but how much better it would be to know why the pancreas stops functioning because then it might be possible to prevent it?

The obvious candidate for the mystery cause of all these diseases is some class of infectious agent that has not yet been discovered. If we could only identify what it was, in the same way that Robert Koch discovered the micro-organisms for tuberculosis, anthrax and the other infectious diseases in the latter part of the nineteenth century, medicine would be immeasurably further on. This is well illustrated by the problem of peptic ulcers, where – and it should be a cause of rejoicing – the causative organism does at least seem to have been identified.

There are a couple of causes of peptic ulcer – notably the non-steroidal, anti-inflammatory drugs used in the treatment of arthritis that erode the lining of the stomach, and, very rarely, a small tumour that secretes enormous quantities of the hormone gastrin, that markedly increases the amount of acid produced in the stomach. But, in the vast majority – 95 per cent – of cases, peptic ulcers just happen. In the past the explanation given has been in terms of the pseudo-causes already mentioned – that they are due to stress and irregular eating habits – which is why over-worked business executives are believed, incorrectly, to be particularly vulnerable. The discovery of wonder drugs in the Seventies – Tagamet and Zantac – which block acid secretion in the stomach, made the search for a cause seem rather pointless because they were so marvellously effective, relieving symptoms within 48 hours and healing the ulcer within four weeks.

There was a catch, though. The reason why these drugs proved so lucrative for the drug companies (the world market is worth about £3,000 million) was not just because they worked, but because, once they were stopped, the ulcer promptly returned. Patients then had to go on 'maintenance therapy', often taking the drugs for years. Ten years ago a couple of Australian doctors reported finding an 'unidentified, curved bacillus in the gastric epithelium' – that is, a previously unidentified bug in the stomach wall, which has subsequently been christened *Helicobacter pylori*. Most of their colleagues were pretty sceptical. Tagamet was seen as such an advance in the medical treatment of peptic ulcers that there was a reluctance to accept that they might be caused by some mysterious organism. *Helicobacter* was dismissed as a 'commensal', a bug like tens of millions that just sit in the gut and don't do any harm.

The Australians, to their credit, were not dispirited by this scepticism, and over the past decade have pieced together the incriminating evidence. One of them, Dr Barry Marshall, volunteered to swallow a flask full of *Helicobacter* and, sure enough, eight days later he developed severe stomach pains, vomiting and halitosis. A colleague who passed an endoscope into Dr Marshall's stomach found it red and inflamed and teeming with the organism. The only certain way of being sure that *Helicobacter* was the cause of most peptic ulcers was to give antibiotics to destroy the organism at the same time as standard anti-ulcer treatment. Then, theoretically, the ulcer should stay healed. And this, indeed, turns out to be the case. Some 82 per cent of ulcers treated with Tagamet alone will relapse within a year, but if antibiotics are given at the same time, the relapse rate falls to four per cent. A great advance indeed.

Colonic Complaints

'I have finally come to the conclusion', wrote the American aphorist Henry Wheeler Shaw, 'that a good reliable set of bowels is worth more to a man than any quantity of brains.' His opinion would no doubt be readily endorsed by the legions of sufferers from the chronic bowel conditions of Crohn's disease, ulcerative colitis, diverticulitis and irritable bowel syndrome. For, besides the many physical symptoms which these illnesses cause, abnormality of bowel function is curiously associated with a lack of psychological well-being – tension and anxiety notoriously give rise to acute bouts of diarrhoea, while constipation is accompanied by a debilitating lethargy and melancholy. Indeed from the 1930s onwards ulcerative colitis (UC) was commonly perceived as a classic example of psychosomatic disorder. The typical patient was described variously as 'intelligent, compulsive, highly strung with an abnormal attachment to the mother', or alternatively as 'passive, dependent and egocentric'.

Nowadays, most gastroenterologists will argue that UC patients are probably no different from anyone else and if they seem more prone to anxiety or depression this is more likely to be due to the chronic condition than a cause of it. Ulcerative colitis remains, however, a mysterious condition. It strikes men and women alike, usually in their early twenties – the lining of the bowel becomes studded with shallow ulcers interspersed with small pus-filled abscesses. It resembles and occasionally can be precipitated by an acute bout of dysentery, yet as Fergus Shannahan, professor of medicine at the National University of Ireland, points out in a review in *The Lancet*: 'Despite extensive investigation over several decades, a simple explanation for the cause of the disorder has not emerged.'

The colon is packed with hundreds of millions of bacteria whose role is generally thought to be beneficial: they reduce the amount of flatus and detoxify potentially harmful compounds such as bile acids. Still, their presence generates a chronic low level of inflammation with lots of lymphocytes known as T cells in the lining of the normal bowel. In some way, these become 'activated', precipitating in Professor Shannahan's words 'a cascade of destructive events'. The T cells secrete 'cytokines' which attract white blood cells whose usual function is to contain and destroy invading organisms by releasing lethal compounds such as nitric oxide. But in ulcerative colitis these noxious chemicals attack 'innocent bystanders' – the cells lining the gut wall. The severity of the resulting symptoms depends on how much of the gut is involved. If limited to the rectal region there will be a discharge of bloody mucus with pain on defecation. At the other extreme, if the whole length of the colon is acutely inflamed the result can be the life-threatening condition toxic megacolon. Here the colon is distended with enormous quantities of gas, and the lining of the gut wall stripped away exposing the underlying blood vessels – leading to profuse haemorrhage. Meanwhile, the natural gut flora escape into the circulation, causing blood poisoning. No single condition in the corpus of surgery so readily demonstrates the dramatic curative power of the surgeon's scalpel. The whole colon must be removed urgently, itself a difficult task made infinitely more so by the almost moribund state of the patient. But as soon as the toxic colon is pulled out of the abdomen, the blood pressure rises and pulse and temperature start to fall. Within a couple of days the patient is out of bed, pushing his drip around the ward and engaging in conversation.

Irrespective of what causes UC, the disease is held in check by drugs that suppress inflammation. Steroids work well in the acute stage and for those in whom the condition is limited to the rectum, steroid enemas or foams are all that is usually required. Sulphasalazine, a combination of antibiotic and an aspirin-like compound, has been the mainstay in preventing relapse ever since it was first used in the early 1940s. There are more potent drugs than this, including azathioprine and cyclosporin, usually given to transplant patients which prevent rejection. These are more effective but their use is controversial.

In marked contrast the surgical management of ulcerative colitis – essentially removing the offensive organ – has been revolutionised in the last 15 years. This has proved vital not only for those who develop toxic megacolon but others whose disease is poorly controlled by medical treatment or who develop cancerous changes in the bowel. Most of the credit here must go to the brilliant innovative British surgeon, the late Sir Alan Parks. The problem with removing a colon was that the patient was left with an unsightly, noisy, odoriferous and incontinent ileostomy protruding out of the abdominal wall, to which a bag had to be attached. The social and psychological consequences can be readily imagined and so even where an operation was clearly indicated it was often delayed or postponed indefinitely. Professor Parks, in a classic paper in 1978, described a procedure where having excised the colon, the last few inches of the remaining small intestine could be enlarged to form a pouch and reattached to the rectum. The anal sphincter was thus preserved and with it continence. At a stroke all the problems associated with an ileostomy were overcome. By removing the colon this operation is curative. And since it dispenses with the need for continued medication and repeated checks to detect early cancerous changes it is now probably the preferred option even for those with moderate symptoms.

At a symposium on ulcerative colitis held at the Royal Society of Medicine in 1909, distinguished surgeons described its gloomy prognosis. There was no medical treatment, ileostomy was virtually unthinkable, and two out of three patients died. Since then, even though its pathogenesis remains as obscure as ever, ulcerative colitis has become eminently treatable and readily curable. As with so many conditions, the success of modern medicine has been based on empirical solutions, rather than a profound understanding of the disease.

Irritable Bowel Syndrome – A 'Dustbin Diagnosis'

Pity the poor patient with irritable bowel syndrome! For years she (the condition is commoner among women) has suffered recurrent bouts where her abdomen swells and is racked by colicky pains. One week, she finds she goes to the lavatory frequently; the next, every visit is frustrating. She has lost count of the number of times doctors have prodded her tummy and nodded knowingly on discovering a tender (and to her, painful) site. She has squirmed in discomfort at treatments involving metal tubes and barium, and been tilted around on the X-ray table, until she has felt seasick.

One specialist 'with an interest' in the complaint persuaded her it would help in making a diagnosis if a balloon was placed in her rectum, which, when filled with air, faithfully reproduced her painful symptoms. And at the end of all this, what is the verdict? 'We can find nothing seriously wrong,' 'We have excluded organic disease' (ie, you don't have a cancer). 'You have a disturbance of bowel motility.' 'Your colon is unhappy.' 'You are suffering from irritable bowel syndrome' – for which there is no known cause, and apparently no effective treatment.

Those with irritable bowel syndrome have been described variously as hysterical, hypochondriacal, depressed, and self-centred but clearly it is not easy to distinguish whether such psychological traits explain the condition, or rather are the consequences of an often exhausting illness which doctors seem unable to influence. Yet there clearly is a two-way relationship between the psyche and the bowels. Anxiety notoriously precipitates bouts of diarrhoea, and experimentally it has been shown that stress in the emotionally vulnerable (induced by immersing their hands in very cold water, or, more unusually, compressing the skull with a metal band tightened by screws) increased the motility of the colon.

On the other hand, constipation has a debilitating and depressive effect, and the cathartic result of purgative drugs is often felt as much in the mind as in the bowel. One of the reported pleasures of the increasingly popular practice of colonic irrigation is the euphoria it induces. Devotees are prone to burst into song at the sheer joy of feeling the cleansing effect of ten litres of water swishing around in their bowel.

Not the least of the problems of finding an effective treatment for irritable bowel syndrome is that in anything up to 70 per cent of cases patients improve as much with the placebo as with the active ingredient, while virtually every sort of psychotherapy, not to mention meditation, hypnosis and relaxation training, can produce a sustained improvement in symptoms.

Doctors then tend to have a therapeutically nihilistic attitude towards their patients. When nothing really works, although virtually everything seems to help a little, there is a tendency to recommend a high-fibre diet, give them anti-spasmodics for the pain, and appropriate drugs for the constipation and diarrhoea, and leave it at that.

An exhaustive review in *The Lancet* has shown that this type of attitude is far from satisfactory. It acknowledges that 'irritable bowel syndrome is a frustrating disorder to treat', but goes on: 'The lack of a universally accepted therapeutic agent does not preclude individualised treatment.'

In essence, this means that although the syndrome is a dustbin diagnosis for a condition without an obvious cause, and to which there is obviously a strong psychogenic component, some of those so labelled will respond dramatically, if unpredictably, to one of a series of different drugs.

For those with diarrhoea-predominant symptoms, a few will be cured by the drug cholestyramine, which mops up excess bile acids; others are improved with anti-depressants, not because they are depressed, but because one of the side effects of these drugs is to slow down the bowel's contractions. Others find relief with verapamil, which is usually used for the treatment of angina and hypertension. Some of those who suffer excess gas are helped by excluding fermenting foods from their diet, such as milk, vegetables and fruit. Women whose exacerbations occur during their periods may be helped by hormone manipulation.

Although there is a sometimes tenuous explanation why these drugs should help individuals, the essential justification for their use is empirical. The only way of finding out if any of them work is by ringing the changes and giving each a therapeutic trial. It might not seem very scientific, but it must be a lot better than therapeutic nihilism.

The Heartburn Hernia

Every year tens of thousands of patients are told, to their utter mystification, that they have a 'hiatus hernia'. Even by the usual obscure standards of medical jargon, this diagnosis is particularly baffling. Hernias, in the public imagination, are rather fearsome things where the gut bulges out in the groin and which can strangulate – requiring an emergency operation. Presumably this must be similar, but most people would be forgiven for not knowing exactly where 'the hiatus' is in their bodies. In fact, the term hiatus is used here in its literal sense of a gap or opening – the gap being in the diaphragm which separates the chest from the abdomen and through which the oesophagus, or gullet, connects to the stomach. A hiatus hernia, then, is a protrusion of the upper part of the stomach upwards through the diaphragm and into the chest.

The public's mystification about the nature of hiatus hernias is compounded by medical uncertainty about their true significance. They are very common, and if looked for, will be found in almost one in three of those over the age of 60, in the vast majority of whom they cause no symptoms at all. But equally they can give rise to a bewildering variety of different symptoms which, in turn can be easily confused with other serious illnesses. Typically, a hiatus hernia causes 'heartburn', a burning pain behind the sternum which may radiate up to the jaw, thus mimicking the chest pain typical of angina. Alternatively, the hernia may be the cause of an intense, boring pain in the upper part of the abdomen which is readily mistaken for a peptic ulcer. Or the hernia may give rise to dyspepsia – indigestion associated with an uncomfortable sensation of bloatedness which can also be suggestive of gallstones.

Underlying these disparate syndromes, their common cause lies in the reflux of acid from the stomach into the lower part of the oesophagus whose walls, as a result, become red and painful. The question of how precisely this occurs was not clear until Drs J. Dent and W. J. Dodds, of Adelaide Hospital in southern Australia, discovered that the answer lay in the science of belching. Despite its vulgar reputation, belching is actually a very important reflex in allowing the air in the stomach – that would otherwise have to travel the length of the gut, thus causing great discomfort – to escape back up through the mouth. Belching is the most conspicuous manifestation of a continuous process where a valve around the bottom of the oesophagus repeatedly relaxes to let small pockets of gas escape in this way. Simultaneously, acid would reflux back upwards to cause heartburn and other symptoms were it not for the support of the muscles of the diaphragm.

But in the presence of a hiatus hernia, where the oesophageal valve is pushed upwards by the protruding part of the stomach, this support is lost with predictably dire consequences. Acid whooshes backwards, the lining of the oesophagus becomes inflamed and may bleed, muscles go into spasm and the patient experiences one or more of the symptoms already described. These, in turn, are brought on or exacerbated by anything which encourages acid to flow across the incompetent valve. This may be a change in position, like bending forwards to tie one's shoelaces or lying in bed at night. Similarly, a rise in pressure within the abdomen precipitated by straining at stool or eating a large meal will have a similar effect.

The lives of patients with a hiatus hernia would be utterly miserable were it not for two types of drugs, both discovered in the 1970s. The first are histamine receptor antagonists, like Tagamet, which reduce the amount of acid in the stomach, allowing the lining of the oesophagus to heal. The second are known as prokinetic drugs, such as anti-sickness pill Maxolon, which by increasing the resting tone of the oesophageal valve minimises the backwash of gastric secretions. When these fail to control the symptoms, there is little alternative other than to resort to surgery to pull the stomach back down into the abdomen and repair the hiatus in the diaphragm.

Many different operations have been tried with varying degrees of success. Their main drawback has been that too tight a repair traps air in the stomach, preventing its eructation back upwards and, as can be imagined, this is very uncomfortable. The option of surgical repair, which ideally would be preferable to the need to take drugs continuously, is now coming back in favour thanks to the work of Alfred Cuschieri, Professor of Surgery at Ninewells Hospital in Dundee. He has described in the *American Journal of Surgery* a technique of repair which does not require the opening of the chest or abdomen at all. Instead, five fine metal tubes, or laparoscopes, are inserted into different sites of the abdomen, through which very delicate surgical instruments are introduced. This technical *tour de force* carried out on eight elderly patients was followed by rapid recovery and complete relief of symptoms.

8

Bones

Fascinating Feet

Cinderella, according to folk historians Iona and Peter Opie, 'is undoubtedly the best known of all fairy stories – a tale whose strangeness has been a wonder to man for a thousand years'. They should know, having traced no fewer than 700 variants of the story across the world. The most striking moment in this tale is where Cinderella slips her foot into the glass slipper – what does it mean? Orthopaedic surgeon Basil Helal, who knows more about feet than anyone else in Britain, has no doubt. In an article, 'The Ascent of Cinderella', in the *Journal of the Royal Society of Medicine* he argues that the resonance of this image lies in its sexual symbolism. 'The foot is the phallus and the shoe the vagina ... the perfect fit ensures a perfect mating and so leads to a happy marriage.' But the foot is not only sexual symbol, it is also, he says, a 'potent source of eroticism' in its own right. Foot fetishism is common and its more famous practitioners included Ovid, Goethe, Thomas Hardy and Casanova. The practice of foot binding in China was a society-sanctioned form of foot fetishism.

By contrast the foot as an object of scientific scrutiny has tended to be neglected, the general impression being that though it is certainly a very useful appendage it is not nearly as interesting as, for example, the hand. Mr Helal finds the comparison invidious. The foot, he maintains, is much more sophisticated and complex, a biomechanical marvel that provides both stability and propulsion for the human frame. Indeed, the human foot is the defining characteristic of Man, his hallmark, which by allowing him to stand upright freed the hands entirely from their weight-bearing function and thus initiated the long climb to civilisation.

The feature that distinguishes the human foot from that of any other animal is the longitudinal arch which separates out the twin functions of stability and propulsion. The stability comes from the outer part, in the semicircle running from the heel to the fourth and fifth toes. This is the weight-bearing surface, and the cushioning of the muscles and ligaments along the highly specialised structure of the heel fat pad act as a shock absorber capable of sustaining the downward force of the human body. The remaining part of the foot focused on the big toe acts as a lever, 'an elastic, mobile dynamic organ of propulsion'.

As is so often the case, it is only when some part of the body goes wrong that its true worth can be appreciated. The big toe is susceptible to the condition, *hallux rigidus*, where there is a limitation of movement in relation to the rest of the foot.

While walking, the stiffness of the toe puts pressure on the surrounding muscles and ligaments, which then become inflamed and very painful indeed. Mobility is obviously severely restricted and, unless adequately and promptly treated, chronic arthritic changes follow which require surgery to correct them.

The renewed interest in the foot in recent years has been fuelled by two developments. The first is the popularity of jogging and the punishing training regimes of professional athletes. The foot is now exposed to forces that even its resilient structure is unable to sustain. The long-distance runner, for example, hits the ground with his heel with a force three to four times his body weight, 800 times for every mile that is covered. Joggers get stress fractures of the small bones in the foot, longjumpers shear the fatty pad off the heel, footballers develop *hallux rigidus* from repeatedly stubbing the toe on the ball, basketball players traumatise the small sesamoid bones under the sole of the foot and so on – the possibilities for injury are enormous. It may be impossible to diagnose these problems without specialist knowledge of the anatomy of the foot and their management may be very difficult – not least because the victims too frequently want to get back to a training circuit as quickly as possible to repeat the traumatic manoeuvres that were responsible for their symptoms in the first place.

The second impetus to scientific interest in the foot arises from the expectation nowadays that the variety of congenital defects with which a child may be born can be corrected surgically. According to Mr John Fixsen, consultant orthopaedic surgeon at Great Ormond Street Hospital, London: 'Children referred to orthopaedic clinics with foot problems or parental anxiety about the condition of a child's feet exceeds all other referrals – it is extremely common.'

He adds significantly: 'It is, however, impossible to give advice unless there is a clear understanding of the natural history and development of the foot in childhood.'

Many of the children referred for a specialist opinion have nothing wrong with their feet, or nothing that requires treatment, and it is a considerable challenge to identify these and thus avoid unnecessary surgical intervention. This is well illustrated by the problem of flat feet which Mr Fixsen divides into two main categories. The first and largest group have no symptoms and the feet are fully mobile. These require no treatment, but he says: 'The position must be carefully explained to often anxious parents that their children's feet are basically normal.' However, where the feet are either painful or stiff, or where there is some demonstrable bony or muscular abnormality, then a careful and thorough examination is essential to allow a definitive diagnosis to be made and corrective treatment undertaken.

Mr Helal draws a teasing analogy between the Cinderella story and the changing role of the foot in orthopaedic practice. For many years it has been misunderstood and neglected, certainly compared to the other joints of the lower limb – the hip and the knee. In recent years, however, the foot has met its Prince Charming in the form of a small group of orthopaedic enthusiasts whose detailed study of its mechanics have revealed it to be an appendage of complex and subtle beauty.

Ankylosing Spondylitis

One of the readiest ways of being labelled a malingerer is to suffer from ankylosing spondylitis (AS), the rheumatic disorder of the spine that combines the two common symptoms of back pain and tiredness, without any apparent cause for either. Physical examination, X-rays, any number of blood tests are all reported as normal, while referral for a specialist opinion draws a blank. The family doctor's suspicions that he is being taken for a ride appear to be confirmed by further vague symptoms of chronic exhaustion and a feeling of being permanently out of sorts – just the sort of problems that afflict the neurotic and depressed. The main reason why AS can so readily be mistaken for malingering is that the site of inflammation – the point where muscles and tendons fit into bone – cannot be visualised on an X-ray. There thus appears to be a gross disparity between the symptoms being complained of and what looks like an entirely normal spine. Only after several years, when the pain and subsequent immobility had altered the movement of the joints relative to each other, will the secondary changes of arthritis become apparent on X-ray.

The medical profession can even fail to diagnose AS in itself – as is shown by the story of Ann Roberts, an intelligent and highly successful consultant now in her mid-forties. Dr Roberts's symptoms started in her medical student days, when she came to dread the protracted clinical ward rounds. After 20 minutes of standing around, moving slowly from one bed to the next, she would begin to feel very uncomfortable. 'I had this fantasy that I wanted to turf the patient out of bed and just lie down on those clean, white sheets,' she says. Difficulty in sleeping came soon afterwards. 'I would go to bed feeling fine, but wake in the middle of the night with pain and stiffness in my back, so I just had to get up, walk about and take painkillers.' She felt chronically exhausted, but her tiredness was more than that which comes from lack of sleep. 'At times I felt as if I could scarcely lift my arms above my head,' she recalls.

Her medical colleagues were friendly but bemused by this multiplicity of symptoms, which now included stabbing chest pains and hot flushes at night. 'They clearly thought I was pretty neurotic, but the trouble was I thought so too.' The crunch came when she seized up after a car journey. 'I felt like a V-registration Ford with bits falling off. I knew there must be something seriously wrong by now, but still felt that things would have to get worse before a definitive diagnosis was made.'

Eventually Dr Roberts took herself off to see Professor Paul Dieppe, a consultant rheumatologist, who told her she had AS. Indeed, he pointed out the diagnosis could have been made much earlier, because her symptoms were actually quite characteristic and different from other types of back pain. The most crucial of these is early morning stiffness, where it can take an hour or more to get going, but which is easily concealed by the other symptoms associated with the illness. Even though she was a doctor, the delay in diagnosing AS had been even longer than the customary eight years; but like so many patients, once the verdict had been given, Dr Roberts embraced it with gratitude. 'It's impossible to describe the tremendous relief at finally being given a label,' she says. 'Even if my condition had turned out to be fatal, I would have died a happy woman.'

AS responds better than any other rheumatological disorder to the healing properties of warm water. At the Royal National Hospital for Rheumatic Diseases in Bath, patients spend an hour or more a day doing exercises in a large swimming pool kept at a constant temperature of 40°C. This is complemented by 'dry land' physiotherapy to strengthen the muscles running up and down the back. Regrettably there is no drug specifically active against AS, though some patients are helped by Salazopyrin. Most, however, find they need high doses of anti-inflammatory drugs, especially when, as periodically and inexplicably happens, the disease flares up. Injecting steroids directly into the inflamed muscles can also be helpful during these exacerbations, and a minority in whom the inflammatory process affects the hips benefit from joint replacement.

Essentially, though, patients have to learn to live with their illness, which may progressively involve the whole spine, rendering it stiff and immobile. As with so many diseases, the prospects of treatment would be enormously increased if the underlying cause could be identified. The main candidate would seem to be a bacterium, *Klebsiella*, a normal and usually harmless resident of the bowel. Antibodies to *Klebsiella* interact with a specific receptor on the surface of lymphocytes (white blood cells) unique to patients with AS. This leads to the release of inflammatory chemicals that initiate the disease. According to Dr Alan Ebringer of the Middlesex Hospital, a combination of antibiotics and a low starch diet (*Klebsiella* thrives on starch) might be sufficient to stop the illness in its tracks. If this treatment were to be effective it would have to be started early on, before the disease process really got going – yet another reason why AS should be diagnosed as early as possible.

The Long and the Short of Shoulder Pain

Different physical illnesses induce quite characteristic mental states which, for those with pain and stiffness of the neck and shoulders, means a constant sense of oppression. Unable to stretch their arms out or throw their head back, sufferers feel almost literally weighed down by the burden of their symptoms. So the two well-recognised shoulder conditions – *polymyalgia rheumatica* and frozen shoulder – cause an almost surprising amount of disability and unhappiness. They are quite distinct. Treating polymyalgia can result in the nearest thing there is to a miracle cure in modern medicine, while frozen shoulder syndrome has proved resolutely resilient to a whole cupboard full of remedies.

There are few more gratifying conditions for doctors to come across than a patient with polymyalgia. Diffuse pain and stiffness around the shoulders complicates even the simplest of tasks, such as brushing one's hair in the mornings, making a cup of tea, or holding a book for long periods. There is a general feeling of fatigue and malaise. Profuse sweating at night may be a feature and loss of weight due to anorexia. As the condition is commonest in those in their seventies and eighties milder cases may be mistakenly attributed to old age, while the more severe may be thought to be due to some sinister condition such as cancer. Either way there is often a reluctance to visit the doctor, so the diagnosis may be delayed for six months or more. The history is so typical that it alone is usually sufficient to alert the doctor to what is going on, and is readily confirmed by the simplest of all blood tests, the Erythrocyte Sedimentation Rate (ESR), which measures the speed with which a column of blood cells in a glass pipette settles. The ESR in polymyalgia is always markedly elevated.

Polymyalgia is much the commonest acute rheumatic condition of the older age group, and it responds instantaneously and dramatically to steroid therapy. Within 24 hours, and following months of malaise and discomfort, the strength in the upper limbs is wondrously restored. But unfortunately that is not the end of the story. The intention of treatment is to give a short burst of high-dose steroids, which are then rapidly reduced to a low maintenance level for the 18 months usually necessary for the condition to burn itself out. Some, however, need a higher maintenance dose, exposing them to the many hazards of chronic steroid therapy – diabetes, raised blood pressure, bruising and even psychosis. This in turn requires a delicate balancing act in which the control of symptoms has to be traded off against the minimally acceptable level of complications.

The symptoms of polymyalgia are due to a pervasive inflammation of the muscles while, with frozen shoulder, the inflammation is in the joint itself. There are three phases in this catchily titled condition: 'freezing, frozen and thawing'. The 'freezing' usually starts abruptly, often at night with pain at rest a prominent feature and the commonest complaint being 'I can't seem to get myself comfortable'. The range of movement gradually declines and after about six weeks the pain recedes, but the shoulder is almost completely immobile, and remains so, often for two years or more until slowly the thaw sets in. Even then there may never be a full recovery.

The first phase is similar to an acute arthritis, while the subsequent immobility is due to loss of fluid in the joint and fibrosis. Logically, then, early intervention with powerful drugs might prevent a very a protracted period of disability. Over the years radiotherapy, ultrasound, steroid injections, heat, exercise, massage and manipulation have all had their advocates, but as one rheumatologist gloomily observed, 'the very diversity of treatments cast doubts on the efficacy of any'. As a result, many doctors confronted with a patient with a frozen shoulder are overwhelmed by a sense of therapeutic nihilism. If nothing really seems to work there is a tendency just to prescribe the usual anti-inflammatory pills and leave them with the advice that the shoulder will eventually loosen up.

Lipmann Kessell, the late and very distinguished orthopaedic surgeon, took a dim view of this pessimism. He advised that the arm should be completely rested in a sling in the early acute phase and generous quantities of painkillers provided. As soon as the pain started to subside, high-dose steroids should be given for two weeks and then, under general anaesthesia, the shoulder joint should be manipulated to disrupt the fibrous adhesions within the capsule. Intensive physiotherapy would then ensure that a full range of movement was maintained. The plan of management, he insisted, could 'reduce the length of disability from a period of 18 months to 18 weeks', which seems eminently worthwhile.

An alternative technique with a similar effect, proposed by Professor Angus Wallace of Nottingham University, is to distend the joint capsule with an injection of a large amount of air and fluid. Two recent surveys of the older age group have found that almost a quarter have some degree of pain or loss of mobility in the shoulders. Rather than putting up with their symptoms they would be well advised to seek a definitive diagnosis and treatment.

Treating Rheumatoid Aggressively

'Rheumatoid arthritis is the commonest potentially treatable cause of disability in the Western world,' writes Paul Emery, specialist at the University of Birmingham, in the *British Journal of Rheumatology*. The phrase 'potentially treatable' is intriguing, because it implies that this grievous disease – which is usually thought of as being rather relentless – is being inadequately treated, and thereby hangs a very interesting tale.

The cause of rheumatoid arthritis is not known, though it has been reported in 11 patients following vaccination for tetanus, suggesting, as many have postulated, that one or more infectious agents precipitate the disease in those genetically predisposed to it. There are other pointers to the possible role of an infectious organism. Despite the stigmata of the crippled and deformed joints of the hands being so readily recognisable, rheumatoid was first described only in 1880. This suggests that it developed quite suddenly, as with other major infectious epidemics, such as syphilis, TB and the plague. Then, just as the ferocity of infections tend to decline with time, so, it appears, is rheumatoid becoming less severe – fewer joints are involved and complications with devastating consequences are less frequently noticed. The question of causation is important, because were the responsible agent to be identifiable, it would be possible to devise appropriate treatments that would stop the illness in its tracks. But the cause is not known, so doctors are left trying to control the effects – the inflammation of the lining of the joints that invades and destroys the cartilage, resulting in crippling deformity.

Over the years, several drugs have been found that do slow down this process – gold, penicillamine, methotrexate and steroids – but they are all potentially toxic, with serious side effects, so tend to be kept 'in reserve'. Initially, patients are usually treated with simple anti-inflammatory drugs like Nurofen, which dampen down the pain and swelling, while this heavy artillery is only rolled out when there is clear evidence of joint destruction. This all seemed plausible enough until, in 1987, Dr David Scott, of King's College Hospital in London, reported on a study in which he had followed up 112 patients for more than 20 years. More than half, he found, had either died or were seriously disabled. 'This underlined the very serious nature of the illness and its often disastrous effects on people's lives,' he said.

The initial reaction was a counsel of despair. The drugs were simply not good enough, and no serious improvement in the outlook for rheumatoid patients could be hoped for until better ones were discovered or, indeed, the underlying cause of the disease identified. On reflection, however, some rheumatologists began to believe that it was not that the drugs were not good enough, but that the philosophy of treatment was in error. Rather than wait for evidence of joint erosion before starting potent disease-modifying drugs, they believed, the illness should be treated aggressively right from the beginning, in the hope of inducing a remission and thus preventing progressive disability. Before this complete reversal of the standard approach to treatment could be initiated, two things had to happen. First, some methods had to be devised of showing that the potent drugs were actually modifying the disease in its early stages. This is not easy. Secondly, if patients were not to be unnecessarily exposed to toxic side effects, it was necessary to find some way of identifying the minority in whom the disease is mild and non-progressive.

Dr Paul Emery's claim that rheumatoid is now 'potentially treatable' is based on the remarkable fact that, over the past five years, solutions have been found to both these problems. A combination of genetic studies, with immunological blood tests, can predict, with 90 per cent accuracy, which patients will go on to develop destructive disease of the joints and so require potent treatment. Further subtle tests of the bone density around the joints can show, long before clear evidence of destruction, whether the disease has been brought under control.

For this radical approach to work, patients with suspected rheumatoid must be referred very early after the onset of symptoms for a specialist opinion – rather than, as usually happens, being treated by their GPs with anti-inflammatory drugs that control the symptoms but do not influence the disease process. In Dr Emery's words: 'With limited resources, efforts must be focused on the time – at the onset of the disease – when intervention is likely to be most effective. We can no longer permit an amateur approach to rheumatoid.' This sounds fine in theory: although in practice it may be more difficult, particularly as NHS waiting lists to see a specialist stretch into the middle distance, so many will be lucky to get an appointment within six months, let alone the six weeks that Dr Emery says is necessary. This leaves the option of paying privately, or pressurising your GP into arranging an urgent referral. Either way, it could make a lot of difference.

Hooray for Hip Replacements

Hip operations are one of the great triumphs of modern surgery. No other operation promises so certainly and offers for so many people such a profound improvement in the quality of their lives. After what seems like years of hobbling around with the teeth-gritting pain of two rough surfaces rubbing together, difficulty in finding a comfortable position for sleep, aches and twinges in the back and knees because the effort to avoid weight-bearing on the hip distorts these other joints as well, the pain is suddenly gone and mobility is returned.

The principle behind the procedure is simplicity itself, although that did not stop its inventor, the late and great Sir John Charnley, from devoting his whole life to bringing it to perfection: the worn and torn femoral head of the joint is cut away and replaced by a metal ball which fits snugly into a plastic socket inserted into the pelvis. Sir John's first results, reported in 1970 after 379 operations, speak for themselves: an average disability of 'a just tolerable pain hampering useful activities, was reduced to 'slight' or 'none'. Thus, after years of bullying my arthritic patients into having their hips replaced, it came as an unpleasant surprise to learn that all is not well. In brief, the early failure rate is unacceptably high, and as many as one in four needs a 'revision' procedure which is fraught with difficulties, very time-consuming and expensive. This was certainly not Sir John's experience: indeed, 95 per cent of those who received a Charnley hip could expect it to last a lifetime. It is clearly important for the 45,000 people who have a hip replacement every year in this country to know what is going on.

The main reason why hip replacements go wrong is that they become loose and, with a chunk of metal rattling around in the bone cavity, pain rapidly returns. In Sir John's day, hip replacements were done almost exclusively on the over-70s, and with obsessive attention to surgical technique and steady improvements in the cement that holds the joint in place, in almost all, the new hip outlived its recipient.

The first problem arose when news of the amazing results of the operation got out, and younger patients began to demand one too. Cement proved an inappropriate fixative, so a series of cementless hip prostheses were developed which had a tendency to become looser earlier, a process accelerated by the fact that the more youthful recipients tended to be much more physically active. The next problem is that in the early days, hip replacements were done by orthopaedic surgeons who had developed a specialist expertise but, as the popularity of the operation mushroomed, everybody, including junior doctors, found themselves 'doing hips' to meet the increased demand. In private practice, too, 'new hips' had become such a lucrative earner that everyone started trying their hand at them.

The end result has been something of a cock-up. The failure rate of this programme of high turnover, indeterminately competent hip replacements has escalated, and those who are any good at them find themselves forced to do increasing numbers of 'revision operations'. These in turn gobble up the resources which should be going to first-time hip replacements, and the waiting lists lengthen even further.

The emphasis in recent years has been to try and find a technical-fix solution, some ideal hip prosthesis that would never wear loose with time. This, according to Michael Freeman, President of the British Orthopaedic Association, is an illusion. 'You don't go to a concert to hear some nonentity playing a Stradivarius; you go to hear masters like Oistrakh, and it is exactly the same with hip replacements. The prosthesis is irrelevant. What is vital is the expertise of the surgeon who puts it in.'

Apart from doubling the number of consultant orthopaedic surgeons and encouraging them to specialise in joint replacement (an unlikely scenario) there clearly will just not be enough of the required level of skill to go round. For those lucky enough to have private health insurance the obvious lesson is the need to be discriminatory about the surgeon they choose to give them a new hip. For everyone else it seems to be a matter of taking one's chances. It might be sensible to have the operation later rather than sooner.

Whiplash: More than just Clunk, Crick

When in the early eighties the wearing of safety belts became compulsory by law almost immediately there was a steep decline in the number of deaths and serious injuries on the road – by about a quarter. In retrospect it just seems remarkable that it took so long to introduce a measure that, at a stroke, saved about 1,000 lives.

Safety belts are none the less something of a mixed blessing, especially for those involved in minor accidents, for they certainly increase the frequency and severity of 'whiplash' injuries to the neck. The fundamental laws of ergonomics dictate that at the immediate moment of impact, the head moves both faster and through a greater range of movements when the body is constrained. As many as six out of ten front-seat occupants have some degree of neck sprain after an accident, and for those unfortunate enough to have been in that situation, the disability is anything but trivial.

The essential problem is a tearing of the muscle fibres and ligaments that support the cervical spine. People are always surprised at just how painful and long-lasting these soft tissues injuries can be, and are dismayed by the pessimistic prognostications of doctors that 'things might start to get better after six or eight weeks'. Even this seems optimistic. Although the precise figures vary from one series to the next, the general impression is that around a half of whiplash victims still have some symptoms after a year. In part, this is because the cervical spine itself is a particularly sensitive part of our anatomy, with many joints, ligaments and nerves all caught up together, so sudden trauma has complex effects which can be difficult to distinguish.

Two factors, however, conspire to make this already difficult problem more intractable. The first is the rather nihilistic attitudes towards whiplash injuries in most accident and emergency departments. The general feeling is that once an X-ray has shown there is no bone injury, then painkillers and a cervical collar and strong reassurance are all that is required. An editorial in the *British Medical Journal* pointed out quite vociferously that this is not good enough. The pain and symptoms persist because the muscles supporting the neck fail to regain their suppleness and elasticity, and this process is only exacerbated by keeping the neck immobile in a restraining collar for weeks. It would seem, and indeed has been demonstrated, that early mobilisation with neck exercises and manipulation performed by physiotherapists both shorten the time before cervical movement recovers and reduces the duration of painful symptoms.

The second complicating factor is that whenever the question of compensation arises for pain and disability or loss of time from work – and this is not infrequent with whiplash injury – it can be virtually impossible to evaluate objectively the severity of symptoms. There is widespread prejudice among doctors that many patients only recover after an injection of a large cheque into their bank accounts. It would be ridiculous to suggest this 'compensationitis' does not exist – indeed it is frequently observed that symptoms improve dramatically following compensation settlements – but there is also now a strong suspicion that some whiplash victims have been unfairly labelled as suffering from 'accident neurosis' and so have not received the sympathy and help they deserved.

The answer, as always, is to prevent whiplash injuries occurring in the first place, by making head restraints a standard feature on all cars. However, because many more car accidents involve impacts from the front rather than from behind, these restraints are more likely to cause facial injuries to back-seat passengers than to prevent whiplash injuries to those in the front. So, if restraints are to be of value, those in the back should also be compelled to wear safety belts, and, to prevent them suffering whiplash injuries, head restraints should also be required on back seats. Nothing in the world is simple.

9

Mending the Mind

Cognitive Therapy – The Talking Treatment that Works

Psychoanalysts are an unhappy lot. Having to listen to the incoherent details of their patients' dreams is tedious enough, but their angst is now compounded by a rising tide of scepticism from their medical colleagues. Psychoanalysis, according to Raymond Tallis, professor of medicine, writing in *The Lancet*, is 'a scientific fairytale'. 'Criticism that it is expensive and ineffective has given way to the grievous charge that it is often dangerous and destructive,' he writes. 'Its peculiar ideas confuse and undermine vulnerable individuals, while its practitioners manipulate the affections and misplaced faith of their clients to ensure continuing lucrative commitment to their remedies.' As for the founder of psychoanalysis, Sigmund Freud, the portrait painted by his most recent biographer, Richard Webster, is of a man of pathological unpleasantness, quite unrepentant about his many diagnostic blunders, and a compulsive manipulator of those around him.

Reacting to this tide of hostile criticism, eighty psychoanalysts and academics gathered in the library of the Anna Freud Centre in leafy Hampstead for a conference on 'science and psychoanalysis'. Under the steely gaze of photographs of the great man which line the walls, Peter Fonagy, professor of psychoanalysis at University College, sought to explain how, in his own words 'we got into this mess'. There are two aspects to the question as to whether psychoanalysis is 'true'. The first concerns the validity of the theory that underpins it. Do young boys fall in love with their mothers and fear castration by their fathers? Are infants driven by libidinal urges to seek sensual gratification through the mouth, anus, and genitals? Does the source of neurosis lie in repressed and painful memories knocking around the echoing chambers of the unconscious mind? Such fundamental concepts are now, according to Professor Fonagy, 'so riddled with controversy' that 'there is no longer a coherent set of principles that could be tested scientifically'.

Psychoanalysis may lack a coherent theory, but its techniques, particularly the relationship with the analyst – otherwise known as the transference – could still be efficacious. So the second question that warrants scientific scrutiny is whether it works – does it make people better, or at least less unhappy? Here, judgement is divided. Many people certainly believe they have been helped, but this could just be from having the opportunity to talk about themselves to someone they are paying to listen, while the specific insights offered by the analyst could be irrelevant. Certainly, when Professor Gavin Andrews, of the University of New South Wales, reviewed all the studies in which the outcome of psychoanalysis had been objectively measured in the *British Journal of Psychiatry*, he was unable to show that it worked better than 'just talking'.

Over the past few years the credibility of psychoanalysis has been eclipsed by the remarkable success of another type of psychotherapy – cognitive therapy – which is based on a theory of neurotic illness that is almost the direct antithesis of that proposed by Freud a hundred years ago. Cognitive therapy dispenses with the couch, with dream analysis and free association. It looks for the causes and solutions of mental problems, not in long-forgotten events from early childhood but in patients' everyday life. Treatment lasts months rather than years and, crucially, it has consistently been shown to be effective even in those conditions usually considered to be 'too difficult' for psychoanalysts, such as serious anxiety states and depression.

Cognitive therapy, as its name implies, is concerned with what, or more precisely how, people think about themselves and the world around them. Thoughts exert a profound influence on feelings and so distorted patterns of thinking (such as the belief that one is unloved), can profoundly affect the emotions. In cognitive therapy such distorted patterns of thinking are identified, and in theory, once corrected, the feelings they cause of depression and anxiety should be ameliorated. It is hard to conceive of a theory of psychological illness more distinct from the Freudian concept of repressed libidinal urges locked up in the unconscious mind. Nevertheless, the roots of cognitive therapy lie in psychoanalysis as described by one of its early pioneers, Aaron Beck. Back in the Sixties, while practising as an analyst in Philadelphia, Beck was treating a young woman with an anxiety state which he initially interpreted in true Freudian fashion as being due to her unhappy sex life. During one session, he noticed that his patient seemed particularly uneasy when talking about her sexual hang-ups, and, on enquiring why, it emerged that she felt embarrassed because she thought she was expressing herself badly and that she sounded trite and foolish. 'These self-evaluative thoughts were very striking,' Beck recalls. 'Because she was actually very articulate.' Probing further, he found that this false pattern of thinking – that she was dull and uninteresting – permeated all her relationships. He concluded her chronic anxiety had little to do with her sex life, but rather arose from a constant state of dread lest her lover might desert her because he found her so tedious.

Over the next few years Beck found he was able to identify similar and quite predictable subliminal patterns of thinking in nearly all the patients who came to him for analysis. He labelled these 'automatic thoughts', which operated at the margins of consciousness, a type of continuous internal monologue of which his patients could be made aware once their attention was directed towards them. When these automatic thoughts were brought out into the open, examined and discussed, his patients reported an enormous improvement in their emotional well-being – much greater than he had achieved from years of submitting them to psychoanalysis. For the first time he felt he was getting inside his patients' minds and beginning to see the world as they experienced it.

For Mark Williams, Professor of Psychology at Bangor University in North Wales, cognitive therapy is 'a liberation' because it liberates people from having to depend on their analysts to interpret their problems for them. In cognitive therapy, the therapist acts as a collaborator, helping to identify and correct the distorted patterns of thinking that lie behind so many neurotic illnesses. 'Cognitive therapy has been criticised for being too simple,' Williams says. 'But why shouldn't it be simple? We can too easily be carried away with the complexity of the human mind, and miss the point that the only really important thing for patients with psychological problems is that they start feeling better, and be offered the means by which they can become so.'

The most damaging legacy of Freudianism, he believes, has been to convince people that there must be some mysterious root cause of mental illness, stemming from repressed events in childhood. Certainly, an unhappy childhood can predispose people to the development of neuroses, but the cause can equally be genetic – a subtle alteration in the biochemistry of the brain – or a reaction to adverse events in adult life. The major advance of cognitive therapy has been to show that, irrespective of the precise cause, the final common path of the neuroses can best be understood in terms of distorted patterns of thinking.

The most convincing evidence supporting the validity of cognitive therapy is that it works. Professor Gavin Andrews, in his review in the *British Medical Journal of Psychiatry* identified it as 'the treatment of choice' in generalised anxiety disorders and depression. Further, it showed 'promising results' in the management of marital and sexual difficulties, in bulimia, in chronic pain syndromes and many emotional disorders of childhood. Since Professor Andrews' review, cognitive therapy has also been used for the treatment of schizo-phrenia, personality disorders and chronic fatigue syndrome. This remarkable scope of cognitive therapy, argues Professor Andrews, has 'devastating implications for the future of psychoanalysis'. The duration and intensity of psychoanalysis means that at any one time analysts can treat fewer than one per cent of those suffering from a neurotic illness who could benefit from psychotherapy, and even for this small minority it has not been possible to show objectively that psychoanalysis 'is better than a placebo'.

Rather, argues Professor Andrews, there needs to be a substantial shift towards cognitive therapy because 'it is important to explain to people what is wrong with them, and if this is done properly the patient feels reassured and more in control'. Currently there are some 250 consultant psychotherapists working in the National Health Service, almost all 'psychoanalytical-oriented'. Professor Andrews is blunt. 'They should switch to practising cognitive therapy or be dismissed to make way for those who are willing to do so.' In Cambridge, two psychoanalysts have been dismissed from their NHS posts and replaced with therapists 'sympathetic' to the cognitive therapy approach. The 'scientific fairytale' of psychoanalysis is heading for oblivion.

Defeating Depression with a Pill

I must have seen thousands of patients over the years, of whom a few are truly memorable. These are my diagnostic triumphs and therapeutic disasters; and some who, for one reason or another, have had a profound influence on my understanding of illness and how it should be treated. One of these was a man in his mid-thirties who had recently joined the practice and came for a repeat prescription of his anti-depressant pills. He told me how he had his first attack of depression while at university about ten years previously. He had tried to conceal his despair but to no avail and he was forced to leave. After a year of psychotherapy, which was interesting but not particularly useful, he started on medication. Within six weeks the sun came out and, as they say, he had never looked back. Since then he had, on his own initiative, tried several times to reduce the dosage of his pills, but noticed that within a few days his original depressive thoughts started to return. He would then up the dose again and they would disappear. He now expected to continue his medication indefinitely but this did not bother him – depression, he said, was no different from diabetes, a chronic disease requiring regular medication to keep it under control.

This matter-of-fact description of a protracted depressive illness exquisitely sensitive to even quite small alterations in medication was curiously moving. More importantly, it contradicted the prevailing philosophy – that anti-depressants should be given for a limited period, after which the dose should be slowly reduced with a view to stopping altogether in six months. There may be circumstances in which such a policy is appropriate as in those with a stable personality who are suddenly laid low by stress or bereavement. But for everyone else, the almost inevitable result must be that their illness recurs. Indeed, the main impediment to successful treatment of depression is that doctors are generally too timid and half-hearted in prescribing medication with most courses of anti-depressants only being taken for three to four weeks. The common myth that anti-depressants are 'addictive' does not help in rationalising people's decision to stop their drug long before they should do so.

There are, of course, several different types and causes of depression, but they are all characterised by chronicity. Indeed, after the first episode of depression, only about a quarter of patients have no further recurrence over the following ten years. According to Greg Wilkinson, Professor of Psychiatry at the Royal London Hospital: 'This confirms the view that depressive disorders are neither trivial, nor transient,' and indicates that 'many patients receive inadequate therapy.' This would certainly seem to be the message of the longest ever trial of anti-depressant drugs in a group of patients who had stayed well on medication for three years. They were then randomised into two groups – one lot continued to take their drugs, while the second were given only a placebo.

Over the following two years two-thirds of the placebo group had a recurrence of their symptoms, compared to only nine per cent of those on drug treatment. What more does one need to know?

Interestingly, just as the evidence of the superiority of drug treatment for depression had become clear, it also seems that cognitive psychotherapy may be equally good. As we have seen, this is not the usual sort of 'talking cure', but rather seeks to change the way in which depressed patients think about themselves. These include 'automatic thoughts', such as 'I'm a bad mother,' and 'logical errors' – focusing on one aspect of a situation while ignoring other equally important ones. Thus a depressive joining a group of friends all but one of whom treat him warmly, will become obsessed with the single apparent rebuff. Cognitive therapy teaches patients to be aware of these patterns of thought and how to avoid them. It is remarkably successful and for those averse to taking drugs might seem an attractive alternative.

Back in 1982 Swedish psychiatrists organised a special education programme for general practitioners. In the following three years the prescription of anti-depressant drugs shot up while that of tranquillisers and sleeping pills declined. The number of hospital admissions for depression declined by two-thirds and suicides fell by three-quarters. It would thus appear that the main problem of depressive patients is not that doctors do not know how to treat them, just that they are failing to do so.

Depression's Disguises

Past the age of 40, forgetfulness is so common as to be unremarkable. When Dr Karen Bolla, psychiatrist at Johns Hopkins University, Baltimore, interviewed a random sample of 200 healthy adults about the nature of their forgetfulness, 'names' came way out in front, following in descending order of frequency by 'recalling phone numbers', 'where things have been placed', all the way down to 'losing the thread of conversation'. To minimise the consequences of these memory lapses, most of those interviewed resorted to the usual ploys of writing notes to themselves and keeping objects in the same place so they would know where to find them. But in general, they were less concerned by their forgetfulness than by the more obvious physical signs of ageing, such as wrinkles and grey hair.

It is a different matter when the memory suddenly seems to get worse. 'I would sit in front of a book, turning the pages, but I was not really taking in what I was reading,' recalls a retired university lecturer Dr Rob Boyle, suspecting that his mind was 'going'. He persuaded his family doctor to send him to a memory clinic at the local hospital where he had the usual panoply of tests, only to be told his memory was 'average' for his age and that the reason he thought his mind was 'going' was because he was depressed. This, apparently, is quite usual. Dr Andrew Barker of St Martin's Hospital, Bath, has described the results of a study of patients who had referred themselves to a memory clinic with a similar number of 'normal' controls. 'The self-referred patients complained of a greater decline in memory in the recent past and were distressed by the perceived deterioration,' but, paradoxically, they scored higher on their IQ tests and there was no objective evidence of memory decline. As with Dr Boyle, however, they are much more likely to be suffering from a mild neurotic illness, such as anxiety or depression.

The influence of the psyche on memory is even more pronounced in those with a form of severe depression known as pseudo-dementia, the symptoms of which can be difficult to distinguish from a 'true' dementing illness. It is, however, crucial that the distinction is made because pseudo-dementia is curable with anti-depressant drugs, or ECT. In a review of 50 cases a decade ago, Charles Wells, Professor of Psychiatry at Vanderbilt University, Tennessee, noted that, as with 'true' dementia, such patients often appear disoriented in time and place, have difficulty in following conversations and are unable to recall obvious facts like the names of family members. 'In the past, the diagnosis of pseudo-dementia has been made usually after the unanticipated recovery of someone who had previously been diagnosed as being demented,' Professor Wells observed. He went on to show how the two conditions could, in fact, be separated out by the manner in which questions were answered.

The most important distinguishing feature is that the 'truly' demented will try to conceal their intellectual deficit, while the pseudo-demented are indifferent. When asked 'Who is the Prime Minister' the former group will say: 'By the time you reach my age, you have seen so many come and go, you don't take any interest any more', while the pseudo-demented are more likely to respond with 'Don't know and don't care.' Those with pseudo-dementia tend to emphasise their disability, making little effort to perform even simple tasks and professing an equal loss of memory for the recent and distant past. Pseudo-dementia is thus a burlesque or caricature of true dementia, but none the less can be readily mistaken for it.

Professor Brice Pitt, of London's Hammersmith Hospital, was asked to see a 70-year-old 'who had waited on his demanding, asthmatic wife since his retirement but had become unwilling to do so any more. He ignored any questions and his few answers were brief and long-delayed.' A year earlier he had been diagnosed as suffering from a dementing illness, but as his condition had not noticeably worsened, Professor Brice Pitt made a tentative diagnosis of pseudo-dementia and advised treatment with ECT. Following this he became 'cheerful, active, alert, sociable, helpful – in fact, his old self,' the professor reports. It is inevitable that intellectual function, and particularly memory, will deteriorate with the passage of years. Indeed, in those lucky enough to reach 90, the brain will have shrunk in size by a fifth and will have lost three thousand million neurons. Nevertheless, this still leaves 12,000 million neurons firing away – and true dementia affects only a small minority of about ten per cent. It is all the more important, then, that treatable forms of memory loss, whether merely perceived or actual, should be identified and dealt with vigorously.

The Closed World of Autism

Of all the bogus theories peddled by psychoanalysts this century, there is none more pernicious than that which sought to explain childhood autism by blaming the 'refrigerator' mother. The autistic child has many complex psychological deficits, but psychoanalysts focused their attention on one in particular – their solitariness. They neither seek out nor reciprocate love and affection: they gaze, not into their mother's eyes, but into the middle distance. They seem unaware of the existence of others, have no social play and make no friends. They are alone, surrounded by an impenetrable wall. Typically, the mother of such a child, according to the famous psychoanalyst Beata Rank, 'gives the impression of being intelligent and well-adjusted, but close investigation reveals her to be narcissistic and immature. The sunshine radiated by the spontaneous, tenderly devoted mother is missing. The child grows up in an orderly scientific atmosphere where routine and dietary prescriptions prevail. To survive in such an atmosphere, the child "retreats" not only from the dangerous mother, but the whole world as well, into another world of fantasy so repetitious, so remote from our feelings and experiences that he appears to us odd, bizarre and dull, intellectually and emotionally.'

The last sentence betrays a certain unease, as if Dr Rank is worried that perhaps there might be more to autism than can be sustained by her specious theorising. As the mother was held primarily responsible for her offspring's problems, then clearly she needed psychoanalysis. And many did, indeed, submit themselves to lengthy, expensive, futile therapy, which compounded their misery and pauperised them at the same time. As the mother of one autistic child, Frances Eberhard, described it: 'I alternated between being overwhelmed with guilt and feeling resentful at being treated like someone who could not face an unpleasant truth. My self-confidence dwindled away and I found myself less and less able to cope with the problems every day brought.'

When eventually Professor Michael Rutter of London's Maudsley Hospital, tested the 'refrigerator' theory by comparing the characteristics of the parents of 19 autistic children with the parents of a similar number of children with simple learning defects he found the following: there was no difference in the incidence of parental psychiatric disease or family stress; no difference in the obsessionality or warmth; no difference in emotional demonstrativeness and responsiveness; and no difference in parental sociability and qualities of friendship. The 'refrigerator theory' was a load of baloney.

The injurious myths of the psychoanalysts were always bitterly opposed by a minority of serious psychologists who have attempted to answer the many complex problems surrounding autism. Autistic children have damaged brains, but the precise site of the damage is not evident even on the most sophisticated of brain scanners. Therein lies a crucial problem: how does one define autism and distinguish it from other types of childhood psychological problems?

Painstaking work over many years has established that autistic children have a triad of impairments. There is the problem of socialisation, already mentioned, but also one of communication – they are unable to initiate or sustain conversation, do not smile or use other facial gestures. And there is a profound lack of imagination; they are unable to pretend or play but are obsessed instead with facts such as timetables and bus routes.

Trying to find a common link between these very disparate intellectual and social deficits proved elusive until very recently when a series of psychological experiments revealed that autistic children cannot understand the meaning implicit in people's speech or actions – as illustrated by the boy who, in response to the request, 'Can you pass the salt', replies in all earnestness, 'Yes.' As virtually every word that is spoken and all our gestures have implicit meanings, the everyday world is simply incomprehensible to the autistic child who is lost, frightened and perplexed in a foreign land, the same deficit explains their impoverished intellectual and emotional lives: they are unable to think about their own thoughts.

Paradoxically, the plight of these sad children provides an insight into the nature of the highest and most subtle level of mental functioning. There must be a discreet part of the brain that gives us the ability to read the minds of those around us, and it is this that is damaged in autism. Curiously, in some this deficit seems to allow space for the extraordinary development of specific talents – the savant phenomenon – usually concerned with numbers or drawing. There can be no cure for autism because it is not possible to replace what is missing. But the patient and remorseless love and attention of those who look after autistic children can help them to make the most of their lives. The contrast with the 'solution' offered by psychoanalysis could not be more damning.

The Painful Thinness of Anorexia

Teenage rebelliousness which, God knows, is difficult enough to live with, seems to be taken to its limits in the perverse self-destruction of anorexia nervosa. There is a bland indifference to personal self-interest, secretiveness, dishonesty and a tyrannical egotism. Admonitions or entreaties to eat more are greeted with outbursts of hysterical aggression which shatter the calm of domestic life. The love and hope invested over many years is reduced to ashes. All this is compounded because, as with so many psychological illnesses, the parents themselves may be blamed for their daughter's condition. Thus, it is said, a specific pattern of relationships within a family predisposes to anorexia – 'enmeshment, over-protection, rigidity and lack of conflict resolution.' It is alleged that, as a child, the anorexic was denied 'a sense of identity', and 'the relentless pursuit of thinness is an attempt to re-establish control over her life and those around her.' Needless to say, it has never convincingly been shown that the dynamics of families with a daughter with anorexia are any different from those with normal adolescents.

So what does cause anorexia? It is more than just a pathological weight phobia, because virtually all teenage girls at some time or another are concerned about their weight and embark on diets, but only a very small minority go on to develop anorexia. Britain's leading authority, Professor Anthony Crisp, maintains that the massive loss of weight, back to pre-pubertal levels, along with the inevitable cessation of monthly periods, provides an escape hatch for teenage girls from the emotional problems of adolescence. It is, in essence, a regression to childhood. 'The anorexic regresses into a restricted, simpler existence and experiences a renewed control over her destiny and renewed experience of safety.'

This concept provides the theoretical rationale of treatment which requires that as a first step, 're-feeding' takes place, usually in hospital, up to a target weight at which menstruation returns. Not until the patient once again inhabits a mature feminine body can there be any hope of a successful psychotherapeutic exploration and resolution of the illness. This approach certainly seems to be effective. In Professor Crips's experience, 70 per cent become 'much better; many still worry about their shape, but not to the same degree as before and probably in a way typical of many women who have never had the condition.'

None the less, anorexia is a bewildering illness and there is growing support for the alternative proposition that, as with depression or schizophrenia, it has an organic basis in an abnormality of the pathways of the brain. What is, after all, a very common practice – dieting in order to lose weight – becomes transformed into a pathological neurosis. Dr Janet Treasure, of the Institute of Psychiatry at the Maudsley Hospital, argues in the journal *Psychological Medicine* that weight loss in susceptible young women may adversely affect the centre in the brain that controls appetite and the secretion of the sex hormones. The common link is the neurotransmitter 5 Hydroxytryptamine (5HT), which is important in controlling appetite, sexual functioning, mediating the effects of stress and certain types of obsessional perfectionist behaviour. In general, anorexia has proved impervious to pharmaceutical therapies, although Dr Harry Gwirtsman, of the US National Institute of Mental Health, has described how the drug Prozac 'diminished the intensity of obsessional thoughts about food and weight' in six patients with chronic anorexia.

Although anorexia is usually perceived as a 'modern' disease, it closely resembles the fasting and asceticism practised in medieval European convents. Nowhere was this combination of spirituality and physical self-denial better expressed than in the cult of St Wilgefortis – the bearded female saint. St Wilgefortis was the seventh daughter of the King of Portugal, who wished to marry her off to the Saracen king of Sicily. She was less than keen and sought divine help to avoid the union. She became ascetic, overcame her appetite and 'begged the Lord to deprive her of her beauty'. God granted her request by causing her to develop a hairy body and grow a beard. The King of Sicily withdrew his suit and Wilgefortis's father, in an uncontrolled rage, had her crucified. Increased hairiness is a feature of anorexia and is thought to be part of the general endocrine abnormalities that follow weight loss and cessation of periods. In England, St Wilgefortis was seen as a woman who had successfully resisted both her father and potential husband under extraordinary pressure. A statue was erected in her honour in Billingsgate and became a shrine for women who wished to rid themselves of difficult, troublesome or wayward husbands.

Taking Hypochondria Seriously

The futility of trying to treat those afflicted with hypochondria is illustrated by the man who went to casualty complaining that a frog was hopping around in his stomach. 'Appearing to accept his diagnosis,' Dr Walter Alvarez, an American physician recalls in a medical journal, 'a fellow doctor and I gave him an emetic to make him sick, and as he was retching, we dropped a small frog into the bowl. The fellow was delighted, but was back the next day, saying there were now dozens of little frogs hopping about inside him.' Reflecting on this experience, Dr Alvarez urges his fellow doctors to 'be kind to hypochondriacs but get rid of them as quickly as possible, because the time they take up is spent to no good purpose.'

It is, however, quite difficult to 'get rid' of hypochondriacal patients, because they keep coming back, although some temporary respite can be obtained by referring them for specialist opinion. The consequences of such buck-passing emerge in a study of the illness careers of thirty-three hypochondriacs, conducted by Dr Christopher Bass, of Oxford's John Radcliffe Infirmary. All 'have been repeatedly investigated for their symptoms', and even though they had no physical illness, two-thirds were being treated for spurious disorders, most commonly 'asthma' and 'angina', and a similar proportion were receiving invalidity benefit on the grounds that they were unfit to work.

Dr Bass describes a typical case. 'A fifty-four-year-old woman who spent most of her time sitting in one room, where her symptoms were aggravated by disturbances in the environment, like the telephone ringing and vibrations from traffic.' Over the past twenty years she had 'attended at least twelve hospitals, often seeing specialists at different hospitals concurrently'. Her symptoms have included abdominal pain, chest pain, shortness of breath, and much else besides. During investigation of these she has undergone endless tests, including six barium meals, four gastroscopies, three barium enemas, three CT scans of the head, two CT abdominal scans and five spinal X-rays. Despite all the medical attention she has received over the years, Dr Bass reports that this lady 'does not trust doctors, claiming they have wrecked her life' – and about this at least she is absolutely right. Indeed, paradoxically, she could even be seen as a victim of medical negligence in that her underlying problem – hypochondriasis – has never been properly diagnosed.

This idea that hypochondria might, after all, be treatable, is quite new, and comes from the understanding that it may be the expression of several different forms of psychological disturbance.

Many hypochondriacs are what is known as 'chronic somatisers', who express their distress in the idiom of physical complaints – although their ailments might be imaginary, their symptoms are not. Virtually any part of the body can be a source of imaginary terrors. Muscle tension in the back of the skull causes headache, readily misinterpreted as being due to brain tumour: worry about the significance of palpitations induces a quite typical form of chest pain just above the left nipple, readily misinterpreted as heart attack.

In the second form of hypochondriasis the imaginary terror is fixated on one disease. Syphilis was most feared in the eighteenth century, leading one doctor to write: 'I cannot be persuaded I am not Pox'd. The losing of my Nose, my Palate, my Eyes possess my fancy for hours together. The horrors of this strike me with such unspeakable Pangs of Grief as no Torture could ever give.' Nowadays, the feared disease is more likely to be cancer or AIDS, and a manifestation of the sort of profound inexplicable fears that are more recognisable as phobias. Lastly, it may be a sophisticated form of malingering. The prospect of a lifetime of drudgery and menial jobs can be avoided by taking refuge in poorly defined illnesses that doctors can never accurately diagnose, but which does not seem to prevent them from signing the invalidity benefit form every thirteen weeks.

Leaving aside the malingerers, some of the other forms of

hypochondriasis are amenable to treatment: psychotherapy can provide chronic somatisers with insight into the cause of their symptoms: depression can be treated with anti-depressants; while 'phobic' hypochondriacs may improve with the drug fluoxetine. For some hypochondriacs, however, relief may only come when they do finally get a definitive disease. 'Ever since I have been ill,' wrote Alice James, sister of the novelist Henry, twenty-four years after her initial bout of hypochondria, 'I have longed and longed for some palpable disease, but must struggle alone under a mass of subjective sensations'. When she did get cancer, she expressed 'enormous relief at this uncompromising verdict'.

10

Men

Prostate Problems

In 1963 Harold Macmillan, certain that his prostatic symptoms heralded the end ('I'm finished, I'll probably die,' he confided to his press secretary Harold Evans), resigned in favour of Alec Douglas-Home. The fortunes of the Tory party collapsed and Britain entered a new political era with the advent of Harold Wilson's Labour premiership. Macmillan's gloomy prognostications were not fulfilled. He underwent an operation and soldiered on for another twenty-three years without any further trouble from that department.

The notoriety of the prostate, and what makes it so popular a conversation topic among men of a certain age, is less to do with the nuisance it causes by obstructing the free flow of urine than with the strong rumour that surgical treatment, though very successful, signals the end of a man's sex life. This was well caught in a conversation I overheard between two kilted Scotsmen in a public lavatory. While standing at the urinal and waiting for something to happen (a classic early symptom of prostatic obstruction), they discussed several disadvantages of having an enlarged prostate. The general conclusion seemed to be that things had to be pretty dire before voluntarily submitting to the surgeon's knife. As one of them said, 'I'm nae ready for the chop yet.'

There is, it must be said, a basis for this apprehension. The definitive treatment for prostatic obstruction is a transurethral resection, or TUR. The prostate, which in youth merely encircles the urethra, grows slowly inwards to obstruct the passage of urine. By passing a cystoscope, a urologist can remove the obstructing part of the gland as if he were coring an apple. The results are excellent, with three-quarters of patients finding complete relief from their symptoms. The main fear of those advised to have a TUR is that 'coring the apple' would damage the delicate apparatus of male sexual function. But as the nerves controlling erection, the *nervi erigentes*, run on the outside of the prostate, they are unlikely to be damaged. Many urological surgeons suspect that the erectile impotence complained of by men after the operation is essentially psychological – a reaction to having been 'tampered with'. Recently, doctors in Israel seem to have confirmed this by showing quite clearly that, if the operation is explained in advance, the incidence of erectile impotence falls markedly.

Many more patients – in fact, about three out of four – have a quite different problem. At the crucial moment of orgasm, muscles around the neck of the bladder contract, forcing semen outwards down the urethra. These muscles may be rendered incompetent by a TUR and, as a result, the semen shoots back into the bladder. This is retrograde ejaculation or a 'dry orgasm'. Although this might seem like no big deal, clearly a TUR does alter the character of orgasm – and, for some, diminishes the pleasure to be derived from it. Although rumours of sexual debility following TUR are exaggerated, they have generated an intense search in recent years for alternative treatments which would leave sexual function completely untouched.

There appear to be three main options. The first is to shrink the prostate by heat. A probe is inserted into the rectum, aimed at the prostate, which is then toasted for an hour at a temperature of 44° C. A second possibility is the drug prazosin, which relaxes the muscles around the prostate, thus partially relieving any obstruction. Then there is fenasteride, also known as proscar. This ingenious drug blocks the hormone dihydrotestosterone, which controls growth of the prostate. It works in the way expected – the prostate shrinking down by a quarter and urinary flow rates increasing – but the precise degree of relief of symptoms is debatable. The general impression from all these treatments is that, although they do not interfere with sexual function and may ameliorate the symptoms of urinary obstruction, they seem considerably less effective than a TUR in actually relieving prostatic symptoms.

The Case Against Circumcision

Circumcision is one of several routinely recommended and apparently quite straightforward types of surgery that can have unanticipated adverse consequences. Two or three times a year concerned mothers ask me to inspect their son's penis (or twinkle, winkler, hosepipe, nudger, little man and a host of other euphemisms), whose foreskin is tight and cannot be retracted, and for which the obvious treatment is circumcision. My opinion, however, has changed radically since reading an impassioned article by a Dr John Warren in the *British Medical Journal*, in which he claimed that 'the foreskin is as important to the penis, as the eyelid to the eye'. The effect of his being circumcised when young, he argued, was that 'throughout childhood and into adult life, the tip of the penis was always uncomfortable, especially when rubbed against clothing'. Once married, he had observed 'remarkably little sensitivity in that region whose skin seemed to thicken with advancing years'. To substantiate his argument that circumcision is unnecessary, Dr Warren cited several papers that show, first of all, that the 'non-retractile' foreskin became 'retractile' in most boys by mid-adolescence and, secondly, that with the help of a local anaesthetic cream the adhesions around the foreskin could be gently separated off, thus avoiding the need for an operation.

There are, of course, compelling religious reasons why some people might wish their sons to be circumcised, but the medical justification is virtually non-existent. None the less, family doctors continue to recommend the operation, and surgeons to perform it, for no better reason than that the 'obvious solution' to a tight foreskin is that it should be removed. I would still be slightly sceptical about the adverse consequences of circumcision were it not that Dr Warren also described the effect of a manoeuvre by which the foreskin can be restored. This entails stretching the penile skin forward as far as it will go, and then strapping it in position with sticky tape to which a ball-bearing is attached, exerting a continuous gravitational pull. After a couple of months, the stretched skin forms a substitute foreskin and, as a result, Dr Warren has found that 'the tip of the penis becomes softer and steadily more sensitive, intercourse becomes much easier, with a great increase in sexual enjoyment'. This increase in the sensitivity described by Dr Warren offers quite convincing proof that the foreskin has an important function. In retrospect, it seems remarkable that doctors should have thought for so long that it is expendable.

The Male Menopause – Myth or Reality?

The author, Gail Sheehy, became interested in the subject of the male menopause while researching her enormously successful book on the female menopause – *The Silent Passage*. Miss Sheehy discovered that many of the women she interviewed were equally concerned about their husbands' faltering virility. This led her to seek the opinion of dozens of experts, psychologists and ordinary men and women, from which she has distilled the essence of the sexual history of modern man. It starts, after puberty, with a period of *unlimited potency*, moves on to the *trajectory from twenty to forty* 'culminating in full sexual mastery', then on to the *faltering fifties* when men 'find a more tender-feeling side that needs to be expressed', and ultimately the *sixties potency crisis*, when a man must 'use it or lose it'. Along the way, having performed like automata for years, men find they are no longer sexually aroused, so they rush off to find new outlets, in adultery or a second wife.

But that is not really the interesting bit, because now, thanks to science, we have an explanation for faltering male virility, and indeed a cure. The cause is the 'male menopause' and the treatment (as with Hormone Replacement Therapy in women) is the male sex hormone testosterone, says Dr Malcolm Carruthers, the director of The Hormonal Health Care Centre in London. Dr Carruthers is virtually unique in Britain for expounding this view, which makes him a rather controversial figure; but there is no doubt he is on to something. If anecdotal reports are to be believed, testosterone treatment certainly boosts libido and much else besides. But he has come in for his fair share of criticism. Gail Sheehy quotes an unnamed American expert as saying: 'He's full of crap.' A professor of psychiatry at Southampton University, Chris Thompson, has commented: 'Treating something called the male menopause with such a powerful hormone fills me with horror.'

So what is going on? The male menopause, or 'viropause' as Dr Carruthers calls it, does not exist as a measurable phenomenon. There is no sudden fall-off in the level of testosterone in the same way that happens with oestrogen levels in women going through their menopause. There is, it is true, a steady decline in testosterone from the fifties onwards, and as Dr Carruthers argues, it is possible in addition that the tissues of the body become less sensitive to the hormone as we get older. The male menopause is thus a relative rather than an absolute phenomenon, which according to Dr Carruthers, causes fatigue, depression, irritability and loss of libido.

Such symptoms could equally be psychological in origin, brought on by overwork or stress, but in the absence of a demonstrable decline in testosterone levels, it is impossible to tell which. Dr Carruthers's empirical approach is to give testosterone and see what happens. In the case of a hereditary peer in his sixties, Miss Sheehy reports: 'I noted a huge improvement in attitude and energy; just generally looking forward to life more.' This is in line with the findings of Professor R. D. Greenblatt of the Department of Endocrinology at the University of Georgia, who found that testosterone produced 'fair to excellent results in two-thirds of patients, with amelioration of fatigue and insomnia, and enhancement of general well-being.'

This does not prove the existence of the male menopause. Even if the peer's symptoms were psychological in origin, they might still have been helped by a testosterone tonic, in the same way that anabolic steroids can improve the performance of athletes. Dr Carruther's treatment is contentious for obvious reasons. If his testosterone therapy is curing a genuine deficiency, albeit a relative one, then that would be medically respectable. But if it is just hormonal tonic, then it is ethically highly dubious. Readers might well think: 'If it works, why not try it?' – which is fair enough, though they should realise there is a rather large fly in the ointment which Dr Carruthers accepts – that, theoretically, testosterone replacement therapy can increase the risk of prostate cancer. He asserts that a thorough screening of prospective patients can anticipate such a risk, but regrettably this is still not clear – thus justifying the medical profession's continued scepticism about his 'hormonal revolution'.

Curing Impotence with Modern Aphrodisiacs

Recently, I have received several letters from older male readers all touching on the same theme, which can be summarised in the words of one correspondent: 'As a pensioner who is not so virile as when I first married, I still feel the need to make love to my wife, but regrettably can't always rise to the occasion.' This is a tricky area in which to offer advice, but I'm encouraged to do so, having attended an interesting international conference of urologists in Bruges. In essence, there has been a major shift in the perception of male sexual problems over the past few years away from the belief that they are 'mostly' pyschological, for which the appropriate treatment will be some form of counselling or sex therapy.

Rather, it now appears that they are 'mostly' physical, especially in the older age group, and therefore amenable to a variety of remedies collectively known as 'the new aphrodisiacs'. The first, and very important, 'physical' cause of impotence is the drugs commonly prescribed for medical conditions, such as raised blood pressure. The two main culprits are bendrofluazide and the beta-blocker propranolol. There are plenty of alternative drugs available for the treatment of hypertension and these are clearly preferable. Next, albeit quite rarely, the cause of impotence may be a low level of the male sex hormone testosterone, for which testosterone pills rapidly restore first the libido and then physical performance. There has been some controversy over whether men whose testosterone levels fall within the normal range may also be helped by testosterone pills on the grounds that their tissues may, with age, have become less sensitive to the hormone and so could do with a boost. Testosterone pills will indeed improve the libido in everyone, and sexual performance may improve as a consequence, but in general their use is best confined to those with clear evidence of hormone deficiency.

Next comes the exciting bit – the realisation that for most men 'the failure to rise to the occasion' is due to an impairment of the action of the nerves that stimulate the blood flow into the member, producing an erection. It is possible to determine if this is the problem by injecting a small dose of a drug called 'Caverjet' into the base of the penis which, in 70 per cent of men, will produce an erection that lasts for up to an hour. Patients can then be trained to give the injection themselves and, according to a recent study in men over the age of 65, this permits 'satisfactory' sexual intercourse in two-thirds. Intriguingly, some find that, having used the drug three or four times, they start having normal erections again. The probable explanation in such cases is that their impotence is indeed partly 'psychological' – due to a fear of failure – and which is improved by the self-confidence that comes from resuming normal sexual relations.

Those whose impotence is cured by caverjet are also likely to be helped by two other drugs. The first is Yohimbine – an ancient African aphrodisiac, which may lead to a resumption of sexual activity in a third of those who take it. This drug is not widely available in Britain, but can be obtained on either private or NHS prescription from the chemists John Bell and Croyden in London. The second drug is an anti-depressant called trazodone. This was discovered to cause erections by a psychiatrist treating himself for depression who, 'when he desired sexual intercourse would take a single dose of 250 milligrams, which reliably induced an erection within four hours that lasted 90 minutes or more.' Trazodone does not work for all, nor does it have a product licence in Britain for the treatment of impotence, but it can still be prescribed for this purpose at the doctor's discretion. It should, however, only be taken under medical supervision as it can cause 'priapism', a prolonged painful erection. To supplement these medical treatments, consultant urologist Christine Evans advises the purchase of a penile ring which snaps around the base of the penis and which can 'bolster a turgid erection'. She also says that vacuum devices can help 70 per cent of those who are unwilling or unable to use the injection treatment.

Some older men whose erectile potency is unimpaired none the less find their sexual relations compromised by premature ejaculation. This, too may have a physical cause and often improves with a small dose of the anti-depressant amitryptyline, one of whose side effects is to delay orgasm. Finally, the most important advice for my correspondents is that they should not be diverted into the arms of counsellors or sex therapists, but rather obtain a referral to a consultant urologist – most of whom, I am sure, are only too willing to help.

The Joys of Changing Sex

A young male university student dropped into the surgery and asked if I could give him a course of feminising oestrogen injections to promote breast development. I must have looked a bit quizzical because he promptly whipped a letter out of his pocket from a consultant psychiatrist which read: 'Mr X is a clear case of gender dysphoria. I suggest that he should have oestrogen injections for the next two years, after which he will be considered for gender re-assignment surgery.'

I was rather taken aback by the tone of this letter, which seemed a bit too straightforward and matter-of-fact, as if giving oestrogen to facilitate a sex change was little different from treating an ingrown toenail. The few transsexuals I have come across in the past have not struck me as being very happy people. They have tended to be histrionic and demanding, obsessed with the question of their sexual identity to the exclusion of everything else.

My views were also coloured by the events ten years ago at the only hospital in the country to perform sex-change operations on the NHS – the Charing Cross – where the consultant surgeon, Mr Grant Williams, publicly stated that he would no longer continue to be involved as so many patients were apparently dissatisfied with their operations. Indeed, he had described gender re-assignment surgery as 'right at the bottom of the list of medical priorities'.

Reflecting on this past experience, I told my young patient that, in theory, I would be pleased to satisfy his request, but would first like to know a bit more about himself and his views on the current status of sex-change operations. He turned out to be immensely well informed: It was important to distinguish, he told me, between genuine transsexuals and the rest. The desire to change sex may be a feature of schizophrenia or personality disorder and is not unusual in certain types of sexual fetishism. But leaving these aside, there remained the true transsexuals, those who have, for as long as they can remember, felt misplaced in their biological sexual roles. In my patient's case, it was quite simple – when young he had always wanted to be a girl. 'I would lie in bed and pray to God, promising I would do anything if he would just perform a miracle for me some day and make me into a girl,' he told me. Surreptitiously, he would try on his sister's clothes and yearned for the presents she got a Christmas. Once past puberty, he realised he was attracted to other men but his yearnings were not homosexual because 'I did not see myself as a man.'

He soon realised that he must be a transsexual, and that sooner or later he must change his sex. 'I didn't resent the fact that nature seemed to have played a trick on me; I just realised it would have to be put right.' I was completely convinced by his story, which raises intriguing questions about the biological determining of our sexuality. It seems there must be a part of the brain that has complete control over all aspects of our sexual identity. Genetically, my patient was a male; as a foetus in his mother's womb, his developing brain had been exposed to male hormones. He had been brought up as a male, but his brain was basically female, and so he would only find security and fulfilment within a female body.

Why, then, do sex-change operations have such a tacky reputation, and why are so many apparently dissatisfied with the result? There seem to be two explanations. First, most such operations are done privately, which meant that, in the Sixties and Seventies, anybody who had the money could have it done. Needless to say, this included many whose transsexualism was a manifestation of mental illness or personality disorder, for whom the operation was entirely inappropriate. Secondly the technique and scope of these operations were not as good, so male-to-female transsexuals were only partly feminised and thus unhappy in their newly adopted sex role. Nowadays, the aesthetic results are said to be 'excellent', with supplementary operations to soften the facial features, contour the body and reduce the prominence of the Adam's apple so the patient looks truly feminine. Consequently, the numbers satisfied with the operation are now much higher: about 90 per cent in a recent study of 150 Dutch transsexuals.

11

Women

Chlamydia Calamities

Doctors may be, and often are, critical of their colleagues in private, but it is unusual, and almost ill-mannered, to express such sentiments publicly. So, when Malcolm Pearce, a consultant at St George's Hospital, London, observed in the *British Medical Journal* that a common gynaecological complaint was treated 'badly' and that his fellow gynaecologists needed 'to radically change their management' of the condition, his criticisms were likely to be well-founded. The gynaecological complaint is pelvic inflammatory disease, usually shortened to PID, an infection of the upper genital tract in women – the womb and Fallopian tubes – by a variety of organisms, but particularly *Chlamydia trachomatis*. PID is associated with a one-in-six chance of infertility, a sevenfold increase in the risk of ectopic pregnancy, a one-in-four chance of chronic pelvic pain, a two-in-four chance of pain on intercourse and a four-in-five chance of menstrual disturbances. 'These complications', writes Mr Pearce, 'can be prevented by early diagnosis and treatment.' But this, it seems, is exactly what doctors are failing to do.

Dr Pippa Oakeshott, of St George's Hospital medical school, describes the case of a 28-year-old woman with pelvic pain of three months' duration who was referred by her general practitioner to gynaecological out-patients. She was certainly thoroughly investigated. The outer surfaces of her pelvic organs were inspected by laparoscopy, her Fallopian tubes were X-rayed, the inner surface of her womb was scraped with a D and C, and her cervix was biopsied. All were reported as 'normal'. Almost a year later she returned to her GP with exactly the same symptoms and on this occasion a swab was taken to test for chlamydia infection. This was positive, the patient and her partner were successfully treated with antibiotics and the pelvic discomfort cured. From this it would seem that her symptoms were caused by chlamydia, despite the absence of signs of acute infection at laparoscopy the previous year. Indeed, this presents an important obstacle to the control of chlamydia infection. The organism can be present in the genital tract without causing symptoms. On the other hand, it can cause the symptoms of PID without overt signs of pelvic inflammation. From this it is clear that the prevention and treatment of PID is not straightforward.

Chlamydia is the commonest sexually transmitted organism in the Western world. It accounts for more than half the cases of 'non-specific urethritis' or NSU in men, while routine investigations identify the organism in the vagina of ten per cent of young women – in whom it is usually clinically silent. To cause PID, the chlamydia organism has to move from the vagina up into the womb and Fallopian tubes by traversing the natural barrier to the passage of infectious organisms – the cervix. This can occur in two ways. The commonest is sexual intercourse, when bacteria can ascend the genital tract on the back of spermatozoa, a process facilitated by the uterine contractions that accompany orgasm. Secondly, chlamydia can gain access to the upper genital tract to cause PID as part of a gynaecological procedure during which the cervix is dilated, as for example with the insertion of an IUD, or termination of pregnancy.

This latter cause of PID is theoretically preventable. In Edinburgh, Dr Donald Scott, consultant in genito-urinary medicine, has ensured that all women seeking an abortion are tested for chlamydia. Those found to be positive are then treated with the antibiotic azithromycin, which is effective as a single dose. To prevent further reinfection the male partner is also asked to attend his clinic, and he too is treated if found to be positive. The much greater problem of PID after sexual intercourse is less amenable to such measures. 'Ideally, all young women should be offered screening,' says Dr Oakeshott, but when she conducted a personal survey of twenty London practices responsible for the care of 140,000 patients, she found only four tested their patients for chlamydia.

The only alternative then, for women who wish to avoid PID, is to visit a sexually transmitted diseases clinic, perhaps once every two years. These are the only places in the NHS where chlamydia testing is done routinely. This might seem a drastic step, but at the moment there is no other option. 'Everyone needs to be much more aware of the potential seriousness of

PID,' says Dr Oakeshott. 'It is not just the promiscuous that are at risk, nice girls get chlamydia as well.' The medical profession's indifference to the problems posed by chlamydia is rather baffling, especially in view of its long-term serious complications of infertility and ectopic pregnancy. Malcolm Pearce's challenge to his colleagues to 'radically change their management' would seem to be as timely as ever.

Understanding Endometriosis

In this age of heightened health consciousness, it is hard to believe that a chronic illness which can ruin the personal, sexual and working lives of young women may be inadequately treated or even go undiagnosed for years. The disease is called endometriosis, an acute inflammatory condition affecting the pelvic organs: the ovaries, uterus, bladder, colon and small bowel. The endometrium is the layer of cells lining the uterus which provides shelter and nutrients to the newly fertilised ovum, and which is shed every month at menstruation. From the beginning of the monthly cycle, glands are formed, blood vessels sprout, supporting fibrous tissue is laid down, all under the influence of the female hormones. If fertilisation does not occur, the arteries go into spasm, the endometrial cells die and fall off the wall of the uterus, to be expelled.

In endometriosis, it is believed, some of these discarded cells, rather than passing out with the menstrual flow, reflex back up the Fallopian tubes and spill over into the pelvis. The following month, these displaced cells will be stimulated to proliferate just as if they were lining the womb, and at the end of the cycle they will atrophy and bleed. But the pelvis and the organs within it are not adapted to coping with these aggressive alien endometrial cells, and react as if they had been sprinkled with acid, becoming diffusely inflamed. This is experienced as deep pelvic pain, the jolting of the ovaries and uterus during sexual intercourse becomes exquisitely tender, while involvement of the bowel wall and bladder can make any call of nature a misery. Despite all this, a survey by the Endometriosis Society reports that the *average* delay in making a diagnosis was 6.8 years, and in a quarter of cases it took ten years.

How this can happen is best illustrated by the experience of Mary Wild, a woman in her late twenties. She first saw a gynaecologist at the age of 18 for severe period pains. He gave the impression she was wasting his time, told her there was 'nothing wrong' and advised her to eat more bran. Two years later her general practitioner misdiagnosed her condition as being due to gallstones, referred her to a surgeon who removed her appendix for suspected appendicitis. Soon after getting married, she again sought medical advice, this time for the pain she was experiencing during sexual intercourse. This was attributed to 'stress' and she ended up seeing a psychiatrist. By now, she says, her life had become 'a seriously unfunny farce'. Her husband resented being married to a woman with debilitating symptoms for which, despite repeated consultations, no cause could be found. 'I began wondering whether I might be imagining it,' she says. Finally, yet another gynaecologist looked inside her abdomen with a laparoscope with told her she was 'riddled with endometriosis', a condition she had never heard of. Her only chance of a cure, she was told, was a hysterectomy to which she consented 'so I could start rebuilding my relationship with my husband. I was desperate to preserve my self-esteem.' Regrettably, her symptoms recurred after the operation and a re-referral to the gynaecologist ended in tears as he told her: 'Let's face it, you are one big pain'. This catalogue of medical misfortune is almost a caricature of common prejudices about gynaecologists – that they can be supercilious, ignorant, prone to making hasty diagnoses and performing unnecessary surgery. Is this fair?

Eric Thomas, professor of gynaecology at Southampton University, says: 'There should be no difficulty in diagnosing endometriosis. Although there are many other causes of pelvic pain with which it may be confused – salpingitis (infection of the Fallopian tubes), irritable bowel syndrome, or dysmenorrhea (painful periods) – if the doctor listens to what the patient is saying, the symptoms alone should tell him what is going on.' The crucial clue likes in the cyclical pattern of the pelvic pain and tenderness on intercourse, which is most marked just before and during the monthly periods when the stimulated endometrial tissue in the pelvis starts to break down and bleed. But Professor Thomas acknowledges that there are genuine ambiguities. Thus, some women having a laparoscopy for, say, sterilisation will have evidence of widespread endometriosis but no symptoms, while others with debilitating pain may have only a few small patches in the pelvis. Paradoxically, then, symptoms of pain and infertility may be falsely attributed to the disease.

Diagnostic questions aside, endometriosis is also a very difficult condition to treat. Drugs that suppress the female hormones will discourage the proliferation of endometrial cells but at the price of inducing menopausal type symptoms, causing weight gain and a general malaise. They are also, in effect, contraceptives, which for those who are finding it difficult to have children anyhow is clearly undesirable. A hysterectomy may provide the only method of controlling symptoms in extreme cases, but this drastic step is unacceptable for many women, especially as persisting patches of endometriosis may continue to cause pain after the operation.

This is most unsatisfactory and it demands almost heroic insight and understanding on the part of the endometriosis sufferer to realise there is not a ready solution, or that treatment may require sacrificing the natural instincts to have children. But similarly gynaecologists are unable to fulfil the demands to provide a cure. In such circumstances, the role of gynaecologists with a special interest in endometriosis is crucial. They will no more have a magic cure than any of their colleagues but their experience gives them an authority which permits the endometriosis sufferer to trust their judgement.

The Misfortunes of Miscarriage

Miscarriages are common. Every tenth pregnancy will end prematurely, usually within the first three months. Though doctors advise bed rest for the premonitory symptoms of pain and bleeding, it is with little hope of influencing the inevitable outcome. These things happen, and there may be some consolation in the fact that in a fair proportion of early miscarriages the foetus has some genetic or structural abnormality. Not all women are able to take such a phlegmatic view. Every miscarriage is a loss, a bereavement. When Dr Sharon Hamilton, of Glasgow's Royal Infirmary, asked women to describe their feelings, half said they cried a lot, felt guilty that the miscarriage might be their fault and worried about becoming pregnant again. When a first miscarriage is followed by a second and even a third, these psychological reactions are enormously exacerbated. As one woman described it: 'Nothing had prepared me for the despair, the emptiness of grieving . . . the sheer murderous anger. The casual attitude of the hospital, the blankness of my GP and the absence of any practical help confused me. Was I meant to behave as if nothing had ever happened?' In at least 80 per cent of cases there is no simple medical explanation for miscarriage. This is partly because so many factors are involved. The anatomical structure of the womb must be normal, with the cervix firmly closed. The lining of the womb has to be receptive to the fertilised egg and this, in turn, depends on the levels of the hormones progesterone and human chorionic gonadotrophin (HCG) in the first part of the menstrual cycle. The cells surrounding the fertilised egg must have the unique property of not being antigenic or the mother will reject it. The blood supply through the placenta must be adequate and increase as the foetus grows. Then, most mysterious of all, there must be some sort of hidden 'communication' between the mother's cells and those of her foetus, so that if it is abnormal it will be recognised and spontaneously aborted.

Over the years, obstetricians have attempted to prevent recurrent miscarriage, focusing on the physiological aspects of implantation. In the 1950s the hormone diethylstilboestrol (DES) was the treatment of choice and continued to be given for several years. It finally fell from favour when the female offspring of treated mothers were found to have an unusually high incidence of abnormalities and developed cancer of the vagina in their early twenties. Since then, progesterone and HCG have been advocated. There has been a vogue for 'cervical cerclage', where a stitch is placed through the cervix to keep it tight, thus, theoretically, preventing the premature expulsion of the foetus. A link between recurrent miscarriage and autoimmune disorders led to the discovery of an 'anticardiolipin antibody' which could be suppressed with a combination of aspirin and a low dose of steriods. Then, most arcanely of all, it was proposed that the immunological tolerance of the mother for the foetus could be enhanced by infusing her with white blood cells from the father.

Britain's leading specialist, Professor Gordon Stirratt, professor of obstetrics at Bristol University is unconvinced by evidence of the effectiveness of any of these treatments. 'The point is that 70 per cent of women who have recurrent miscarriages will eventually have a live birth, so it is almost impossible to show that any of these interventions makes a difference,' he says. 'The crucial question is whether any specific treatment has a better outcome than the caring and sympathetic approach all patients have a right to expect.' His own policy is to perform a few investigations, check the hormone levels, exclude possible infections and assess the competence of the cervix and only try to correct quite specific abnormalities. 'But most often "masterly inactivity" is the appropriate response,' he says.

This is not mere nihilism. The problem as Professor Stirratt sees it is that most obstetricians realise they are impotent to prevent recurrent miscarriages. They can try to play this down, in which case their reaction is readily interpreted as being unsympathetic. Alternatively, they can jump onto the latest therapeutic bandwagon. It would seem much better for doctors to acknowledge their ignorance, but make a firm committment to provide strong emotional support.

'Should I Have a Caesar?'

There are signs of revolt against the almost unchallengeable assumptions of the past decade in favour of the joys and benefits of natural childbirth. One of its great exponents, Sheila Kitzinger, was mocked in an article in *The Times* for claiming that the experience of labour was 'passionate, intense, thrilling and, for some, the nearest thing to overwhelming sexual excitement'. Not a bit of it, says journalist Mary Anne Sieghart, who was debilitated by the pain of her 12-hour ordeal. 'At the end, all I could feel was a sense of despairing relief . . . I was too exhausted even to turn round and look at my baby.' She accuses Sheila Kitzinger of betraying a generation of women with threats and blandishments in favour of natural birth: 'The threat that pain-killing drugs might harm the baby, the blandishment of an unforgettable quasi-spiritual high.' There is as little point in trying to get through labour without drugs, Mary Anne Sieghart concludes, as in banging one's head against a brick wall for 12 hours.

In the Seventies, the natural childbirth protagonists clearly had a point. Twenty years ago, when I dabbled in obstetrics, medical intervention was the rule. Rather than allowing women to go into labour naturally, they were booked into hospital on a specified date and I would spend the first hour of the day going from one bed to the next putting up a drip to 'start them off'. They then had to lie on their backs – no suggestion that they might adopt more physiological positions – and moaned and groaned with much recourse to pethidine and gas and air for however long it took for the baby to be delivered. Now, thanks in large measure to Ms Kitzinger *et al.*, such mindless intervention is no more, but, like all crusaders, they went too far by caricaturing any sort of medical assistance as wrong and unnatural. They ended up doing a disservice to women by deceiving them into thinking it was worthy, and even desirable, to suffer the excruciating agonies of labour.

Obstetricians are still accused of intervening too readily – as is shown by the continuing rise in the number of Caesarean sections performed. In Britain they now account for 12 per cent of all deliveries, and in the US an astonishing 25 per cent. The main reason for this trend, according to a recent survey of British obstetricians, is the fear of litigation and, in particular, of being sued for negligence if the baby is born with, for example, cerebral palsy. The indications for a Caesarean have widened to include breech pregnancies, protracted labour and for 'precious babies' who have been conceived with difficulty.

Interestingly, increasing numbers of women, obviously unimpressed by the arguments of the natural childbirth enthusiasts, are actually requesting to have a Caesarean. This almost certainly accounts for the much higher rate in women delivered privately, though presumably the obstetrician conspires with the patient by devising some pseudo-reason why it should be done. But the practice now seems to be spreading to the NHS. Recently, obstetricians at Leighton Hospital in Cheshire reported that 'patient demand' was now the third commonest reason for the procedure. Women requesting it had either had a very unpleasant first labour and no desire to repeat the experience, or, alternatively, had been so impressed by their previous hassle-free Caesareans that they wanted another. Paradoxically, this can be seen as a consequence of the success of the natural childbirth movement in asserting the autonomy of women to determine what sort of delivery they should have. As the obstetricians from Cheshire point out: 'Women are no longer passive recipients of care . . . they are more assertive, and demand to have a say in how they are looked after.' It is difficult to see why this should not extend to deliberately opting for a Caesarean to avoid the rigours of a natural delivery.

Birth and Your Bottom

The controversy between 'natural' and 'hi-tech' childbirth has subsided in recent years as obstetricians seem to have taken on board the criticism that they have been over-zealously interfering in a normal physiological process. Their current view would seem to be that having a baby should be as fulfilling an emotional experience as possible, with medical intervention limited to the judicious use of forceps or Caesarean section only in special circumstances. This all seems very sensible, were it not that in private a considerable number of obstetricians take a rather different line. Mr Raghdad Al-Mufti, an obstetrician at Queen Charlotte's Hospital, London, sent a questionnaire to nearly 300 of his colleagues asking what type of delivery they would personally favour if they, or their partners, were pregnant for the first time. Nearly a third of the female respondents said they would like to have their baby by Caesarean section, and this figure rose to two-thirds if the baby's estimated weight was more than 9 pounds. Similarly, about half of female obstetricians would wish to be delivered by Caesarean if they were expecting twins or their baby was in the breech position. These finds are really quite extraordinary. What is it that so concerns female obstetricians that their personal choice about the method of childbirth should be so at variance with the advice they offer to their patients? The answer, in a word, is their bottoms.

Vaginal delivery obviously traumatises the tissues, and any subsequent muscle laxity can be corrected with regular pelvic floor exercises. However, and this is the hidden secret of modern obstetrics, approximately one-third of women will also damage the anal sphincter and in 10 per cent this causes problems with continence. There is a loss of voluntary control over the passing of wind, which can occur unexpectedly and in socially embarrassing circumstances. In addition, the summons to open the bowels has to be acted on promptly if accidents are to be avoided. I had no idea these problems were so common, and to find out more I arranged a visit to St Marks Hospital, London, where more is known about the maladies of the rectum and anus than anywhere else in the world.

As he showed me the splendid new premises attached to Northwick Park Hospital in North London, the clinical director, Mr James Thomson, reminded me that civilised society depends on the proper functioning of the anus. This crucial part of the anatomy, although just over an inch long, is a masterpiece of intelligent design, with five quite separate mechanisms interacting together to preserve continence. It has, in addition, an extraordinary rich nerve supply to discriminate with complete accuracy between the presence of gas, liquid or stool in the rectum. Thus, we can pass wind discreetly about ten times a day without fear of embarrassment, and control our calls of nature in a socially acceptable manner.

It has been recognised for a long time that the function of the anus can be impaired by childbirth, but there has never been much interest in the problem because it was thought there was little to be done about it. Until very recently it was believed that the baby, as it descended through the birth canal, stretched and damaged the nerves in the pelvis, thus impairing the action of the circular muscles around the anal sphincter. This, however, has proved to be incorrect. A few years ago Michael Kamm, physician at St Marks, had the ingenious idea of visualising the sphincter muscles with an ultrasound machine and discovered, to his astonishment, that in more than 90 per cent of cases there was clear evidence of structural damage. The attitude to continence problems following childbirth immediately changed completely, because structural damage to a muscle – unlike damage to a nerve – can be treated by surgical repair. And then, as so often in medicine when some condition becomes treatable, doctors become much more aware of it. Thus, the hidden secret of obstetrics has finally come out of the closet, which is presumably why so many female obstetricians now favour Caesarean section.

Luckily, the success rate of sphincter repair is gratifyingly high, with restoration of continence in virtually all cases, although some women may still find they occasionally pass wind dramatically and unexpectedly. This issue has been neglected for so long that presumably there must be many thousands of women who have had no alternative other than to arrange their lives to minimise the inconvenience and social distress caused by anal incontinence. They, too, however, may benefit from surgery, and at the very least should ask their doctors to refer them to St Marks so the precise nature of their problem can be properly investigated. In a recent heartening study of a group of women, with an average age of 66 and 'an average duration of continence problems' of 17 years, surgery restored 'complete control' in precisely half and a considerable improvement of their symptoms in virtually all the rest.

Choosing Your Baby's Sex

There are more than enough problems in the world to be concerned about without getting bogged down in ethical pseudo-controversies. A classic example was the birth to Gillian and Neil Clark of a healthy baby girl – thanks, allegedly, to the sex selection techniques offered by Dr Peter Liu at his London Gender Clinic. The Tory MP Jerry Hayes hit out at 'a potentially dangerous perversion of nature'; the Shadow Health Secretary, David Blunkett, called for the banning of sex selection 'for social reasons'; and a spokesman for the saintly Cardinal Basil Hume commented: 'The birth was not consistent with the Catholic view of procreation.' These days, any birth of a much-wanted child to a happily married couple should be cause for celebration rather than condemnation. In theory, sex selection could, in addition, contribute to the nation's genetic stock. I have come across several attractive, intelligent couples with two or three children of the same sex who would willingly have another, if they could be sure it would be of the opposite sex.

I say 'in theory' because, desirable as sex selection might be for individual couples and, indeed, the nation, I doubt if it works as claimed – which also happens to be the opinion of most experts in reproductive physiology. As people should know, but many surprisingly do not, the sex of a child is determined by whether the ovum is fertilised by a sperm carrying the usual twenty-three chromosomes and the female sex X chromosome, or twenty-three chromosomes and the male sex Y chromosome. They are called X and Y because of their shape: the only physical difference between the two is that the Y chromosome is missing one arm's length of DNA, so the sperm carrying it is infinitesimally slightly less heavy.

Clearly, if sex selection is to work, it is necessary to separate the two types of sperm, and there must be some other distinguishing physical characteristic that allows this to be done. In 1979, an American doctor, Landrum Shettles, maintained in his book *Your Baby's Sex: Now You Can Choose* that the Y-bearing sperm swim faster and so, other things being equal, they should get to the ovum first and many more boys than girls would be born. But this is balanced, he claimed, by the fact that the X-bearing female sperm, though less speedy, are more resilient and so less likely to be destroyed by vaginal secretions, which are more acidic around the crucial time of ovulation.

It is thus theoretically possible to practise do-it-yourself sex selection. Couples wishing to have a girl should first douche the vagina with a diluted teaspoonful of acidic white vinegar and be sure to have sexual intercourse at the time of ovulation – which can be determined by a slight rise in body temperature or the presence of a clear, jelly-like vaginal discharge. For a boy, the vagina should be douched with a diluted alkaline solution of sodium bicarbonate, and sexual activity should occur either just before or just after ovulation. Dr Shettles subsequently proposed a further modification. Based on the observation that the lubrication associated with female orgasms tends to be alkaline, he suggested that only couples wishing to have a boy should try to achieve this pleasurable state. By all accounts, Dr Shettles sold a lot of books, presumably because, even if his method was completely valueless, half of all the couples following his advice would, by chance, end up with a child of the right sex.

The technique used by the London Gender Clinic also presupposes that the Y-bearing sperm swim faster and is based on a method developed by a Dr Ron Ericson, first reported in the journal *Nature* in 1973. This described how, if sperm were encouraged to swim through several layers of the protein albumen, the swifter Y-bearing sperm would win the race. The first batch would thus be more likely to result in a boy, while the second batch would produce a girl. Two years later, researchers from the Western General Hospital, Edinburgh, reported, also in *Nature*, that they were unable to confirm these findings. That should have been the end of it, but Dr Ericson, who firmly believes in his technique, has carried on and, last year, claimed a 76 per cent success rate in giving couples a child of the desired sex. His article in the journal *Fertility and Sterility* was followed, most unusually, by a note from the editor that 'Not everyone has been able to duplicate the results reported', which is science-speak for saying he did not believe them. The last word comes from Professor Robert Winston from Hammersmith Hospital, who told a conference last April that genetic analysis of the sperm-sorting technique yields X and Y-bearing sperm in a ratio of 50:50. None the less, there are good reasons for hoping that an effective technique will be found. According to the *New Scientist*, Roy Jones – working at the Institute of Animal Physiology in Cambridge – is looking for differences in the proteins on the surface of male and female sperm. If present, it will be a simple matter to add an antibody against the male sperm, which, by inactivating them, would give a 100 per cent guarantee of a baby girl.

Is It Normal

My mother assures me that during her child-bearing years it never crossed her mind that her babies would be anything other than perfect. How different things are now! The first four or five months of pregnancy are permeated with anxiety lest one or other antenatal test will find something terribly wrong. Will the amniocentesis show the foetus has Down's syndrome or some other chromosomal abnormality? Will the blood test for alpha-fetoprotein raise the spectre of a baby with spina bifida? Will the ultrasound show defects of the brain, heart or kidneys? Taken together, these tests, and others, add up to a medical programme of eugenics – seeking out and destroying foetuses that are less than perfect. The moral issues raised by the programme are countered by doctors with the utilitarian argument that parents want to have a normal baby, and the doctor's job is merely to provide the technological means by which that wish can be fulfilled. Yet it is becoming increasingly clear that antenatal testing has a more adverse effect on women's experience of pregnancy than was previously realised.

Take, for example, the triple test – the blood test to screen for Down's syndrome. This has two possible results – 'screen positive' or 'screen negative'. Screen positive does not mean that the foetus has Down's syndrome but rather that the risk of it being so affected is at least one in 250. Many women understandably find this a difficult concept to grapple with. Although all it really means is that the risk is sufficiently high to warrant amniocentesis. As five weeks may pass between first having the triple test and receiving the result of amniocentesis it is clear that the scope for needless anxiety is very considerable. A recent study from Cambridge of twenty women who were found to be 'screen positive' illustrates the problems. Several did not know they were being screened for Down's. Some found the hospital staff seemed to have a poor grasp of the implications of the result, one being told that it meant she 'had no hope', while the result of another was dismissed because the test was 'unreliable'. Eight found it difficult applying the 'one in something' risk to their own pregnancy, and though those who were eventually found after amniocentesis to have a normal baby 'reported enormous relief initially', worries often emerged later: 'if the baby does not have Down's syndrome, what does it have?' Such experiences, it seems, are typical, forcing Dr Theresa Marteau, director of the Psychology and Genetic Research Group at Guy's Hospital, to admit ruefully in the *British Medical Journal*: 'No matter how good a test is technically, screening of uninformed, unsupported patients by unprepared staff is a recipe for at best confusion and at worst great distress.'

Those women who do have an abnormal baby and decide to have an abortion are, not surprisingly, distressed by the consequences, but again the degree of that distress has also been poorly appreciated. The general assumption has been that parents would ultimately be grateful to be spared bringing up a handicapped child, but it seems the emotional complications of aborting a wanted, if abnormal, baby run very deep. Two years after a termination for foetal abnormality, 20 per cent of the women in a study from Glasgow 'still experienced a level of sadness, fear, guilt, anger and failure that interfered with their mental well-being'. Typical comments included 'Why did I have to make such a decision? . . . nobody can understand how difficult it was' and 'I thought if this could happen to me, what other mishaps are in store for me or my children?' Commenting on these findings, the authors write: 'Support after leaving hospital following termination was minimal or non-existent – there was a lack of understanding of the turmoil, ambiguity and reticence that couples felt.'

The putative benefit of antenatal testing – the increased likelihood of having a normal baby – have been bought at the cost of a loss of innocence. No longer can pregnancy be the happy, carefree experience it was for my mother's generation. Modern mothers are clearly prepared to accept this – but they should not have their fears compounded because their doctors fail to make clear the implications of their tests and to support them in acting on the consequences. All prospective mothers should buy *The Antenatal Testing Handbook* by Vivienne Parry, published by Pan, which provides excellent advice in this fraught area.

12

And Children

Teething Troubles

It is standard medical teaching that teething in babies causes no symptoms. Nelson's classic *Textbook of Paediatrics* says that 'teething can lead to intermittent localised discomfort' and little else. However, mothers bringing their babies to surgery attribute a bewildering variety of symptoms to teething, including poor sleeping, refusal to feed, earache, diarrhoea and fever. The situation calls for considerable tact on the doctor's part. There seems little point in saying that teething is a non-existent condition which has never reliably been shown to cause any distress. So a sensible compromise is to examine the baby to see if there is any obviously treatable cause for its symptoms, and if there is not to advise a treatment for temperature or diarrhoea, or whatever the baby is suffering from.

It now transpires that mothers have been right all along. Researchers at the Tel Aviv School of Medicine asked 46 of them to take their babies' temperatures and monitor their symptoms in the two weeks before the eruption of their first tooth. Sure enough, its appearance was associated with a distinct fever, which in some babies rose as high as 38°C (100.4°F). There are complex reasons why doctors deny what can so easily be demonstrated, but in the case of teething I am sure there is a strong historical element of guilt. From the sixteenth century, doctors propagated the view that teething was responsible for a multiplicity of childhood illnesses, including convulsions and death, and recommended as a protective measure that babies' gums should be lacerated 'to liberate the death'. Besides being extremely painful, this often resulted in a nasty infection leading to many problems that they attributed to teething itself. The custom fell out of favour at the turn of this century and I suspect that, as a reaction to the damage the treatment caused, the contrary view that teething is harmless has been passed down through generations of doctors.

Breast Versus Bottle

By all accounts human breast milk tastes like watered-down milk fortified with teaspoonfuls of sugar. If this over-sweet liquid was the only gustatory experience of the newborn, one might expect them to get bored with it fairly quickly. But the flavour of breast milk varies markedly depending on the maternal diet. Many mothers report that their babies' feeding habits seem to depend on what they themselves have had to eat and this even extends to the flatus-inducing properties of beans and lentils, after which both mother and child pass a lot of wind. Similarly, maternal onion eating is said to cause infantile colic; spicy foods and acidic drinks lead to stomach upsets and chocolate notoriously results in diarrhoea. Alcohol is held to be doubly beneficial, both increasing milk production (malt beer is particularly recommended) while its appearance in breast milk is soothing and sleep-inducing. There is no evidence that in moderation this is harmful though there is one account of a woman who took the 'alcohol is good for nursing mothers' rather too literally and whose consumption of 50 lagers a week produced signs of chronic alcoholism in her baby.

Drs Julia Menella and Gary Beauchamp, of the Chemical Senses Center in Philadelphia have investigated the subject, trying to tease out the fact from the folklore. With the help of a panel of sniffers they have been testing the separate effects of alcohol and garlic on the smell of breast milk and infant-feeding behaviour. The sniffers easily detected both substances and in the case of alcohol the intensity of the smell correlated well with the actual amount that was present. Perhaps surprisingly, the babies seemed to prefer the garlic-flavour milk, sucking much more vigorously and for longer than when offered the alcohol-laced variety. So in addition to the established putative benefits of breast milk over bottle feeding – cheapness, convenience, protection against infection and promotion of bonding – it would seem appropriate to add 'taste variety'.

The popularity of 'breast v bottle' has fluctuated markedly over the last 50 years. While in the 1940s three out of four babies were breast-fed, by 1970 this number had dwindled to one in four. This low point was followed by a resurgence attributed to the combined efforts of medical opinion and the influence of organisations like the

215

National Childbirth Trust. The 'health benefits' of breast feeding have always been fairly hypothetical, especially in the West where the incidence of infectious diseases is low. More recently, there has been a reaction against the dowdy unsexy image the NCT personifies and now the bottle is once again in the ascendancy. This appears very clearly in a survey of 550 recent mothers conducted by a public relations firm which identified two distinct groups – the nurturer ('I would never consider anything other than breast-feeding') and the modernists ('I am completely happy with bottle-feeding') with the rest occupying a position in the middle ('I would like to breast-feed but I can't').

The nurturers see themselves as 'caring individuals who put their babies first' and were uniformly hostile to the bottle-feeding modernists ('Tarts back in ski-pants three weeks after the birth'). By contrast the modernists saw themselves as 'smart, organised, good-looking young women who want to go on working and seeing their friends' and were disparaging about the nurturers who they saw as 'wearing cheese-cloth skirts and sandals and whose husbands are wimps'.

The nurturers tend to be older, better educated, of a higher social class and married. The modernists felt that breast-feeding prevented a 'normal life' and were keen to start sexual relationships again as soon as possible after the birth. The nurturers can console themselves that their babies at least will have a much more varied (and exciting) taste experience in the early months.

Colic Cures

Human babies cry far longer and more loudly than the offspring of any other species. So loudly, indeed, as to be literally deafening, as Mrs Charlene Bostrom of Minneapolis found after a particularly shrill outburst from her 11-month-old son. A friend, Mr Loren Swanson, an acoustics engineer, offered to monitor the screams with his 'decibel sounds level meter'. The measurements were made at a distance of six inches, equivalent to the space between the mother's ear and the mouth of the infant when being held. The peak noise level recorded by the metre was 117 decibels, only just less than that of a pneumatic drill. Little wonder Mrs Bostrom had been deafened.

Compared with other abilities of small infants, this vocal facility is exceptionally highly developed both in power and duration, and no doubt for good reason. It is not enough for the baby to alert its parents to the need to be fed or changed, but their lives have to be made sufficiently unpleasant to force them to react – and very effective it is, too. Regrettably, some infants cannot be consoled. The nightmare of young parents, these are difficult babies, who, particularly in the evenings, cry inconsolably for hours at a time, despite every conceivable attention. Typically, the baby draws up its legs, clenches its fists and emits high-pitched screams for several minutes, then stops for a while and then starts again.

The question as to why they should do so has, over the years, generated an enormous number of fanciful theories: the babies are overfed or underfed, or fed the wrong things; they suffer from allergy or 'hypertonicity' – heightened muscle tone; the fault lies with the parents, who 'pick the baby up too much' or 'bounce it too much after its feeds'. It has even been suggested that persistent crying is a form of malingering. 'I feel sure of one thing – such infants are certainly not as distressed as they appear or their parents think they are,' one paediatrician wrote.

The persistence of such psychosocial explanations is all the more remarkable because they were completely demolished by the late R. S. Illingworth, Professor of Paediatrics at Sheffield University. He convincingly showed that the reason for persistent crying in infancy was that the baby was in pain induced by intestinal spasms. Everything fits this explanation: the rhythmical paroxysms of screaming; the accompanying loud bowel sounds; the temporary cessation following the passage of wind. Most convincingly, Professor Illingworth showed that an anti-spasmodic drug, dicyclomine, was 'strikingly successful' in preventing attacks. Regrettably, dicyclomine can no longer be given to babies after some poorly substantiated reports of adverse reactions, so parents must now soldier on with less effective remedies – although Professor Illingworth maintained that the best alternative treatment was a small amount of alcohol.

Small Can Be Beautiful

Height should not matter – but it does. Tallness, particularly in men, has always been a valuable biological characteristic, distinguishing the ruler from the ruled, the rich from the poor. We 'look up' to our betters. Even today those fortunate enough to be six foot tall or more benefit from a pervasive positive discrimination in their favour. Employers prefer the taller of equally qualified candidates and give them more generous starting salaries. The taller of the two candidates for the American presidency has won 80 per cent of the elections this century – a point made much of by commentators following the famous television confrontation between Bush and Dukakis in 1988. The short by contrast consider themselves at a disadvantage when seeking a mate. They are more prone to depression and low self-esteem and hyponchondriasis. They lack, it is said, 'an appropriate aggressive drive'. Gulliver's impression that the dwarf-sized Lilliputians were petty, suspicious and deceitful reflects a common prejudice.

Two factors have encouraged doctors and parents in the hope that the social stigma of short stature with its psychological consequences might be surmountable. Height is powerfully determined by the genes inherited at birth but the consistent rise in average height over the past 200 years reveals that environmental factors must also be crucial. Further, genetically engineered growth hormone has been widely available since 1986 with the promise that short stature may turn out to be 'treatable'. This hope, it seems, may have been misplaced.

Average height has certainly continued to rise. Dr Michael Preece of the Institute of Child Health has devised a new set of 'normal' growth curves to monitor children's growth which are approximately half an inch greater for each age group than the previous set devised in 1966. An extra half an inch appears trivial, but when compared with similar data stretching back over the past 200 years, the environmental contribution to human height is truly astonishing. Today the mean height of a 15-year-old is around 5ft 6in which 100 years ago would have been a respectable 'average' and 100 years before that would have been considered tall. The differences in average height over time conceal an even more marked differential between the social classes. In 1750 the upper-class recruits to Sandhurst were an amazing 7½ inches taller than the humble recruits to the Marine Society. Even in 1950 there was a 3-inch difference in adult height between the social classes.

Improved nutrition combined with the prevention of infectious diseases in childhood are the two commonly cited reasons for this rise in height. To this more recently must be added improvements in antenatal care, so babies are now born longer, an advantage they carry into adult life. The problem for those hoping to boost the stature of the small by improving these important influences in the early years is the limit to what is biologically achievable.

There will come a time when even the children of the least well off have enough to eat, and access to the best maternity services is universal – and then most children can be guaranteed to reach their optimal height. The narrowing of the class differential in height to a minuscule quarter of an inch suggests this point has almost been reached.

The opportunity to improve the prospects for the short therefore now rests with growth hormone treatment. Growth hormone is secreted by the pituitary gland at the base of the brain. A deficit causes dwarfism, and an excess – usually due to a tumour – causes gigantism. Though first used therapeutically in 1959, its method of preparation – distilled from 20,000 pituitaries from corpses – was arduous and expensive. In 1986 Genentech, the US genetic engineering company, successfully inserted the gene-for-growth hormone into bacteria, allowing production of virtually limitless quantities in a pure form. An editorial in the *New England Journal of Medicine* soon afterwards emphasised the implications of this breakthrough: 'A large group of children with short stature not due to a deficiency of growth hormone may now benefit from treatment.' The inevitable ethical controversy over the legitimacy of improving on nature by treating 'normal' children was muted by the finding of subtle differences in growth hormone secretion between the tall and the small. Dr Peter Hindmarsh, lecturer at the Middlesex Hospital, recalls: 'Back in 1987 this seemed very exciting. Everyone believed that boosting levels in those who were relatively growth-hormone deficient would accelerate their growth rates.'

Indeed it did. Children responded to their thrice-weekly injections with a rapid increase in growth velocity so that at the end of three years Dr Hindmarsh was able to report the predicted final height in a group of 16 young patients had increased by 2½ inches in boys and 1¾ inches in girls. This early optimism has now evaporated. 'We are still waiting to find out what their ultimate achieved adult heights will be,' Dr Hindmarsh said. 'But we will be lucky if we have gained an extra inch.' With ten years' treatment costing about $80,000 a child, this scarcely seems worthwhile. The advantages of growth hormone in increasing speed of growth seems to have been lost in the pubertal growth spurt which occurs earlier but lasts for a shorter time.

The hope of a technical fix for the 'linearly challenged' has proved a mirage. They might console themselves with the aphorism that 'small is beautiful' and that excessive tallness, now an increasing problem because of the upward shift in average height, is if anything even more of a social disadvantage.

Failing to Thrive

Every week consultant paediatricians are asked for their opinion on one or two children with the tentative diagnosis of 'failure to thrive'. The most obvious physical feature is faltering growth, though the children tend also to be apathetic and behavioural disorders are frequent. There will be an underlying physical cause in about a quarter in whom, almost invariably, there are other physical symptoms as well, such a diarrhoea and distension of the abdomen. A simple blood test will show anaemia caused by malabsorption of one or other of the vitamins necessary for making red blood cells. Investigations of the gut will usually result in a diagnosis of coeliac disease – intolerance of gluten – and when the diet is switched to exclude gluten, a constituent of wheat, recovery rapidly follows. But no matter how many tests the paediatrician orders, in three-quarters of children all the results will come back negative. Then the explanation for failure to thrive lies elsewhere. Often, but not invariably, it is associated with psychological problems in the child, usually attributed in the past to emotional neglect.

This phenomenon was first described in the 1940s in children hospitalised for long periods who, despite adequate amounts of food, were 'listless, emaciated and pale, unresponsive to stimuli and had an appearance of unhappiness'. A similar picture has been observed recently in children brought up in orphanages in Eastern Europe. The contribution of love and emotional security in promoting growth in children was unintentionally confirmed by the distinguished British nutritionist Dr Elsie Widdowson in her study of children in two German orphanages after the war. Her main purpose was to investigate the degree to which food supplements in undernourished children could accelerate growth rates. To her surprise the children in the first orphanage, who were only given the standard post-war rations, grew more rapidly than those in the second, who were given supplementary bread, jam and orange juice, representing an added 20 per cent of calories to their daily food intake. The difference, Professor Widdowson believed, could only be explained by the personality of the director of the second orphanage. She was 'stern and forbidding, ruling the home with a rod of iron . . . Children and staff lived in constant fear of her reprimands and criticisms, which were often quite unreasonable'. But the director had her favourites who, over the year in which the experiment was conducted, put on an extra kilogram in weight and centimetre in height compared with the other children in the orphanage.

The mechanism by which emotional neglect can lead to poor growth rates, has however, never been clarified. In the last few years it has become accepted that the underlying cause must be malnutrition. So, even if children are presented with adequate amounts of food everyday, emotional problems within the family leading to poor appetite or perverse feeding behaviour mean they do not consume enough for their needs. Dr David Skuse, a child psychiatrist in London, has suggested two possible ways in which this might happen. In the first, the mother is depressed or anguished, resulting in a tense child who does not feed well. She reacts badly to her infant's lack of enthusiasm for the food she is offering and so stops meals prematurely, leaving her child angry and hungry, and a vicious circle develops. Alternatively some children are intrinsically less lovable than others, whether in physical appearance, crying habits or response to affection. This can affect the mother's desire to nurture, which in turn results in feeding problems.

Paradoxically over-concern about a baby's diet can also lead to failure to thrive. Dr Harvey Marcovitch, a paediatrician from Horton Hospital in Banbury, was perplexed when, back in the 1980s, he noticed increasing numbers of children referred for 'failure to thrive' came from apparently stable and prosperous middle-class families. The mothers tended to be over-anxious and to focus their concerns on the prevailing shibboleths about a healthy diet. They cut out milk and dairy products to protect their offspring against hardening of the arteries, and refused to give them any processed foods in case the colouring agents and additives they contained might induce hyperactivity. The healthy diet they imposed instead – containing lashings of fibre and bran – not only gave the children colic but proved so unappetising that they were getting insufficient calories. This 'muesli-belt malnutrition' was readily resolved after mothers were encouraged to widen the dietary choice available for their babies.

Nevertheless, failure to thrive is more common among children in problem families, and care proceedings followed by fostering can lead to dramatic gains in height and weight within a few weeks. But deciding when such drastic measures are appropriate is not easy.

As Dr Skuse says: 'Parents are at risk of being regarded as guilty of emotionally abusing their children unless they can prove their innocence – but sufficient grounds to disprove such a suspicion may be hard to find.'

Cleft Palate Repairs

'I expected to swim through it,' is how Mrs Liz Weston recalls her feelings when admitted to the obstetric ward of a London teaching hospital in 1991. This was her third pregnancy, there had been no complications and all her scans and blood tests had been normal. But when, after a short labour, her son, Tom, was delivered he had a large gap running through his upper lip and into the palate. Though extremely distressed, she was reassured to be told her baby's cleft palate could be fixed almost immediately, and within a week the hospital's plastic surgeon sewed the two sides of the upper lip together. A few months later the hole in the palate was patched over. Soon after the second operation Mrs Weston and her family moved to Bournemouth and, having been told that Tom might need speech therapy, she made the appropriate enquiries and was delighted to learn that a surgeon working at the town's main hospital, Tony Markus, had a special interest in children with Tom's condition.

Their first meeting she remembers as 'a terrible shock'. 'He was obviously terribly nice and sympathetic but he told me that Tom's operation would have to be completely redone. I could not believe it. I thought as his repair had been performed at a London teaching hospital he must have had the best possible treatment, but now it seems he would have to have another two major procedures over the next 18 months. Both my husband and I were deeply sceptical.' For nine months they prevaricated, but having met and talked to parents of children with the same problem, 'Eventually we were convinced. Mr Markus's results were obviously very good; what really decided us was that his arguments seemed to make such good sense.'

The face is formed in early embryonic development from sheets of tissue that grow inwards from either side and upwards to unite in the middle. Failure of fusion results in several deformities, varying in severity from a cleft or hare lip on one side to a wide gap on both sides of the nose that stretches up and back through the tissue of the gums into the nostrils all the way to the back of the palate. Over many years operations have been devised to repair the defect which all involve sewing the skin and muscles on either side of the cleft together again. Initially there is usually a good aesthetic result and the face appears normal. But as the child grows various anomalies appear. The nose becomes skewed to one side and the shape of the face in profile becomes abnormal with a flattened central part and protuberant jaw. The child develops speech difficulties with a marked nasal intonation. The cause of these late complications – which in turn require further corrective surgery and extensive orthodontic treatment – was thought to be the same genetic abnormality that had given rise to the cleft lip in the first place, a deficiency in the growth potential of the tissues of the face.

There is, however, a very different explanation. It might seem obvious that the growth of the face through childhood into adult life is primarily determined by the underlying bony skeleton, but this is not the case. To grow in harmony, all the soft tissues, the overlying skin, the muscles, the tongue and the teeth have to interact with each other and with the underlying bone, moulding the shape of the skull as it enlarges. Thus the eruption of the teeth of the lower gum is dictated by the downward force exerted by the teeth in the upper gum, and vice versa. The muscles of facial expression around the mouth and nose exert traction on the underlying bone and pull the centre of the face forward. From this perspective the late complications of cleft lip surgery are not necessarily inevitable, but may rather be caused by the surgeon's failure to fully restore the anatomical relations disrupted by the embryonic failure of fusion. This explanation in turn requires that the initial operation needs to be much more extensive to achieve what is known as a 'functional repair'.

Whereas the standard cleft lip procedure involves reuniting the *orbicularis oris* muscle that surrounds the mouth; with a functional repair the other muscle groups around the nose are also mobilised and reconnected to the underlying bone. In a review of these two approaches in the *Journal of Oral and Maxillo-Facial Surgery*, Professor Ulrich Joos of the University of Munster, Germany, reports normal development of the mid-face in all children with a functional repair compared with only 20 per cent of those who have the standard surgical procedure. Mr Markus has had similar results prompting the question of why everybody has not switched to the new techniques, or rather why he thinks it necessary to redo cleft palate operations performed by other surgeons.

In Britain cleft palates have usually been dealt with as if they were primarily a cosmetic defect, requiring the skills of the plastic surgeon. The concept of the 'functional repair', however, has been pioneered by Mr Markus's speciality – oral and maxillo-facial surgeons whose training focuses on and requires a detailed understanding of the complex anatomy of the face. Recently plastic surgeons have come to recognise their results have been less than satisfactory, certainly compared with those obtained in other West European countries. They believe, however, the explanation lies in the fact that too many surgeons have been doing too few operations. Professor Bill Shaw of Manchester University is a firm protagonist of this view and with some difficulty has managed to persuade 15 of the 18 plastic surgeons in the North West to give up cleft palate work in favour of three of their colleagues who now do all the operations.

This is certainly an advance but as Mr Markus points out: 'Numbers [of operations] are important and the more experienced the surgeon the better the results.' But the key issue, he maintains, remains the technique – the extensive type of operation that maximises the chances of a truly functional repair. Mrs Weston has no regrets about placing her trust in his judgement. 'As an artist I have been taught to look at people's faces and it is obvious that their shape and symmetry is determined by the structures underneath. Agreeing that Tom should have a major revision of his original operations remains the most difficult decision I have ever made.' But the result, she says, is 'simply wonderful'.

13

Cancer – The Dread Disease

When Cancer Cures Itself

There is no more dramatic or perplexing event in medicine than the cancer that cures itself. It happened to a family doctor of my acquaintance, Hugh Faulkner, who, having retired after 30 years in practice, was found to have a tumour of the pancreas. He declined any offer of treatment, which would only have been palliative, and resolved to live out his last few months in Italy, his chosen country of retirement. On his way through Heathrow Airport, Dr Faulkner bumped into an old friend, a Japanese doctor, who hearing of his plight, suggested that he should try a macrobiotic diet which involves cutting out all meat and dairy products in favour of beans, lentils and so forth. With nothing to lose, Dr Faulkner cast aside his natural scepticism about this type of 'alternative' cancer cure and was astonished to find that over the next few months he began to feel a lot better. A repeat scan of the pancreas showed his cancer had shrunk, and he lived on for almost another decade.

It is tempting to think the macrobiotic diet did the trick, but this cannot be the case. The 'spontaneous regression' of cancer is always coincidental to, rather than a consequence of, any alternative treatment being taken at the time, and it is never possible to replicate the amazing cures attributed to them. It is important to be fastidious about such pseudo-explanations because they distract attention from just how remarkable is the phenomenon of spontaneous regression, with its implication that the body must have some means of eradicating malignant growths. Find out why it happens, or how these self-healing properties could be harnessed, and who knows what benefits might result.

From an analysis of all the reported cases of spontaneous regression of cancer, Dr G.B. Challis, of the University of Calgary, has been able to make some general observations. The phenomenon has been noted in virtually every type of cancer and at every stage. He describes the case of one woman with cancer of the rectum, in whom it was found at operation that her pelvis was 'so extensively invaded with cancer that only a palliative excision would be attempted'. She lived on for 17 years, and an autopsy after her death reported 'no detectable tumour tissue present'. And why did it happen? The straight answer is that nobody knows, but the favoured explanation is that some event, perhaps the trauma of an operation, or an infection, stimulates the production of antibodies that destroy the cancer. Theoretically then, stimulating the immune system in some non-specific way might be beneficial in cancer, and this has subsequently been demonstrated, particularly in treating the skin cancer, melanoma.

An appreciation that spontaneous regression occurs can also protect patients against being over-treated. Cancer specialists have taken considerable pride in the very high cure rate – almost 100 per cent – of the childhood cancer neuroblastoma, with anti-cancer drugs. Recently, however, it has emerged that when such cancers are left alone, they often shrink to a fraction of their original size, at which point they can be removed with a simple operation. Spontaneous regression may also occur in non-malignant conditions, such as an enlarged prostate and the narrowing of the coronary arteries in heart disease. So here a policy of 'watchful waiting' may be considered preferable to immediate medical intervention. Thus, almost a third with prostatic symptoms of obstruction of urinary flow will improve without surgery over a five-year period, and in a further 50 per cent their symptoms will get no worse. Similarly, coronary arteries which are so narrowed as to warrant treatment may with time widen of their own accord, thus restoring blood flow to the heart muscles. Anyone witnessing spontaneous regression of cancer cannot help but be moved by what appears to be an almost miraculous event. But in a sense, it is just one instance, albeit a remarkable one, of an even greater miracle – the hidden and mysterious ways in which the body sustains and heals itself.

Carried Away by Fear

Due to a clerical error in the X-ray department at Musgrove Park Hospital in Taunton, Somerset, Mrs Dorothy Cushing was told she had lung cancer, for which she was duly treated with a full course of chemotherapy. She had time to choose the clothes for her burial and pick the hymns for her funeral service, and then after five months the mistake was discovered. 'It is impossible to realise the trauma it has caused,' she remarked. A decade or so ago, and by default, this problem would not have arisen because cancer patients were rarely told the truth. No doubt Mrs Cushing would have been informed she had 'a patch of inflammation on the lungs'. Treatment would not have been offered for her non-existent tumour – and certainly not on the basis of a single X-ray and no other confirmatory evidence.

She would have carried on attending the hospital out-patients until her continued good health would have struck someone as being rather odd, a further X-ray would have been requested and the mistake uncovered. I do not suggest there is any intrinsic virtue in doctors concealing the truth from their patients, but this alternative scenario is a reminder of just how fearfully people view the diagnosis, and that perhaps blunt honesty is not necessarily for the best. Honesty may indeed be lethal, as illustrated by the case of the man 'killed by a word', reported in *The Lancet* by Dr Colin Hewlett. This man, in his mid-fifties, who had not been told his diagnosis, had chronic lymphatic leukaemia, which was being kept under control with small doses of steroids and a drug called chlorambucil. He remained very well until one month he missed his usual appointment and soon after was admitted 'in a very neglected state'. It turned out that he had looked over his GP's shoulders, seen the word 'leukaemia' in his notes and concluded the worst. His subsequent progress, Dr Hewlett writes, 'was rapidly downhill and within three weeks he was dead. His blood count had not changed and no cause for his rapid decline was found during life or at autopsy.' Perhaps this morbid reaction would have been avoided if the nature of the illness had been fully explained. But there are some for whom 'the truth' is such a terrible blow that they are quite unable to cope and for whom not knowing is much to be preferred.

This type of 'self-willed' death is very similar to the effect of the voodoo hex or 'pointing the bone' where the victim dies from the fear of an evil spell cast upon him. Both are due to excess stimulation of the parasympathetic nervous system, which slows down the heartbeat, breathing rate and lowers the body temperature. Just as the victim may be saved from 'the hex' if the spell is found to be defective or is overridden by a more powerful witch doctor, so self-willed death can be reversed in Western man. Professor George

Milton, a specialist in skin cancer at Sydney Hospital in Australia often finds himself in the position of being 'the more powerful witch doctor'. 'My clinic often admits patients with incurable melanoma, demonstrating all the features of self-willed death,' he writes. 'As soon as they feel something is being done to help, even if all that can be achieved is to show an interest, the improvement may be so dramatic that there is a danger of medical staff believing their treatments have actually prolonged life.' The last word on the matter goes to Dr B. S. Mantell, senior cancer specialist at the Royal London Hospital. 'In speaking to patients with cancer,' he says, 'I follow two principles: (1) One must never lie but must be judicious in telling the truth; (2) No patient should be worse off for seeing a doctor.'

Twenty Years of Modest Progress

Twenty years ago cancer specialists would rightly congratulate themselves on their phenomenal success in curing previously incurable cancers – especially those affecting children, leukaemia and lymphoma, and testicular cancer in young men. They key to their success lay in cytotoxic chemotherapy, drugs which, given in combination, kill off the cancer cells more completely and effectively than normal cells. But these now curable cancers still represented only a tiny minority of the total, and so the challenge was to apply the lessons learnt to those that afflict people in their sixties and onwards, known as solid tumours, because they arise from solid organs – the brain, the lung, breast, gut, and so on. Lung cancer, being the commonest of all, was an obvious candidate for chemotherapy, especially as it is only rarely curable – when caught early enough to be surgically removed. The results of a comparison of chemotherapy versus 'no treatment' in nearly 200 patients with lung cancer was reported in *The Lancet* in 1975: those given 'no treatment' lived longer and with a better quality of life than those treated with chemotherapy. And that, effectively, was the end of that. The chemotherapy which worked so well in the sorts of cancer that affect young people regrettably seemed ineffective in the solid tumours. And so, for the past two decades in Britain most patients with solid tumours have not had chemotherapy, unless as part of a clinical trial comparing the merits of new anti-cancer drugs.

During that time, however, three important things have changed. 'We have moved on from the indiscriminate and largely valueless use of chemotherapy in situations where there could be no justification other than a doctor's desire to do something,' says Dr Jeffrey Tobias of the Middlesex Hospital. Cancer specialists are much more focused about what role chemotherapy might play in different types of cancer. Secondly, as Dr Tobias points out, the commonest and most grievous side effects of chemotherapy – nausea and protracted vomiting – are now controllable with new drugs. Thus, chemotherapy becomes a more acceptable notion, especially for older and sicker patients; being less toxic, it is now more justifiable to treat patients in anticipation of only a modest benefit, such as an extra few months of life. Thirdly, vast numbers of trials of chemotherapy over the past 20 years have revealed some circumstances in which it really does make a difference.

And what does all this add up to? It depends to whom you talk, or, as Alexander Pope put it: ''Tis with our judgements as our watches, none/Go just alike, yet each believes his own.' Chemotherapy does work but the controversy is over whether it works well enough. Writing in the *British Medical Journal*, Graham Mead, a cancer specialist at Southampton, argues that 'routine treatment is not yet justified', because of 'the side effects, inconvenience and financial costs of chemotherapy – without significant improvement in symptoms or survival'. David Cunningham from the Marsden, however, claims there has been 'important progress in treatments . . . resulting in major improvements in quality and quantity of life.' This controversy is well illustrated by an overview of chemotherapy in lung cancer – how much further have we moved from 20 years ago, when 'no treatment' was the better option? Take 100 patients with the best prognosis – whose lung cancer can be surgically removed – and 50 will still be alive five years later. Give them all chemotherapy in addition and the figure rises to 55. Take 100 patients with the next stage – whose cancer is inoperable but still contained within the lung – give them radiotherapy, and 10 will still be alive five years later; 12 if they are all given chemotherapy. For those with advanced disease, chemotherapy adds about an extra month of life.

It is a similar picture with most of the other solid tumours: chemotherapy gives a small overall improvement at each stage. But if by chance one is lucky enough to be one of those whose life is prolonged by chemotherapy, then it matters not one whit that the 'overall' benefit is small. This is a good argument for giving all (or most) cancer patients chemotherapy – as happens in the United States – but it will not happen. This is partly because of cost, and partly because cancer specialists find it difficult to convince themselves it is worthwhile giving chemotherapy to 100 patients to prolong the life of two of them. But the main reason it will not happen is that there are not enough cancer specialists to go round. The United States has 100 times as many per head of population and, without a major expansion in numbers (very unlikely), 'chemotherapy for all', even if desirable, is a mirage. So doctors will continue to use their discretion about who to treat (and, more often, who not to), but there is more than enough evidence now to justify giving chemotherapy to those who wish it.

Catching Prostate Cancer Early

An ex-Army officer in his 70s writes to tell me that, in the past year, three of his wartime comrades have been diagnosed as having cancer of the prostate. There seems to be a lot of it about, and he is anxious to know how he can avoid their fate. In particular, he asks if I could advise on some new-fangled blood test he has read about that can pick up this type of cancer early enough for it to be curable. My correspondent is quite right to be concerned. The number of cases of prostate cancer seems to be rapidly on the increase, but as the organ from which the tumour arises is concealed deep in the pelvis, it has the unfortunate tendency of creeping up on people, so that in over a third of patients the tumour is already widespread at the time of diagnosis, which is obviously bad news.

Fifteen years ago, it was found that in such patients a chemical in the blood known as the Prostate Specific Antigen (PSA) is markedly elevated. More recently, it has become apparent that the PSA is also raised, albeit to a lesser extent, in those in whom the tumour is still confined to the prostate gland and so potentially curable. Logically, then, all men should routinely have their PSAs measured, which, if found to be moderately raised, should initiate a search for the tumour. If present, this could be extirpated either by surgery – a radical prostatectomy – or by X-ray treatment, thus saving the patient's life. With this rationale, screening for prostate cancer has mushroomed in the United States. Any man over the age of 50 visiting his doctor is unlikely to escape without having his PSA measured, and the number of radical prostatectomies has risen fivefold in as many years.

In Britain, however, the Department of Health has resolutely refused to get involved in promoting this type of screening, and many reputable doctors take a dim view of the whole business. There is much talk of 'substantial resource implications', of subjecting patients to 'potentially damaging ineffective treatment' and, indeed, of a 'prostatectomy holocaust' – all from an innocent blood test. The PSA raises strong emotions, and it is useful to know why. First, although the mortality from prostate cancer is high – 8,000 deaths a year – its incidence is much higher. Indeed, it has been estimated that 1 million men in Britain between the ages of 50 and 70 may have the pathological features of cancerous change in their prostates. Obviously, then, in many men, either the tumour is indolent and does not progress to threaten their lives, or they eventually succumb to some other illness, in which case, harbouring a few cancer cells in their prostate is irrelevant.

Secondly, radical prostatectomy, as its name implies, is a major procedure, which carries a substantial risk of incontinence and impotence, and thus is not to be undertaken lightly – especially if the question of whether the cancer being removed is life-threatening cannot be unambiguously answered. From all this, the best advice might seem to be to try and forget all about it and just get on with your life. None the less, the possibility remains that a simple blood test like the PSA could save some lives, and for those who wish to take the matter further, this is what to do.

Drop in to see your family doctor and ask him politely if you can have your PSA measured. He is under no obligation to accede to your request, in which circumstances the options are either to seek out a private GP or seek a private referral to a consultant urologist. If the test result is normal, that's fine. If it is very high, the cancer has already spread and appropriate NHS treatment should be arranged. If it is in the medium range, it is usual for an ultrasound of the prostate to be done, which, in a third of cases, shows 'hot spots' suggestive of a tumour. This whole procedure is likely to cost about £340, so it helps to be rich if you are thinking of having it done on a regular basis. Even though you may have been tested privately, those found to have a tumour will be treated on the NHS by the urology consultant at their local hospital. He will arrange further investigations, including a biopsy and, depending on the results, either advise a policy of watchful waiting or definitive treatment. Good luck!

Hope at Last for Stomach Cancer

The usual medical reaction to a patient with stomach cancer is one of regretful despair. The only hope of salvation lies with the surgeon, but as the tumour is usually far advanced, too often he ends up opening and closing the abdomen, having concluded it is inoperable. The statistics tell it all: only 5 per cent of patients survive five years. This situation is changing rapidly with a marked improvement in prognosis which, one might imagine, could have been achieved only by some breakthrough such as potent new anti-cancer drugs. Not at all. The changing prospects for stomach cancer have been achieved by an ordinary consultant surgeon, Mr Henry Sue-Ling, working in Leeds, who became convinced that progress lay simply in a more systematic application of current knowledge.

'Back in the 1970s, I looked very hard at the appalling results with stomach cancer and I felt sure it must be possible to improve on them,' Mr Sue-Ling recalls. He turned for inspiration to Japan where stomach cancer is so common that there is a mass screening programme, using the fibre optic endoscope. This permits the lining of the stomach to be thoroughly scrutinised and any areas which look suspicious can be biopsied. The cells are then examined under a microscope for evidence of malignant change. The Japanese have also pioneered a radical surgical operation where, in addition to removing the cancerous part of the stomach, they methodically excise all the lymph nodes to which the cancer might have spread. With this two-pronged attack a third of stomach cancers are detected at the earliest stage, and all but 10 per cent are cured by surgery. Stomach cancer is essentially a curable disease in Japan, and Mr Sue-Ling believed similar results were achievable in Britain. 'Our results were so poor that British surgeons had just been burying their heads in the sand, refusing to learn from the Japanese experience,' he says. 'We needed to go back to basics to try to diagnose these cancers earlier and to review thoroughly our surgical procedures.'

A screening programme similar to that in Japan was out of the question because stomach cancer is so much rarer in Britain – although it still accounts for more than 11,000 deaths a year. However, prompt endoscopy of patients over the age of 40 with dyspeptic symptoms should pick up a fair proportion of cancers at an early stage. Accordingly, Mr Sue-Ling organised a service where general practitioners could refer their patients directly to hospital without the requirement that they be seen initially by a consultant. The number of endoscopies quadrupled over a decade but, as Mr Sue-Ling had expected, the proportion of those whose cancers were still at the early stage rose from 4 to 26 per cent.

In addition Mr Sue-Ling decided to adopt the radical surgical techniques pioneered by the Japanese. This was not without its problems. Not only is the operation very arduous, taking up to four hours to perform, but British patients, on average, tend to be 11 years older with a higher incidence of obesity, diabetes and heart disease. The initial rate of post-operative mortality and complications proved to be unacceptably high, and although this has improved with greater experience, it still does not compare with those in Japan. Nonetheless, Mr Sue-Ling has been vindicated. His results, published in the *British Medical Journal*, are described by a fellow surgeon, David Kerrigan of Manchester Royal Infirmary, as 'outstanding'. Two-thirds of patients undergoing a curative resection now survive for five years. 'The traditional British view of stomach cancer as a fatal disease is out of date,' Mr Sue-Ling says. 'The results of surgery now approach those found in Japan.'

Part 3

The Hazards of Everyday Life?

1

Healthism

Healthism – The Rampant Disease

Alcohol misuse among the older age group is much more prevalent than is widely believed, two doctors have excitedly reported in the *British Medical Journal*. Their findings were based on a systematic survey of the alcohol consumption of a group of senior citizens (average age 77, the oldest 94), admitted to hospital with an acute illness. Applying the ludicrous definition of 'excessive drinking', as the equivalent of more than two glasses of wine a day, they found that one in twenty were 'misusing' alcohol. But probing further by inquiring whether and how often they added a 'tot' to their tea or coffee, this figure doubled to one in ten. This is not a joke. The impertinence of cross-questioning seriously ill patients about the minutiae of their drinking habits is matched only by the absurdity of the conclusion that alcohol tots pose some significant hidden health hazard. Indeed, as every sane person knows, far from being a threat, alcohol promotes longevity. Mrs Charlotte Hughes, the longest living Briton, who died at the age of 115, attributed her good fortune to her daily breakfast of brandy, bacon and eggs, and to observing the ten commandments. The world's oldest person (according to the *Guinness Book of Records*), Shigechiho Izumi, a Japanese who died in 1986 at the age of 120, attributed his longevity to rising at six every morning and drinking a flask of pure sugar cane spirit with his dinner every evening.

The false depiction of a group of innocent old-age pensioners as alcoholics is an example of 'healthism', the belief that life's main goal is the pursuit of health by strict adherence to a healthy lifestyle – in which, regrettably, tots of alcohol do not feature. In his book entitled *The Death of Humane Medicine*, Professor Petr Skrabanek of Trinity College, Dublin, argues that 'healthism' now threatens the fundamental principles and purpose of medical practice.

The traditional professional ethic where the doctor saw his role as being the individual servant of the individual patient has been eroded by the belief that the doctor's main task is to modify people's behaviour in their own best interests. Lurking behind this shift in emphasis is a scientific falsehood that most illnesses are self-induced, the result of an 'unhealthy' lifestyle, and thus preventable. Accordingly, human activities are divided into approved and disapproved, prescribed and proscribed, responsible and irresponsible. Irresponsibility extends well beyond smoking and not wearing a condom, to failing to have regular medical check-ups, failing to take enough exercise and failing to eat the right sort of food.

The main success of the healthist tendency in medicine has been to persuade the Government of the need to compel the public into changing their behaviour in the approved direction. So, Professor Skrabanek writes, 'health education has been replaced by health promotion propaganda, family doctors are given financial incentives to perform regular "health" screening. Goods deemed to be unhealthy are excessively taxed and the advertising of legal products interfered with'.

Healthism is particularly difficult to combat because its pretensions appear so intrinsically beneficial. Who can argue with measures the ostensible purpose of which is to make everyone healthier? It does, however, represent a significant erosion of individual liberty. 'The only freedom which deserves the name is that of pursuing our own good in our own way,' wrote John Stuart Mill. Professor Skrabanek quotes a further passage that could almost have been written specifically to refute the claims of healthists: 'Neither one person, nor any number of persons, is warranted in saying to another human creature of ripe years that he shall not do with his life for his own benefit what he chooses to do with it . . . all errors he is likely to commit against advice and warning are far outweighed by the evil of allowing others to constrain him to what they deem is good.' It might seem a long jump from investigating the drinking habits of the over-seventies to the philosophical observations of John Stuart Mill, but it is not. Prying into people's alcohol consumption with the express intention of identifying those in whom it exceeds the approved 'safe' limits, and then cajoling them into reducing it, is a denial of individual freedom.

It is a reflection of the powerful grip that healthism now exerts on the minds of doctors that so many should utterly fail to understand this. Professor Skrabanek's merciless exposure of these philosophical and scientific errors may succeed in rescuing medicine from this folly and restoring its humanity. Meanwhile, we should follow the advice of the *Regimen Sanitatis* published in the fourteenth century. 'If you want to stay hale and healthy, stop worrying about trifles, have a light lunch, and do not strain too hard when at stool. If there are no doctors around, do not worry: the best doctors are a happy mind and moderation in all things.'

Pleasure Promotes Longevity

'A glass of good wine', wrote Sir Walter Scott (and presumably he would have included a good Havana), 'is a gracious creation and reconciles poor mortality to itself, and that is what few things can do.' Doctors are, on the whole, a sober, unimaginative lot, naturally unsympathetic to such opinions. Indeed, in recent years, they have taken to propagating a puritanical view of the world with a missionary zeal. Each of the pleasurable pursuits that give life its flavour and piquancy – alcohol, tobacco (of course), tea, coffee, good food and sex – have all been anathematised in one way or another, implicated as the cause of misfortune, disability and death. This is all very peculiar, because, by definition, the pursuit of pleasure must be good for us. Clearly we are motivated, at least in part, to feed and water ourselves by means of good food and pleasant wine, and to propagate our species by the joys of sex. But the pleasure pathways in the brain are so potent that their biological role must extend well beyond material self-preservation to serve some higher function.

Two questions therefore arise. How and why have medical experts tried to show that our pleasurable pursuits are harmful, and, contrariwise, what is the evidence that pleasure is actually good for us? Central to the distorted emphasis of the experts' pronouncements is the difficulty in measuring the experience of pleasure – exactly how, for example, does champagne ease and amplify the happy occasions of birth and marriage? By contrast, the damage caused by excessive alcohol, leading to cirrhosis of the liver, is readily amenable to statistical measurement. The upshot is that any health evaluation of the costs and benefits of alcohol is heavily biased in favour of the costs which can be counted, and against the benefits – in terms of the pleasure alcohol gives – which cannot.

The next reason for the anathematisation of pleasure lies in the dubious scientific techniques deployed in the search of the causes of disease, where one group of people with an illness are compared with another 'control' group and differences between them are sought. There will be vast differences, but the easiest to record turn out to be pleasurable habits – what and how much people eat and drink, and so on. Positive statistical correlations with these pleasurable practices are then presented as the cause of the disease. The farcical nature of this enterprise is well illustrated in the case of coffee. Coffee gives enormous pleasure to millions: it starts the day off with a kick; it is a pleasurable accompaniment to watching the world go by from the vantage point of a café table; and it is an indispensable conclusion to a meal. But coffee, the experts tell us, is implicated in raised blood pressure, heart attacks, strokes, hip fractures, diabetes in children, premenstrual syndrome, as well as cancers of the pancreas, bladder, colon and ovary. The sheer profusion of these alleged coffee-related ailments only serves to underline the worthlessness of the scientific methods by which they were discovered. Anyone credulous enough to switch to decaffeinated coffee will find no succour there, either. The solvent used to remove caffeine from coffee, methyl chloride, is under a cloud for causing cancer as well – though, it has subsequently emerged, only if given in doses equivalent to twenty-four million cups of decaffeinated coffee a day. Spending one's working life producing this scientific gibberish can obviously affect one's sanity, and, indeed, a further reason for the medical crusade against pleasure is that some of those involved seem to have a screw loose. When it was revealed that generous quantities of wine every day might be good for the heart, an American doctor said: 'I think that in our society even suggesting this possibility is fraught with danger.'

But what of the contrary evidence for the benefits of the pursuit of pleasure? One clue lies in the universal social class differential in health. Compared with the professional classes, the semi- and unskilled have a higher incidence of virtually all diseases, which is usually attributed to genetic differences, cultural habits and 'poverty'. But perhaps, as Dr Bruce Charlton of the University of Newcastle has suggested in *The Lancet*, this is the wrong way round, and a more plausible reason for the health differential lies in the benefits of being relatively wealthy and the greater opportunity this provides for enjoying the pleasures of life. This view is supported by a study of an unfortunate group of people who are psychologically incapable of enjoying pleasure, a condition known as anhedonia. They are impervious to the joys of eating, smells and sounds, and indifferent to the pleasures of the company of others. Not surprisingly, anhedonia is common among those with a depressive personality. Those so afflicted have a high risk of committing suicide but they also have a mortality rate from other causes twice that of the general population. The pleasures of life should be enjoyed on their own account, and do not require to be justified by showing that they do us good. But this evidence that pleasure can prolong one's life might serve as a useful antidote to the moralistic self-righteousness of so many doctors.

The False Promises of Prevention

Common sense is an absolute requirement for the practice of medicine. Doctors have to get it right, as error, whether in diagnosis or treatment, results in misery – or, indeed, can be fatal. They get it right, not just by reference to the vast corpus of knowledge that is 'medical science' but by possessing a discerning intellect that can distinguish illusion from reality and is the only sure protection for the ill against the false solutions of quackery. Further, when confronted by the untreatable, a different type of intelligence is required, one that appreciates and can cope with the tragedies of people's lives. These attributes are not universally found in society but are, to a greater or lesser extent, found among doctors. Each week, in the obituary column of the *British Medical Journal*, one reads of men and women, the defining characteristic of whose lives was that they were sensible, practical people.

And yet there is a feeling that, increasingly, medical advice and opinion seems to be rather unbalanced. Trivial or, indeed, non-existent threats to health from what we eat or the air we breathe are exaggerated out of all proportion. Patently erroneous propositions – as, for example, 'AIDS does not discriminate' – are sedulously propagated. Judgementalism is rife and the public are burdened with gratuitous advice at every aspect of their private lives. What lies behind this change in tone? The medicine as practised by the paragons of the *BMJ* obituary columns was essentially a straightforward affair. When people fall ill, whether with cancer or a cold, the doctor's job is to make them better, if possible.

But recently the scope of medicine has become much more ambitious. Doctors should not just try to make the ill better, but stop the healthy getting ill. 'Prevention' is after all better than 'cure'. And if this aspiration is to be fulfilled, then the concern of medicine must stretch well beyond the sick to encompass the healthy as well, who must be advised, admonished and cajoled if they are not to fall ill.

Now, prevention certainly *can* be better than cure. The traditional form of preventive public health relied on engineering and hard science, as in the provision of clean water and the development of vaccines which have a proven record in dramatically reducing disease. But this new type of public health relies on dubious statistics, mass persuasion and the manipulation of people, and does not work. This would not matter very much were it not that this belief that prevention is cheaper and better than cure has proved very seductive to politicians who have decreed that it should form the basis of Government health policy. Indeed, the document *Health of the Nation* sets out specific targets to be met. These include 'preventing' 30 per cent of suicides, even though serious mental illness is not preventable; 'preventing' 50 per cent of teenage pregnancies, even though no one has any idea how this is to be achieved; reducing the rate of heart disease by 40 per cent by getting people to eat less fat, even though it is already falling dramatically without any significant changes in the patterns of food consumption; reducing the number of people who drink the equivalent of three glasses of wine a day, even though there is no evidence that two, or even three, times this amount poses any risk to health; reducing cancers of the cervix and breast with very expensive screening programmes, despite the absence of evidence in this country that they work. And so on.

It is quite clear that this type of prevention may not only be much more expensive but, by wasting precious resources, be much worse than cure. The scope for prevention is after all very limited in a society such a Britain where most people live out their natural life spans to die from, or be incapacitated by, illnesses strongly determined by ageing. Propaganda campaigns to change people's lives are a poor substitute for the proper task of medicine in alleviating those illnesses. Certainly there are many misfortunes in life it would be nice to avoid, but the promise of preventing cancer or heart disease or anything else without the ability to do so is quackery.

2

Environmental Alarums

The Broad View

Virtually every aspect of our daily lives has been implicated, in one way or another, in causing cancer. So comprehensive is the list of suspect foods, beverages, household goods, cleaning products and so much else besides that, were the alleged risks to be taken at face value, it would be a brave man or woman who would contemplate getting up in the morning. This supposition is so absurd that the only rational response to each new cancer scare might be a sceptical shrug. But doubts remain. Certainly the experts who bring these problems to our attention may be guilty of exaggeration or special pleading but if they were right only a fraction of the time, this would still be important. How to tell? The ordinary citizen is in no position to come to an informed decision as that would require studying in detail hundreds of scientific studies every year, while even a determined effort to make sense of the data and obscure scientific terminology would leave one none the wiser. It is, however, no longer necessary to attempt such a heroic task because it has been done by Professor Aaron Wildavsky, of the University of California with his post-graduate research students. Their findings have been published as *But Is It True? A Citizen's Guide to Environmental Health and Safety Issues*. Their verdict? The alleged environmental risks to health are 'false, mostly false, unproven or negligible'.

The first priority, argues Professor Wildavsky, is to distinguish between 'high-level' exposure to potentially harmful chemicals that might occur in certain occupations and 'low-level' exposure – the minuscule, virtually unmeasurable quantities of pollutants and toxins in the air and water to which the general population is exposed. Self-evidently, high-level exposure can be harmful, after all any chemical at a high enough dosage can be damaging and this is as true for arsenic as it is for carrots. Central to the environmentalist's case is that the evidence of harm from high-level exposure can be extrapolated to low-level exposure, but fundamental laws of biology show this is not the case: just because drinking a bottle of whisky a day for five years causes liver cirrhosis does not mean that eating a whisky flavoured plum cake once a year for thirty years has the same effect. This does not happen because, as Professor Wildavsky points out, the human organism is actually remarkably robust with a whole repertoire of self-repair mechanisms to deal with potentially harmful substances: wounds heal, bacteria are repulsed and toxins at low levels are detoxified.

The second reason for being sceptical about these environmental health scares is that the main evidence incriminating chemicals in cancer – toxicity tests in rats and mice – is highly suspect. It was never very likely that feeding rodents vast quantities of chemicals would be very informative about whether exposure at infinitely lower doses might threaten man. The validity of these tests was discredited in 1990 by the American scientist Dr Bruce Ames who found that natural chemicals in 27 types of food, including bananas, apples, celery and tomatoes, were equally capable of producing cancer in rodents. Indeed, there are more cancer-causing chemicals in a single cup of coffee than that which the average person could consume in a year from pesticides and other man-made chemicals. Those worried by these matters, Professor Wildavsky suggests, should drink one less cup of coffee a year.

These reservations about the scientific basis of health scares would be irrelevant if it were possible in only one instance to show quite unequivocal evidence of harm. But it cannot be done. Time and again, Professor Wildavsky finds that the alleged claims are based on one type of evidence while other sources that challenge or contradict them are either marginalised or ignored. Nitrate fertilisers have been implicated in stomach cancer because when ingested they form compounds that are carcinogenic to animals. And so, with the widespread rise in such fertilisers since the war, the rates of stomach cancer should have risen. But over the last 50 years its incidence has fallen by half. Far from causing stomach cancer, it would seem that nitrate fertilisers protect against it. As Professor Wildavsky consistently answers the question 'But is it true?' with an emphatic 'No', one can only surmise that for the last 20 years the public has been systematically deceived by environmentalists, scientists and regulators about the threats to health in their everyday life.

Radiation Not Guilty

In one of the longest, most complicated and certainly the most expensive civil actions ever heard before a British court the High Court judge, Mr Justice French, ruled that in the case of the Sellafield cancers British Nuclear Fuels could not be held responsible for the death from leukaemia of a ten-month-old girl or the infertility of a 27-year-old woman following her treatment for lymphoma. The implications of this verdict in understanding the health hazard of radiation are so important that it merits further elaboration. The saga of the Sellafield cancers began almost by accident some years ago when a young television producer, James Cutler, noticed, as he wandered through the churchyard of the Cumbrian village of Millom, that the dates on the more recent gravestones showed that several had died while still young. He checked their death certificates at Somerset House and found they had almost all died of radiation-associated cancers like leukaemia and lymphoma – and drew the obvious conclusion. The programme he made linking these deaths to the nearby nuclear reprocessing plant at Sellafield caused an uproar.

The official enquiry that followed, headed by the former president of the Royal College of Physicians, Sir Douglas Black, confirmed an unusually high incidence of cancers but maintained they were 'unusual but not unique'. Further investigations revealed that Sellafield was indeed 'not unique'. Children living near other nuclear plants at Aldermaston and Dounreay were also found to be at increased risk of radiation-induced cancers. The case against British Nuclear Fuels seemed to be overwhelming except for one intractable problem – the amount of radioactive discharge from Sellafield, or any other nuclear plant, was much too small to cause cancer. A simple mathematical calculation makes that clear. We are all exposed to natural sources of radiation from cosmic rays and the earth's core, estimated at 2.5 millisieverts (msv) per year, of which nuclear discharges are held to contribute around 0.1 per cent, or 0.0025 msv. Radiation-induced cancers only start to occur at levels of exposures of 100 msv, therefore, children near Sellafield would have to have been exposed to levels of radiation 40,000 times greater than normal if their cancers were to be attributable to radioactive discharges. Clearly this is impossible.

There had to be an alternative mechanism, and this was suggested by the late Professor Martin Gardner in 1990, who showed that the fathers of affected children working in the nuclear plant were much more likely to have been exposed to high levels of radiation while at work. These levels, he argued, could damage the sperm cells so that the genes they passed on to their children would induce cancer. The outcome of the case held before the High Court centred on the validity or otherwise of this explanation. It was rejected on three counts. First, there is no evidence of increased leukaemia rates in the offspring of those exposed to much higher doses of radiation at Hiroshima and Nagasaki; secondly, it is not conceivable that radiation would consistently cause the same type of genetic damage in the sperm cells that would give rise to a specific type of cancer, especially as there was no other evidence of genetic damage; thirdly, a further study of workers published since then failed to confirm Professor Gardner's findings.

So we are left with a conundrum. By any stretch of the imagination, the circumstantial evidence seems overwhelming, but everything else we know about radiation and its effects on biological systems argues against the discharges from Sellafield being the culprit. Counter-intuitively and against all our prejudices, there is no alternative other than to exonerate British Nuclear Fuels. There must be a reason for the cluster of cancer cases in the vicinity of nuclear plants, but we must look elsewhere for the explanation.

The Myth of Falling Sperm Counts

There are few more potent myths than that 'something' in the water supply is having an adverse effect on the male reproductive organs. The 'something' are pollutants – pesticide residues and chemicals known as PCBs, which have similar biological properties to the female hormone oestrogen and have been incriminated in an alleged decline in the male sperm count and an increase in the frequency of cancer of the testes. It all sounds pretty frightening and, not surprisingly, Greenpeace and other environmentalist organisations have called for urgent preventive action to be taken. The only problem is that it cannot possibly be true.

Many of the foods, particularly the vegetables, we consume, contain very small amounts of naturally occurring oestrogenic substances, so the first thing to establish is how much more of the pollutant-derived oestrogens we might be consuming over and above that which is a normal part of the diet. In a report from the Medical Research Council, Professor Lewis Smith of

Leicester University gives the answer. The minute amounts of naturally occurring oestrogens in our food are still 40 million times greater than the amount derived from pesticides and PCBs – or, put another way, pollutants contribute 0.0000025 per cent of the oestrogenic substances in our diet.

Nor is that the end of the story. Back in the Fifties, obstetricians misguidedly believed that miscarriages might be prevented by administering the oestrogen DES during pregnancy. The doses varied but worked out at about 10 milligrams a day, which means the foetus was exposed to levels of oestrogen 10 million million times greater than that from oestrogenic pollutants. Hundreds of thousands of women were treated with DES, and their children are now aged between 35 and 40, so if foetal exposure to these high levels were to have had an adverse effect, this should now be apparent in the male offspring. An increase of vaginal cancer has been observed among the female offspring, yet, according to a study published in the *New England Journal of Medicine*, there is no evidence that male sexual function or fertility has been adversely affected. Nor, indeed, compared with men not exposed to DES, do they have a greater risk of cancer of the testes.

Clearly, it is completely inconceivable that oestrogenic pollutants could be the cause of either the decline in sperm count or the rise in testicular cancer. So what is? The answer to the first part is easy. The evidence for the decline in sperm counts over the last 20 years is poor and contradictory. The most likely explanation for the 'decline', then, is that it is a myth – and, certainly, doctors who treat men with infertility problems do not believe it is any commoner now than in the past. As for the increase in testicular cancer, the honest explanation must be that, as with virtually all cancers, we do not know its cause, not why its incidence should change over time.

The Lead Scare Scam

Diesel fuel is a health risk according to a report which argues that exhaust emissions from diesel cars could trigger 'asthma attacks, heart disease and cancer in thousands of people'. Like the myriad of other putative environmental hazards we have been warned about in recent years – pesticides, chemicals, fertilisers, and so on – it is almost impossible to evaluate whether diesel fuel might harm health in the ways suggested. Only a handful will be bothered to read the report in any detail, and even then the scientific details are likely to be so obscure that it will be difficult to make up one's mind.

Environmental campaigners thus have carte blanche to generate public neurosis. They alone have the drive and propaganda skills to establish the agenda, and are prosecution, judge and jury about almost every new hazard. Nonetheless there is a general feeling that they are a good thing, keeping industry on its toes by discouraging it from polluting our green and pleasant land. No doubt many would say that even if the health hazards of any specific pollutant are not clear, this does not matter because in general the less we have of chemicals in the water supply and noxious gases in the air the better.

The interesting thing about this diesel scare, however, is that it is a direct result of an earlier campaign – indeed the most successful there has ever been – to remove lead from petrol, thus forcing the public to use more 'environmentally friendly' fuels like unleaded and diesel. So although it may seem merely perverse to ask whether it was a good thing to remove lead from petrol, it is still interesting to try to assess whether the expected benefits have been realised.

At the time of the campaign, spearheaded by the tireless Mr Des Wilson, it all seemed pretty clear cut. Lead in petrol contributes significantly to the amount of lead in the atmosphere and so could result in low-level lead poisoning in children which it was alleged has an adverse effect on children's IQ, is responsible for behavioural problems, and is a 'likely' cause of still-birth and malformations. Of course there were dissident voices. Dr Peter Ellwood, of the Medical Research Council, compared the average levels of blood lead on traffic-free Sark with those in the Welsh valleys and found they were almost the same, forcing him to conclude that lead in petrol probably contributed only a fraction of the total amount compared to other sources such as dust, paint and lead pipes. In vain did the lead industry argue that its product made car engines more efficient so the move to unleaded petrol would increase the amount of petrol used, which in turn would increase the quantities of carbon dioxide (later to implicated in the greenhouse effect) pushed out into the atmosphere.

But Mr Wilson's campaign proved to be unstoppable, and in 1983 the Royal Commission on Environmental Pollution recommended a phased removal of lead from petrol. But the victory was a Pyrrhic one. The most influential study on adverse effects of lead on children's IQ was conducted by Herbert Needleman of

Harvard University who found that children with lead levels of 35 microgrammes per decilitre (a figure only very rarely found in even children living next to lead smelters) had on average an IQ score four points lower than a control group. The relevance of this trivial difference to Britain where children's blood levels were three times lower than this even before lead was removed from petrol is obviously highly dubious. Further, serial measurements of children's IQ have shown enormous increases of the order of 25 points in the four decades after the war – during which time, of course, the amount of lead piped into the atmosphere from cars increased enormously. Roy Harrison, professor of environmental health at Birmingham University has calculated that the cost of switching to unleaded petrol as between £400 and 600 million a year.

Asthma and Pollution – 1

The part of London where I work includes one of the capital's busiest traffic intersections. Every hours, thousands of cars pour across Vauxhall Bridge and hasten down the Embankment. When the temperature soars into the nineties, there is an almost palpable blanket of stagnant air polluted by exhaust fumes. Not surprisingly, the Department of the Environment issued warnings about ozone levels and the television news featured concerned doctors advising the public on the dangers to their health. Meanwhile, I was in the surgery, with nebuliser in one hand and syringe in the other, fully prepared for hordes of wheezing patients. Nothing happened. Even questioning those whom I knew to be asthmatic as to whether their symptoms had deteriorated drew a blank.

Perhaps my experience was unusual, or the most badly affected had simply gone straight to hospital. Nonetheless, it seemed worthwhile to take a closer look at the evidence behind the universal belief that the dramatic rise in the number of asthma cases over the past thirty years has been caused by the escalating number of cars on the road. It seemed best to start with a 'literature search', courtesy of a marvel of modern technology called Ovid Medline at the Royal Society of Medicine Library, which provides almost immediate access to over one-and-a-half million medical papers on every conceivable topic published during the past four years. It contains, for example, over 16,000 references to AIDS, which would take the best part of a fortnight to scrutinise fully. Having keyed in my request for anything on 'asthma and car exhaust', the system thought for a moment before flashing up on the screen that there were exactly zero references on this important subject in its database. This does not mean nothing has been written on the topic, but does suggest that, in the pecking order of important medical issues, the link between asthma and car pollution does not rate very highly.

Seeking further enlightenment, I turned to three very substantial reports produced in recent years by a group of genuine experts. These have examined the adverse effects of the three main photo-chemical pollutants – sulphur dioxide, ozone and oxides of nitrogen, better known as Nox. Here, I discovered it is really quite straightforward to define, with a fair degree of accuracy, their adverse effects. To find out what toxic levels are necessary to produce respiratory symptoms all that is needed is to take a group of people, some with asthma and some without, and put them in a special chamber, exposing them to the pollutant of interest and see what happens.

It is useful, before providing a synopsis of their conclusions, just to review the grounds for the concern that car exhaust fumes are so harmful to our lungs. Over the past thirty years, the number of cars on the road has almost tripled – from 8 million to 18 million – during which time the incidence of asthma has almost doubled. This looks convincing, though other allergic diseases not obviously related to car ownership such as hayfever and eczema have also doubled, suggesting there may be some other single underlying mechanism. Further, though air pollution can certainly exacerbate symptoms in asthmatics, it would actually need to *cause* asthma to explain this rise in frequency, and this has never been demonstrated.

Nevertheless, the image of toxic car fumes causing wheezing and breathlessness is a very potent one, and during the past few years many environmentalist groups, medical charities and journalists have vigorously campaigned on this issue. Could sulphur dioxide and acid aerosols be responsible? In the early Fifties, these by-products of the burning of fossil fuels led to the pea soup fogs, which reached staggering levels of up to 1,350 parts per billion (ppb). The chamber studies show that it takes levels of around 400 ppb in asthmatics and 1,000 ppb in non-asthmatics to cause symptoms. Since the Clean Air Act, levels in Britain have fallen dramatically and now hover around 30 ppb, so clearly they cannot be the culprit for the rise in asthma. What about ozone, the notorious villain of the Los Angeles smogs? Levels in Britain have remained fairly constant over the past 20 years, peaking in the summer months with average levels of around 70 ppb were recorded. The chamber studies show that the exposure levels twice as great as this have only a small effect on lung function; so ozone, too, can be exonerated. That leaves us with Nox, the main pollutant from car exhausts whose quantities have almost doubled over the past ten years, coinciding with the asthma 'epidemic'. Here the experts tell us that 'changes in lung function in normal and asthmatic subjects are trivial and inconsistent following exposure to concentrations of 1,000 ppb'. The levels recorded in Britain are 10 times lower than this. Ergo, the epidemic of asthma over the past 30 years cannot be blamed on car-exhaust fumes, and those looking for a reason should look elsewhere. They are undoubtedly unpleasant, but the concentration of their toxic constituents is just much too low to cause significant symptoms. The mysterious non-appearance of scores of wheezing breathless patients in my surgery is explained.

Asthma and Pollution – 2

Besides its great natural beauty, the Isle of Skye is one of the least polluted parts of the kingdom – no toxic emissions from factory chimneys, no traffic-congested roads contaminating the air. Indeed, virtually the only man-made airborne pollutant is the smoke from household fires rapidly dispersed by the prevailing winds from the Atlantic.

And yet when Dr Jane Austin, paediatrician at Inverness's Royal Northern Infirmary, investigated the prevalence of asthma among the children of school age on the island, she found it to be commoner than in the rest of the Highlands, commoner than in Aberdeen, commoner even than in Cardiff. Her careful measurements of lung function showed a deterioration following exertion in one-third of the island's school children, while the equivalent figure in Cardiff is 8 per cent.

Dr Austin's findings are quite unexceptional: doctors and scientists have found little or no relationship between the severity of airborne pollution and the numbers affected by asthma. Certainly those who already have asthma are often made wheezier and more short of breath by the photochemical smog from vehicle exhausts, but pollution does not seem to cause the illness or account for its increased frequency.

'There is no evidence of the significant rise in pollutants that would have been necessary to cause the increase in asthma,' says Professor Anthony Seaton, of Aberdeen University, citing as evidence a remarkable study of children in Leipzig and Munich. Before the fall of the Berlin Wall, most of the factories in East Germany manufactured little else other than pollution, and Leipzig was no exception. In 1989 the concentrations of sulphur dioxide and particulate matter in the air were respectively 30 and ten times higher than in Munich. Yet the study found asthma to be commoner in Munich than in smog-ridden Leipzig.

There is a profound disparity between popular belief and expert opinion on this matter. While for the public and environmentalists a causative link between air pollution and asthma is self-evident, the experts are not convinced. 'Air pollution as a cause of asthma has the seeming merit of appealing to common sense,' writes Anthony Newman Taylor, professor of respiratory medicine at London's Royal Brompton Hospital in *The Lancet*, yet the relationship, he says, 'has not been observed'.

So why do people, particularly children, suffer from asthma? Asthma has much in common with two other allergic illnesses – eczema and hay fever – and collectively the three of them are known as the 'atopic diseases'. These diseases are characterised by an excess of production of an antibody called IgE which, in the presence of some allergens, causes symptoms. Thus for the atopic individual a high pollen count may the cause the itchy eyes and runny nose of hay fever; chemicals and foods may cause itchy, dry skin of eczema, while air pollutants, the house-dust mite and viral infections may cause the wheeze of asthma.

The main features of these three atopic illnesses are remarkably similar. They all run strongly in families suggesting that the same genes are involved. Thus, those with asthma are much more likely to suffer from eczema and hay fever, and their children are much more likely to suffer from these illnesses. They all tend to start in childhood and get better or disappear altogether with the passage of time. They have all become a lot more frequent since the war as shown by a comparative study of thousands of children in Aberdeen in 1964 and 1989. Over this 25-year period, the prevalence of asthma and eczema doubled and that of hay fever trebled.

They are also, virtually uniquely, 'diseases of the advantaged' – they occur more frequently in children born into professional compared to working-class households. They are also more common in small rather than large families – 'only' children are four times more likely to develop hay fever than those with several siblings and three times more likely to develop eczema. Further, as already noted, asthma seems to be commoner in isolated communities such as Skye than in towns, and in affluent cities such as Munich than in impoverished Leipzig.

Clearly, then, something to do with the body's immune system has changed, increasing the prevalence of these three illnesses. The obvious candidate – that fits in with all the other observations to do with social class and family size – is the decline in exposure to infection. Commenting on the relationship between eczema, hay fever and family size, Dr David Strachan, senior lecturer at St George's Hospital medical school, observes it is best explained 'if allergic diseases are prevented by infections in early childhood transmitted by contact with older siblings'.

Professor Newman Taylor of London's Brompton Hospital has made a similar point about asthma which he says may have reached 'epidemic status in affluent societies because falling family size reduces the chances that toddlers and infants encounter infections sufficiently early'. The rise in atopic illness certainly coincides with the precipitous decline during the postwar years in the major childhood infectious diseases, so perhaps they are the price that has to be paid for modern vaccines, the miracle of antibiotics and social progress.

The Nonsense Over Nitrates

A medical journal has reported the results of a study investigating the health consequences of having one's water supply cut off, apparently an increasingly common occurrence as people struggle to meet their ever-escalating water bills. The researchers failed to find evidence of outbreaks of infective diarrhoea or hepatitis but the report concluded that, in general, the denial of access to a clean water supply was likely to have adverse health effects in the long term. I am sure they are right. A major cause of these water disconnections is the rising cost of water to the consumer. This has been passed on by the water authorities in meeting EC regulations on water purity – which are intended to promote public health by protecting us against chemicals and pesticides. Indeed, in January 1992, the Advocate General of the European Court, Karl Otto Lenz, found Britain guilty of failing to implement a 1980 directive that the maximum level of nitrates in our water supply be reduced from 100 to 50 parts per million, because of their alleged role in causing

Blue Baby Syndrome and stomach cancer. As fertilisers are a major source of nitrates the aim of the directive was to force farmers to use alternatives, and the cost incurred in implementing it has been estimated at £400 million.

So which poses the greater threat to health – minuscule quantities of nitrates, or having one's water supply disconnected? To answer that we have to look at the evidence of the harm from nitrates. When ingested in excess nitrates react with the haemoglobin molecule in red blood cells, preventing them from carrying oxygen, which becomes apparent as cyanosis, a blue discoloration of the skin – hence Blue Baby Syndrome. The process is readily reversible with treatment. In Britain since the last war there have been no more than 13 reported cases of Blue Baby Syndrome due to the presence of nitrates in the water, the most recent case being in 1972. An investigation by the Department of Health into these cases found the evidence 'not convincing', either because the diagnosis was not adequately established, or because the cases arose from circumstances in which there was bacterial contamination of the water (almost all cases concerned water from wells which is particularly liable to such contamination. This, by itself, causes the nitrate level to rise.)

Nitrates have also been incriminated as a cause of stomach cancer because, when ingested, they form compounds that at high doses are carcinogenic in animals. But what about the evidence in humans? While the use of nitrate fertilisers has become widespread since the war, the incidence of stomach cancer has fallen by half. In 1985, Dr Shirley Beresford, of the Royal Free Hospital, compared the varying rates of stomach cancer in different parts of the country with nitrate levels in the local water supply and found an inverse relationship – the higher the nitrate concentration, the lower the incidence of stomach cancer. This was confirmed by Professor Richard Doll, who found that nitrate levels in the saliva were actually lower in people living in those areas with a high incidence of stomach cancer when compared with areas where the rate was low. So if nitrates are implicated in stomach cancer, the only logical inference from these three consistent strands of evidence is that, far from causing the disease, they actually protect against it.

Were Britain to fulfil the EC directive, it is thus inconceivable that there would be any beneficial effects – either on the non-existent problem of Blue Baby Syndrome or on rates of stomach cancer – while the adverse consequences of rising water bills, with resulting disconnections, is likely to be considerable. This is not just one further example of EC idiocy, but a single illustration of an issue of enormous importance. It is now a truism that environmental pollution poses considerable threats to human health, but it is not easy for most people to grasp the often complex scientific detail involved. They must take it on trust when environmental activists say that chemical A causes cancer or chemical B genetic abnormalities. This, in turn, has placed enormous power in the hands of the regulators, enabling them to control or interfere in industry and the lives of individuals to reduce the putative risks, in anticipation of some health gain. But time and again, critical examination of the claims of the environmental lobby shows it to be, just as with the example of nitrates, either trivial or false. It is easy to shrug one's shoulders and say, 'Perhaps it is not possible to show exactly the degree to which these pollutants harm us, but the less we have of them the better.' However, the costs involved are colossal, and take up money that would be better spent on mitigating environmental problems that might actually improve the quality of our lives – such as the threat to the rainforests and the loss of biological diversity.

3

Fags, Booze and a Suntan

Tobacco – A Serious Hazard At Last

I narrowly defeated the Chancellor, Kenneth Clarke, to win the coveted Services to Smokers' Rights Award, presented by Forest – the Freedom Organisation for the Right to Enjoy Smoking Tobacco – for bringing to the attention of *Sunday Telegraph* readers the beneficial effects of smoking in protecting against Parkinson's Disease and Alzheimer's. Winners of less flattering awards, most of whom failed to turn up to collect their handsome plaques, included Secretary of State for Health, Virginia Bottomley – the 'Jackboot' award – and a Mr S. Mittler, director of services at Southampton General Hospital, who appointed a *gauleiter* to sniff the hospital grounds for lurking smokers, earning the accolade for 'maximum effort in increasing intolerance towards smokers'.

It was, as can be imagined, a most congenial evening. I was pleased to be able to contribute to the gaiety of the occasion by reporting the latest research from that week's *New Scientist*, which shows that smoking protects against another disease – severe acne. Rather than being victimised for their habit, smokers should be honoured every year by a grateful nation for their prodigious contributions to financing public services through taxation, and by dying early not being a burden on the state.

My main purpose in writing about smoking, however, is to strengthen the resolve of those who have decided to quit, and to discuss recent developments in screening for and treating lung cancer. Those who smoke throughout their lives are 22½ times more likely to die of lung cancer before the age of 75 than non-smokers. Set against this, all other hazards of everyday life, such as being run over by a bus or falling off a mountain, are utterly trivial. The best reason for quitting is that over a ten-year period this markedly increased relative risk to smokers declines back to that of non-smokers. Regrettably, this is not precisely the case and depends rather on when the decision is made. Thus, a smoker giving up in his thirties will still have a two-fold greater chance of developing lung cancer than non-smokers, and for those who wait until their fifties, the risk is five-fold. So the message, predictably, is the sooner the better. The temptation to switch to cigars or pipes should be avoided. Although the chance of getting lung cancer for those who have only ever smoked tobacco in this form is just three times that of non-smokers, for those who have switched from cigarettes, the risk does not fall – and so in health terms they might as well not have bothered.

I now turn to the difficult question of whether it is possible, by having regular chest X-rays, for lung cancer in both smokers and ex-smokers to be picked up early enough for it to be curable. The simple answer is a qualified yes. Three-quarters of those lucky enough to be found, usually by chance, to have a tumour at its earliest stage with no spread to the local lymph nodes, will, after surgical removal, still be alive in five years' time – which is obviously highly desirable. The limitation of regular X-ray screening, even done as frequently as every six months, is that by the time most tumours are detected they have already spread and the chances of cure have become very small. None the less, a study in the late 1960s showed that a quarter of those whose tumours were detected by screening survived five years, compared with the usual figure of about 7 per cent. This might seem modest, but as lung cancer is itself so common, this does add up in absolute numbers to quite a lot of people whose lives must have been prolonged or even saved by screening. The NHS decided against providing a national programme for smokers, but it seems quite sensible that those who have been heavy smokers in the past, and who want to maximise their chances of not dying from their habit, should seek a private consultation and discuss the possibility of having regular chest X-rays.

Finally, there is the question of the best treatment for those found to have lung cancer which is not potentially curable by surgery. The usual treatment is palliative radiotherapy, which without altering the prognosis, can make the symptoms more bearable. I have been advised by Dr Stephen Spiro, consultant physician at University College Hospital, that this alone should now be considered inadequate. He argues that chemotherapy, currently only given to 2 per cent of those with lung cancer, should be more widely used. Nine out of 10 of those with 'small cell' lung cancer respond to chemotherapy, and although it does not prolong life it does markedly improve the quality of their remaining months by reducing the amount of coughing, breathlessness and pain. As for those with 'non-small cell' lung cancer, chemotherapy can result in a 'cure' in 5 per cent of cases, which works out at more than 1,500 people a year. I apologise to those who still enjoy the sweet and calming pleasures of tobacco for the killjoy nature of this column, but it is always useful to know the facts. If persuaded, there is now no excuse for even the most committed smoker not to quit, as the nicotine patches and chewing-gum now available are so demonstrably effective in abolishing the craving for tobacco.

Feeling Better For a Smoke

Heretical as it is to say, smoking can be good for your health. Indeed, much of the credit for the worldwide dissemination of tobacco must go to the initial enthusiastic advocacy of doctors and in particular to Nicholas Monardes and Juan de Cardenas, two Spanish physicians. 'To seek to tell the virtues and greatness of this holy herb,' de Cardenas wrote in 1578, 'the ailments that can be cured by it, the evils from which it has saved thousands, would go unto infinity.' Two factors contributed to its popularity in medical circles. Tobacco was thought to have properties of being 'hot and dry', which within the sixteenth-century understanding of disease meant it counteracted a surfeit of 'wet humours' that were the major cause of illness. As a remedy to restore humoral equilibrium, tobacco had clear advantages over bleeding and purging. Then, tobacco clearly had a pharmacological effect, which is more than could be said for most of the other contemporary herbal remedies. Dr Monardes cited no fewer than twenty specific ailments, from toothache to cancer, for which tobacco was considered a cure. Later, tobacco still had many medical uses. It was inhaled as an anti-spasmodic for asthma, inserted as an enema for the relief of intestinal obstruction, and regularly prescribed in lunatic asylums as snuff.

Tobacco is no panacea, but as a potent pharmacologically active compound it would be most unlikely if it did not have some therapeutic effects, though the now implacable medical hostility to smoking almost guarantees that these are ignored. In fact, smoking both protects against and improves the symptoms of three serious diseases – ulcerative colitis, Parkinson's disease and Alzheimer's disease. In each the evidence is similar and consistent. Martin Osbourne, a surgeon at the Royal Free Hospital, London, says: 'It is beyond doubt that smokers are protected against ulcerative colitis, and the more that is smoked the greater the protection – so those on 25 cigarettes a day or more have a risk as little as one tenth that of non-smokers.' Many patients recognise that smoking improves their symptoms of pain, diarrhoea and mucus. In a typical case described by Dr John Rhodes, a consultant gastro-enterologist at the University Hospital, Cardiff, a 36-year old woman who had smoked a packet a day for 15 years, and then quit at the age of 32, developed ulcerative colitis a year later. She started smoking again 'and noticed a marked improvement within a week . . . since then she has stopped and started on two further occasions with exactly the same effect.'

In ulcerative colitis, the precise mechanism of the beneficial effects of smoking is unclear. But in the case of Parkinson's and Alzheimer's there is a plausible explanation for the protection provided by regular smoking – that it increases the number of nicotine sensitive receptors in the brain, which in turn influence the amount of the important neurotransmitter acetylcholine. Smokers have a 50 per cent reduced risk of developing Alzheimer's – and the more smoked the greater the protection. A similar figure, though less consistently, has been found for Parkinson's.

Nicotine also has a therapeutic effect, which is particularly important for patients with Alzheimer's for whom there is no treatment of any value. Dr Gemma Jones, of London's Institute of Psychiatry, has reported the results of injecting small doses of nicotine under the skin of twenty-four patients and found their levels of 'attention and information processing' almost reached those of a group of people without disease. Regrettably, however, there was no change in short-term memory. Theoretically, nicotine skin patches might be equally beneficial, though there is no doubt that the optimal method of drug delivery is by smoking which ensures nicotine rapidly gets to the brain. The overall health hazards of tobacco certainly outweigh those of preventing these diseases, but these hazards only become more apparent after 20 years or more. Doctors could encourage people after, say, the age of 60 to take up smoking (or to use nicotine patches daily) as this would not significantly reduce life expectancy but increase the likelihood of a sparkling senescence.

The Smokescreen of Passive Smoking

There is a lengthy list of diseases attributed to what the Americans call Environmental Tobacco Smoke but is better known as 'passive smoking' and which now includes asthma, glue ear in children, breast cancer and brain tumours. Dr Stanton Glantz, of the University of California, has recently asserted that in America alone passive smoking causes 50,000 deaths a year. Not only humans but pets, it seems, are affected. A Californian veterinarian has found a slightly increased risk of lung cancer in dogs where there is a smoker in the home and the death from the same disease of a six-year-old, blue-feathered budgie called Peter was blamed on his owner's 40-a-day habit.

There is certainly an association between the number of adult smokers in a household and acute exacerbations of asthma in children – but much of the rest of the evidence indicting passive smoking is a nonsense. It was never likely to be easy to prove a link between passive smoking and lung cancer but back in the 1970s researchers hit on the idea of comparing the rate of lung cancer in the non-smoking wives of smoking husbands with that where neither partner smoked. There have been thirty such studies with contradictory results – some showing a small positive effect, but others indicating that being married to a smoking husband might even protect against lung cancer. There were also some anomalous observations from the positive studies: one of the earliest showed that passive smoking was more dangerous than active smoking, as the non-smoking wives of heavy smokers seemed to have a higher rate of lung cancer than smoking wives.

In 1986, Professor Nicholas Wald, of St Bartholomew's Hospital, pulled all the data together in a statistical overview and concluded that passive smoking increased the risk of lung cancer by between 10 and 30 per cent, accounting for around 300 deaths from the disease a year in Britain. Since then, numerous worthy committees have endorsed this conclusion and the experts have become more emphatic in their pronouncements. Professor Wald now believes the evidence to be 'compelling' and Dr David Burns of the University of California, writing in the *Journal of the National Cancer Institute*, says: 'The causal relationship between Environmental Tobacco Smoke and lung cancer is now clearly established.'

The trouble is, it isn't true. There are essentially two types of lung cancer. The commonest are squamous cancers which arise from the cells lining the airways. The second are called adenocarcinomas, which arise from glandular tissue in the air sacs in the periphery of the lung. In the early 1950s, when Sir Richard Doll and the late Sir Austin Bradford-Hill first proved that smoking caused lung cancer, they made the important distinction that the cancers caused were of the squamous type and there was 'no marked association with smoking and adenocarcinoma'. On the rare occasions that non-smokers do get lung cancer, it is almost always of the adenocarcinoma type. But in the passive smoking studies it is just this adenocarcinoma type whose rate is allegedly increased among non-smoking wives of smoking husbands. It is therefore necessary to suppose, if the passive smoking story is to be believed, that carcinogenic cigarette smoke as inhaled by smokers over many years causes one type of cancer, and that the same smoke, as inhaled by passive smokers at doses of tens of thousands of times lower causes an entirely different type of cancer, not usually associated with smoking and in a different part of the lung.

Dr Clark Heath, of the American Cancer Society, in an attempt to explain this anomaly away, writes in *The Lancet*: 'Presumably this histological and anatomical shift from squamous cancers in the central bronchi to adenocarcinomas in the periphery reflects the smaller particle size of Environmental Tobacco Smoke allowing deeper penetration of carcinogens into lung tissue.' If you believe that, you'll believe anything. A better explanation is provided by Professor Alvan Feinstein of Yale University Medical School: 'As the evidence fails to comply with the prime requisites of scientific reasoning, the prosecution simply ignored these inconvenient results.' In the same article Dr Feinstein revealed that he 'recently had heard an authoritative public health expert say "yes it's rotten science, but it's in a worthy cause. It will help us get rid of cigarettes and become a smoke-free society".' There are indeed many good reasons for giving up smoking, but the fear of giving other people lung cancer is not one of them.

Alcohol – 'The Most Hygienic of Beverages'

It is hard to imagine the man in the street taking much notice of the latest guidelines on 'safe' drinking. These now permit him an extra half pint of beer a day, taking him up to a grand total of two, while his wife is advised to call it a day after a pint and a half, or a couple of glasses of wine. This is still quite a lot less than is necessary to become even vaguely merry, and anyhow has no more objective rationale than earlier more stringent limits. Rather, the evolution of these 'safe' drinking limits over the past few years shows how genuine concern about the harmful effects of excess alcohol has been exploited by the Government and doctors to justify their wider ambitions of nannying the nation. Thus, in 1979, the Royal College of Psychiatrists, having examined the relevant evidence, recommended that 'reasonable guidelines' for the upper limits of drinking should be 56 units a week – twice the level currently permitted and the equivalent of four pints of beer or a bottle of wine a day. This, they said, 'accords with the scientific findings of the relationship between drinking levels and risks to health', as indeed it does, for only above this amount are people at significant risk from alcohol-related diseases.

These guidelines, however, exceed by quite a large margin the average amount of alcohol consumed, which is not much use to those who wish to interfere in the lives of as many people as possible – for their own good, of course. This could only be achieved by bringing the 'safe' level down, and it has been gradually whittled down to 21 units for men and 14 for women, by which time they have become 'relevant' to virtually everybody. The public may not adhere to these strict limits, but none the less their effect has been to mislead many people into thinking that moderate levels of alcohol consumption are much more dangerous than they are. Now the news is out – that alcohol protects against heart attacks. Grudgingly, 'they' – experts, health professionals, and the usual busybodies – have conceded that it might actually be a good thing to drink a couple of glasses of wine a day.

What they have concealed, however, is that the evidence shows that we can all consume even more than this. Indeed, the greatest protective effect of alcohol is with four drinks a day and that even those on six drinks have a lower risk of heart disease than those who do not drink at all. A well-kept secret. In fact the benefits of alcohol stretch well beyond this. Alcohol boosts milk production in lactating mothers and provides restful sleep for those afflicted by insomnia. It relieves the symptoms of colds and flu when taken with a glass of milk at night, while a small tot relaxes the muscles, thus relieving pain throughout the neck and shoulders. It is dramatically effective in the condition of benign essential tremor, rapidly abolishing the fine trembling of the fingers. Finally, its mild euphoric properties put people at their ease, allowing them to enjoy Christmas parties.

The risk of damaging one's health from drinking too much is, in any case, a very personal matter. Certainly, virtually all those who develop cirrhosis of the liver – at least in the Western world – are alcoholics, but it is not inevitable because two-thirds of alcoholics never do so. The explanation probably lies with genes and, in particular, the way in which alcohol is metabolised in the body. The important issue for people then, is not how much the government tells people they are allowed to drink but whether any given level of alcohol intake is actually doing them damage. Most of those who drink too much know it already, or are at least told so by their friends or spouses. But a simple method of confirming it is to visit your general practitioner and ask for a blood test of liver function known as the gamma GT, which, if raised, is highly suggestive of alcoholic liver damage. Further alcohol also increases the size of the red blood cells and this is detected by a simple blood count in which the mean corpuscular volume (MCV) is greater than 96. Those with a raised gamma GT or MCV should restrict their drinking until these tests have returned to normal. Everyone else should take comfort from the great French scientist Louis Pasteur's sensible observation 'Alcohol is the most helpful and hygienic of beverages.'

Talking Sense About a Suntan – 1

No prolonged spell of good weather can be considered complete nowadays without Cassandra-like warnings of the folly of exposing our sensitive skins to the warming rays of the sun. In *New Scientist* magazine, ultra-violet radiation is described as 'a poison which is now exacting its toll ... what began as a post-war fetish for sunbathing is rapidly developing into a health crisis' – and the Cancer Research Campaign has rammed the message home with full-page advertisements of a couple relaxing beside a swimming pool and the blunt message: 'A thousand people die of skin cancer each year.' This is serious stuff. For millions, sunbathing is an innocent pleasure – a special sort of sensuous, if mindless, relaxation. It is also, to be blunt, about sex. It is not possible to be on a beach or even in a central London park surrounded by scantily clad and gilded strangers without thinking about such matters. One would expect the experts – before disturbing the peace of mind of the nation's sunlovers with fears of cancer – to have a pretty watertight case that sunbathing really is dangerous. I am not convinced.

The ultra-violet light from the sun certainly does increase the risk of two types of 'cancer' – the basal cell carcinoma (better known as a rodent ulcer) and squamous cell cancer. I put the word cancer in inverted commas because, in the commonly accepted sense of the word, they are not malignant. Rather, they are highly localised patches of abnormal skin, which do not spread to distant parts of the body, and are in no way life-threatening. Predictably, they occur on exposed areas like the face or the back of the hands and are particularly common among farmers, fishermen or others with outside occupations. Prolonged exposure seems essential as they only occur in the later decades of life or, as in Australia and South Africa, where those of European descent spend virtually their whole time on the beach or beside the swimming pool. These 'cancers' are easily cured by a short course of X-ray treatment or by surgical removal.

The focus of recent anxiety are the much more sinister malignant melanomas. The incidence of these little black tumours, which can spread rapidly and fatally, have doubled in the past 20 years. The Cancer Research Campaign advertisement links these directly to sun exposure, with the cautionary tale of 'Diana', aged thirty-two, who ignored an itchy mole on her left ankle and six months later was dead. 'We know that sunburn in childhood can trigger melanomas in later life,' the advertisement tells us. The connection is easily made – but it is justified? The characteristics of melanoma are almost the exact opposite of the skin 'cancers' – rodent ulcers – which are indeed sun-related. They occur on non-exposed parts of the body like the trunk and the back of the legs rather than on the face or hands. They are much more common on those who work indoors – the professional and technical classes – than on those with an outside occupation. Consistent sun exposure, therefore, clearly does not contribute to melanoma.

Perhaps, it has been suggested, the danger lies in intermittent high doses of ultra-violet rays sufficient to cause sunburn on parts of the body that are normally clothed, and certainly patients with melanoma report past episodes of bad sunburn twice as frequently. However, as it is the fair-skinned who are most likely to suffer from sunburn, it is necessary to ask whether skin complexion alone is itself a risk factor for melanoma – which indeed it is. The fair-skinned are 70 times more likely to have a melanoma than the dark-skinned, making it impossible to determine whether sunburn makes any contribution at all. What then about the claim that the rise in cases of melanoma is caused by the rise in numbers taking holidays abroad? A study from the University of Glasgow investigating this question tried to discern whether patients with melanoma were more likely to have spent their summers abroad than those without. They found 'no significant difference between the two groups in the numbers of Continental holidays and total numbers of days spent in sunnier climes.'

Altogether, the link between sunbathing and melanoma seems very tenuous indeed – and, whatever the causes of the marked increase in melanoma in the past two decades, sun exposure does not seem to be one of them. We should not be surprised by this as the incidence of most cancers rises and falls over time without anyone providing a satisfactory explanation. Malignant melanoma is no exception. The Cancer Research Campaign's advertisement anathematises people's private pleasures by stating as fact what is for the most part refutable conjecture. Roll on the next health scare.

Talking Sense About a Suntan – 2

The intention of 'Sun Awareness Week' – specifically aimed at children – has been to promote 'sun awareness in appropriate curriculum areas'. 'Consideration should also be given to the development of shaded areas in school playgrounds and the sun protection afforded by school uniforms,' says the handout from the Health Education Authority. So far so worthy, but one wonders what effect all this might have on impressionable minds. Having 'caught the sun' after a day on the beach, will they now worry lest they die from skin cancer, unaware that the risk of such an eventuality is infinitesimally small?

The putative dangers of the sun's rays are placed in a more rational context by noting that for fifty years the most potent treatment available for the ravages of childhood rickets and tuberculosis was sun therapy (or heliotherapy). Such was the enthusiasm for the healing powers of the sun that in the early Twenties the Sunlight League was founded in London, and one of its aims was 'the education of the public to the appreciation of sunlight as a means of health; teaching the nation that sunlight is nature's universal disinfectant, as well as a stimulant and tonic'. These were no idle claims, coming after the discovery that sunlight killed a whole range of bacteria. A Danish physician, Niels Finsen, won the Nobel Prize for demonstrating the advocacy of sun therapy in curing tuberculosis of the skin. As for the 'stimulant' properties of sunlight, these were first commented on by a French doctor in 1815: 'The influence of sunlight on the morale of man is very powerful. The physician will prescribe sun for the sad and the weak, which, when taken with moderate exercise, restores courage.' He goes on to point out that the British aristocracy migrated to the South of France in the winter months 'to ease the disorder of temper caused by the spleen . . . or at least to get away from the misery of their cloudy climate.'

The value of sun therapy in curing rickets and tuberculosis has been supplanted by modern drugs but is still advocated as a treatment for common skin disorders, such as eczema and psoriasis. According to Brian Tiffey, professor of photobiology at Durham University, 'Scandinavian dermatologists prefer to send their patients suffering from psoriasis to the Dead Sea for a period of four weeks rather than admit them to hospital.' The Dead Sea is particularly favoured because, being below sea level, the sunlight contains far fewer burning UVB rays, so the patients can sit in the sun for longer. Finally, as Professor Tiffey also notes, 'for more than fifty years reports have appeared suggesting that regular sun exposure protects against cancers of the breast and colon'.

It is easy to be puzzled as to why medical advice should be so vulnerable to the vagaries of fashion – but, as we see here, it is all a matter of emphasis. Focus on the life-enhancing aspects of sunshine, its essential role in the prevention of rickets and skin infections, its proven ability to cure skin diseases and hint that it may also protect against cancer, then one of the healthiest ways of spending one's holiday is to lie on the beach sunbathing. Contrariwise, lump all skin cancers together but fail to distinguish the majority – the benign rodent ulcers – which do follow prolonged exposure to the sun from the rarer but more serious malignant melanomas, where the evidence is much weaker; throw in a warning that too much sun causes premature wrinkles – and then the last thing we should be doing on our holidays is acquiring a sun tan. You pays your money, and takes your chances . . .

Those who do develop premature wrinkling of the skin from over-exposure to the sun – otherwise known as photo-ageing – may feel there is not much to be done. But as Laurence Lever, consultant skin specialist at Northwick Park hospital points out, this is not the case. 'The most reliable method of improving the appearance of the photo-aged face is a surgical face lift,' he writes in the journal *Dermatology in Practice*. The face may be further enhanced by inserting under the skin fatty tissues taken from elsewhere in the body. This type of fat transplantation can also be used to improve the appearance of photo-aged hands. In addition, individual wrinkles can be corrected by the injection of collagen or silicone under the skin.

4

The Non-Science of a Healthy Diet

Eat Your Heart Out

Over the past decade, the belief that fatty foods cause heart disease has, in popular culture, achieved the same status of self-evident veracity as the link between smoking and lung cancer. There has, it must be said, always been a difference of opinion on the matter which divides more on professional than scientific grounds. Public health doctors and nutritionists have been vigorous protagonists, citing the experience in the United States which shows, they claim, that a switch to healthy eating has been rewarded by a decline in heart disease. Heart specialists tend to be much more sceptical. The late Sir John McMichael, widely credited for making post-war Britain an international centre of medical excellence, observed: 'It is a sobering thought that our profession has been brainwashed by propaganda into accepting a fashionable belief that can only be transient.'

These contradictory views have been reconciled in the past rather unsatisfactorily, by a show of hands around tables of expert committees – although, as another noted sceptic, Professor Tony Mitchell, of Nottingham University, said: 'The claim that the collective beliefs of a prestigious committee can provide a substitute for facts is all too prevalent . . . We can never be sure of the relationship between their opinions and the truth.' The widely publicised reports of many expert committees – in which the protagonists have always outnumbered the sceptics – have, like the steady drip of water on a stone, had the desired effect of convincing the public of the potential harm of fatty foods. So successful has this strategy been that healthy eating has become the central plank of government health policy.

Now, however, it seems the experts are finding it more difficult to reach their consensus as the alleged link between diet and heart disease has been dealt a series of body blows from which it is difficult to see how it can recover. Dr George Davey Smith, writing in the *British Medical Journal*, has reviewed all the trials in which healthy people with high cholesterol levels have been treated with cholesterol-lowering drugs and found there has only been an extremely modest, about 1.5 per cent, fall in number of heart attacks compared to controls. This seems a very poor return for giving expensive drugs – all of which have side effects – to otherwise healthy people. In these cost-conscious days when prescriptions for these drugs have risen sixfold in the past six years, there are obviously considerable pressures on the Department of Health to discourage their use – except in a very small minority who, due to a genetic disorder, have massively raised cholesterol levels.

An even more fundamental question arises inevitably from Dr Davey Smith's reviews. If cholesterol-lowering drugs have only a marginal effect in those with high levels in reducing the amount of heart disease, what hope can there be that dietary admonitions for the mass of the population to reduce their fat intake will work? In their defence the protagonists might argue that fat consumption is only one factor that needs to be considered, and, though admitting the situation is confused, nonetheless justify their advice as being prudent. The public, bullied for a decade into giving up, for example, egg and bacon for breakfast, should rightly demand something more rigorous. Clearly one only has to look at the much higher incidence of heart disease in the West compared with Japan to realise that fat has something to do with it – but what?

The answer lies in the pattern of heart disease in the Western world over the past 50 years, which is very striking. Very rare before the 1920s, its incidence increased every year throughout the Forties, Fifties and Sixties, peaking in the United States, Canada, Australia and New Zealand in the late 1960s (and in Britain and Europe a few years later), since when it has declined equally dramatically. Throughout this period, the amount of fat in the diet as a percentage of total energy consumed has remained virtually unchanged. There have been some alterations, particularly in the United States, but these have been both too late and too insignificant to have had any measurable effect. Fat in the diet, therefore, cannot be a *determinant* cause of heart disease, though it is probably fair to surmise that whatever is responsible has its most marked effect in those societies with a relatively high fat consumption such as the West, or within those societies, in those individuals with a genetically determined markedly raised cholesterol level.

By distinguishing between a direct and indirect role for fat consumption and heart disease, all the problems – why even powerful cholesterol-lowering drugs have such a marginal effect and why dietary changes make so little difference – are resolved. There are important questions to be asked in the future about the motivation of those who have, by failing to make this distinction, given the public an utterly misleading understanding of the role of diet in illness. For the moment it is enough to realise that the central pillar of health education policies of the past decade with its malign implication that those with heart disease have only themselves to blame – has been skewered.

Pass the Salt, Please

With the passage of time, words can acquire quite different connotations. 'Stroke', so resonant of gentleness and seduction for the young, becomes in later life a sudden and dramatic felling. The catastrophic loss of power and intellect that may result is probably the most grievous of all misfortunes, eminently justifying the sensible precaution of having one's blood pressure checked regularly and taking appropriate medication if it is found to be raised. A group of government-appointed experts has proposed that the toll of strokes – responsible for 30,000 deaths a year – would be further reduced were everyone to lower the amount of salt they consume by a third: for example, cutting down on salty foods, limiting the amount added at cooking and not adding it at table.

A reasonable suggestion certainly, and well worth adopting, were it not that many doctors, including specialists in studying and treating raised blood pressure (hypertension), disagree. When the same recommendation was made ten years ago, it met a very cool response. Thirteen hypertension experts representing eight specialist units in this country and abroad wrote collectively to *The Lancet* expressing concern that 'the usual scientific standards for weighing evidence and giving advice have been forgotten in an evangelical crusade to present a simplistic view of the evidence'. The proposal was, they said, 'unjustified and irresponsible', while the 'potential harmful consequences have not been examined'. They clearly thought that yet another dietary fad was unjustifiably being foisted on the public. But to understand why, it is necessary to take a closer look.

The blood pressure is primarily determined by muscles in the walls of the arteries which, by altering their diameter, can change the resistance to the flow of blood, and thus the pressure required to push it around the circulation. The maintenance of a steady blood pressure is without doubt the most important physiological requirement of the body, for the fairly obvious reason that the brain must have a constant blood supply. Were the blood pressure to fluctuate when, for example, we stand up or lie down, the brain would be deprived of oxygen with predictably dire consequences. The blood pressure is therefore the best defended of all physiological functions, with half a dozen separate homeostatic mechanisms backing each other up to guarantee its stability – pressure receptors in the artery walls, hormones secreted by the kidneys, monitors of the amount of body fluids and several others besides. These mechanisms operate independently of each other; it has been shown in animal experiments that it is possible to strip away one control system after another, and still the blood pressure remains unchanged. With the blood pressure so well protected, modest changes in salt consumption are unlikely to be very influential, not least because the concentration of salt itself in the body is rigorously controlled, so any excess is rapidly excreted, while with salt deprivation, it is rigorously conserved in the kidneys.

Nonetheless, the cause of persistently raised blood pressure is not known (except in a small minority of cases), and there is some evidence that salt consumption may be implicated. Thus primitive societies where little salt is consumed have a very low frequency of hypertension, and in addition the blood pressure does not rise with age as it does in the West. Further, migration from 'low' to 'high' salt societies is usually accompanied by a rise in blood pressure. This has been shown many times in communities as disparate as the Easter Islanders moving to the South American mainland, and rural Zulus moving to urban areas. Not all agree that differences in salt consumption explain this phenomenon, suggesting rather that the rise in blood pressure may be due to the stresses of urbanised Western living. Support for this 'stress' theory comes from a study comparing the blood pressure of 144 nuns in a secluded monastic order in Umbria with a similar number of women living in close proximity. The nuns follow the Rule of St Benedict – *ora et labora* – spending their days in absolute silence praying, doing domestic chores and gardening. Whereas the blood pressure of those living outside the walls of the nunnery rose steadily over a period of 20 years, that of the nuns remained completely unchanged. As the amount of salt consumed by the two groups was exactly the same, Dr Mario Timio of the University of Perugia – who conducted the study – attributed the difference in blood pressure to convent life which 'is virtually devoid of conflict, aggression and competition for power and money'.

Much the simplest way of determining whether salt contributes significantly to hypertension is to change the amount consumed and see what happens. Extreme salt restriction does seem to lower the blood pressure, and in the early 1950s, before the discovery of effective anti-hypertensive drugs, the only treatment was a salt-free, monotonous and very unappetising diet of rice and fruit, which not surprisingly very few patients were able to stick to for any length of time. Studies of more modest reductions in salt have given contradictory results, showing either a small effect or none at all, and in some a paradoxical increase in blood pressure. Despite this uncertainty Dr M.R. Law of St Bartholomew's Hospital, London, was able to report in the *British Medical Journal* that combining the results of 45 separate studies, it was possible to show that if everyone reduced the amount of salt they consumed by three grammes a day, this would lower the blood pressure sufficiently to prevent 15 per cent of all strokes.

Regrettably this did not end the controversy, as Dr Law was promptly criticised for having heavily skewed his conclusions by including large numbers of poorly conducted studies. A more rigorous overview by John Swales, Professor of Medicine at Leicester Royal Infirmary, published later the same year, found that reducing salt 'had no significant effect in those with normal blood pressure', while 'a small fall' was detectable in those with hypertension, 'but only with substantial sodium restriction'. 'It is necessary to make a sharp distinction,' Professor Swales argues, 'between advising patients being treated for hypertension to change their salt intake, and making similar recommendations to the general public. The former may help a little, the latter does not.'

5

Four Essays on Fatness

Can the Fat Child Blame His Genes?

Fat children may be unhappy, bullied by their classmates and a
constant source of anxiety to their parents, but attitudes on how
to help them are vitiated by an unwarranted optimism – 'It is just
puppy fat; he (or she) will grow out of it.' The likelihood is that
he will not – fat children grow up to become fat adults – so it
seems important to try to influence eating habits from an early
age. This would be relatively straightforward if 'nurture', or how
children are brought up, was the main determinant of childhood
obesity. There is some evidence to support this. In the United
States, and it is probably the case in Britain, the proportion of
obese and super-obese children has doubled over the past two
decades, strongly suggesting that hamburgers and chips in front
of the television is proving a more popular leisure-time activity
that knocking a football around. Certainly, the amount of time
adolescents spend viewing has increased over this time by a third
to an astonishing average of four hours a day.

Further, it seems the eating patterns of fat children are different
from others, which is in marked contrast to the situation with adults,
where it is difficult to show that the fat eat more than the thin.
Marjorie Waxman, a psychologist at the University of Pennsylvania,
painstakingly compared obese boys with their non-obese brothers
and found they ate considerably more (over 1,000 calories at one
sitting, versus just over 600) and ate twice as fast. None the less, the
main cause of fatness in both children and adults is now believed to
be genetically determined. This has been shown both by studies of
twins separated at birth and brought up in different families (here
the body mass of identical twins turns out to be much closer than
that of the non-identical) and of adopted children (where the body
mass much more closely resembles the true rather than the adopted

parents). The role of genes is anyhow clearly demonstrated when one walks down the High Street and is confronted by the spectacle of the striking physical resemblance between a grossly fat mother and her equally large adolescent daughter. As everyone knows, you can't change your genes, so in contrast to parental false optimism, doctors, health visitors and others tend to be rather pessimistic that much can be done about childhood fatness.

This, it now seems, is only partly correct, as Dr Leonard Epstein of the University of Pittsburgh has shown in a report in the *Journal of the American Medical Association* entitled: 'A ten-year follow-up of behavioural family-based treatment for obese children'. This had two components: a 'traffic-light' diet and behavioural manipulation. The diet involved coding foods by colour, depending on how fattening they were, ranging from green, which the child was encouraged to eat, through yellow to red, like sweets and sugar drinks, which were forbidden. The behavioural therapy involved setting up 'contracts' and promoting 'social reinforcement'. The treatment period under Dr Epstein's supervision lasted only eight weeks but, remarkably, ten years later the effects are still obvious. The children are marginally too plump (reflecting the genetic contribution to obesity), but this is in marked contrast to a control group where the children are, on average, half as heavy again as they should be. This is obviously highly encouraging.

Pleasantly Plump *or* Just Plain Fat?

My favourite uncle's motto was 'Laugh and grow fat', and it is an auspicious sign that that this is the theme of a book appropriately entitled *You Don't Have To Diet!* Plumpness has much to commend it. Fatter mothers give birth to bigger babies who are less likely to get diabetes or heart disease in later life. The plump in middle age are less prone to infections and more likely to survive heart attack. Fatter oldies do not suffer from brittle bones or, if unable to pay their heating bills, from hypothermia. By contrast, those who worry about their size and whose weight yo-yos up and down as they lurch from one dietary fad to another, are more prone to depression, attacks of gout and gallstones, and are at increased risk of dying suddenly from abnormalities of heart rhythm.

None the less, the pleasantly plump spend a billion pounds a year in Britain trying to become unhealthily thin. They are, according to the authors, nutritionist Dr Tom Saunders and foodie personality Peter Bazalgette, victims of an 'evil and exploitative diet racket'. The authors do not mince their words when it comes to dismissing the best-selling diet books of the past decade. Rosemary Conley's *Hip and Thigh Diet* (2 million copies sold) 'perpetuates myths, encourages faddy eating and exaggerates the health risks of fatness in women'. As for the very successful *Food Combining Diet* by Kathryn Marsden, which urges readers to avoid 'foods that fight' – so protein and carbohydrates should not be eaten together – this is based on theories that are 'discredited and unsubstantiated by modern science'. Their own solution is straightforward and unrevolutionary. Those who wish or need to lose weight should not make dramatic changes in their diet, just eat less of what they normally consume, and this should result, they claim, in shedding around two pounds a week or a stone every two to three months.

This defence of plumpness, animosity towards the dieting industry and advice just to eat less is the current medical orthodoxy – and none the worse for that. It is plausible, but dodges several crucial questions. First, while plumpness is entirely acceptable, fatness is not, on either aesthetic or medical grounds. Though the proportion of the population so afflicted is small, at around 3 per cent, in absolute numbers this still adds up to a million or more. Secondly, the cause of obesity is not known. The orthodox line is that physiologically the fat are no different from anyone else in terms of digestion or metabolic rate or the way they lay down fat stores, but differences there must be. The fat do not necessarily eat more than the thin and everyone knows of people who can eat three meals a day and remain thin as a rake. It is now quite clear there must be a gene that predisposes to fatness. Thus, a Danish study of 3,850 adopted children found that 'genetic influences are important determinants of all degrees of adiposity, ranging from extreme thinness to marked fatness, and family environment alone has little or no influence on the development of obesity'. Similarly, a Swedish study of twins reared apart came to exactly the same conclusion. Whatever this mysterious fatness gene might be, it must be responsible for some as yet undiscovered physiological disturbance that distinguishes the obese from the non-obese. Every day in my predominantly working-class practice, I see levels of obesity running through two or three generations of the same family that would be highly remarkable among the middle or upper classes.

Thirdly, those who fail to lose weight on standard medically approved, calorie-reducing diets are usually accused by their doctors of not trying hard enough – that it is their own fault. This is almost certainly unfair, as shown by a study in *The Lancet* in the 1970s in which 29 women with a long history of 'unsuccessful' dieting were isolated in a country house on a low-calorie diet. After three weeks, 20 of the 29 had either lost no weight or, at most, one pound. So if we do not understand the cause of fatness, and a fair number of the obese are obviously highly resistant to a simple reduction in the amount of calories consumed, it seems patronising and unhelpful to dismiss the 'alternative' diets out of hand.

The pseudo-scientific explanations put forward by their protagonists of why they work may be simplistic, but that does not mean they may not work. On theoretical grounds, there seems no reason why some people might respond to sugar or carbohydrates by producing too much insulin, and so might be helped by sticking to a high-fat diet of meat and dairy products. Alternatively, some may absorb high-calorie fatty foods too readily, and so are best sticking to carbohydrate-based foods like bread and potatoes. As for the much-maligned food-combining diet, the columnist Mary Killen and her husband attest to its remarkable efficacy. Together they have shed stones in weight, while still consuming generous amounts of food. There is, it seems, much to be said for keeping an open mind on this matter and refusing to accept the orthodox medical line that if you cannot lose weight, then it's your own fault.

Roly Poly Swings and Roundabouts

It would seem that the German Chancellor, Helmut Kohl, has an appetite to match his achievements as a great European statesman. Having enjoyed a five-course VE Day banquet dinner at the Guildhall (lobster, Atlantic turbot, roast beef of old England, iced soufflé and petits-fours), he rounded off his evening with a further substantial meal at Sir Terence Conran's famous restaurant, Le Pont de la Tour. 'The restaurant manager forbore to reveal the exact specifications of Herr Kohl's second meal,' reports *The Times* Diary, 'but confirmed the Chancellor did indeed take full advantage of the three-course menu'.

The Chancellor, it is true, has a generous waistline but, increasingly, it would appear that the relationship between food intake and size is as much to do with how one eats as how much. Herein lies the clue to one of the more pleasing ironies of our time, that our American cousins, despite their obsession with 'healthy food', are getting fatter and fatter. To be precise, throughout the Eighties the number of fat Americans rose by a third, so that now one in three is overweight. The Americans have apparently taken to heart the message of the virtues of reducing the amount of fat they consume and switched to 'low-fat' crisps, milk, ice-cream and so on. But they are eating much more of these foods than before, while simultaneously taking less exercise. As important, they have become a nation of bingers, eating vast quantities at a single sitting, and this, paradoxically, is caused by their enthusiasm for dieting in an attempt to lose weight.

Binge-eating is usually associated with bulimia nervosa, the distressing condition where young women eat anything up to 3,000 calories at one go, but keep their weight normal by throwing it all up again with self-induced vomiting. Recently, however, it has emerged that in around a quarter of people who are seriously overweight, the cause of their obesity is that they are secret bingers. There are, according to Peter Cooper, Professor of Psychology at Reading University, 'several triggers' for bingeing. Most frequently, the binger is simultaneously trying to diet in an attempt to lose weight, as one woman describes: 'If I look in the mirror and see I am too fat, immediately I want to eat. I know this is silly when I really want so desperately to be thin, and I feel that I can't cope any more and I might as well just give up and eat.'

This curious relationship between weight loss and bingeing was originally observed in a study of Canadian veterans captured during the ill-fated Dieppe raid of 1942. As prisoners of war, they experienced serious food restriction, and so, not surprisingly, when released in 1945 they had lost an average of two stone. Subsequently, nearly 60 per cent reported bingeing on a regular basis. It is also said, although I have never seen it confirmed, that the high death-rate after liberation among the tragic victims of the Belsen concentration camp was due to 'over-eating'. Their shrunken stomachs and compromised circulatory systems could not adjust to the sudden availability of adequate amounts of food. It is clear that starvation, whether relative in the case of dieters, or absolute, as in the case of Allied prisoners of war and Holocaust survivors, must throw a switch in the brain that induces binge-eating.

The explanation lies in the mysterious mechanisms by which the body maintains a steady weight. Over a period of 20 years, for example, most people will put on only around 10 per cent of their body weight. Clearly, however, our food intake and energy output vary widely on a daily basis – Chancellor Kohl presumably does not have two dinners every evening. So there must be some kind of thermostat in the brain which, without us knowing it, alters our behaviour to keep our weight steady. This thermostat varies our appetite and thus the amount of food we consume, as well as the amount of exercise we take; more subtly it alters our metabolism, thus varying the amount of energy that is burnt up. When a person deliberately attempts to lose weight, the reaction of this thermostat is to try to increase the desire for food, leading to bingeing – unfortunately, it now seems that messing around with the thermostat can have serious long-term consequences, because bingeing persists even in those who have long since over-compensated for their weight loss through dieting, so even though obese, they carry on bingeing and so put on even more weight.

That, at least, is the theory, and it certainly explains why it can be so difficult to lose weight in the first place and why the most successful dieters are those who attempt it gradually, thus slowly resetting their thermostats. There are two treatments for bingeing. The first is behaviour therapy and the second, anti-depressant drugs which may work by treating the underlying depression that so frequently accompanies eating disorders, or may suppress the appetite, thus reducing the urge to binge.

Sloth Is the Villain

Every year many readers resolve to lose a stone or two by switching to a 'healthy' diet. But before they kiss farewell to bacon and eggs, full cream milk, salted butter and similar delights, I would like to draw their attention to the experience of two intrepid explorers, Dr Mike Stroud and Sir Ranulph 'Ran' Fiennes. A couple of years ago, when the pair walked across Antarctica, the weather was a bit parky, with temperatures down to minus 50 degrees centigrade and winds of 100 mph. Just to add to the challenge, they pulled their own sledges.

To simplify matters they ate the same food every day: breakfast – porridge fortified with butter; elevenses – soup with added butter; lunch – more soup with more butter; tea – flapjack biscuits covered in butter; supper – freeze-dried meal with added butter. They also allowed themselves four bars of chocolate a day. This high-energy, high-fat diet works out at about 5,100 calories a day, which is twice the amount they would normally consume. Almost two-thirds was made up of the much-maligned 'saturated fat' which is twice the daily intake officially recommended by medical experts.

And what was the effect of this 'unhealthy' diet? During the four months of the expedition, both Dr Stroud and 'Ran' lost a considerable amount of weight: 3 and 3½ stone respectively. Their metabolic rate increased – an important observation, because when people try to lose weight by cutting down on food, the rate tends to fall as the body adapts to burning fewer calories. The fat content in their body fell from 18 per cent to zero and, to cap it all, their cholesterol levels remained completely unchanged. These results are as effective a repudiation as one could look for of the prevailing wisdom about what constitutes a healthy diet. The simple truth is that if you take enough exercise, you can eat what you like, including indulging in butter six times a day and four bars of chocolate.

This point is further emphasised in an investigation by a Cambridge scientist, Andrew Prentice, into why it is that the 'average' Briton is now one stone heavier at an equivalent height than 50 years ago, while the numbers of the 'clinically obese', that is, seriously fat, has doubled in a decade. Is this, asks Dr Prentice, due to gluttony or sloth? One might imagine, with the advent of big supermarkets with their prodigious amounts of high-quality food, that gluttony would be the major cause of the fattening of Britain. But it is not so. Astonishing as it might seem, we are eating one-fifth less food than we were in the Seventies. Dr Prentice then turns to the evidence implicating sloth. Seventy per cent of households now have central heating, which, he points out, reduces the body's need to expend energy to maintain a constant core temperature. In addition, the rising incidence of obesity is directly paralleled by a doubling in the number of hours spent watching television. The number of cars per household has also markedly increased, and very few people now walk more than a couple of miles at a stretch. Sloth, of course, is a pejorative term, and one could as easily describe these trends to people making greater use of 'improved personal transport and domestic leisure facilities'. But, irrespective of the terminology used, the verdict is inescapable – that lack of exercise rather than too much food is the critical factor.

None the less, the seriously fat find the amount of exercise necessary to influence their weight both uncomfortable and embarrassing. They are left little alternative other than to diet, at least initially, to slim down sufficiently to be able to take up jogging or join an exercise class. There is no doubt that self-help groups such as Slimmers' World and Weight Watchers are immensely useful in the early stages of dieting, in marked contrast to the use of 'slimming pills' which, in my experience, do nothing for those to whom I have prescribed them in the past.

Finally, there is the vexed question of surgery. This fell out of favour in the mid-Eighties because the standard operation, in which the small intestine was by-passed, was associated with a wide variety of undesirable side effects, including intractable diarrhoea, liver disease and kidney stones. However, Christopher Royston, senior plastic surgeon at Hull Royal Infirmary, has reported on another procedure where the size of the stomach is reduced – called vertical-banded gastroplasty. After an appropriate interval, this is followed by a 'tummy tuck', in which the excess folds of skin following weight loss are removed. And the results? Most patients halved their weight from about 17 to 10 stone and were reportedly pleased with the aesthetic results of the tummy tuck. I'm sure we will be hearing more about this operation in the future.

6

Keeping Fit

Marathon Man, Take It Easy

A fitness specialist at the Freeman Hospital in Newcastle, Dr Gary Ford, has appealed for marathon runners over the age of 65 to take part in a study of 'how to stay young'. The record for geriatric marathon running is held by a 79-year-old man, who completed the 26-mile course in just under four hours. This is, to be sure, about twice as long as it would take someone half his age, but as many people in their forties feel knackered just running for a bus, it is indeed remarkable. No doubt Dr Ford's findings will confirm the value of regular vigorous exercise in maintaining muscle strength and the robustness of the heart and lungs. But this does not answer the question of the wisdom of pursuing this goal.

An authority on fitness in the old age group, R.J. Shepherd, professor of applied physiology at the University of Toronto, has observed rather enigmatically: 'Though strenuous exercise may be recommended as the basis for a happier life, it is not necessarily a guarantor of a longer one.' Put bluntly, it can be lethal. The reason is simple. Exercise pushes up the pulse rate, reducing the amount of time blood has to pass down the coronary arteries between each contraction of the heart muscle. As everyone over the age of 65 has some degree of narrowing of their coronary arteries, this can critically reduce the amount of oxygenated blood reaching the heart muscle. It is therefore relatively deprived of oxygen, resulting in a serious abnormality of heart rhythm – or, indeed, a heart attack.

It is not easy to quantify the exact risk of such a possibility. Professor Shepherd ingeniously examined the time of day that 250 middle-aged businessmen had their heart attacks, and found considerably fewer than expected occurred while the men were asleep or at work; but they occurred six times more frequently while doing 'odd jobs' or taking part in some sporting activity. On this basis, he estimated that one might expect one 'cardiac event' for every 500 man-hours of vigorous exercise, which compares very badly with the figure for bus driving: one cardiac event for every 500 man-years of sitting at the wheel. Dr Ford's marathon volunteers might stay young, but not for long. It is more sensible to go for a brisk walk for an hour a day instead, which has the added advantage of not causing the orthopaedic problems – small fractures, tendonitis, ligament tears – that can so easily incapacitate, if not kill, the elderly marathon man.

Sporting Dangers

The modern athlete often seems a poorly creature, vulnerable to a host of minor and major ailments. Indeed, the *Oxford Textbook of Sports Medicine* spends the best part of 800 pages describing in exhaustive detail – and without hint of irony – the many ways that exercise is harmful to health. Sudden death, debility from over training, susceptibility to viral illnesses, neurosis, hypochondriasis, a bewildering variety of acute injuries to bone and muscle, not to mention overuse syndromes, all lie in store. These hazards are inescapable given the driving dynamic and fascination of sport, the Olympic motto *Citius, Altius, Fortius* – Faster, Higher, Stronger – which over the past 100 years has produced a relentless improvement in world sporting records.

Many factors have contributed – technical innovations, science and doping – while modern training techniques have pushed the limits of human performance beyond their natural boundaries. The great British physiologist and Nobel laureate, A. V. Hill, commented on the extraordinary achievement of the human athlete. 'The magnitude of the bodily changes involved in severe exercise is such that it is difficult to appreciate,' he wrote in 1927. 'A man running 100 yards at a top speed does enough mechanical work to lift his body 85 yards into the air – about one-third the height of the Woolworth building in New York City.' The 'sportive fatigue' that comes from transgressing these limits, wrote the pioneering French sports physician Philippe Tissie in 1919, 'produces a kind of experimental disease in the healthy. The athlete is a sick person [*une malade*].'

In addition, every sport has hazards unique to itself as shown in the following round up:

Cycling

The initial medical reaction to cycling was generally hostile. The main concern being that it would precipitate unnatural sexual desires in women, or as the *British Medical Journal* rather opaquely put it: 'The friction produced by the saddle may cause bruising, even excoriation of the sensitive external genitalia, and in women of a certain temperament may lead to other effects on the sexual system which we need not particularise.' A Dr J.W. Ballantyne warned that women of 'advancing years, especially if near the menopause, should be extremely careful' as she had come across many cases of harm from cycling including 'goitre, appendicitis, dementia and hysterical seizures.'

More specific hazards of cycling including 'cyclist's spine', an unfortunate condition in which side to side movement of the pelvis causes muscular strain at the base of the spine, precipitating chronic back pain. There was also 'cyclist's sore throat', attributed to the inhalation of bacteria and leading to recurrent tonsillitis and 'bicyclist's faces', a curious distressed look in which the physical effort of cycling was said to lead to permanent facial contortion.

When these hazards failed to warn the public off, the *British Medical Journal* brought out its big gun: cycling was bad for the heart. 'There must be few of us who have not seen the effects of over-exertion on a bicycle,' an editorial observed. 'Cycling causes dilation of the heart from thickening of its walls. The condition may give little concern to those affected, but a medical man will view it with considerable distrust and apprehension.' In 1992, a century after promoting these risks, real or imagined, from cycling the British Medical Association conceded that it might after all be healthy. Since then, however, two further hazards have been reported – the skin cancer, malignant melanoma, from cycling in shorts when young and the numb penis syndrome in young men for whom long hours in the saddle have traumatised the all-important pudendal nerve.

Running

In the United States, ageing runners are advised to go out in twos so that if one keels over with a coronary, the other is on hand to raise the alarm and start resuscitation. The value of this advice was confirmed by a study in the *New England Journal of Medicine* which estimates that 75,000 heart attacks a year follow severe exertion, and that 40,000 Americans drop dead while exercising to improve their health. Depending on the degree of physical fitness, the increased risk of a coronary during exertion ranges from twofold to a hundredfold.

Those with a classical education will recall that in 490 BC the first marathon runner, Pheidippides, running from Marathon to Athens to tell its citizens the Persian armada had been defeated, dropped dead after his last words – 'Rejoice, we won.' Tempting fate, a participant in the 17-kilometre Morat-Fribourg mountain race in Switzerland wore a T-shirt emblazoned with the message: 'You haven't really run a good marathon until you drop dead at the finish line. Signed Pheidippides.' The man was 49, and that was just how he died.

Besides injuries to bone and muscle, the other main hazard to runners is 'the trots' – cramping abdominal pains with profuse and often bloody diarrhoea. Derek Clayton, who set the marathon record in 1979, remembers: 'Two hours later, the elation had worn off. I was urinating large clots of blood and vomiting black mucus and had black diarrhoea.' This would have been caused by a critical reduction in the amount of blood reaching the gut, which has been diverted instead to supply the needs of the leg muscles.

To its credit, jogging more than any other form of exercise has the richest repertoire of exotic ailments. These include jogger's nipples – pain and inflammation from friction against the shirt in women who fail to apply a precautionary layer of petroleum jelly; jogger's testicles – discomfort in the perineum and pain during urination due to gravitational pull on the prostate and urethra; jogger's penile frostbite in those jogging in sub-zero temperatures while insufficiently clad; jogger's infertility – the suppression of ovulation in women running more than 30 kilometres a week. Joggers are also prone to attack from birds of prey, dogs and malicious onlookers – in one survey almost ten per cent reporting having been hit by a thrown object including cans, bottles, ice and a rock-filled bag.

Tae Kwon Do

The most dangerous contact sport of all is tae kwon do – the Korean 'art of foot and hand' in which the participants kick their opponents' heads. At the sixth tae kwon do World Championship held in Denmark, 5 per cent of the competitors required hospital admission with fractures to the jaw and cheekbone, fractures of the forearm, concussion and 'facial contusions and lacerations'.

Water-Skiing

Water-skiers hitting the water in the sitting position with legs apart run the risk of an unwanted rectal enema leading to 'abdominal pain, an intense desire to defecate and the passing of large amounts of blood-tinged fluid.' Women are vulnerable to an unwanted vaginal douche sufficiently forceful to tear the cervix or shoot backwards up the Fallopian tubes into the abdomen, resulting in peritonitis.

Bingo

Players are prone to 'bingo brain', a syndrome of chest pain and confusion due to lack of oxygen from sitting in a bingo hall with heavily smoking players. Convalescence in a smoke-free environment leads to complete recovery.

Bull-fighting

Matadors who have been pursued by angry bulls are at great risk of suffering trauma to the anal sphincter, Carlo Magallon, rectal surgeon from Valencia informed a group of British surgeons at the Royal Society of Medicine.

Russian roulette

The most dangerous sport of all is undoubtedly Russian roulette. This 'deadly game of chance in which the revolver cylinder holds only one bullet' is made even deadlier by its more ardent practitioners. They raise the stakes by putting in two or three bullets at a time and by firing twice or more each turn. This game is responsible for just under one per cent of all 'suicidal' deaths in the United States.

Part 4

Diversions

1

The Other Side

Familial Telepathy

'If you were a bit younger I would say you were probably pregnant,' I observed to a women in her mid-fifties who had just regaled me with an impressive list of pregnancy-like symptoms – early-morning sickness, heartburn and breast tenderness. 'Funny you should say that, I think you might be right,' she replied, making me sit up with some astonishment. 'Not me, of course, I know I'm past that sort of thing: it is my daughter. She has her third on the way and every time I feel as if I am the one who is going to have the baby.' She went on: 'It is only the oldest, mind you. When my other two daughters fall pregnant, I never feel a thing.' 'And why do you think that is?' I asked. 'I'm not sure. My eldest is the only one I had normally, the other two had to be delivered by Caesarean section. Perhaps that is the difference.' Perhaps it is.

The matter-of-fact style in which this story was recounted made it particularly compelling and, in the absence of any other obvious explanation, this woman's remarkable physical sensitivity to her daughter's pregnancy seemed to be a classic example of 'Family telepathy'.

No doubt many people could describe similar experiences – usually involving the uncanny talent that young children seem to have for telepathic communication. To be sure, most instances tend to be prosaic: a mother just returned from shopping is about to tell her young daughter that she saw a big black dog with curly hair when her daughter tells everyone at the dinner table that 'mother has just seen a big black dog with curly hair'.

Dr G. N. M. Tyrell, a leading psychical researcher of the 1940s, made a point of collecting particularly striking anecdotes of this type. In one example, the child 'recalls' something his mother has forgotten: 'I was telling my youngest son why a certain school was called Arnold House and explained that Dr Arnold had altered the English schools a great deal and had been headmaster of one whose name that moment I could not remember. 'A few minutes later he said 'What did you say about somewhere called Ruggy?' I replied I had not mentioned anywhere with this name and did not know what he was talking about. He looked very puzzled and went on repeating the word to himself. Then I remembered we had spoken of Dr Arnold and I said, 'Is it where Dr Arnold taught? Do you mean Rugby?' He looked much relieved and said, 'Yes that's right, Rugby.' I had not consciously thought of Rugby at all.'

Sometimes the content of the telepathic communication can be a lot more dramatic than this. The journalist Cassandra Eason was inspired to write her book *The Psychic Power of Children* after being told by her son over breakfast that 'Daddy's gone poly-boys on his motorbike, but he's all right.' ('Poly-boys', she explains, was a playful expression she used when rolling her son on the floor while he was being dressed.) Daddy, it seems, was expected home at any time. Two hours later, when Miss Eason had already 'started to plan the tea service after the funeral', he did finally turn up on a very battered motorbike.

There have been various attempts to explain this type of telepathy between parents and their children in biological terms. The argument goes something like this: the close relationship between mother and child is impaired in the early years by difficulties in communication. 'In the pre-verbal and non-verbal phase signals are exchanged in a way that runs far ahead of the infant's capacity to make himself understood.' Telepathy fills this gap, but, in later years, becomes superfluous.

However, it is necessary to go back over sixty years to find rigorous scientific evidence for the validity of telepathy in a series of experiments conducted in the 1930s by Dr J. B. Rhinne, a psychologist at Duke University in Baltimore. He devised a pack of twenty-five cards, each featuring one of the five simple symbols: a circle, waves, a cross, a square or a star. The experimenter shuffled the cards, turning the pack into an unknown order of twenty-five random 'events', and turned them over one after the other. The telepathic subject at some distance could then write down the symbols as they were dealt, and the experiment would be repeated several times. While an ordinary person, with luck, would guess the right symbol five times out of twenty-five, telepathic subjects regularly turned in 'hit' rates of eighteen and upwards. The odds of this happening by chance are in the order of one in 1,000 million. By contrast, most medical experiments examining, for example, whether a drug does what is claimed for it, are said to be 'significant' where the likelihood of the results being a chance finding is in the order of one in 100.

By these criteria, telepathy becomes one of the most convincingly proven of biological phenomena. Its explanation remains a mystery, but of its reality there can be no doubt. Familial telepathy can certainly make telephoning a very frustrating business. As one woman put it: 'Countless times I have heard "engaged" signals when ringing my daughters because they were trying to ring me.'

Numerical Superstitions

There is a common superstition amongst hospital staff that misfortunes or disastrous events tend to come in threes. Thus, a casualty officer who admits two patients with heart attack in one evening will stay up waiting for a third. A surgeon who has had two post-operative deaths will be fearful that a third is imminent, and physicians comment on how patients with unusual diseases also tend to come in threes. There is unlikely to be any sound statistical basis for this piece of medical folklore which only reflects the well-known tendency of people to be struck by, and therefore remember, remarkable coincidences. The 'Rule of Three' has, however, an interesting parallel in the more general belief that personal misfortune also comes in threes – or, more comfortingly, that three misfortunes in a row signal the end of a run of bad luck.

The number three has both lucky and unlucky connotations; in fact (unlike thirteen which is universally held to be ominous), it can be life-giving, as with the Blessed Trinity and the mystery of birth – where from the relationship of two people a third emerges. But, in the Russian Orthodox Church it is also strongly linked to death: the way of a departed spirit is illuminated by three candles lit from a single taper. A better known example is in trench warfare, when lighting three cigarettes from the same match made the holder a target for enemy marksmen.

Richard Blacher, professor of psychiatry in Boston, has found the morale of patients to be seriously depressed by the ominous implications of this Rule of Three, even though they recognise their fears to be irrational. Without exception, those who have had two heart attacks believe their third will be fatal while, commonly, someone is much more likely to believe he will not survive an operation if he has recently lost two relatives, making his own death almost inevitable.

It is the very nature of this type of superstition that no amount of reassurance is of value. Professor Blacher argues rather that doctors should try to seek out these hidden fears and exorcise them with some form of 'counter-magic'. In a particularly telling example, he described the case of a 50-year-old woman who was unable to sleep because of her fear she would die in the night after her cardiologist had told her she had had two cardiac arrests in the intensive care unit after complicated bypass surgery. Professor Blacher's response was that during the operation itself her heart also had to be stopped, which meant in fact she had had 'three cardiac arrests'. The patient commented. 'That makes me feel a lot better. If it stopped three times, it must be very strong to come back.' She called him a few days later to say she was now sleeping soundly.

Seeing One's Double, Sensing Trouble

A man in his early fifties was sitting quietly alone in his sitting room one evening when he had the feeling there was someone else in the room. He looked up to see a greyish figure close by who, he rapidly realised, was not only wearing the same clothes as him, but was indeed himself. This meeting with his double or *doppelgänger* had, not surprisingly, been rather disconcerting, and he turned up at the surgery wanting to be reassured he was not going mad – or, indeed, suffering from some potentially lethal illness, as such visions are commonly thought to be an omen of impending death.

The curious and most disturbing aspect of seeing one's double is that it is obviously much more than just an hallucination. As the distinguished French neurologist Jean Lhermitte described it: 'The subject not only believes he can see his own image as if it were reflected in a mirror, but also has the knowledge that in this image there is a part of himself. He feels connected to it by spiritual and material links. Indeed, he has the illusion that he lives in this image, which thinks and feels like himself.'

My patient's initial reaction had been to doubt the authenticity of his vision, but reality proved compelling. 'It seemed as if I was in the presence of my own soul,' he said. Not that it did anything very interesting other than appearing to mimic his movements before vanishing. He was reassured when a 'thorough check-up' failed to show evidence of any illness that might have led to an early appointment with the grim reaper. But I did refer him to a neurologist lest the appearance of his *doppelgänger* was caused by some abnormality of brain function such as epilepsy or migraine.

The clue to understanding the *doppelgänger* experience, it appears, lies in the nature of our 'body image'. Besides awareness of the appearance and feeling of our bodies, we also have a sentiment of ownership; that it belongs to us. Perturbations of the part of the brain where this body image is located will therefore necessarily not only generate the hallucination of one's physical appearance but the psychical element of being part of it as well. Despite this mundane materialist explanation, there are two situations in which the appearance of one's double can certainly prove to be inauspicious. The last phases of any serious illness are often accompanied by an alteration in consciousness, drowsiness or incipient coma in which hallucinations, including those of one's double, can appear, and thus are indeed a harbinger of one's imminent demise. When the major infectious illnesses, smallpox, typhus and the plague were rampant, the high fevers they produced could have this effect. Thus, Aubrey, in his *Brief Lives*, written in 1696, describes how 'the beautiful Lady Diana Rich, daughter of the Earl of Holland, as she was walking in her father's garden in Kensington met her own apparition, habit [clothes] and everything as in the looking-glass. Soon after, she died of smallpox.'

Secondly, there is a recurring theme in the fictional works of writers like Poe and Dostoyevsky in which a *doppelgänger* haunts the life of the main protagonist from which the only escape is death by suicide. The hero in De Maupassant's *Le Horla*, having attempted and failed to murder his own double, exclaims: 'No . . . no, he is not dead. I suppose then I have to kill myself!' This might seem like little more than Gothic fantasy but Peter Brugger, a Canadian neurologist, has described the case of a 21-year-old man with epilepsy who jumped from his third floor window, sustaining serious injury, to escape from his double who had been lying in his bed. 'He first tried to wake the *doppelgänger* by shouting at it, and then became more and more scared by the fact that he could no longer tell which of the two he was. Looking out of the window, he decided to jump out "in order to stop this intolerable feeling of being divided in two".'

Thus, exceptionally, the *doppelgänger* can be a harbinger of death. But in reality it is just an artefact of the brain – so, when meeting one's double, it is only polite to greet him in a friendly rather than suspicious manner. He is, after all, the best friend one has. Incidentally, the neurologist could find no cause for my patient's hallucination, and put it down to a transient epileptic seizure in the body-image part of the brain.

Supernatural Encounters

'Whenever five or six people meet around a fire at Christmas, they start to tell ghost stories,' remarked Jerome K. Jerome over a century ago – a custom he attributed to the 'close atmosphere at Christmas that draws up ghosts like the dampness of the summer rain brings out frogs and snails'. Victorian interest in the supernatural was particularly heightened at Christmas 1894 because of the enormous interest generated by a survey that revealed just how many people had had (or claimed to have had) encounters with ghosts. Of 17,000 people interviewed for the Census of Hallucinations, almost one in ten answered 'Yes' to the question 'Have you ever, when believing yourself to be completely awake, seen or been touched by a living being; which impression, so far as you could discover was not due to any external physical cause?' Some ghosts had come to haunt the living for a purpose, to point out hidden caches of money with which debts could be paid, but on the whole, as the Census report points out, 'there is an absence of any apparent intelligent action on the part of the ghost. If their visits have an objective, they certainly fail to reveal it.'

The Census of Hallucinations has long been considered a curiosity of little scientific merit, but in a sympathetic discussion in the journal *History of Psychiatry*, Dr T. R. Dening, a psychiatrist at Fulbourn Hospital in Cambridge, writes: 'By the standards of the time, the methodology was good and well thought out.' Dr Dening selects for special mention the evidence from the Census of the phenomenon of 'death coincidences', where people claim to have seen images of friends and relatives whom they thought hail and hearty, but whose ghostly appearance, it subsequently transpired, occurred at the moment of their death. Thus, Mr Walker-Anderson, a Yorkshireman who had emigrated to Australia, described how he awoke on the evening of 17 November 1891, and saw the figure of his aunt, 'Mrs P.', standing near the foot of the bed, looking older and stouter than when he had last seen her three years earlier. Her lips moved, and although he heard no sounds, he seemed to catch that she meant to say 'goodbye'. The following morning, he told his wife of his apparition and wrote down on a piece of paper: 'I believe Aunt P died on the 17th November' and put it in a drawer. In due course, the English newspapers for that week arrived by boat and, sure enough, there was a death notice of his Aunt P. who had indeed died on that date. Subsequent correspondence with his mother revealed that, taking into account the time difference between Melbourne and Greenwich, Aunt P. had appeared in Australia 'three hours after her death in England'.

At one level there is a straightforward explanation for Mr Walker-Anderson's vision of his aunt. There is a state of clouded consciousness between wakefulness and sleep when 'waking dreams' occur, and it is not uncommon for people to see figures, hear music or someone calling their name. These are called hypnagogic hallucinations, and as Mr Walker-Anderson 'saw' his aunt having just woken from sleep, his experience clearly falls into this category. The problem is to explain why she appeared when she did – was it mere chance that Mr Anderson's hallucination of his Aunt P. occurred at the time of her death? There were thirty similar instances reported in the Census, and the possibility that they all occurred coincidentally with the death of a friend or relative must be very small indeed. Dr Dening emphasises the great care taken by those conducting the survey to avoid elements of bias and seek independent confirmation of the reports. The results of the Census, he says, 'challenge the notion that hallucinations are necessarily pathological'.

The Census was repeated on a much smaller scale in 1977 when only 800 people were interviewed. Exactly the same proportion, about one in ten, reported personal experience of having seen or been touched by a ghost. Some are distinctly modern such as the ghostly hitchhiker and others less than modest – an Anglican vicar described being embraced by the ghost of a naked young woman.

The Hallucinations of Widowhood

A recently bereaved widow once confided to me that every morning she would wake early to hear her late husband's footsteps on the landing outside her bedroom. At other times, she would hear him call her name from the sitting room and once she even saw him sitting, as was his custom, in his favourite armchair. Despite the realism of the ghostly apparitions, she was pleasantly surprised at how unthreatening, even reassuring, they were. She had gone so far as to enquire of her local vicar whether they might be evidence of life after death.

In a classic study of the hallucinations of widowhood, Dr Dewi Rees, a family doctor in Montgomeryshire (as it was), found they occurred in more than half of the recently bereaved and persisted for many years. Those who had enjoyed a happy marriage were particularly prone to such hallucinations and the opportunity to remarry was specifically declined by some because of an active sense of disapproval from the late spouse. One 71-year-old woman, however, who had been widowed twice, reported the confusing sensation of feeling the presence of both her late spouses in her house at the same time.

In societies that practise ancestor worship, such hallucinations are even commoner. A survey of widows in Tokyo found that they were virtually universal – probably because the widows actively sought to maintain links with their late husbands with daily offerings at the family altar. As one widow put it: 'When I want to talk to him I just light some incense. Then if I'm happy I smile and share my good feelings, and if I am sad I know my tears are in his presence. When I look at a photograph of his smiling face I see he is alive, but then I look at the urn and know he is dead.' Visual hallucinations are particularly common among the Hopi Indians of North America. In a typical example described by a psychiatrist, Dr William Hatchett, a 60-year-old woman started seeing her son (who had died from exposure) at her window. To stop this she nailed a blanket over the window, but then he took to 'visiting her every night'. She would berate him for having left her and then switch on the light, at which point her hallucination disappeared.

It is very difficult to make sense of this phenomenon. Hallucinations are, of course, a feature of many altered brain states. Mountain climbers, polar explorers and shipwrecked sailors during periods of prolonged stress have the feeling a guardian angel has joined them – summarised in one account as: 'a benign, recognised and comforting male . . . who conveniently did not argue.' The same sense of 'the presence of another' may also be a feature of an epileptic fit or the paranoid delusions of schizophrenia, and can be induced by drugs, particularly those for treating Parkinson's disease. However, the hallucinations of widowhood are qualitatively different. They are more than a psychological response to the trauma of bereavement because they continue long after the acute pains of grieving are over. Then, unlike pathological hallucinations which tend to be stereotypic (the 'presence' being an anonymous stranger) and occur repeatedly during an illness and not at other times, the widows' hallucinations are spontaneous, unpredictable and emerge from a consciousness that is otherwise impaired.

This qualitatively distinct nature of the hallucinations of widowhood, together with their ubiquity, presumably explains why a belief in the after-life is so prevalent among Eastern religions – a belief so fundamental that its validity does not lend itself to argument. In Western cultures, by contrast, there is almost a conspiracy to deny the significance of hallucinations. Not only is it not generally known how common they are (none of the participants in Dr Rees's survey had mentioned his or her experiences to others for fear they might be thought to be losing their marbles), but the hallucinations are perhaps too readily dismissed as being no different from other pathological varieties. The only puzzling thing is why, if the dear departed do make a habit of returning to visit us, they do so in such an oblique manner. They should be more upfront about their presence rather than enigmatically wandering up and down corridors in the early hours. This would have the added advantage of obviating endless controversy among us mortals over whether there really is life after death.

2

The God Slot

The Greatest Miracle of All

Seeing the Christmas story through the eyes of small children is to be reminded of the extraordinary accessibility of Christianity to the youngest minds. They may not grasp the full philosophical implications of God Made Man, but this central truth of the Christian faith could not be portrayed more evocatively than by the nativity scene with, at the centre, the baby in a manger, doted on by Mum and Dad, the donkey and oxen in the background and the three magi kneeling in homage. For the great mystics of the English church, such as St Ambrose and the Venerable Bede, the appeal of the nativity story was perceived as being deliberate – a sign from God to 'pierce the heart', and thus support the call to conversion which the gospel contains. 'It should be carefully noted,' says St Ambrose, 'that the sign given of the Saviour's birth is not a child enfolded in Tyrian purple, but one wrapped round with rough pieces of cloth. He is not to be found in an ornate gold bed, but in a manger. Although he was Lord of Heaven, he became a poor man on earth that we might win the Kingdom of Heaven.'

There is nothing intrinsically exceptional about being born into poverty. But the nativity story evokes our sympathy because of the unusual location where Christ was born – in a stable. There seems to be something particularly arresting about babies being born in unusual places, for such stories in modern times are invariably newsworthy. There are several instances of a situation analogous to that in which Mary and Joseph found themselves in Bethlehem on Christmas Eve when there was 'no room at the inn', but in modern times a father accompanies the mother in labour to the maternity hospital only to find it is locked. This happened to Nicola Georgiadis and her boyfriend, who arrived at the University Hospital of Wales in Cardiff soon after midnight. There they found a notice which read: 'Please ring for admission, 1 a.m. to 6 p.m.' Shortly afterwards a midwife did appear, but by then an eight-pound baby girl had already been born on the pavement outside.

Alternatively, the couple may never actually get to the maternity hospital because something happens on the way. For Mr and Mrs Jagota, of Tyne and Wear, their Saab 9000 skidded off the icy road into a ditch at three in the morning. Luckily Mr Jagota had a mobile phone and was able to call an ambulance. When the paramedics arrived, the baby's head was already beginning to show and Mrs Jagota, still sitting in the passenger seat, was shouting, 'It's coming, it's coming!' After it was all over, one of the ambulancemen said: 'I wrapped the lovely little girl in a hypothermic blanket and handed her to her mother. It was a very emotional moment.'

In the most extraordinary of these unusual births, the baby is born while the mother is sitting on an old-fashioned train lavatory, which opens directly on to the track. The baby falls through but miraculously survives. For Roxanna Ramirez, the 21-year-old daughter of a US Sergeant stationed at an air base in Pordenone in northern Italy, her baby was born when the train had stopped at Mestre station. Miss Ramirez felt unwell, and sat down to prevent herself from falling over. 'I felt something pushing, I felt very hot,' she recalls. A traveller on the opposite platform saw the baby fall on to the tracks and alerted the station guard. A similar story was reported from Tokyo, although in this case the train was travelling at 40 miles per hour. The mother afterwards told the police she thought she had given birth, but it was not until five hours later and after several trains had passed over him that railway workers found the 6b 14 oz boy, who had a scalp laceration requiring four stitches. In each of these instances, one can imagine the event almost as it occurred, as indeed one can evoke the details of a mother giving birth in a stable in Bethlehem, which is why, 2,000 years on, the image of the child 'wrapped in swaddling clothes and lying in a manger' resonates so powerfully.

'*And is it true?*' asks John Betjeman, in his wonderful poem *Christmas*: '*And is it true,/This most tremendous tale of all ... The Maker of the stars and sea/Became a child on earth for me?*' That, of course, is a matter of faith, but there is another way in which a modern perspective can illuminate the Christmas story. Two millennia ago, the Jews in Palestine had no idea of how precisely conception took place, or indeed of the developmental changes that resulted in the birth of a baby. But now thanks, to techniques of in-vitro fertilisation, not only doctors and biologists but most people have some idea of the extraordinary events following fertilisation. How is it that a flat sheet of cells can, within a few days, transform itself into a bilaterally symmetrical being with a back and a front, a right side and a left side, and with different tissues and organs beginning to form?

In describing this phenomenon, even the most hard-bitten of scientists cannot restrain their awe: 'No one who studies the development of the embryo can fail to be filled with a sense of wonder and delight,' writes Professor Lewis Wolpert, in his book *The Triumph of the Embryo*, adding: 'Understanding the process of development in no way removes that sense of wonder.' Indeed, the more that science can explain how the genes switch themselves on and off, making a liver cell here, inducing the formation of a limb there, the more wondrous it becomes. And even were it possible to describe in precise detail each and every mechanism by which the embryo is formed, one would still be left with the greatest mystery of all: that two cells, an egg and a sperm, which alone will survive for only a few days can, when fused together, become a living being. From this perspective, the human embryo appears as a natural miracle, the imparting of form to matter in a way that makes possible the emergence of what is alive and conscious, from what is, in itself non-living and non-conscious.

The Christmas story focuses our attention in a particularly dramatic way on this natural miracle. And if St Ambrose thought the nativity scene was intended to 'pierce our hearts' and open them to the truth of Christianity, perhaps a better appreciation of the miraculous nature of the event it celebrates can do the same in our more secular age.

The Return of the Soul

Modern theology no longer allows that the soul should leave the body after death to flap heavenwards to spend an eternity with the Almighty. According to John Habgood, formerly Archbishop of York, 'nothing departs the body when we die', but rather that 'the continuity of self' – life after death – 'is held in the mind of God.' Interestingly, just as the Archbishop is anxious to play down the reality of the soul, it – or something very like it – is making something of a comeback in medical thinking.

Eighteenth-century physiologists were convinced of the material existence of the soul by the admittedly rather crude animal experiment of decapitating frogs and chickens and watching them make purposive movements for half an hour or more. Clearly such movements could not be merely mechanical, but were, the physiologists inferred, evidence of a sentient principle, a life-force best conceived of as an immaterial soul. The demise of the scientific proof of the existence of the soul came with the discovery of the spinal reflex. Both the perception of physical sensation such as pain and movement, it was found, could be mediated by nerves in the spinal cord without any involvement of the higher centres of the brain. The enigma of the apparently purposeful movements of the headless chicken was thus explained. The soul had become redundant and it was discreetly dropped from the discourse of scientists.

This has, however, left a lacuna – how to conceive of or understand those aspects of man's consciousness, quite separate from the workings of the mind, which might be called 'spiritual'. This encompasses virtually everything an individual values most highly – the aims and purpose of life, the sense of human solidarity with others, the recognition of the moral dimension of one's actions, the distinction between good and bad, and an awareness of God. The 'spiritual' here is not an abstract or ethereal concept, it has a physical reality that informs and determines people's judgements and actions. And for want of a better word, one might call it the soul.

Doctor Andrew Sims of the University of Leeds maintains that doctors and psychiatrists have committed a grave error in failing to recognise the potency of the spiritual in people's lives. 'We ask patients to which religion they ascribe,' he says, 'but we neglect the much more important question, 'what does your religion mean to you?' This omission is serious, Dr Sims argues, because it prevents a proper understanding of those aspects of human behaviour which reflect a disturbance of the spiritual in people's lives.

Consider, for example, the case of ghost-possession in a 22-year-old Indian man who had been imprisoned for theft and kidnapping – as described by Dr Anthony Hale of St Thomas' Hospital in London. As a young man his jealous aunt had fed him 'cursed sweet rice' thus making him susceptible to possession by spirits – which took the form of a foggy cloud which entered through his nose and mouth and made him wretch and wheeze, and took control of his body. While possessed by this demon he felt forced to engage in petty pilfering, car-theft and similar crimes, all with the purpose of bringing shame and stigma on himself and his family. The prison chaplain offered independent confirmation of the man's story claiming to have seen the ghost in the form of a 'descending cloud'. Leaving aside the reality or otherwise of the demonic cloud, Dr Hale noted that his patient's symptoms – his withdrawal, lack of a sense of personal identity and responsiveness to hallucinations – were very similar to that of a schizophrenic psychosis. Treatment was started with powerful tranquillisers, after which the episodes of ghostly possession apparently ceased.

The reverse of this perverse exaggeration of spiritual beliefs is their complete absence, as seen in those dangerous psychopaths labelled as having a 'personality disorder' who have a complete absence of guilt, no concern for the feelings of others, an inability to form relationships and high levels of aggression. Such people are defined by their complete lack of spiritual or moral values. They might be said to have no soul.

The fascination of medicine is how the pathological illuminates the normal. We understand the complex physiology of the heart by studying the consequences of what happens when it becomes diseased. Similarly, between these two extremes of psychotic religiosity and a pathological absence of spiritual values, it is possible to discern the reality and importance of the 'human soul' that guides and controls our lives. It may not be demonstrable by experiment as the eighteenth-century physiologists maintained, and it may not flap heavenwards at our departing, but it exists.

Mystical Moments

Christianity, or indeed any religious belief, could be nothing more than an abnormality of brain function. There is the view, for example, that Paul's conversion on the Road to Damascus, was an attack of temporal lobe epilepsy and certainly 'the light from Heaven', the auditory hallucinations ('Saul, Saul why persecutest thou Me?') and the subsequent temporary blindness, are quite compatible with this diagnosis. Similarly 'the strange and violent tremblings of the body' and celestial visions of St Theresa of Lisieux could be interpreted as being epileptic in origin.

Psychiatrists at the Maudsley Hospital studying patients with both mental illness and epilepsy found that mystical delusional experiences were 'remarkably common' and not infrequently associated with dramatic conversions. One, a bus conductor, was suddenly overcome with a feeling of bliss ... 'he carried on collecting his fares correctly, telling his passengers at the same time how pleased he was to be in Heaven'. Another 'had a dreamlike feeling, saw a flash of light, and suddenly knew he could have power from God if only he asked for it'. Mind-altering drugs can have a similar effect. Famously, Aldous Huxley came to believe that mescaline had revealed to him the personal presence and certainty of God. Contrariwise, religious belief can be extirpated by psychiatric treatments with drugs or psycho-surgery. The late psychiatrist William Sargant reported the case of a women obsessed with the belief that she had sinned against the Holy Ghost. Immediately on recovering from her leucotomy, she reported that she had 'now lost all belief' in its existence.

For those not afflicted by such neurological or psychological problems, revelation, in the form of new beliefs suddenly arrived at, may often occur in the highly charged atmosphere of intense religious ceremony. Much of the success of John Wesley's revivalist movement has been attributed to his ability to induce in his audience great states of anxiety about their sinfulness, their helplessness to save themselves from the wrath to come and the impossibility of salvation from Hellfire, except by the sudden acquisition of faith. Alternatively, the ultimate mystical experience of achieving unity with God can come from the opposite extreme, when, distanced from the world, the mind is emptied of everything other than the search for enlightenment. Mary of the Incarnation described this as 'knowing with great power and certainty that here is Love Himself, ultimately joined to me, and joining my spirit to His'.

The validity of any religious belief would seem to be compromised by the facility with which self-induced hysteria or abnormal discharges of the brain can so easily simulate Divine Revelation, and, indeed, some agnostics justify their belief on just these grounds. This must be a superficial view. Religious faith is indeed a broad church, ranging from the voodoo worship of the Haitian magic man to the high intellectual argument of Cardinal Newman, from primitive demonology to ethical monotheism. And just as it is easily possible to discriminate between these polarities (and their intrinsic worth), so it is possible to distinguish the ecstatic experience of the epileptic fit from that acquired as a culmination of a prolonged period of intellectual and spiritual contemplation. It would be possible to share the rationalist's scepticism if mystic revelation was the sole basis for religious belief. It is not and the real authority rests on the more secure foundations of Reason and Tradition.

The Lourdes Miracles

The Catholic newspaper *The Universe* has reported on its front page that 'prayer power' has saved the life of a young woman, Anne Connolly, three years after she was diagnosed as having a brain tumour. An exploratory operation was complicated by a stroke leaving her 'paralysed and unable to speak'. Following prayers for the intercession of the Venerable John Henry Newman and a visit to Lourdes 'the tumour has dispersed and her only disability is an impaired right hand and sight'. A recent brain scan now shows 'dead tissue instead of tumour'.

This being the 150th anniversary of the birth of St Bernadette, more people than ever will be seeking spiritual and physical solace by making the pilgrimage to Lourdes so perhaps this is an appropriate moment to take a dispassionate look at miraculous cures. The Lourdes cures, unlike other forms of faith healing, are relatively easy to assess because of the extensive documentation required by the church before they are deemed scientifically inexplicable and therefore miraculous. First it must be proved that the illness existed and a diagnosis established; then, that the prognosis with or without treatment was poor; and finally that the cure was instantaneous and permanent. Three separate panels of physicians must agree these criteria have been met. This all seems very impressive and one would imagine that having passed through all these hurdles, the more recent cures deemed by the church to be due to divine intervention would be well authenticated.

But this is not the case, as Dr D. J. West makes clear in his book on the cures recognised since the War, *Eleven Lourdes Miracles*. As a research officer for the Society for Psychical Research, Dr West would be expected to be generally sympathetic, but he finds, rather, 'carelessness in presentation of data', 'lack of consideration of alternative diagnoses', and 'an extensive bias in interpretation'. Two cases must suffice: Gabrielle Clauzel was cured of her rheumatic spondylitis of the spine suddenly while attending Mass at Lourdes in 1943. She had been chronically ill for six years, first with an attack of rheumatoid arthritis, followed by epileptic seizures and gastric trouble with the vomiting of food and bile. By the time she set out for Lourdes she was bed-bound, but during Mass she expressed a desire to get up off her stretcher which she did, to the great astonishment of those about her. She walked back to her hotel where 'she lunched with a big appetite and since then she has experienced no further troubles'. Dr West comments: 'the most obvious feature is the severity and variability of this lady's symptoms in the absence of signs of disease sufficient to account for them. The X-rays both before and after her "cure" certainly showed she had arthritis of the spine, but this is a common enough condition and by no means enough to account for all her florid symptoms.' Despite the thoroughness with which the case was investigated, his overall impression of the reports were that they were 'curiously imprecise and unsatisfactory'. In his opinion Mlle Clauzel's illness must have been hysterical.

Then there was Rose Martin who was diagnosed in 1946 as having cancer of the cervix, for which she underwent a hysterectomy. Subsequently she was found to have a large mass pressing on the rectum which was presumed to be a recurrence though this was never confirmed by biopsy. While taking the waters at Lourdes, her pain disappeared, her bowel movements returned to normal and examination two days later found no evidence of the rectal mass. The 'large mass' could as easily have been a chronic abscess liable to draining spontaneously and indeed the nurse accompanying Mme Martin reported she had passed a large amount of offensive matter while on the train to Lourdes. 'I fail to see why her recovery was considered "miraculous" or even remarkable,' Dr West writes, and goes on, 'close examination of these eleven modern miracles yields scant indication of any absolutely inexplicable recovery. Some are in fact readily explicable in ordinary terms and only appear as evidence of the supernormal by virtue of over-enthusiastic interpretation and much special pleading.'

The reason, paradoxically, lies in the very stringency of the criteria for cures to be miraculous – that they be instantaneous and permanent. This is unrealistic and corresponds to the ancient belief that divine intervention must by necessity be dramatic and complete. 'Concern with fulfilling these criteria,' Dr West argues, 'means that the doctors involved fail utterly to preserve a detached frame of mind so essential to a fair consideration of the merits of all possible interpretations. They cannot let themselves be carried along by the facts, but must strive to carry the facts with them.'

There is no doubt that swift and profound physiological changes can occur as a result of a visit to Lourdes but to demonstrate them it will be necessary to conduct a serious scientific study of a whole group of sick pilgrims and compare the results with a group of 'controls'.

The Mystery of the Stigmata

It is around Easter that one of the more curious of religious epiphenomena – the stigmata or wounds of Christ – commonly occur. The most recent medically documented report, albeit in the late 1970s, was of a young black Baptist girl from Oakland, California, whose stigmata lasted on and off for three weeks. Dr Loretta F. Early, a psychiatrist at the University of California, describes how she bled variously from her right palm, her left foot, right thorax and from the middle of the forehead (the site of the crown of thorns). The blood appeared to well up spontaneously over about five minutes and, once wiped away and the site examined with a magnifying lens, the skin was found to be intact.

On Good Friday she bled from all the sites simultaneously on waking and commented she felt 'it was all over'. Standard blood test investigations were all normal and subsequently it transpired that she had also experienced a repetitive auditory hallucination, 'Your prayers will be answered', which ceased on Easter Sunday. There was no doubt she was deeply religious; much given to quoting biblical verses and dreamt frequently of Christ. Discussing the case, Dr Early comments: 'Self-induced trauma is almost impossible to rule out in such cases, but we believe the likelihood to be almost nil.'

Since the time of St Francis, the first person to have received the stigmata, there have been 320 further instances – almost all young Italian women of a nervous disposition. St Francis's stigmata, unlike that of Dr Early's patient, persisted after his death as marks on his hands, which looked 'as if nails had been driven through them: round on the inner side, on the outer side they were elongated, and small pieces of flesh took on the appearance of the nails, bent and drawn back and running through his flesh,' reported his biographer, Thomas of Calano.

The Catholic church has always been slightly embarrassed by the stigmata phenomenon and maintains there is no intrinsic connection with sanctity because the wounds on the hands, at least, are in the wrong place as the crucifixion nails were driven through the wrist and not the palms. The two most famous stigmatists were a young Belgian girl in the nineteenth century, who bled every Friday – except on two occasions – for 15 consecutive years, and Theresa Newman, who bled every Friday from 1926 to 1962. Both were repeatedly scrutinised by eminent doctors. In the case of Theresa Newman, a Dr Warnhorst tested the authenticity of the bleeding by placing, on a Thursday evening, a specially sealed glass cylinder over the whole arm. The next morning the seals were unbroken but there was blood in the glass of the cylinder.

The prevailing medical explanation is a rare condition among those with hysterical traits in which they become sensitised to their own red blood cells. Under hypnosis, bruising can be successfully induced at suggested sites.

3

The Power of the Mind

Scared to Death

Several years ago an American psychiatrist, George Engel, described nearly fifty cases of people who had been 'scared to death'. Most occurred during or immediately after a disaster, such as an earthquake or explosion. Fear was implicated in most cases, although two women involved in a shipwreck 'gave up' when realising their children had been swept overboard. Occasionally, the minor repetition of an earlier incident was responsible, as in the case of a fifty-year-old man who survived a major earthquake only to die sitting at his desk during a minor tremor a few months later. The youngest case was a terrified four-year-old girl, who died while having some milk-teeth extracted. Three deaths were ascribed to violent and bloody scenes depicted on television. There is no theoretical difficulty in explaining how these deaths come about. Fear releases a vast surge of adrenalin into the bloodstream to prepare us to fight or flee. The blood pressure rises dramatically and there is an increase in the heart-rate, which can result in either a stroke or a heart attack or uncontrolled fibrillation of the heart muscle.

Nonetheless, as Dr Engel acknowledges, impressive as these anecdotal reports appear to be, many doctors remain sceptical, wondering if perhaps such deaths are merely coincidental. Like the Apostle Thomas, they would like to see definitive proof. This is easy enough in an experimental laboratory, and there are lots of grisly accounts of stupid scientists inventing ways of scaring dumb creatures to death – it has even been shown to occur in cockroaches. But with humans, self-evidently, the ethical problems posed by such investigations would be insuperable. The *Journal of the American Medical Association*, however, has published the findings of a 'natural' experiment that should convince the most doubting of doubting Thomases.

In the build-up to the 1991 Gulf War, Saddam Hussein repeatedly threatened to launch a chemical attack against the civilian population of Israel. Gas masks and automatic syringes containing atropine (to neutralise the effects of chemical weapons) were distributed to the entire population and every household was urged to prepared a sealed room. Then, on 18 January, one day after hostilities began, the first of seventeen missile attacks from western Iraq exploded in and around Tel Aviv and Haifa. 'This situation provided the unique opportunity to study the effects of a well-defined and acute, stressful event on mortality,' said Dr Jeremy Kark, of Hadassah University Hospital in Jerusalem; or, to phrase it more comprehensibly, would there be more deaths than usual (leaving aside those caused by the missiles themselves) on the days of the attacks?

The answer, perhaps predictably, was 'yes', quite spectacularly so, with an almost 50 per cent increase through the country – but fascinatingly, this only occurred on the first day, after which the mortality rate promptly returned to normal. This, then is pretty convincing evidence that it is possible to be 'scared to death', although a handful of cases were attributable to some other misfortunes – three adults were suffocated by incorrectly fitted gas masks. But this seems to be a less interesting observation than the remarkable way in which ordinary people appear to be able to adapt so promptly to the most stressful situations.

Typecast

In the popular alternative medicine handbook *You Can Conquer Cancer*, author Ian Gawler describes the typical personality profile of cancer patients: 'They try to please other people, to act as others want them to. There is often an overtone of personal subservience. They want to be liked.' A similar publication describes the sort of person who gets rheumatoid arthritis as 'extremely dependent, inadequate, [with] difficulty in coping with other people and with severely blocked emotional expression.' It is easy to imagine how the impressionable who turn to these books for guidance might well end up more despondent than ever – believing they are somehow to blame for their misfortunes.

This nonsense is not limited to the alternative medicine brigade. Mainstream medicine is full of studies – usually contradictory – which define personality types for virtually every illness. Patients with ulcerative colitis, for example, have been described as 'intelligent, compulsive, highly strung, with an abnormal attachment to the mother' – or, alternatively, as 'passive, dependent and egocentric'. This is all unimpressive, for the simple reason that people tend to have not one but several personality types, moving from one to another according to the circumstances. Depending on the company I am in, or whether my mood is manic or depressive, I can just as easily be an introvert as a extrovert.

The one clear exception is the highly competitive 'Type A' personality who, according to American heart specialist Dr Meyer Friedman, has anything up to a fourfold risk of having a heart attack. This has come to mean that any pushy, middle-aged executive who keels over with a coronary 'had it coming' – which is clearly ridiculous. Dr Friedman's Type A personality is much more specific: a rare if readily recognisable breed of men of almost pathological unpleasantness, who have two main characteristics. The first is Time Urgency – he walks and eats fast, is fetishistically punctual, thinks of other things when his wife is talking, never reads a magazine or relaxes in front of the TV, and never 'finds time to sit and daydream, recall old memories or carefully scrutinise flowers, trees birds or animals'. The second characteristic is Free-floating Hostility, so he loses his temper while driving, does not believe in altruism, often lies awake at night furious about what someone has done, and is readily irritated by trivia: indifferent shop assistants; late arrival of the mail and so on.

Dr Friedman, who has been studying interview video tapes, now reports that Type As are also identifiable by certain physical signs such as rapid speech, chronic beads of sweat on the forehead, clenched hands during a casual conversation and a loud hostile laugh. Readers, I am sure, will get the picture, and, if at all possible, will have steered well clear of any Type As they might have met.

Thirty separate studies have demonstrated that Type A behaviour – which is 'reliably rated, a deeply ingrained and enduring trait', carries an increased risk of heart disease. There is not much one can do about this because, almost by definition, Type As are unapproachable and unwilling to listen to advice. Their tune changes, however, if they survive their first coronary. Then they become much more willing to submit to psychological therapy. According to a study from the United States, those who are prepared to modify their exaggerated emotional reactions, change their beliefs and establish more realistic goals, halve their chances of having another heart attack.

Not only personality but emotions such as grief and fear carry an increased risk of heart disease. In the year following the Aberfan disaster, the mortality rate among the bereaved was seven times higher than among those who did not lose a close relative. People who suffer from 'phobic anxiety', a sense of fear and apprehension, have a fourfold increased risk of a fatal heart attack. The precise mechanism is not clear, but there is a clear analogy with the well-recognised observation that pigs (whose circulatory and nervous system is very similar to humans) often 'die of fright' en route to market. In a rather pointless experiment, scientists found that inducing a heart attack in pigs by tying off one of the coronary arteries had a very different outcome, depending on the animal's state of mind. Those who were fed, petted and handled before the experiment survived, while those unfamiliar with the laboratory became withdrawn, developed rapid uncontrollable fibrillation of the heart muscle and died. Recognising the potentially fatal consequences of these emotional states is very important. Theoretically, by helping the bereaved to overcome their unhappiness or the chronically anxious to overcome their fears with either drugs or psychological support, it might also be possible to save their lives.

The Secret of Longevity

Somewhere in the Queen Mother's serene smile on her 94th birthday walkabout was a slightly bemused air suggesting that she herself is surprised that she is still going. Obviously it helps that she is a woman, and perhaps all those gins and tonics have had a preservative effect. The envious might suggest that her longevity is not unconnected to a lifetime of privilege with somebody always on hand to carry her favourite corgi on and off the royal flight. But longevity is just as possible among those 'downstairs' as 'upstairs', a point well illustrated by Dr Richard Asher, the distinguished physician, in a description of 'an unusual case of health' which he reported in the *British Medical Journal* 'The lady I describe here is healthy not only in the sense of never being ill,' he writes, 'but in the more practical fashion of being hard at work for 76 (76!) consecutive years with only ten days' illness.' Dr Asher's knowledge of this interesting case was 'purely social', as Fanny, the 90-year-old lady in question, never consult doctors. Fanny works as a cook at a girls' day school in London. An accompanying photograph shows a spry, lively woman standing beside her oven as her main responsibility is to cook for 90 people every day, in addition to acting as housekeeper to the headmistress.

Dr Asher tells us that Fanny rises at 6.30 a.m. takes herself for a walk and then cooks breakfast for four people. At 9.30 a.m. she goes shopping, and at 11 a.m. starts cooking the school lunch ready for 1 p.m. At 1.30 p.m. she sorts out the dirty crockery, and then at 4 p.m. prepares tea for the staff of seven teachers. At 6.30 p.m. she prepares supper for the headmistress, and three hours later takes herself for another walk before retiring. On Saturday she does the cleaning and polishing and, on Sunday, her own washing in the morning, cooks and serves lunch, and then takes the afternoon off! Dr Asher, though recognising that many people can be quite active at 90, maintains the singularity of this case, which merits his reporting it to the *British Medical Journal*, is that 'Fanny should perform quite so much responsible work at this age, and that she should have worked for so many years without absence through illness.'

Perspicacious readers will have guessed that this is not a contemporary account. Nowadays, Fanny's conditions of employment would have attracted the attention of the Health and Safety Executive and would have been found in breach of a fistful of regulations requiring her forcible retirement – Dr Asher's report was published in 1958. At the time, it generated a lot of interest and speculation as to what might be the cause of this type of rude good health. Dr Norah Devon, pointed out that a survey of children in Kent had found that the two factors 'showing the closest correlation with good health' were 'attendance at Sunday School, and parents who believe in corporal punishment'. Even at that time, though, she thought that these methods might prove 'unpopular'.

More importantly, perhaps, the longevity of both the Queen Mother and Fanny might be attributable to a combination of good genes (Fanny's mother lived to 100, and her three siblings all survived late into their ninth decade), and 'personality'. It is impossible not to think that personality must be influential, but very difficult to pin down exactly how and why. For Professor Hans Eysenck of London University's Institute of Psychiatry, the main guarantor of good health is 'autonomy' – belief that control of one's life lies within oneself rather than in externals, such as upbringing, education or the class system. This, he contrasts with those who are 'over-patient and suppress their emotions or, alternatively, are constantly angry, blaming some person or circumstance for their unhappiness'.

The impression that personality has something to do with health is also due to the fact that those like Fanny, who are self-reliant and phlegmatic, make a point of not visiting their doctor and thus appear to be 'healthier'. Indeed, when they do turn up to the surgery, the slimness of their medical records sets alarm bells ringing. When those with 'slim notes syndrome' seek a medical opinion, clearly something truly serious is going on to have forced such reluctant patients to visit their doctor. When they do, their problems merit urgent and thorough investigation. History does not record whether Fanny passed her century, but it is to be fondly hoped the Queen Mother will still be with us to greet the new millennium.

Virtue Rewarded

Virtue has its rewards. The conscientious, truthful child will live longer than the lazy and deceitful, according to a report in the American journal, *Science*. Such psychological generalisations are never very convincing, but this is a fascinating exception.

In 1921, Lewis Terman, an American psychologist, scoured high schools in San Francisco and Los Angeles looking for children of exceptional intelligence. He found 1,528 boys and girls with an IQ of 135 or above, whose lives have been scrutinised at regular intervals ever since, providing much valuable information about the relationship between high intelligence and subsequent achievement. They have done very well, with seven out of ten graduating from college – ten times more than a random group of comparable age. The majority of the women – as was the custom in the 1940s and 1950s – became housewives, but still the numbers cited in the *Dictionary of American Scholars* and *Who's Who* is many times more than would have been expected. Eighty-six per cent of the men ended up in the two highest occupational categories – the professions and business – and 4 per cent were in *Who's Who* before the age of forty.

There is nothing here to substantiate the common stereotype of the 'brain nerd': the 'Termites', as they were called in deference to Dr Terman, were successful across a wide range of activities, and were in general sociable and well adjusted. As for the few – less than 10 per cent – for whom things turned out badly, they were either struck down by mental illness or alcoholism. So, high intelligence is a great blessing – which is scarcely a revelation, although it is interesting to see it confirmed. But that is not the end of the story. The Termites are now, gradually, dying off. Dr Howard Friedman, of the University of California, has systematically correlated their age at death with both their psychological profiles, as determined by Dr Terman in the 1920s, and their family circumstances. He has found that for the men, the 'conscientious and truthful' who were brought up in stable families have lived, on average, an astonishing seven years longer than the 'unconscientious and lazy', whose parents were divorced. This is partly explained by the proverbial 'unhealthy lifestyle', as the unconscientious were more likely to be smokers and drink more alcohol. But even when this is taken into account, the difference in longevity persists. Why?

Clearly these very intelligent boys were successful in adult life – but there are different types of success. Most of those identified as talented when young grow up to be unremarkable adults. They will be proficient in their chosen fields, but their particular expertise – whether as doctors, lawyers or in business and academia – will be routine rather than pioneering. They may be content with their lives, but they often have a sense that they have not fulfilled their potential. So though outwardly successful, they are discontented, frustrated at not having realised their childhood ambitions. Yet some with precisely the same amount of talent will grow into highly accomplished adults, creative forces in their chosen field, effortless experts or 'natural masters'. They, too, are usually content with their lives, but their state of mind will be qualitatively different – for they have fulfilled their potential.

So intelligence itself is not enough. The great Victorian scientist Sir Francis Galton, in his analysis of eminent men, observed that in addition to innate ability, his subjects also had 'zeal' and 'the power of doing a great deal of work', motivated by the belief that honesty and perseverance will lead to success. They were both talented *and* conscientious. It is the frustrated and discontented who, for various mysterious reasons, tend to have shorter lives, while the factors that permit the full flowering of childhood talent turn out to be the determining factors in longevity are personality and family relationships. Examination of the early lives of great achievers found 'they came from homes that were intact. What characterises their households was high moral demands and insistence on meeting standards of excellence in one's work.'

There are exceptions of course and other factors are undoubtedly important – particularly luck, the knack of being in the right place at the right time, and the quality of teaching at school and university. But the bedrock requirements for the fulfilment of talent, a creative and successful career and a long life would seem to be conscientiousness and a stable family upbringing.

The Meaning of Life

We Britons are apparently becoming more neurotic and less happy as revealed by a comparison of the results of two large surveys of 10,000 ordinary people – using the well-validated General Health questionnaire – the first conducted in the mid-1970s and the second ten years later. The later survey elicited many more negative answers to the question 'Have you recently been feeling hopeful about your future?' and more affirmative answers to the gloomy enquiry: 'Have you recently felt that life is entirely hopeless?' Reporting the results in the *British Journal of Psychology*, Dr Glyn Lewis of the London School of Hygiene estimates that the prevalence of 'psychiatric morbidity' – neurosis, anxiety and depression – has increased by an astonishing 40 per cent over this period: up from one in five of the population to almost one in three. 'An increase of this magnitude has disturbing implications both for public health and treatment provided by the NHS,' says Dr Lewis. Although the trend he has identified is probably correct it is hard to believe that a third of the country is chronically unhappy and it is certainly doubtful that we need a lot more psychiatrists to cheer us up.

None the less, the issue raised by Dr Lewis is an interesting one. What does make people happy? Not, it seems, economic prosperity. The Japanese are not happier than the Indians; Europeans not obviously happier than Latin Americans. For what it is worth, a sociological study of the 'personal happiness ratings' of different countries found that Nigerians, with a Gross National Product of just over 100 dollars per head, were on a par with West Germans, with a GNP per person of nearly 14,000 dollars. Rather, the essential component of personal happiness, or what the psychologists call: 'psychological well-being' seems to be having a 'meaning in life', defined as 'the recognition of order, coherence and purpose in one's existence, the pursuit and attainment of worthwhile goals and an accompanying sense of fulfilment'. Those privileged to have this 'meaning in life' tend to embrace traditional values, with strong religious beliefs or self-transcendent values and have a personality disposition described as 'hardiness' which allows them to remain healthy under stress.

This sounds plausible enough, if rather vague, but two New Zealand psychologists, Sheryl Zika and Kerry Chamberlain of Massey University, have empirically tested this link between 'meaning' and 'well-being'. They subjected two groups of people – 200 young mothers and 160 retired people – to several psychological tests: the 'Purpose in Life' test; a 'Life-Regard Index' and a 'Sense of Coherence Scale' (which 'assessed the extent to which the world is perceived as sensible, ordered and predictable'), and compared the results with conventional measures of psychological health. 'The overall results', they found, 'lead strongly to the conclusion there is a substantial and consistent relation between meaning in life and psychological well-being.' More than half of the variation in the happiness of individuals turns out to be attributable to 'a recognition of order and purpose in one's existence'.

Why then should we have become more miserable in the ten years covered by these two surveys? Dr Lewis 'finds it difficult to provide evidence of a link with the election of a Conservative Government in 1979'. Indeed, the second survey in the mid-1980s was conducted at a time of general optimism and of peak popularity for Mrs Thatcher, who is generally credited with having restored British self-esteem. But three factors at that time could well have contributed to a greater sense of 'meaninglessness'. Most important of these was unemployment – the percentage of young people out of a job had risen from 3.6 to 13.7, clearly paralleled by a rise in the suicide rate in this age group by a third. The mid-Eighties also saw the continuing decline of the two pillars of civil society – organised religion and the institution of marriage – both strongly and independently linked with 'meaning', and so happiness. There is, in general, a fatalistic acceptance of these trends. No doubt another survey in a few years' time will show that we have become even more miserable. Oh dear.

Jealousy – The Green-Eyed Monster

Jealousy is a universal human emotion. When the New Zealand psychiatrist Dr Paul Mullen investigated its prevalence, he found that, of the 400 people he questioned, every single one had experienced pangs of jealousy at one time or another. Nor is jealousy without virtue. St Augustine's famous observation '*qui non zelat, non amat*' – he who is not jealous does not love – emphasises how it may be as much a reflection of solicitousness and devotion as of suspicion and distrust. Jealousy may even have a social function – well described by Dr Charles Mercier in 1918: 'The institution of marriage and the instinct of jealousy serve the same purpose. Love selects, jealousy stands guard to repel others from entering the sacred fold.'

Modern liberal notions of individual freedom have undermined the commitment to exclusivity in personal relationships, and jealousy's reputation has suffered as a result. The best that can be said for it now is that, in small doses, it need not be unpleasant – conferring a *frisson* of danger and excitement. Some, indeed, may be flattered that their spouse still cares enough to feel jealous.

The borderline between normal and morbid or pathological jealousy is ill-defined, not least because the most rational person under jealousy's influence behaves irrationally, rifling through pockets – and worse – looking for clues of sexual infidelity. It is relatively easy to make the distinction when the jealousy is a feature of some psychiatric syndrome like schizophrenia or paranoia, or where the conviction that the partner is being unfaithful is demonstrably false. But jealousy can also be morbid, even in the absence of such delusional beliefs, when the individual responds with abnormal facility and intensity to events which appear, albeit remotely, to place the partner's fidelity in question.

According to Dr Paul Mullen, who, incidentally, is the world authority on the green-eyed monster, the source of this form of morbid jealousy varies but it is usually associated with low self-esteem, a sense of insecurity and of inferiority. Like all morbid reactions, it feeds on itself; the suspicions of infidelity can never be laid to rest, leading to a constant state of sadness and apprehension – depressive symptoms which further distort reality. The desires of the morbidly jealous tend to be irreconcilable and contradictory. There is a wish both to expose and punish the supposed infidelity while at the same time retaining the relationship. The morbidly jealous fear loss but promote division. No marriage can withstand such a corrosive influence. In a serious of eighty cases described by the psychiatrist Professor Michael Shepherd, 'the quarrels, accusations, recriminations, remorse, verbal abuse and physical assaults, led in virtually every case to either separation or divorce'.

A Sad Case of Being Too Happy

It sometimes seems as if virtually everyone coming through the surgery door is depressed for some reason or other. Yet patients afflicted by the other end of the mood spectrum – the chronically or ecstatically happy – seem very rare indeed. There is no doubt that such a phenomenon exists which is seem most clearly in those suffering from mania. Having just recovered from an episode, Charles Lamb wrote to Coleridge: 'I look back with a gloomy kind of envy, for while it lasted I had many, many hours of pure happiness. Dream not, dear Coleridge, of having tasted the grandeur and wildness of Fancy until you have gone mad.' Another mania victim describes 'the intense sense of well-being which is physical as well as mental. The digestive system functions particularly well and an inner warmth pervades me so I can walk about naked out of doors on quite cold nights.'

Patients with multiple sclerosis, especially in the early stages of their illness, may also appear much happier than they should be. Indeed the sometimes bizarre disparity between their mood and their degree of disability – which is also a feature of hysterical paralysis – led not infrequently in the past to MS patients being labelled hysterics. Dostoevsky's fits were famously pleasurable. 'For a few moments I feel such happiness. It is so strong and so sweet that for a few seconds of this enjoyment one would readily exchange ten years of one's life – perhaps even all of it.' Harold Klawans, a Chicago neurologist, describes a variant of this called orgasmic epilepsy. A patient told him of 'this intense, warm feeling . . . as if I'm having the strongest of orgasms. And then I'm at peace, and everything is warm and beautiful.' Rather surprisingly, she insisted her epilepsy be treated, commenting: 'I do not need to have these orgasms while driving the children to the dentist.'

Besides these dramatic examples, Dr Richard Bentall, senior lecturer in psychology at Liverpool University has suggested that there may be a more low-grade variant of chronic happiness which can almost be classified as a psychiatric disorder in its own right. The chronically happy, he points out, are a minority and their general gaiety and gregariousness clearly demarcates them from the norm. They may show defects in cognition, such as refusing to dwell on unhappy events in the past, or exhibit irrational thought patterns like over-estimating their own achievements and those of others. So far chronic happiness has evaded medical scrutiny, but it is probably because those afflicted see little point in visiting their doctor and may indeed be unaware about their mental state at all.

The unfortunate family doctor is thus stuck with the thankless task of trying to cheer up as best he can all those who are palpably unhappy – the depressed, anxious, lonely, panic-stricken and so on. As happiness and depression are both clearly physico-chemical states, the simplest way to achieve this would be to prescribe 'happy' pills. In this, however, doctors are severely hampered because the relentless campaign against the best legally prescribable happy drug of all – the benzodiazepines like Valium (and its many equivalents) has meant that they are reluctant to prescribe them, and those who are most likely to benefit are very reluctant to take them. In my experience, no other drug takes the edge off misery and despair so quickly and so safely, or guarantees sleep and relaxation to the exhausted; yet I have lost count of the times I have almost had to force my patients to take them.

The anti-Valium hysteria has been kept on the boil by lawyers acting on behalf of patients who allegedly became dependent, but there are signs it is on the wane. Dr Michael King, a senior lecturer at the Royal Free Hospital, has said: 'The risks of these drugs have been much exaggerated. We must not patronise patients by believing they cannot handle them. Short-term prescribing is humane.' His views are echoed by Ian Hindmarch, Professor of Psycho Pharmacology at Surrey University: 'Benzodiazepines are the safest drugs we have for people with anxiety and sleep disturbance. The legal profession has been dining out on these drugs which doctors should be able to prescribe in freedom.'

Vive la Différence

In a deliberate parody of the current enthusiasm for finding a genetic cause for everything, Dr Jane Gitschier of the University of California has reported in the journal *Science* that the genes for several characteristic male traits – 'addiction to death and destruction movies', 'interest in the sports pages of newspapers', 'inability to express affection over the telephone' – have all been found on the male Y chromosome. The deterministic belief that we are all prisoners of our genes is increasingly prevalent – but at least it is a useful antidote to the contrary view still widely peddled in academic and feminist circles that anyone who dares to suggest that there might be substantial differences in skills and attributes between the sexes must be a sexist reactionary.

Rather, if current research is to be believed, not only psychological differences but the very structure of the brain itself is as different between men and women as chalk and cheese. Psychological tests consistently show that men are better at 'target-directed motor skills', such as throwing darts and kicking balls, at remembering directions and understanding the complexities of three-dimensional objects. Women are demonstrably superior at fine motor skills, at remembering people's names and noticing if something is out of place. Professor Doreen Kimura of the University of Western Ontario provides a plausible if speculative explanation for these attributes in evolutionary terms. In primitive, hunter-gatherer societies, she argues, where men had to go out and forage for food, it would clearly be advantageous to be able instinctively to find one's way about, and, by deploying 'target-related motor skills', throw one's axe at a passing antelope with an even chance of hitting it. These skills are obviously unnecessary for women guarding the family hearth, for whom fine motor skills such as the ability to recall where objects had been put down would be more useful.

The difference in psychological traits is reflected in distinct anatomical differences between the brains of the two sexes. In the male it is asymmetrical, with a thicker right cortex; in the female it is more integrative, with a larger *corpus callosum* – the bridge of neurons connecting the two hemispheres of her brain. These anatomical differences are undoubtedly influenced by the sex hormones. Testosterone secreted by the male testes in early foetal development is crucial in determining male sexual characteristics, so there is no reason why it should not also influence connections in the brain. Conversely, girls who have been exposed to high levels of testosterone in the womb prefer to play with typically masculine toys like cars and grow up to be more boyish and aggressive than their unaffected sisters.

The genes also have a direct influence on psychological behaviour quite distinct from the effects of hormones as shown by studies of people with an aberration in the number of sex chromosomes. Best known are XYY males who, with an extra Y chromosome, have an 'extra dose' of masculinity. They are tall, not very bright and have an exaggeration of certain 'male' traits. They tend to be impulsive, lack emotional control and have a weak concept of self. As a result, they are 18 times more likely to end up in prison. By contrast, women born with only one X chromosome, a condition known as Turner's Syndrome, are short, and infertile, and seem to have a deficit in typically female traits, as shown in a study in *The Lancet* from Dr Declan Murphy of the US National Institute of Health. Psychological tests on women with Turner's showed that, compared with controls, there is impairment of female memory attributes, such as recalling events and names.

The missing X chromosome is also linked with immaturity in the development of the female psyche, so those with Turner's tend to exhibit childish behaviour, are conformist, non-aggressive and lacking in intellectual originality. It is difficult to know exactly what all this adds up to; but it would seem that Dr Gitschier's parody in which genes directly determine a whole range of male and female behavioural attributes is probably much nearer the mark than she anticipated. *Vive la différence!*

Dream Analysis

In contrast to the arcane world of Freudian dream interpretation, current medical theories on the purpose of dreaming tend to be unimaginative. Dreams are 'auditory and visual hallucinations induced by signals from the brain stem' or 'designed to reinforce memories stored during waking life' or 'like a computer "dumping" unwanted programmes, a means of forgetting useless information'. Yet for doctors with the time and interest to enquire, dreams can provide fascinating insights into the lives of patients and their experience of illness.

Indeed, dreams, and particularly the emotional stress of nightmares can actually precipitate episodes of migraine, asthma and even heart attacks. Dr Harold Levitan of Montreal has studied migraine sufferers who developed their headaches at night and found 'the outstanding feature of the dreams, culminating in migraine, was a powerful negative effect'. He cites a typical example: 'I was in a shipwreck . . . many people were drowning. As I swam away, I looked back and saw the others were being eaten by sea monsters . . . it was very scary. Then I woke with a terrific throbbing headache.' Similarly, acute asthmatic attacks with narrowing of the airways has been shown to be strongly related to emotional dreams. And a distinguishing feature of patients with peptic ulcers is that intense dreams increase the secretion of gastric acid, eroding the stomach lining.

Dr Daniel Schneider, a New York psychotherapist, has described the dream of a 45-year-old man that ended in a coronary. He was about to give a violin concert before a glamorous audience. 'I came out to tremendous applause,' he said. 'I bow and the hush deepens. I turn towards my violin case and take out – not a violin but a gangster-style machine gun and swiftly put the muzzle to my mouth, and, rat-tat-tat, I blow my brains out.' He awoke with a severe crushing chest pain and on admission to hospital was found to have had a severe heart attack.

Dr Robert Smith, a psychiatrist at the University of Rochester, New York, has found that dreams may reflect the severity of physical illness. He studied the dreams of patients admitted to a cardiac unit for 'references to death' featuring graveyards, wills and funerals. The greater the degree of cardiac disability, the more often were these death-related dreams reported, suggesting that they were in some subtle way warning the patients of their prognosis.

In this way, dreams can contribute to the distress of illness. At least some of the despair of those with early dementing illnesses can be attributed to the dismal nature of their dreams, which symbolically focus on lost resources: wandering in a strange place, looking for help, being left behind or losing something familiar. The emotions, reported Kenneth Altshuler, a New York psychiatrist, included not a feeling of fear but rather 'a vague sense of apprehension, increasingly helplessness or strangeness'. As the dementia progresses, these dreams become stereotyped and endlessly repeated.

By contrast, the dreams of young people struck by some devastating misfortune such as paraplegia are notable for strong elements of denial and wish fulfilment and are characterised by energetic physical activity, 'expressing a reluctance to give up their former body image'. Many paraplegics, though invariably impotent and denied the pleasure of sexual enjoyment, report dreams which culminate in the full sensation of orgasm. This observation demonstrates how cerebral eroticism plays a central role in sexual gratification quite independent of the sensations in the genital region. Changes in dream content can equally reflect an acceptance of disability. Dr Larry Burd, of the University of North Dakota, describes the case of a 35-year-old man who lost both forearms after an accident sawing logs. He had initial difficulties in adjustment, and particularly expressing physical affection to his wife and children. 'He then reported he knew the time he had accepted his amputation because he began to dream of himself with hook hands.'

Another group in whom changes in dream content are significant are people undergoing sex change operations. Dr Vamik Volkan, professor of psychiatry at the University of Virginia, describes a man who after the operation to remove his penis 'dreamed he was a young man fighting others aggressively with sticks. He then threw his stick away and turned a corner, opening his arms and saying "Come to me". His feeling was that he expected gentleness from the others.'

The doctor prepared to listen to dreams can gain a rare insight into a patient's state of mind, as a fascinating study of the serial dreams of a man terminally ill with cancer of the colon reveals. The dreams start with the typical 'frustration' type, with the dreamer trying but failing to get into his surgeon's office even though late for an appointment, and move on, while being treated with chemotherapy, to dreams of being 'tortured and battered about by several people who were supposed to be my friends'. These are followed by premonitions of the end, a 'shadowy figure stands by my bedside. He leads me out of the hospital to a place I've never been before. He is somehow very comforting.' Lastly, he dreams it is all over. 'My friends are enjoying themselves and I put on a record but they cannot see me. It is as if I am a ghost. The record ends but the turntable keeps spinning. I shout "It's all over, turn it off" but they cannot hear me.'

Twin Traits

As a twin, I have always had a personal interest in 'twin studies', where psychological research into the differences between twins is used to tease out how much of our personalities can be attributed to nature (our genes) or nurture (our social upbringing). The simple answer has always been that, to varying degrees, both are important. Recently, however, psychologists have come to believe that striking results from twin studies have clarified one of the great mysteries of the human species: why it is that we are all so different. If nurture, or social upbringing, were the dominant influence, then, given the enormous cultural differences in our lives, it is difficult to explain how such distinct personality traits as conscientiousness, laziness, friendliness, aggressiveness and so on, are so readily recognisable in all social classes. But if nature, or our genes, were dominant, this presupposes an element of rigidity which cannot be reconciled with the way some people seem able to 're-invent' themselves, acquiring entirely new personas.

The balance has been shifted decisively in favour of 'nature' by a study of 100 sets of twins separated in infancy and reared apart, which has been conducted over the past 15 years by Dr Thomas Bouchard, a psychologist at the University of Minnesota. His main finding has been that identical twins brought up apart are as much alike as if they had been brought up together. Far and away 'the most significant factor in the variation in measurable personality traits is due to genetic influence', he announced in the prestigious journal, *Science*. Included in Dr Bouchard's study are the 'Jim twins' – Jim Lewis and Jim Springer – separated at birth and only reunited at the age of 39. Besides being, predictably, the same height and weight, they had both married twice, first to women called Linda and then to women called Betty; they had christened their firstborn with the same name, and shared the same taste in beer and cigarettes. When Dr Bouchard met them for the first time he was 'staggered by the similarity of their gestures, voices and the morphology of their bodies; these two men had lived entirely separate lives and yet, if he closed his eyes, he could not tell which Jim was talking,' writes Lawrence Wright in the *Guardian*.

But the parallel lives of these twins raised apart goes well beyond such personal and anecdotal impressions; when subjected to in-depth psychological testing of the five 'superfactors' (the traits which most comprehensively describe personality) of extroversion, neuroticism, conscientiousness, agreeableness and openness, the results were virtually indistinguishable. From this study, Dr Bouchard estimates that two-thirds of measurable personality traits are directly attributable to genetic influence. Put another way, the similarities we notice between biological relatives – mothers and daughters, fathers and sons, aunts, uncles and cousins – 'is almost entirely genetic in origin'. This leaves only a minor role for parental upbringing and family attitudes, which, argues Dr Bouchard, are only relevant at the extremes. Self-evidently, gross deprivation and maltreatment will have a deleterious effect, while what he calls 'charismatic, dedicated parents' can 'make all their children share the same interests and values'. Such exceptional situations aside, Dr Bouchard might seem to want to make us prisoners of our genetic inheritance, which is clearly not the case. Rather, he says, each individual picks and chooses from a range of stimuli and events, largely on a basis of their genes, and creates a unique set of experiences; that is, 'people help to create their own environments'.

This powerful genetic component to personality explains why, over time, it changes so little, and the determined toddler turns into a determined adult. For Professor Sandra Scarr, a leading American child psychologist, it could not be otherwise: 'If personality development was so vulnerable as to be diverted off its tracks by slight variations in parenting, the human species could never have survived,' she says. This is in many ways a rather depressing conclusion because it implies that a deliberate attempt to try and improve a child's personality is likely to be ineffective: 'We know how to rescue children from extremely bad circumstances and return them to normal developmental pathways,' writes Professor Scarr. 'But for children whose development is on a predictable but undesirable trajectory, and whose parents are providing a supportive environment, any intervention will only have limited effect.'

The results from Dr Bouchard's studies of identical twins are certainly compelling evidence in favour of a dominant role for nature in the development of personality. Yet almost immediately the doubts start creeping in. Parental interest and the quality of schooling have an important influence for good or ill on how children turn out, while most people's personalities do change, albeit subtly, for better or worse as they get older.

4

Diversions

Plum Pudding Perils

Writing in the December issue of *Tribune* for 1946 George Orwell reminded his readers, 'The whole point of Christmas is that it is a debauch . . . it is not a day of temperate enjoyment, but of fierce pleasure,' which we should be willing to pay for 'with a certain amount of pain'. In that long-gone era of austerity and rationing, the quality and diversity of what most of us typically consume on Christmas Day would have seemed wonderfully extravagant. But people are never content. So in this puritanical age, the excesses of Christmas are tantamount to mortal sin and the ascetic and, allegedly healthier, dietary habits of post-war Britain are viewed with a misty-eyed nostalgia. Orwell was right. The point of Christmas is: 'The battle with platefuls of turkey, the flaming plum pudding and Christmas cake with almond icing an inch thick,' even if there is 'peevishness the next morning and castor oil on December 27'.

For physiologists and doctors, Christmas provides another opportunity, a classic experimental situation in which to study the effects of a large calorie intake on the human organism. John Hampton, professor of medicine at Nottingham University, has examined the strain on the heart imposed by a typical Christmas lunch (a standard festive meal of poultry, mince pies and wine) in six healthy volunteers. He found that the amount of work done by the heart – the cardiac output – increased by a third in order that more blood should reach the stomach to facilitate digestion. This rise in cardiac output may put a strain on the heart in those whose coronary arteries are narrowed by atheroma and can even be lethal as a pathologist observed in a letter to *The Lancet*, 'I have noted full stomachs in several people with severe heart disease who died of an acute heart attack,' he comments. 'Such patients are definitely at risk following a large meal, the danger being compounded by alcohol, which further raises the cardiac output.' Christmas lunch is thus clearly hazardous, but there can be few more pleasant ways to go than passing out on the sofa, and then passing on to the next world, having enjoyed one last meal in the bosom of the family.

In a further experiment that bears directly on the traditional dilemma of whether it is better to sleep off a heavy Christmas lunch in front of the fire, or burn it off by taking the dog for a brisk jog, the thirteenth-century Holy Roman Emperor Frederick II 'caused two men to be given a good meal', after which one was allowed to rest and the other made to perform strenuous exercise. 'Subsequently,' according to a former professor of physiology at London University, 'he had them both disembowelled in his presence.' The rested man's stomach was empty, he having obviously digested his meal, while that of the man forced to exercise was still full.

More sophisticated investigations have added little to Frederick's original observations, which were confirmed six centuries later, albeit in dogs, by the great Russian scientist Pavlov. Exercise inhibits digestion by slowing the gut, so it remains slopping around in the stomach, causing nausea and discomfort. Nonetheless doctors at Guy's Hospital found 50 years ago that exercise only inhibits stomach emptying if it is unpleasant whereas amicable walking and talking actually enhance it.

There are a further series of prosaic dangers associated with the Christmas festivities. A 40-year-old man was admitted to Greenwich Hospital on Christmas Day with acute obstruction of the gut which was found at operation to be due to a large orange balloon stuck in his duodenum. He made an uneventful recovery, as did a woman aged 86 who developed peritonitis on Boxing Day and from whose abdomen was retrieved the plastic robin used to decorate the Christmas cake whose beak had perforated her gut wall.

More tragically Dr Ann Savage, of Selly Oak Hospital in Birmingham, has described a late complication of Christmas. A 38-year-old man was admitted 'pale, confused and with no recordable blood pressure'. Attempts at resuscitation failed and at necropsy half a cocktail stick was found to have perforated through the oesophagus into the main blood vessel – the aorta – running behind it. 'At the inquest,' Dr Savage writes, 'his wife stated that on Christmas Day they had been eating sausages wrapped in a piece of bacon, secured by a cocktail stick. These were difficult to see and she herself had found one in her mouth and removed it. Her husband jokingly said he must have swallowed his' – as indeed he had.

These hazards of Christmas aside, few could disagree with George Orwell's stirring conclusion to his *Tribune* article: 'One celebrates a feast for its own sake – so let there be no gloomy voices of vegetarians or teetotallers to lecture us about the things we are doing to the linings of our stomachs.'

Rejuvenation – More than Meets the Eye

'Youth is the one thing worth having,' Lord Henry told Dorian Gray in Oscar Wilde's novel. 'It is one of the great facts of the world, like sunlight or springtime. It cannot be questioned. It has its own right of sovereignty. It makes princes of those who have it.' And so it is that for everyone who is the wrong side of 40 each New Year is always tinged with melancholy – one step further away from the springtime of youth towards decrepitude, to creaking joints and wrinkled skin, slower reaction times and furred-up arteries. If only there were some simple rejuvenation remedy that could throw this process into reverse – without having to forfeit one's soul, like the hapless Dorian Gray.

But rejuvenation, so fashionable in the middle decades of the century, has been discredited, reduced to a footnote of medical history in which quacks and fraudsters preyed on the vain and the gullible. Or has it? Perhaps surprisingly, the reputations of two of its richest and most successful practitioners, Serge Voronoff and Paul Niehans, have been at least partly rehabilitated in recent years.

The Russian physician Professor Voronoff, at the peak of his fame in the 1930s, was doing ten monkey gland operations a week in which three thin slices of monkey testicle were grafted (with silk stitches) on to the inside of the scrotum. He was, as a result, a very wealthy man. He occupied the whole of the first floor of one of Paris's most expensive hotels, surrounded by a retinue of chauffeurs, valets, personal secretaries and two mistresses. It was an impressive achievement for someone whose claim to success rested on just one book containing portrait photographs of patients before and after receiving their grafts. The changes he described were similar to those in the ageing sheep which had been the subject of his early experiments. 'Like my old rams, they become young in their gait, full of vitality and energy.' A 65-year-old man even required a second graft after two years, having been 'over-prodigal of the vital energy supplied by his first one'.

The following decade, those seeking rejuvenation made their

way to Professor Paul Niehans in his mansion overlooking Lake Geneva, a house stuffed with Italian and Dutch Old Masters and furnished with tapestries and carpets which had once belonged to Napoleon. The names of his patients read like a *Who's Who* of the rich and famous, including Gloria Swanson, Marlene Dietrich and Lillian Gish, Somerset Maugham and Noel Coward. Tito, de Gaulle, Churchill and the Windsors are believed to have been on the list. And there was the greatest catch of all: Pope Pius XII, who, in the summer of 1953, sought Professor Niehans's help for his unexplained chronic poor health. For his services the professor was invited to join the Vatican's select group of scientists, the Pontifical Academy.

Professor Niehan's rejuvenation technique involved injections of cells taken from lamb embryos which, according to his book, *Introduction to Cell Therapy*, migrate to the appropriate organs of the body. So, foetal brain cells bolster a fading intellect, foetal heart cells strengthen the heart muscle, foetal kidney cells keep the urine flowing, and so on. A French aristocrat, Cornel Lumière, described the treatment as 'Not a particularly pleasant experience, but it mattered little. For years to come I would feel grateful for those injections. Their benefits are too great, too good for anyone to forgo.'

In time both of these rejuvenation remedies fell into disrepute. Professor Voronoff's reputation was badly damaged by detailed scientific studies of a French veterinarian who claimed to demonstrate that the transplanted monkey testicles were rapidly overwhelmed by the body's own cells. '*Une zone d'invasion cellulaire massive.*' In 1952 a distinguished British surgeon, Kenneth Walker, described the work as 'no better than the methods of witches and magicians'. And, in another memorable phrase, the monkey grafts were swiftly dismissed as 'nothing more nor less than a piece of dead meat put in the wrong place'.

As for Professor Niehans, he lived long enough to hear himself denounced as a pious fraud by Dr Gerald Dorman, president of the American Medical Association, who argued: 'He carefully selects patients who are likely to respond to treatment which includes rest, good care and excludes liquor and tobacco. That is enough to ensure that many will feel better. But there is absolutely no scientific evidence his cellular therapy has any value.' And yet many, probably, most, of those who had these treatment reported a remarkable improvement in wellbeing. It seems unlikely that Professors

Voronoff and Niehans would have amassed their vast personal fortunes merely on the basis of a placebo response to useless therapies.

In November 1991 an editorial in *The Lancet* suggested that the file on Voronoff's work be reopened and in particular that 'the Medical Research Council should fund further studies on monkey glands'. The fate of organs transplanted from one species to another is inevitably one of rejection, but perhaps the testes are different. Without using immunosuppressant drugs, researchers from Lanzhou in China have successfully transplanted the steroid-secreting adrenal glands, so perhaps, the editorial observes, 'any organ whose predominant function is the synthesis of steroids (which includes the testes) might be less liable to rejection than others.' Nowadays doctors treating the 'male menopause' with synthetic testosterone claim similar results to those of Professor Voronoff. Professor R.D. Greenblatt, of the University of Georgia, has found 'fair-to-excellent results in two thirds of patients with amelioration of fatigue and enhancement of general wellbeing'.

As for Professor Niehans, his rejuvenation therapy would appear to be vindicated by a study of the effects of human growth hormone in men over 60 by Dr Daniel Rudman, published in *The New England Journal of Medicine*. Growth hormone is secreted by the pituitary, a gland at the base of the brain, and promotes the strength and viability of tissues generally. Dr Rudman reported that after six months of treatment his patients appeared ten to twenty years younger, with stronger muscles, less fatty tissue and better nourished skin. 'There was a dramatic change in physique; the men had the appearance of being much fitter and in better condition.' Now it so happens that one of the 12 injections in Professor Niehans's treatment contained ground-up foetal pituitary gland packed with this reinvigorating hormone which probably produced the beneficial effects that so many reported. Professors Voronoff and Niehans thus seem to deserve at least a qualified apology from the orthodox medical establishment who were so dismissive of their work. Now that the scientific basis of their results has been elucidated, perhaps many more will seek to follow the example of Dorian Gray and stay youthful with injections of growth hormone or testosterone.

When Illness Strikes the Leader

The health of politicians might be thought to play only a small role in the destiny of nations, but it has significantly influenced British post-war history on three occasions: in 1951, 1956 and 1963. During the Labour Party Conference in 1951, Clement Attlee was laid low by an exacerbation of a peptic ulcer, and vainly tried to reconcile the factions of his party from his hospital bed. In fact, the reforming zeal and competence of the Labour administration had already been severely compromised by the ill-health of several Cabinet ministers. Four years earlier in 1947, Ellen Wilkinson had died from either an asthma attack or a drug overdose and the Chancellor of the Exchequer, Hugh Dalton, who had been boosting his spirits with a stimulant drug, Benzedrine, was forced to resign after an indiscretion to a journalist. His successor, Sir Stafford Cripps, fared even worse. A strict vegan, he spent several months in a Swiss clinic with a mysterious illness, and was forced to retire in 1950. Then Foreign Secretary Ernest Bevin, a walking textbook of the complications of heart disease, which he self-treated with liberal doses of alcohol, died in 1951. Clement Attlee's hospital bed diplomacy, on top of all this, proved unsuccessful and, to no one's surprise, the Tory Party was returned at the General Election a few months later.

In 1956, Anthony Eden's response to the Suez Crisis was interrupted by a nasty attack of cholangitis, an infection of the biliary tract, associated with an earlier unsuccessful operation on his gall-bladder. On his return to the House of Commons, a Labour member observed: 'His face was grey except for black-ringed caverns surrounding the dying embers of his eyes.' At this crucial time, when he needed all the help and advice he could get, three of his Cabinet colleagues – Butler, Nutting and Monckton – were incapacitated by stress and the Leader of the House of Lords, Lord Salisbury, had a heart attack. Then, in 1963, Harold Macmillan developed acute retention of urine, due to an enlarged prostate. Under the influence of sedative drugs and the prospect of a major operation, he was persuaded to resign. It was, according to the medical writer Dr Hugh L'Etang, an unnecessary decision and one that Macmillan later bitterly regretted.

So with the wisdom of hindsight, it is possible to substantially rewrite the past 50 years of British politics. Without Attlee's peptic ulcer, Labour might have won again in 1951 and there would have been no Suez Crisis. Without Eden's cholangitis the Suez Crisis might have been successfully resolved, and Macmillan would never have succeeded to the Prime Ministership. If Macmillan had not resigned to be replaced by the ineffectual Douglas Home, Labour might never have won the election in 1964.

Probably the greatest beneficiary this century of this fact of political life was that old monster Stalin. Fate smiled on him twice. On Lenin's death in 1923, Trotsky was in the Crimea, incapacitated by a bout of dysentery. In the two weeks before he was able to return to Moscow, Stalin effectively took control of the party machinery. Twenty-two years later at Yalta, Stalin repeated his *coup*, extending Communist influence over China and most of Eastern Europe against minimal opposition from an unusually compliant Churchill and a seriously ill Roosevelt. The rest, as they say, is history.

The Heroic Self-Sacrifice of Scientists

No matter how exotic the location or worthy the subject, international medical conferences are invariably of a mind-numbing tediousness. To liven things up during a meeting on impotence a few years ago, one participant walked round to the front of the podium, dropped his trousers and injected a new drug directly into his limp organ. The audience, it is reported, greeted the robust erection this produced with a prolonged round of applause. Unusual as this behaviour might appear, it follows a long and heroic tradition in which doctors and scientists have put their theories to the test by experimenting on themselves.

One of the greatest self-experimenters was the British scientist J.B.S. Haldane. Concerned about the problem of excessive heat in the mines, he observed the physiological effects on himself of remaining fully clothed in a room heated to 150° Fahrenheit. Investigating the effects of cold on divers, he spent hours in a pressure chamber immersed in a pool of freezing water. In a related experiment, looking for ways of preventing 'the bends', his spinal cord was injured by a bubble of inhaled helium, which produced persistent pain in his lower back and down both legs. For Haldane, the 'ideal way of dying' would be as a result of investigating how diseases were transmitted.

This was indeed the fate of John Hunter, surgeon to George III and the most celebrated anatomist of his day. He sought to resolve the burning issue of his time – whether gonorrhoea and syphilis were the same thing or two different diseases – by inoculating himself with the pus of a victim of veneral disease. Regrettably, this brave experiment only added to the confusion because, unknown to Hunter, the patient from whom he obtained the specimen was suffering from both diseases. So, after developing the signs of a gonorrhoeal infection, ten days later there appeared the typical sore of primary syphilis. His autopsy at the age of 65 revealed the syphilitic infection had progressed to cause a ballooning dilation of the main blood vessel in his chest – the aorta.

Hunter's heroic self-sacrifice was followed by many others. While studying how yellow fever might be transmitted, Dr Stubbons Ffirth injected the black vomit of a sufferer directly into his veins; Dr Max von Pettenkoffer swallowed a cup of bouillon laced with cholera bacilli to prove his (mistaken) theory that the cholera organism alone was not sufficient to cause death from the disease.

This tradition of self-experimentation has continued to the present day. In the early 1980s an Australian, Dr Barry Marshall, drank a cocktail containing the organism *Campylobacter pyloris* and rapidly developed the symptoms of gastritis – abdominal discomfort, nausea and halitosis. A colleague then passed an endoscope down his throat, which showed the stomach wall was absolutely teeming with the bugs. Both gastritis and peptic ulcers, Dr Marshall concluded, were not just due to excess acid but were actually infectious diseases. He predicted, and was subsequently proved right, that peptic ulcers could be prevented from relapsing with large doses of antibiotics.

To self-experimenters we owe our understanding of the nature of many infectious diseases, their incubation periods and how they are spread. Surgery would be inconceivable without the anaesthetic gases developed by doctors experimenting on themselves. If Dr Werner Forsmann had not passed a tube into his own heart in 1929, we would never have had open-heart surgery. If Dr G.S. Brindley had not injected his penis hundreds of times with different drugs, the best treatment we have for male impotence would never have been discovered. Heroic as these self-experimenters undoubtedly were, the discomforts and misery they inflicted on themselves must have been compensated by the sheer exhilaration of furthering the cause of scientific truth. Dr Gail Dack, a strong believer (amid general scepticism) that a bacterial toxin could cause food poisoning, fed himself with a suspicious piece of sponge cake. A couple of hours later he rushed to the bathroom where, between paroxysms of vomiting and diarrhoea, his wife overheard him muttering: 'Oh, this is wonderful.'

Phantom Fables

Among the many stories recounted by readers is that of a North Yorkshire farmer who lost his leg following an accident while driving his tractor. Like virtually all amputees, his missing leg was replaced by a 'phantom' which was so life-like he often forgot his limb was missing. When he retired to bed, however, his phantom foot became intensely itchy and, bizzarely, he had found that this was best relieved by scratching at the site the foot would have occupied had it been there. Phantom sensations are not limited to loss of a limb. A phantom breast, which seems to fill out the padded bra, is often described by women following a mastectomy breast cancer. The internal organs such as the uterus and stomach may also develop phantom symptoms after their removal – so period pains may persist after a hysterectomy. Patients with spinal cord injuries who can feel nothing below the waist can still wake after an erotic dream having experienced a 'phantom orgasm'.

But phantom limbs are much the best-described of this type of phenomenon – thanks to a remarkable paper written by two British neurosurgeons, W.R. Henderson and T.E. Smythe, who were captured by the Germans in 1940 and spent the war studying the effects of amputation on 300 of their fellow soldiers held in prisoner-or-war camps. They found that patients are aware of the phantom immediately they recover from the anaesthetic; indeed, it feels so natural that 'at first the impression is that the expected amputation has not been done until it is discovered that the limb, though still felt so vividly, is in fact absent.' The phantom limb can also be moved voluntarily, the ankle can be flexed and extended and the toes, especially the big toe, moved up and down. Over time, the phantom limb appears to shorten or telescope, and the foot or hand appears to move closer to the stump. Similarly, the facility with which the phantom can be moved declines with time, and it seems to become much stiffer. The phantom limb has a ghostlike quality, being able to move through solid objects like a wall or table, and is famously sensitive to changes in the weather, being most noticeable in cold and wet conditions, while 'involuntary movements of the absent digits are unfailing precursors of an East Wind.'

There are two possible explanations for the phantom limb. The first is that they arise from nervous impulses in the parts of the brain concerned with the missing limb. This would seem plausible enough, but it is actually rather difficult to imagine how our bodies could have two separate existences – the physical reality of the bone and flesh of a limb and a parallel, equally realistic reality, albeit a metaphysical one, in the brain. Doctors Henderson and Smythe described several very curious cases in which phantom limbs seemed to 'remember' their previous life. In one instance, a soldier jumping from a truck sprained his ankle and so fell behind his companion. A few minutes later he was wounded in the same leg, was taken prisoner, and required an amputation. He described how he could still feel the pain of his sprained ankle in his phantom limb, but not the much more severe pain of the bullet that had necessitated the amputation.

An alternative theory for phantoms put forward by the biologist Dr Rupert Sheldrake is that the limb severed at amputation still 'exists' as a field of energy. He cites the experience of Dr Barbara Joyce, head of a nursing programme, who claims to be able to reduce the sensations of pain and itchiness in phantom limbs by massaging them. This is essentially the experience of my North Yorkshire farmer who could only obtain relief from the itching of his phantom foot by scratching. Dr Sheldrake described an experiment which seems to confirm this hypothesis. There were two participants, Mr Casimir Bernard of New York, who lost his right leg below the knee while in action in France in 1940, and a Mr Inigo Swann. Mr Bernard moved his phantom limb up and down while Mr Swann – sitting opposite him – with a hood covering his head, 'guessed' its position. Initially, Mr Swann's guesses were no better than would have been expected by chance but, dramatically, after 100 attempts, 'the results started to show something'. Mr Swann had 'learned' to feel Mr Bernard's phantom limb as it passed through his hands, which he perceived as an unpleasant sensation. Dr Sheldrake's suggestion of an 'energy field' could also explain how it is that when a prosthesis is fitted to the amputated limb, the phantom functions to control its movements. 'The lifeless appendage seems to be animated by the living phantom.'

Tattooing Tales

In one of Parliament's more revealing moments the Tory MP for Billericay, the ever-youthful Teresa Gorman, told the chamber that she had tattooed eyebrows. She informed a hushed chamber that as a young girl she had plucked so vigorously at her eyebrows that they had never regrown again, leaving her no alternative other than to simulate artificially what nature could no longer provide.

Plastic surgeons use tattoos to achieve other desirable aesthetic effects. Hilton Decker MD, from Florida, has reported good results from replacing nipples lost during surgery of the breast with tattooed replicas: 'The central portion representing the nipple is tattooed with a dark brown pigment. The surrounding area is tattooed with medium and light brown pigment creating a stippling effect.' Now women with poor eyesight, arthritis or a tremor who find the delicate task of applying makeup to their eyelids too difficult, can opt for the permanent alternative of having them tattooed.

Tattooing remains endemic within the Armed Forces – a survey of a garrison in Salisbury found that almost half sported one or more motifs. A British tattooist who placed an astonishing 90,000 designs on soldiers during the two World Wars felt they can have a very positive effect on morale. 'A good tattoo can help a serviceman,' he commented. 'It strengthens his self-confidence and lets even a mummy's boy feel like a man.' Tattoos have rightly been described as a poor man's coat of arms, featuring many of the symbols that can also be found in the heraldry of the upper classes, while the accompanying motifs 'True Love', 'Mother', 'Death before dishonour' are a caricature of the aristocrats' Latin epigrams. Interestingly, the only time the upper classes took to tattooing in a big way was during the First World War, when there was a craze among officers to have an image of the Kaiser represented on the buttocks.

The other important social groups in which tattoos are commonly found are the dispossessed, criminal and psychopathic. In one case study, almost a fifth of the corpses of 1,000 teenage drug addicts found in New York were tattooed usually with very negative themes: 'Born to lose', 'I don't believe in friends', 'Hard luck', and so on. Truman Capote in his novel *In Cold Blood* gives a vivid description of the tattoos worn by the murderer: 'A blue-fanged tiger stalked along his left biceps, a snake coiled around a dagger slithering down his arm and elsewhere skulls gleamed and tombstones loomed.' Most surveys of psychopathic murderers have found that a quarter to a third will have equally gruesome tattoos.

It all seems a far cry from the Polynesians, whose enthusiasm for 'tattawing' (from which our word originates) so impressed Captain Cook on his voyage to the South Sea islands, but most tattoos are really quite innocent and sometimes very witty. A casualty officer examining a punk rocker with abdominal pain was taken aback to see that her pubic hair had been dyed green. Tattooed above it was the warning: 'Keep off the grass.'

Risking Death for a Sexual Thrill

The practice of throttling one's sexual partner to heighten sexual excitement is allegedly common among the Eskimos and South East Asians. The earliest well-documented case in Europe was in 1791 when the musician Koczwara, regarded by Bach as the finest bass player of his time, persuaded a prostitute to hang him for five minutes. He could not be revived, and she was tried, acquitted and 'took resolutions for a better life'. Needless to say, the Marquis de Sade, in his novel *Justine*, has one of his characters engage in erotic asphyxiation, after which he exclaims: 'Oh, these sensations are not to be described, they transcend all that one can possibly say.'

Sexual stimulation is also a well recognised consequence of asphyxiation by hanging, as an old English poem makes clear:

> *The townsfolk saw with great dismay*
> *His organ rise in boldest way,*
> *A sign to all who stood around*
> *That pleasure e'en in death is found*

Deep-sea divers and pilots whose oxygen supply is impaired also report sexual euphoria due to the brain being starved of oxygen. It is presumed that, in response to carbon dioxide building up in the bloodstream, the arteries to the brain dilate, increasing the blood supply to the libidinal centre.

In general it would seem that being temporarily asphyxiated by one's loved one is fairly harmless, the danger comes for those who try to go it alone with the help of ropes or ligatures controlling the pressure on the neck in a variety of ways. Understandably, things can go wrong – in the form of giddiness or loss of consciousness – and then the results can be fatal. These auto-erotic asphyxial deaths are of special interest to forensic pathologists, who need to distinguish them from suicide or even murder. The distinction is important as it influences the reaction of family and friends – and, indeed, life insurance payments that depend on whether the death is deemed an accident or suicide.

337

Dr Robert Hazelwood of the University of Virginia, writing in the *Journal of Forensic Science* describes the case of a 33-year-old security guard found dead in a warehouse, naked except for a leather belt around his waist and a pair of handcuffs, and his clothes stacked neatly some distance away. A rope attached to the wall behind him passed over a beam ending in a hangman's noose around his neck. The secluded location, incomplete suspension and bondage were, according to Dr Hazelwood, 'all typical features of the death scene of an auto-erotic fatality'. Interviews with his workmates, however, revealed that the victim had been suffering from a depressive illness, and on several occasions during the previous week had expressed a desire to kill himself. An open verdict was returned.

By contrast, a lecturer in forensic medicine at Leeds University, Dr S. Sivaloganathan, describes a case that looked suspiciously like murder: a 36-year-old male teacher wearing a bra and make-up was fished out of a river with his hands and feet tied by a clothes line, and a stone attached to his left ankle. 'The question was whether he was responsible for getting himself in this predicament or someone had put him there, perhaps outraged by his perverse activity,' Dr Sivaloganathan writes. Police divers found several other large stones at the bottom of the river, also with clothes line attached and each with a loose free end suggesting it had been cut, probably with a pair of scissors. 'The conclusion was that the deceased used a novel method of asphyxia, achieving sexual stimulation by partially drowning himself and then, when he had enough, he would cut himself free.' On this occasion he had failed. The medical verdict was of accidental death from auto-erotic drowning.

Mr Bobbitt's Misfortune

True human sympathy can rarely stretch beyond one's immediate family and closest friends. Or, as the French philosopher La Rochefoucauld put it: 'We all have strength enough to endure the misfortunes of others.' Sometimes, indeed, the misfortunes of others may be so curious or bizarre as to be amusing. Such, no doubt, will have been many people's reaction to the tale of the unfortunate Mr John Wayne Bobbitt, whose penis was amputated by his wife, Loretta, and thrown onto a motorway verge. Luckily the publicity following Mr Bobbitt's misfortune did not precipitate an epidemic of penile amputation by vengeful wives and girlfriends, such as occurred in Bangkok in the 1970s and which gave rise to the enigmatic Thai saying: 'I'd better get home or the duck will have something to eat.'

Traditional Thai homes are elevated on pilings, with the windows open for ventilation and the family pigs, chickens and ducks kept underneath. Thai wives who had been humiliated by their philandering husbands would wait until they fell asleep and then sever the penis with a sharp knife before throwing it out of the window, where, indeed, it might be swallowed by a passing duck. If the erring husband was lucky enough to hang onto his now disembodied organ, the place to go to was Bangkok's Sririaj hospital where the chief surgeon, Mr Kaslan Bhanganad, became very adept at coping with this type of emergency. At the beginning of the epidemic, things did not go too well, due to lack of experience. In the *American Journal of Surgery*, Mr Bhanganad says: 'For the first cases, the clinical course was stormy, complicated by diminution in organ size and inability to achieve an erection.' With time, however, his technique improved so he was able to achieve 'acceptable' results. Mr Bhanganad said: 'We believe penile reimplantation should be successful, provided the amputated part is not mutilated, decomposed or partially eaten by a duck.' The viability of the organ proved surprising, with a successful outcome in one case being achieved after a delay of eight hours, and in two others after the organs had first been fished out of septic tanks, having been flushed down the toilet by angry wives.

Most of Mr Bhanganad's later cases regained normal function though there was a loss of sense of touch and pain in the reimplanted organ with many describing it as being 'numb'. Mr Bhanganad was surprised at how little this defect seemed to concern them, until it was pointed out that a numb organ could increase sexual enjoyment because it meant ejaculation was delayed and coitus could be prolonged.

Such details will no doubt appeal to those with a black sense of humour – an almost essential requirement for doctors working in casualty departments, who have to cope with an endless stream of those for whom this has not proved their lucky day, having fallen off ladders or under buses or had a coronary on the way to work. Writing in the *Journal of Emergency Medicine* recently, Dr Robert Slade has described what he calls 'emergency room folklore': accounts of misfortunes encountered in casualty, which, though endlessly repeated, turn out to be mythological. A classic example is the 'exploding toilet seat'.

One Sunday morning, so the story goes, a father retires to the lavatory for a few moments' solitude with the papers without realising that his wife has just vacated the bathroom, having sprayed the residue of her highly inflammable hairspray down the loo before throwing the empty cannister away. The father settles on the loo seat, extinguishes his half-smoked cigarette by dropping it between his legs into the bowl. The result is a terrific explosion that blows him off the seat, inflicting serious burns on his anatomy. When the ambulancemen arrive they laugh so much they drop the burnt breadwinner off the stretcher, causing further injury. Dr Salde writes: 'There are multiple versions of this story recounted in casualty departments across the country, but all of them are without any solid evidence. In experiments in my own bathroom, I could not produce an explosion of any significant force, although I did succeed in singeing a large water-melon.'

[A few weeks after this column appeared a former RAF pilot from 244 Squadron recounted the following experience from his time in the Persian Gulf. 'The toilet facilities were thunderboxes over unpleasant depths, disinfected daily by one of the local walids (boys). Early one morning I was close at hand when an airman disappeared inside. After a moment's peaceful silence a figure erupted at the rate of knots, after the unmistakable but unnerving sound of a petrol explosion. Aircraft fuel, not water, had 'cleansed' the lats. It did occur.']

Murder Most Sophisticated

Poisoning is much the most interesting and sophisticated method of homicide – and the one with the highest chance of going undetected – usually by the administration of a poison whose deadly effect is difficult to distinguish from death by natural causes. Thus the symptoms of phosphorous poisoning are very similar to those of yellow atrophy of the liver, while thallium simulates the symptoms of polyneuritis – an acute inflammation of the nerves. An Australian woman successfully disposed of two of her husbands in this manner before a detective, suspicious of the similarity of their deaths, ordered their bodies to be exhumed. Toxicological tests revealed massive levels of thallium in the tissues of both.

The Newcastle surgeon and chairman of the BMA's Ethical Committee, Mr Paul Vickers, induced a lethal aplastic anaemia – destruction of the bone marrow – in his wife with the anti-cancer drug CCNU. This was a perfect murder in every respect, and Vickers would certainly have got away with it, had he not later called off the marriage to his girlfriend and accomplice – who then went to the police and revealed all.

Despite the many advantages of murder by poisoning, it remains a rare means of homicide, though, according to Professor Michael Green, forensic medicine specialist at Sheffield University, this could be because most cases go undetected. 'It is suspected that some illnesses and death, especially amongst the elderly, are deliberately drug-induced – notably by overdosage with digoxin [a heart drug] and sedatives,' he says. Further, trends in the forensic-pathology service have reduced the thoroughness of investigations into cases of sudden or unexpected death, thus increasing the chances that death by poisoning will be overlooked. The number of autopsies is certainly falling – and, Professor Green alleges, so is their quality. As a result of financial constraints, it is now more difficult to persuade hospital laboratories to screen for drugs and other toxic substances. 'Poisoning', Professor Green urged, 'should always cross the minds of those dealing with an unusual case of sudden illness or death.'

There could be no better illustration of the importance of this advice than the very unusual case of a mystery illness, described by Victor Dubowitz, professor of paediatrics at the Hammersmith Hospital. Early one Sunday morning Professor Dubowitz was phoned by a doctor in Qatar and asked if he would admit a 19-month-old girl who, over a period of ten days, had become increasingly drowsy and lethargic and was unable to sit upright or walk. By the time the young girl arrived at the Hammersmith Hospital she was semi-conscious and unresponsive to commands. She made continuous restless movements when disturbed, had a hoarse cry and seemed to be sweating excessively, even though her temperature was normal. Professor Dubowitz suspected a viral infection of the brain, or encephalitis, and was disconcerted when all the investigations that might support such a diagnosis were entirely normal. The girl's condition continued to deteriorate to a point where she need artificial ventilation. While this was being discussed on a ward round, the nurse sitting by her bedside interrupted to say she thought the diagnosis was thallium poisoning.

In response to the somewhat surprised reaction of the medical staff, she pointed out that the Agatha Christie novel she was reading, *A Pale Horse*, described several cases of thallium poisoning, in which the victim's symptoms were remarkably similar to those of the girl. In addition, the one consistent feature stressed in the book – loss of hair – had just become apparent that morning. Professor Dubowitz ordered an urgent toxicological analysis, which revealed very high urine levels of thallium – a domestic poison widely used in the Middle East to eliminate cockroaches and rodents, with which she may have been deliberately poisoned. Luckily, the girl responded to treatment, although even four months later she still needed support when standing and walking. 'We are indebted to the late Agatha Christie for her excellent and perceptive clinical description,' Professor Dubowitz concludes in his report. And to the nurse's powers of observation, it would be fair to add.

Choking

It might seem a rare enough possibility, but when a guest rises from your dinner table, blue-faced and distressed after his food has gone down the wrong way, he might be about to experience the sixth commonest form of accidental death – which probably claims 1,000 lives a year in Britain. The first recorded case of choking to death was by the Roman historian Suetonius, who reported the untimely death of a son of the Emperor Claudius after inhaling a small pear that he had, in sport, thrown into the air and caught in his mouth. Nowadays, gluttony is the major contributory factor, especially if the victim is a talkative eater. The risk is also increased in those who wear dentures (and so inadequately masticate their food) and in the inebriated, who bite off more than they can chew.

The problem for those present is to know what to do before the ambulance arrives. The first imperative is to make the correct diagnosis – and, particularly, to distinguish this life-threatening event from a heart attack. Here, luckily there is one vital clue: the victim is silent. The obstructing piece of food, as well as preventing air from getting into the lungs, prevents air from passing over the vocal cords, which is necessary for speech. All that is necessary to recognise the emergency is to point at the dinner plate and ask: 'Can you speak?' If the victim cannot, one can be sure he has food stuck in the throat – and be equally sure he will die in a few minutes unless someone, anyone, acts fast. The more medically minded might also note the pulse is rapid and bounding due to retention of carbon dioxide which is quite unlike the pulse following a severe heart attack which, though also rapid, is weak or even impalpable.

The commonest initial reaction is to stick the forefinger and middle finger into the victim's throat in the hope of extracting the bolus of food. This is not a very good idea, as quite apart from the danger of having one's digits severely bitten, it can precipitate spasm at the back of the throat, which only makes matters worse. However, if the victim can be encouraged to explore the back of his own throat, it is sometimes possible to get a hold of the obstructing matter, particularly if it is a large piece of meat. Another instinctive and time-honoured reaction is to thump the victim vigorously on the back. This, too, is unlikely to do much good, although it may stimulate a coughing fit which can disimpact the obstruction. By contrast, back-slapping may do the trick in small children if they are also held upside down to benefit from the added effect of gravity. Back blows were condemned by the American surgeon Henry Heimlich as 'death blows' because of their potential to drive the piece of food further and deeper into the airway. In its place he proposed the technique which bears his name – the Heimlich manoeuvre: a sharp blow in the mid-line just underneath the diaphragm forcing air out of the lungs under pressure. The mechanism can be simulated by inserting a cork into the mouth of an inflated balloon and then squeezing it forcefully. The cork flies out, similar to the opening of a bottle of champagne. Mr Heimlich's manoeuvre was based on painstaking experiments on beagles. He inserted a piece of raw hamburger into the creatures' larynx and then 'I pressed the palm of my hand deeply and firmly into the abdomen. After one or two compressions the hamburger was ejected and normal respiration was established.'

In the 20 years since Mr Heimlich first described his manoeuvre, its efficacy has been confirmed many times. Objects expelled from the throats of choking victims have included apples, hot dogs, beef, chicken, coins, pills and sweets. One mother found her nine-month-old infant blue and lifeless in her cot and noticed that foam rubber had been gouged out of the mattress cover. A quick upward thrust on the baby's abdomen and the missing wad of rubber flew out of the child's throat. There have also been reports of successful self-administration of the technique. This is particularly important because, commonly, the choking victim leaves the dining table silently (of course), remarkably unnoticed by the other diners to seek refuge in the nearest lavatory or kitchen. Hitting oneself in the abdomen is likely to be met by a reflex tightening of the muscles, so it is probably best to fall on the arm of a chair or over a balustrade.

If the Heimlich manoeuvre fails, then truly drastic measures are called for, justified on the grounds that death is now imminent and there is nothing to lose. Place the victim on the floor with the neck extended over a cushion. Then, with the sharpest knife available, saw briskly back and forward just beneath the Adam's apple, and thrust down vertically with the point of the knife. Once the larynx has been entered, the knife should then be rotated through a right angle to open up the space. The patency of this artificial airway can then be maintained by slipping the barrel of a retractile ball-point pen into the space. To minimise bleeding, the victim should then be placed in the lateral recovery position with the held tilted downwards. With luck, the ambulance should arrive soon after to transport your frightened but grateful guest to the safety of the hospital.

Sneezing

Sneezing – of which there is a lot about in the summer months – is under-appreciated. The main group of chronic sneezers are hay-fever sufferers who think it a nuisance. While for everyone else it is just a useful way of dislodging irritating particles from the nose. But there is much more to sneezing than this. It is a curiously pleasurable phenomenon and, indeed, may be a sign of pleasure – dogs often greet their returning master or mistress with a vigorous bout of sneezing and, for some humans, sexual excitement can similarly instigate a bout of sneezing.

There are two distinct phases of sneezing. In the first the lining of the nose responds to some irritating particle by becoming engorged and secretes a clear mucus substance in which it will be expelled. This nasal engorgement, in turn, stimulates a series of deep rapid inspirations storing a large volume of air within the chest. The second phase starts once the pressure in the lungs has passed a critical point. A combination of the elastic recoil of lung tissue and the contraction of muscle in the chest and abdominal wall, hurtles air back out of the lungs at a speed of 100 ft per second, expelling the mucus droplets in a fine mist to a distance of around six feet. This is obviously a very efficient method.

Many other factors, hormonal changes, psychological mood and sexual stimuli can also produce nasal engorgement thus precipitating a bout of sneezing. The sexual precipitant of sneezing relates to the surprising anatomical similarity of the lining of the nose to other better known erectile tissues of the body such as the penis. This observation was first made by an ENT surgeon from Baltimore, John Mackenzie, who argued that 'sexual stimulation causes an excess congestion and inflammation of the nasal passages' and cited the experience of one of his patients, 'a man of sanguine temperament who, every time he caressed his wife, sneezed three or four times'. Sneezing is also of interest to psychiatrists. Professor Linford Rees, a psychiatrist at St Bartholomew's Hospital, was struck by how many of his patients who were suffering from chronic nasal irritation or rhinitis admitted that emotional moods, like anger, resentment and indignation, precipitated a bout of sneezing. Conversely he also noted that attacks of sneezing can relieve emotional tension.

The downside of sneezing is that the convulsive pressure changes that occur can be disastrous: it is a well-known, if rare, precipitant of a stroke and has been reported to cause retinal detachment and even miscarriage. For the same reason the great physician William Harvey found the sneeze useful in stimulating childbirth. Called to a woman in protracted labour who had 'fallen into a swoon', he thrust a feather with strong sneezing powder towards her nostrils. 'By this she was aroused. As often as I applied the feather to her, her delivery was advanced and, finally, a healthy and living child was born.'

So sneezing is a response to both noxious and pleasurable stimuli and accordingly in mythological terms it can be both a good or ill omen. The Welsh think it is unlucky; East Anglians think it a good premonitory sign; for the Chinese, a sneeze on New Year's Eve will bring bad luck throughout the year, and the Japanese believe that when they sneeze someone is talking highly of them. In the Old Testament it is both a sign of life and impending death. When Elijah revives the dead son of the Shunamite woman, we read: 'He stretched himself upon the child and the flesh of the child waxed warm; and the child sneezed seven times and opened his eyes.' But for Jacob, sneezing was a sign that his soul was about to depart his body, leading him to pray: 'I have waited for my salvation, give me time to bless my sons.'

Yawning

Yawning is a neglected subject of scientific enquiry, being commonplace enough and mistakenly thought to be of little significance. Yet it is, along with the 'stretch' that frequently accompanies it, fascinatingly complex.

Excessive yawning can be a sign of serious brain disease. It was frequently observed in those with *encephalitis lethargica* – the diffuse brain inflammation that followed the massive flu pandemic after the First World War. It can occur after a brain haemorrhage or signal the presence of a brain tumour. It may be a feature of an epileptic attack or migraine and is common in those with Huntingdon's chorea. Each of those conditions affect the yawning centre in the mid-brain and the treatment, if any, is of the underlying condition.

More importantly, protracted yawning may indicate the incapacitating, but treatable, condition known as 'primary disorder of vigilance'. Here, vigilance is markedly reduced and those affected find it difficult to concentrate and stay awake. Dr Warren Weinburg, a neurologist at the University of Texas, describes the case of a nine-year-old boy whose teachers thought he was lazy and immature. He yawned a lot and was easily bored. He disliked reading and was unable to concentrate on any task. Dr Weinburg treated him with amphetamine-like stimulants 'with immediate improvement . . . he read 59 books in four months and built a model of the Hoover Dam out of 25,000 toothpicks'. This 'primary disorder of vigilance' is distinguished from other causes of excessive sleepiness such as narcolepsy because it tends to run in families and the children affected have a quite characteristic temperament – usually described as being kind, caring and compassionate.

Although interesting, these pathological types of excessive yawning do not help to clarify what its functions might be, for there are likely to be several. Yawning is a response to different situations: tiredness, obviously, but also boredom, hunger, bad ventilation or even 'infectiousness' – *cum enim qui videt alium oscitare, ipse quoque oscitandum invitatur* (to see another yawn is also an invitation to yawn).

Yawning due to boredom is said to be primarily social – the physical expression to others of an inner emotion – just as we laugh when we are happy and cry when we are sad. Yawning is thus an 'involuntary signal' to the bore to stop talking, or to guests who have overstayed their welcome that it is time to go home.

Yawning when tired – which is more frequently associated with stretching – is an attempt to regain, albeit only temporarily, a state of alertness. The original theory was that yawning was intended by nature to be a 'gymnastic . . . an automatic impulse caused by bad air in the lungs which awakens the respiratory organs into activity'. It certainly seems plausible that the large intake of air that accompanies the initial inspiratory effort might boost the oxygen supply to the brain. This, however, has been discounted in the absence of evidence that tiredness is due to oxygen deficiency. More recently it has been suggested that the stretching of the arms and respiratory muscles is the crucial factor, revitalising the body by counteracting the loss of muscle tone that comes with tiredness.

Yawning is without doubt good for one. This is clearly illustrated by the adverse consequences for those in whom the reflex is inhibited, because they suffer from its only significant complication – recurrent dislocation of the jaw bone. A Canadian professor of psychiatry describes the case of a 25-year-old woman who was drinking coffee, yawned and found that her jaw had locked with the mouth open. 'She was unable to speak and experienced a lot of pain. Eventually her husband struck her on the right side of the jaw, returning the joint to its normal position, and she was able to close her mouth again.' This occurred on several occasions until she became so frightened of yawning that she rapidly suppressed any incipient urge by cupping her hand under her jaw. Deprived of the pleasure and relaxation that yawning brings, she became irritable and depressed.

Belching

The facility to expel unwanted gas from the gut, either upwards or downwards, is essential for human happiness. The great virtue of belching is that is permits pockets of air trapped in the stomach to eructate upwards, rather than having to travel the length of the intestine before being released. Those with a deficient belch reflex suffer grievously, as illustrated by the case of a 25-year-old female chemist, described by Dr P. J. Kahrilas, physician at the Medical College of Wisconsin. This woman's symptoms followed a predictable pattern. She felt fine in the early part of the day, but from midday onwards became increasingly distressed by an audible gurgling sound emanating from her chest and a pressure-like pain building up behind the sternum. Over the years several doctors had informed her that her problem was 'emotional in nature', but Dr Kahrilas's investigations proved otherwise. A barium X-ray showed a large air bubble trapped in the upper part of the stomach, while studies of the sphincter at the lower end of the oesophagus showed its function to be impaired. When Dr Kahrilas passed a tube down into the stomach, the patient gave a loud and prolonged belch as the trapped air escaped and, gratifyingly, her pain promptly subsided.

This failure of the belch reflex is difficult to treat, but its consequences are a reminder of just how essential belching is to our sense of well-being. Rather than feeling embarrassed when belching, we should rejoice that the reflex is in working order. Luckily, this type of problem is rare, whereas difficulty in passing flatus is all too common a feature of a bout of constipation, where gas trapped in the colon causes colicky pains and abdominal distension. More dramatically, the trapping of flatus is crucial to the condition known as toxic megacolon. The fortuitous discovery that its elimination can be curative provides one of the more diverting medical stories of recent times.

Toxic megacolon is just as nasty as it sounds: a life-threatening complication of inflammatory or infectious bowel disease, in which the lining of the colon is stripped away so that blood and mucus leak through the rectum, while, simultaneously, the colon becomes grossly distended with vast quantities of gas. Those affected are very ill indeed, and frequently the colon has to be removed in its entirety if a fatal outcome is to be averted. Recently Dr M. Z. Panos, of the University of Birmingham, reported how a chance observation by one of his patients radically transformed the management of this condition. A 38-year-old man had developed toxic megacolon following an episode of salmonella poisoning, which he had contracted while on a visit to Thailand, and, says Dr Panos, 'surgery was considered'. While trying to make himself more comfortable, the patient adopted the 'Mecca position' – kneeling on the bed bent forwards, with his arms outstretched in front of him and his bottom sticking up in the air. In this position, he passed a monumental quantity of flatus 'which continued for some minutes'. Immediately he felt much more comfortable, so he repeated the manoeuvre several times 'with similar results'. He described his experience to an astonished surgeon, who measured his abdominal girth and discovered that he had indeed become a lot slimmer. 'Over the next fortnight his condition gradually improved, at which point he was discharged fully recovered.' Subsequently, it has become standard practice for surgeons to recommend the 'Mecca position' in these circumstances, and no doubt many colons that would otherwise have ended up in the surgical bucket are still functioning happily in their owners' abdomens. Such is medical progress.

The expulsion of intestinal gases is thus both pleasurable and healthy, but it is always possible to have too much of a good thing; the over-production of wind can pose serious social problems. The case of a 28-year-old man, currently the acknowledged world record holder for the passage of flatus – 140 times in one day – is instructive. Like others so afflicted, he found it difficult to persuade the medical fraternity to take his problem seriously, until his plight came to the attention of Dr Michael Levitt, of the University of Minnesota. Intestinal gases are derived from the fermentation by bacteria in the colon of undigested food residues; hence an excess of wind is likely to be due to a failure to absorb certain types of food. Dr Levitt found his patient was intolerant of the sugar lactose, present in milk and dairy products and, indeed, it was when he was restricted to a milk-only diet for two days that he produced his record-breaking performance. The elimination of lactose-containing foods had a dramatic effect in reducing the frequency of passing flatus down to 25 times a day, although this is still slightly higher than the 'normal average' figure of 14 times a day. According to Dr Levitt, his patient 'is assiduously testing a wide variety of foods in an attempt to develop a flatus-free palatable diet.'

Smelling

There was a time when a doctor would sniff his way to a precise diagnosis. Surgeons who attended British soldiers fighting for the Empire during the nineteenth century suspected yellow fever if the patient exuded the smell of a butcher's shop. If the armpits of someone with a rash and fever exuded the aroma of freshly baked bread, nurses would confidently diagnose a case of typhoid fever. When diphtheria was endemic, a discriminating physician could pick out a case from a queue of sickly children because of the characteristic sweetish odour. In the field hospitals of the First World War, surgeons were alert to the pervasive stench of rotten apples, indicating gas gangrene. If a wound gave off the sweet whiff of grapes, it had been infected with the bacterium *pseudomonas*.

These exotic diseases are rarely seen nowadays and a physician's olfactory skills are limited to more mundane disorders. The 'secret' drinker is readily sniffed out by the strong whiff of peppermint on his breath which still cannot disguise the distinctive smell of alcohol secreted through the sweat glands on the skin. A whiff of ammonia from an old man suggests urinary incontinence usually from an enlarged prostrate. Similarly, a comatose young man taken to casualty whose breath smells strongly of acetone almost certainly has diabetes.

More important in contemporary medical practice are those unfortunate people who emit unpleasant odours, with all their attendant social and psychological problems. Halitosis – caused by rotten teeth and gums and readily preventable by strict dental hygiene and regular visits to the dentist – is the commonest. But if the teeth are healthy, there may be other causes. A chronic nasal infection often associated with obstructing polyps may be responsible and is treatable by surgical removal and a course of antibiotics. Foreign objects inserted by children in their nostrils can give rise to the vilest of odours, which can take a surprisingly long time to diagnose. Dr Michael Farnham, a Miami paediatrician, has described a typical case. 'For a couple of months, a two-year-old child had been afflicted by a body odour so unpleasant that the teacher at her nursery school banned her from the classroom – even the girl's mother could not stand to be near her,' he writes. 'A thorough examination of the nose disclosed a piece of bathroom sponge with the same foul odour as that coming from the child. Within an hour of its removal, the smell had disappeared.'

A further hidden source of halitosis only recently identified is a chronic infection of the stomach by the organism *helicobacter pylori*, which has also been incriminated as a cause of gastritis and peptic ulcers. This can now be confirmed by testing the saliva for antibodies to the organism, which can be eradicated by four weeks' worth of antibiotics.

Those plagued with excessive flatulence may also have their lives made a misery by the disagreeable odours they produce. Regrettably, many of those with bad 'wind problems' consider their ailment too trivial or embarrassing to seek medical help. The problem may fade if flatus-inducing foods such as baked beans are avoided and charcoal tablets that absorb intestinal gas are chewed. If these measures have no effect, it is possible the problem is due to a missing gut enzyme leading to malabsorption of sugars or to the presence of large numbers of methane-producing bacteria in the colon.

There are also a group of rare congenital syndromes known exotically by the offensive odours they cause: cat's urine syndrome, sweaty feet syndrome and rancid butter syndrome. Most of these are lethal in childhood but fish odour syndrome is an exception. Eleven cases have been described in *The British Medical Journal*. The breath and sweat smell strongly of rotting fish producing 'strong feelings of shame, social isolation, paranoia and depression with educational and career disadvantages and a failure to maintain relationships with the opposite sex'. The underlying problem is an inability to metabolise and so render odourless an amine, trimethylamine, derived from the diet, which is present in large amounts in eggs, liver, offal and saltwater fish. The patients had been badly served when trying to seek medical help. Some were told by psychiatrists that they were obsessional, while others who consulted dermatologists were advised to improve their personal hygiene. Though the condition is incurable, they were apparently much helped by learning that they suffered from a recognised clinical disorder. Dietary advice to avoid exacerbating foods, and the use of acid soaps and body lotions which convert the trimethylamine in the skin to an odourless compound are also useful.

Hair Shock

Sudden whitening of the hair is such a curious phenomenon that many people suspect it is a myth. How can pigment just drain out of a hair follicle overnight? In *The Natural History of Nonsense*, Bergan Evans notes: 'Commonest of all fictions about the hair is that as a result of some harrowing experience it may turn white overnight. Perhaps the night air has something to do with it; hair never seems to turn white over day.'

There are, however, more than enough anecdotal reports to suggest that it does indeed occur. It happened to Marie Antoinette after she returned to Paris, and was confronted by the revolutionary mob after unsuccessfully trying to flee the country; and to Sir Thomas More on the eve of his execution. Twenty-six attested cases in medical literature are all preceded by catastrophic emotional stress – most frequently on the battlefield or after a shipwreck or railway catastrophe.

It is possible that some of these episodes may have been artificial. The distinguished dermatologist, Sir Richard Sutton, in his book *Diseases of the Skin*, observes: 'Reliably reported episodes of blanching are doubtless the result of the removal of cosmetic coloration or the application of bleach.' It has been suggested, for example, that the whitening of Marie Antoinette's hair might have been explained in this way. 'She was determined to present herself well and in dignified style for her execution, and had carefully reserved a large stock of hair powder for this, her final public appearance.'

Alternatively a plausible scientific explanation has been put forward by Dr Ashley Robins of Cape Town Medical School in South Africa. From the thirties onwards any head of hair consists of pigmented and white strands. With 'sudden whitening' there is a preferential and massive loss of the pigmented ones, while the white ones left behind give the appearance that the hair has turned colour. This certainly occurs in the balding condition *alopecia areata*, where over a matter of weeks pigmented hair follicles are systematically lost. Why and how this should occur so suddenly in reaction to shock remains, for the moment, unexplained.

D-I-Y Brain Surgery

Ever since a charming West Indian car mechanic cured his sciatica by crashing his car, I have taken an interest in unusual and dramatic forms of self-treatment, whether these are deliberate or involuntary. A week earlier my patient had pulled his back while fixing an engine. Stoically he carried on working but his pain gradually got worse and started to radiate down the back of his leg – a classic symptom of sciatica usually due to a displaced disc. As he was driving to work one morning, his car skidded and crashed into a lamp-post. He emerged shaken but unhurt to find his sciatica had completely disappeared. Indeed it was this instantaneous recovery that finally brought him to the surgery for a check-up as he feared he must have harmed himself in some other way. I assured him he had not, and that he had benefited from an unusual, if expensive, form of self-treatment – 'auto-manipulation'.

Another method of self-treatment discovered by a farmer in Illinois subsequently proved to be life-saving in the South American jungle. The farmer, hyper-allergic to bee stings, found by chance that applying a high-voltage shock to the place where he had been stung prevented the usual severe reaction. Hearing of this, an Ecuadorian doctor, Ronald Guderian, used the same technique on thirty-four consecutive patients with snakebite and found that 'within fifteen minutes' all the pain had gone and the usual complications of an untreated bite – swelling, bleeding, shock and kidney failure – did not develop. He speculated that the electric shock must constrict the local blood vessels, preventing the spread of the snake venom.

Sometimes self-treatment may be unintentionally life-saving. An

Australian ratcatcher regularly dosed himself with rat poison, the anti-clotting drug Warfarin – as a general preventive measure against having a heart attack. One day he took a little too much and started haemorrhaging through the rectum. Investigation in hospital revealed the source to be a small operable cancer of the lower bowel. If it had not been for the Warfarin-induced bleeding, the tumour may not have been detected until it was too late.

The most dramatic example of self-treatment is do-it-yourself brain surgery. Writing in the *British Journal of Psychiatry*, Professor L. Solyom, of the University of Columbia, described the case of a young man, severely afflicted with an obsessive disorder centred on cleanliness, who would spend up to six hours a day just washing his hands and taking showers. This, naturally enough, interfered with his ability to lead a normal life and as a result he became depressed and then suicidal. He decided to end it all by shooting himself through the head – from which injury, with the help of neurosurgeons at the local hospital, he surprisingly recovered. To the patient's relief and the amazement of his psychiatrists, he was now no longer depressed and his obsession with cleanliness was limited to insisting that his mother kept the bathroom and kitchen spotlessly clean. Two years later he was found to be 'consistently calm and cheerful' and had completed his high-school education. A brain scan showed the bullet had damaged part of the frontal lobe of the brain, fortuitously mimicking the technique of lobotomy used by brain surgeons for the treatment of intractable mental illness.

However, the award for the most consistent and ingenious method of self-treatment goes to a farmer in Northern Ireland who, over a period of thirty years, discovered several cures for the recurrent bouts of palpitations caused by his abnormally fast heart rhythm. This condition – known as a supraventricular tachycardia – is usually treated by drugs, though often responds to 'shocks' of various types. When the farmer first got his palpitations he would jump from a barrel and thump his feet very hard on the ground when landing. This became less effective with time, so his next cure involved removing his clothes, climbing a ladder and jumping from a considerable height into a cold-water tank. Later he discovered that the simplest treatment was with one hand to grab hold of his six-volt electrified cattle fence, earthing the shock by simultaneously sticking a finger of the other hand into the ground. Ingenious as all these treatments were, his cardiologist advised that a more up-to-date approach was probably called for – and the farmer now has a special pacemaker which recognises when his heart rhythm shoots up to 150 beats a minute, and administers two small electric shocks which restore it to normal.

Robinson Publishing, PO Box 11, Falmouth,
Cornwall TR10 9EN
Tel: +44(0) 1326 317200 Fax: +44(0) 1326 317444
Email: books@Barni.avel.co.uk

UK/B.F.P.O customers please allow £1.00 for p&p for the first book, plus 50p for the second, plus 30p for each additional book up to a maximum charge of £3.

Overseas customers (inc Ireland), please allow £2.00 for the first book plus £1.00 for the second, plus 50p for each additional book.

Please send me:

_____ Backache: What Exercises Really Work £5.99

_____ Arthritis: What Really Works £7.99

_____ Arthritis: What Exercises Really Work £5.99

_____ The Family Encyclopedia of Medicine and Health £9.99

NAME (Block Letters) ....

ADDRESS ....

....POSTCODE ....

I enclose a cheque/PO (payable to Robinson Publishing Ltd) for _____

I wish to pay by Switch / Credit card

Number _____Card Expiry Date _____